T5-BQA-876

MODERN
INTERNATIONAL LAW

By the same author

Prisoners of War, 1963
Indian Extradition Law, 1969
International Law through the United Nations (Ed), 1972

MODERN INTERNATIONAL LAW

R.C. HINGORANI

OCEANA PUBLICATIONS, INC., DOBBS FERRY, NEW YORK
1979

ISBN 0-379-20439-8

Published by an arrangement with Oxford & IBH Publishing Co., 66 Janpath, New Delhi 110001, India

Published by Oceana Publications, Inc., Dobbs Ferry, New York. Printed in India

Dedicated to
Third World Countries

PREFACE

At the outset, I must admit that days of writing textbooks are gone. Today is an age of specialisation where the tendency is to know more and more of less and less. Nevertheless, I have undertaken the task of writing this little monograph essentially to serve the sole purpose of reflecting Afro-Asian views on various aspects of international law.

During my quarter century of experience in teaching international law, I have found myself at pains to agree with whatever Western authors have written. Whenever I have tried to present the views differing from printed views of the Western world, these have looked strange to students who have been almost brainwashed by the enormity of Western writings. Unfortunately, there has so far been no concerted effort to project views of the developing nations on various aspects of international law. These States do not subscribe to all that has been given to them by the Western countries. They have their own misgivings and reservations to what is being passed on to them as international law in the formation of which they had no hand or say. This prompted me to embark upon the stupendous task of writing a book on international law which reflects the aspirations of the Afro-Asian States. No aspect of Western international law can be binding on them unless they consent to it, expressly or impliedly.

Developing nations have not rejected Western international law in its entirety. They have accepted such norms to which there can be no serious objection. They have rejected norms which are inconsistent with their new status as equal, sovereign independent States. My effort in this book has been to re-write international law in the light of the above considerations. However, I must hasten to say that the views are not officially sponsored by any Government. I have written the book as I interpret it as a Professor from a developing country. While most of the topics covered are common here as well as in Western books, some new trends have also been discussed.

In between the completion of this work and its publication, there have been some important developments in the world community which could not be incorporated in the text of the book. There has been the bloody *coup d'etat* in April, 1978 in Afghanistan when Daud was replaced by Taraki. The Law of Sea Conference was held in April-May, and again in Aug-Sept, 1978 but without achieving any success. There has been the Trijunction Agreement signed in June, 1978 between India, Thailand and Indonesia demarcating the sea boundary near the Andamans from the median line.

There has been a special General Assembly Session in May-June, 1978 on Disarmament. The Conference urged upon nations to channelise funds, otherwise spent on armaments, for welfare activities. It declared that "enduring international peace and security cannot be built on accumulation of weaponry by military alliances nor be sustained by precarious balance of deterence on doctrines of strategic superiority." In its opinion, "nuclear weapons pose the greatest danger to mankind and civilisation." Therefore, it was considered essential to halt and reverse the nuclear arms race in all its aspects in order to avert the danger of war involving nuclear weapons. The Final Document signed on 1st July, 1978 established the Committee on Disarmament consisting of 32 to 35 members, Disarmament Commission consisting of all U.N. members and chalked out the Programme of Action.

The Soviet Union has ratified the Additional Protocol II of Tlatelolco Treaty of 1967 declaring Latin America as a Nuclear Free Zone. In 1975, the General Assembly had exhorted upon the Soviet Union to sign and ratify the Protocol. There has also been an agreement on Namibia in July, 1978, a long standing issue ever since the establishment of the United Nations.

The historic 'Camps David' Summit between President Carter of the U.S.A., President Sadat of Egypt and Prime Minister Begin of Israel, was concluded on 17th September, 1978 with the signing of two agreements. One relates to "A framework for Peace in the Middle East." The other is called "Framework for the Conclusion of a Peace Treaty between Egypt and Israel within Three Months." This summit could be the pace-setter for bringing peace to the strife-torn Middle East.

This is a maiden attempt at writing Modern International Law. Some aspects may have been left out. Others dealt with briefly. It is a one-man effort and I do not claim perfection. I hope to benefit from comments which may be offered from time to time. The lacuna would be removed in my next edition.

Finally, I must thank the University Grants Commission (India) for financing this project. I take this opportunity to thank various persons who typed my manuscripts, checked the typescripts and verified the footnotes. I thank Phil Cohen of the Oceana for associating its name with the book.

R.C. HINGORANI
Dean, Faculty of Law,
Patna University

September 30, 1978

CONTENTS

INTRODUCTION

International Law is at the cross roads today. Until the mid-twentieth century, the world community comprised fifty odd States. The Hague Conference of 1899 was attended by 46 States out of which only five were from Asia—China, Japan, Korea, Persia (Iran) and Siam (Thailand). There was none from indigenous Africa. In the subsequent Hague Conference of 1907, there were only four of the above States from Asia, Korea having been dropped. The Geneva Conference of 1929 on Prisoners of War was attended by the same number of States; six Asian States attended the Conference—China, Egypt, India, Japan, Persia (Iran) and Siam (Thailand). India was then a colony but attended the same as a member of the League of Nations. The United Nations started in 1945 with 51 States; only eleven of them were Afro-Asian States, including India which was then a colony.

Today, of course the United Nations has a membership of 149 States. About one hundred States have become independent in the post-World War II period thus causing proliferation in the world community's membership. Africa alone accounts for about 50 States. Few are from the American continent and the rest are from the Asian and Middle East regions.

Until recently, international law remained dominated by Europe. It was mostly influenced by the Christian States of Europe. England and France had a dominating role in the formulation of this law. Even the United States of America played a secondary role initially. That is why President Monroe introduced in 1823 the doctrine of non-interference in American continent by European States in exchange for a similar promise of non-interference in European Affairs. The Christian States of Latin America had no say in the formulation of international law rules. That is why they tried to develop regional international law like diplomatic asylum, Calvo clause and Drago doctrine. Turkey, a European but non-Christian State, was considered as a sick State of Europe, having no say in the formulation of international law. Thus it was European international law in the nineteenth century. It developed into Euro-American law in the twentieth century with active participation of the United States of America.

A hundred new States which have become members of the world community in the recent past have been confronted with the problem of acceptance of the Euro-American International Law. They are not ready to accept everything passed on to them as universal international law. They have to resort to the policy of pick and choose. They do not, however, propose to reject all rules of international law as inherited by them. They accept such rules which are not inconsistent with their new status as sovereign States. They reject other rules which compromise their sovereign status. Similarly, they reject everything which is the result of domination. They equally reject the rules which may better be labelled as national policies of some States than as international rules.

There is the problem of succession by new States. There is no univeral succession. International law being based on consent, new States only succeed to what they consent. They raise the basic issue: how far international law developed by a few Western nations is binding today on more than the hundred newly born States? Naturally, it cannot bind new States unless they consent to its continuance. They accept some of the pre-existing norms which do not prejudice their legitimate interests. They reject the other norms which were borne out of national interests or balance-of-power politics of yester-years. The Third World wants new norms based on equality, natural justice, morality and human values.

New States were immediately confronted with the problem of succession to treaties which were applicable to their territories earlier as colonies. Three trends were noticed in this connection. Some States declared to start with a clean slate. Others accepted the treaties on the basis of inheritance agreements. A third set of States tried to pick and choose from among the pre-existing treaties. However, it needs to be stressed here that in the latter two cases, it is not only the new State whose choice would determine the validity of a treaty; the other party to the treaty may disown it as well. This is not an uncommon practice among States.

There have been some new developments in the domain of international law. There has been a demand for a new economic world order; this has given rise to the Charter of Economic Rights and Duties of States. Terrorism and peacetime espionage have been quite frequent and agonising. These have to be tackled on an international plane. There has been a stress on recognition of the role of an individual, right of self determination and human rights. President Carter's projection of human rights as a factor influencing his country's foreign policy has added a new dimension to human rights. Multinationals have assumed menacing roles. There has been a fear of environmental pollution which poses a great danger to the living conditions of the world community.

There is also a need for reorientation regarding the so-called right of intervention in some cases. Western nations have justified intervention in some cases in the past. Today, it remains a thing of the past. The United Nations resolutions and the Helsinki Agreement have unequivocally condemned the concept of intervention.

The rules of war have been greatly influenced by the Western nations, particularly England and the United States. It has been felt that some of the rules are not universally recognised. Yet others have been imposed by dint of gun-power and victory. So they need to be sorted out and reshaped.

The United Nations has grown to be a universal organisation. Its purposes and principles have been elaborated. Various organs of the United Nations have been dealt with to assess their working. The functioning of the International Court of Justice has been examined in more detail and indeed critically.

ANNEXURE

Growth of United Nations Membership, 1945-1977

Year	*Member States*	*Original Members*
1945	51	Argentina, Australia, Belgium, Bolivia, Brazil, Byelorussia, Canada, Chile, China, Colombia, Costa Rica, Cuba, Czechoslovakia, Denmark, Dominican Republic, Ecuador, Egypt, El Salvador, Ethiopia, France, Greece, Guatemala, Haiti, Honduras, India, Iran, Iraq, Lebanon, Liberia, Luxembourg, Mexico, Netherlands, New Zealand, Nicaragua, Norway, Panama, Paraguay, Peru, Philippines, Poland, Saudi Arabia, South Africa, Syria, Turkey, Ukraine,

		Union of Soviet Socialist Republics, United Kingdom, United States of America, Uruguay, Venezuela, Yugoslavia
		New Members
1946	55	Afghanistan, Iceland, Sweden, Thailand
1947	57	Pakistan, Yemen
1948	58	Burma
1949	59	Israel
1950	60	Indonesia
1955	76	Albania, Austria, Bulgaria, Cambodia, Finland, Hungary, Ireland, Italy, Jordan, Laos, Libya, Nepal, Portugal, Romania, Spain, Sri Lanka,
1956	80	Japan, Morocco, Sudan, Tunisia
1957	82	Ghana, Malaysia
1958	100	Benin, Central African Republic, Chad, Congo, Cyprus, Gabon, Ivory Coast, Madagascar, Mali, Niger, Senegal, Somalia, Togo, United Republic of Cameroon, Upper Volta, Zaire
1961	104	Mauritania, Mongolia, Sierra Leone, United Republic of Tanzania
1962	110	Algeria, Burundi, Jamaica, Rwanda, Trinidad, Tobago, Uganda
1963	112	Kenya, Kuwait
1964	115	Malawi, Malta, Zambia
1965	118	Gambia, Maldives, Singapore
1966	122	Barbados, Botswana, Guyana, Lesotho
1967	123	Democratic Yemen
1968	126	Equatorial Guinea, Mauritius, Swaziland
1970	127	Fiji
1971	132	Bahrain, Bhutan, Oman, Qatar, United Arab Emirates
1973	135	Bahamas, Federal Republic of Germany, German Democratic Republic
1974	138	Bangla Desh, Granada, Guinea-Pissau
1975	144	Cape Verde, Comoros, Mozambique, Papua New Guinea, Sao Tome and Principe, Surinam
1976	147	Angola, Samoa, Seychelles
1977	149	Djibouti, Vietnam

SECTION I

GENERAL PRINCIPLES

CHAPTER 1

DEFINITION AND CONCEPT OF INTERNATIONAL LAW

Definition

International law may be defined as a body of such rules which nation-states consider as legally binding upon them in their relations *inter se*. Such rules may either comprise international treaties or international custom which has acquired the force of law in the world community.

Generally speaking, international law means such law which is operative in the international community. Therefore, it may not be correct to classify international law into particular, general and universal as is done by Oppenheim [1]. According to Oppenheim, particular international law is operative among a few States, general international law among many States and universal international law among all States. International law is applicable to all the States and, therefore, is necessarily universal. There may be some rules of international law arising out of a given treaty which has been ratified by most of the States but not by all the States. Nevertheless, such a treaty borders on universality since the number of non-ratifiers may be negligible. In any case, if a treaty does not have ratification by most of the States, it hardly attains the status of international law. It may only be treated as a treaty applicable to some States.

Belief has also been created that Grotius is the father of modern international law. While one does appreciate his contribution in the field of international law in the form of his famous book, *De Jure Belli ac Pacis* in 1625, it is difficult to agree with the title given to him if it were to connote that he is the first jurist to have written a book on international law. This wrong impression is possibly based on two assumptions. One that international law was initially operative only among Western-cum-Christian nations which were supposed to be the only civilised nations then, and secondly because ancient writings like *Manusmriti* and one by Kautiliya were not accessible to Western authors, or these writings were ignored by them. History has proved that international law was practised even in old days and there were regular rules relating to diplomatic relations, war, etc. in ancient India [2]. There was application of international regulations between Greek City States. The Roman period also witnessed the growth of international law. Whatever the quantum of contribution of these periods may be to the development of international law, it cannot be denied that international law was operative during these periods and many of the international rules which are operative today were no less operative then. Contributions of jurists like Belli in 1563 [3] and Gentili in 1598 [4] are equally outstanding.

Nature of International Law

Despite the fact that international law has regulated relations among States since last so many centuries, one is often confronted with the question whether international law is law in the real sense. Doubts as to that crop up whenever there is violation of international law rules by a given State and the victim finds no redress against the violating State.

Controversy as to the nature of international law arises from Austin's definition of law as command of a sovereign attended by sanction in case of violation of the command. On the basis of this definition, Austin has categorised international law as positive morality lacking the force of law. According to Austin and like thinkers, it is asserted that since international law regulates regulations between sovereign nations having no common superior to whose command these sovereign States may be subordinate, it lacks the basic essential of law inasmuch as there is no sovereign to command and enforce sanctions against the violator of the command in the domain of international law.

If Austin's definition of law were to be considered as absolutely correct, it must be admitted that international law does not fit in within the category of law. But as things are, Austin's concept of law is very controversial and cannot be wholly relied upon. One has, therefore, to analyse whether international law is law or not. This would raise the question as to what one understands by the word 'law'.

'Law', as one should understand, is a code of conduct to

which people should conform in the interests of organised society lest the violator may be penalised for not conforming to it. This concept of law is as much correct with respect to municipal law as in the case of international law. The difference may, of course, lie in the fact that while municipal law regulates relations within a given State, international law regulates relations among sovereign States. Otherwise, both municipal law and international law prescribe a code of conduct which would no doubt invite censure whenever the same is violated. In this sense, international law is just like conventional law, i.e. contract law, which creates legal relations through consent of parties. Therefore, if conventional law could be considered as real law, one wonders why international law cannot be considered as law in the real sense.

In the above circumstances, Holland's remark that international law is the vanishing point of jurisprudence is hardly tenable. Undoubtedly, nation-states and international institutions have sometimes felt helpless in vindicating the rule of international law in world community but this is due to the non-proof of violation on the part of a given State or sometimes due to the fact that a powerful nation may violate international law with impunity. While the first ground is equally true in municipal law where the accused is set free for want of evidence, the second ground is peculiar to the field of international law. Here also, if analogy is slightly extended, it will be found that the second ground has also some parallel in civil law inasmuch as powerful accused may be instrumental to causing the disappearance of evidence through threats or otherwise or he may not be punished either because of immunity which he may be enjoying or his conviction may be commuted or condoned.

It cannot be denied that there are some enforcement measures in international law also. Self help is one of such measures. This measure may not be very desirable but this kind of redress existed in ancient societies and to some extent today also as part of law. The present Charter of the United Nations prescribes enforcement measures under Articles 5, 6, 41 and 42 against the violating States. These measures have the semblance of taking action against the wrong-doing States.

Therefore, it is safe to say that international law is as much law as any other law although it is not free from criticism that it may be weaker than the ordinary law of the land. Mere violations in the realm of international law should not dishearten the protagonists because violations occur both in municipal and international law.

History of International Law

International law has its origin since the days two nations conducted relations between themselves. It is, therefore, not correct to say as Oppenheim has said that, "the conception of Family of Nations did not arise in the mental horizon of the ancient world [5]." International law was very much in the mental horizon of the ancient world and was actually practised. Following few pages will trace out the history of international law in the early days.

International law was practised by Jews in their relations with other nations. Inviolability of diplomatic agents was recognised and maintained. They recognised humanitarian rules of warfare. Sanctity was attached to treaties. The Jews also had envisaged the idea of one world during the days of Isaiah. Any cruelty perpetrated during war was not the monopoly of the past only. Even the present century would bear out inhumanitarian treatment meted out to adversaries during war.

Greeks also practised international law. Small city-states observed rules of international law in the same way as Christian nations observed in later days. It was during Greek period that the rule of international law requiring prior declaration of war was developed. The dead were given a decent burial even during the fury of war and prisoners of war could be exchanged. It is said that Greeks did not consider international law as legally binding but only religiously binding. It is difficult to say which had more sanctity then—legally binding rules or religiously binding rules. If religion enjoyed the same sanctity which law enjoys now, it is immaterial whether international law in those days was religiously or legally binding. Probably it may not be wrong to say that religiously binding rules then were as sacrosanct as legally binding rules of international law today, if not more.

Romans have contributed a fair amount to the rules of the international law as they exist today. *Jus Gentium*—international law—was the Roman device to deal with foreigners. This law consisted of commonly accepted rules among States based on laws of nature. The rule of acquiring territory through means of occupation has been borrowed from Roman Law. Romans had drafted elaborate rules of warfare and the doctrine of postliminium as we know today is based on *Jus Postliminii.*

In ancient India too, international law was practised [6]. It operated in the vedic age from 4000 B.C. to 100 B.C. between tribal heads known as Rajahs. Incredible though it may look to Western authors, the fact is that international law was as much in vogue in ancient India as it may have been in the seventeenth and eighteenth centuries of the Christian era. Paradoxically, international law as practised in ancient India was more universal than the so-called Western international law. As late as in 1937, Mussolini claimed that laws of war were not applicable in the Ethiopian War as Ethiopia was outside Christendom. Hindu international law applied irrespective of religion and civilisation [7]. This was despite the fact that basis of international law in India was religious teachings like Manu's *Dharam Shatras.* Kautiliya's *Arthshastra* is another documentary proof of prevalence of international law in ancient India. International law then had more sanctity because it was based on *Dharma* which was sacrosanct for all Indian States.

Then India was divided into many kingdoms having the same religion. They conducted their foreign relations through *rajdoots* who are known today as ambassadors. *Manusmriti* prescribes qualifications of a good envoy and his functions [8]. Megasthenes came to the court of King Chandragupta Maurya in 303 B.C. as an envoy of King Seleukos Nikator of Babylon and Syria. *Manusmriti* provided that an ambassador must be well versed in all branches of knowledge. He should be of noble lineage, of pure character, efficient and able to read minds through gestures and postures [9]. Kautiliya expected the envoy to be endowed with power of persuasion, well trained in arts and with foresight, memory and enthusiasm and industry in addition to being in the enjoyment of good physique [10].

Mitakshra gave three types of *dootas—Niststartha,* who has authority of a king, *Samdistartha* who is a messenger of communication from one king to another and *Sasanhara.* The letter of credentials was called *Sasana.* Envoys enjoyed privileges and dignities and were immune from arrest or being killed. A king who killed an envoy was condemned to hell. There were no permanent envoys although ambassadors were exchanged for *ad hoc* purposes.

According to Manu, territory could be acquired by inheritance, recovery from usurper and conquest as a result of enforcing of some right or settlement of dispute or by occupation of territory which was unoccupied. Cession of territory by *dana* (gift) to avoid war or as a token of matrimonial settlement was also prevalent.

Residents were divided into two categories—citizens and non-citizens. Citizens were called *Svadesiva* and non-citizens were called *Prajana*. Allegiance to the king was mandatory. Foreigners were allowed entry by royal warrant—which we term as visa today—and they had to report at points of entry. There was a separate department for foreigners during Chandragupta's period which looked after foreigners and watched their activities [11]. There was practice of grant of asylum to political refugees who sought protection [12]. However, criminals were extradited.

The principle of *Pucta Sunt Servanda* was not alien to Hindu international law. Kautiliya required faith and honesty in carrying out international obligations. Mostly treaties were bilateral and they were binding on parties. They were sworn by fire, water, plough, brick of fort wall, shoulder of elephant, hip of horse, front of chariot or weapon [13].

War was resorted to as the last step when everything else failed. War must be preceded by conciliation, gift or by causing dissention. When all these attempts failed, war may be waged. Like the Kellog-Briand Pact of 1928, Emperor Ashoka renounced war as an instrument of national policy during his rule between 274-237 B.C. [14]. Wars were divided into two categories : just war which was termed as *Dharma Yudha*, and unjust war—*Adharma Yudha*.

There was difference between combatants and non-combatants. There was fully developed system of laws of war based on rules of humanity and chivalry. These rules were applied to civil wars also. Belligerents were expected to abide by these rules in all circumstances whether the war was between believers and non-believers.

Article 23 of the Hague Regulations prohibiting the infliction of unnecessary suffering was operative then also. King Rama instructed his brother Lakshmana not to use weapons of mass destruction. Arjun did not use *Pasupathastra* (a hyper-destructive weapon) during the *Mahabharata* war. A non-combatant and a combatant who had surrendered were not killed.

Geneva Convention IV of 1949 relating to the protection of civilians during war was equally operative then. The king and residents of occupied territory were treated with humanity and chivalry. There could not be any destruction of royal race, God and customs of the country. When Paurva surrendered to Alexander in 300 B.C., he expected a royal treatment as a king.

Prisoners of war were also treated with humanity. In 1367, Bahmani and Vijayanagar kings entered into an agreement for humane treatment of prisoners of war and sparing of lives of the enemy's unarmed subjects [15].

Apart from several international law rules which were prevalent in ancient India, the scriptures and *Arthashastra* are full of other rules on statecraft and foreign relations. It is not necessary to give details of all these rules here. Only some important rules have been given above to illustrate that international law was equally developed and operative in ancient India. This has been conveniently ignored by Western authors.

Basis of International Law

It is said that consent is the basis of international law. Obviously, international law is law governing relations among nations which do not recognise any authority superior to them. In such a situation, international law is treated as conventional law which is created by consent of the parties which happen to be sovereign nations. No law can be imposed on such nations to which they have not agreed. It is immaterial, however, whether such consent is express or implied.

Consent as the basis of international law is greatly true, whether it is customary international law or treaty law. While in the former, it is implied; in the latter, it is expressed. It is because of lack of their consent that newly independent States want the restructure and revision of European-oriented international law in the making of which they had no hand. However, these newly independent States are confronted with *fait accompli* of the entrenched rules of international law which gives them very little discretion to reject established rules of international law. While Afro-Asian States have accepted some rules of international law as they existed at the time of their emergence, they have challenged some of the rules which run counter to their newly acquired status as sovereign independent States. They cannot afford to be absolute non-conformists because any wholesale deviation from established rules of international law would create an adverse atmosphere for them in the world community. They have got to be little cautious and selective in the rejection of some parts of international law. In some cases assertion of right by a new State creates impediments for her recognition as an international person. Bangla Desh's insistence on the prosecution of war criminals in 1972 and 1973 cost her the initial rejection of her request for membership to the United Nations and recognition by Pakistan.

Here comes the role of reason in international law. It may be noted that international law comprises such rules which have been considered as reasonable by the international community. There is no rule of international law which may be considered as generally unreasonable. Therefore, newly independent States accept reasonable rules of international law without any grudge. However, if a given rule of international law causes some hardship to a new State, it may disown the same on the ground of it being prejudicial to its national interests. But this does not normally happen in the case of customary and conventional international law. This happens only in bilateral or multilateral treaties. Strictly speaking, such treaties do not form part of international law and, therefore, new States may disown the same if it imposes undue burden upon them.

Different Theories Regarding International Law

There are two leading schools relating to science of international law. These schools are better known as naturalists and positivists. They are discussed below in some detail.

Naturalists

The seventeenth century saw the rise of naturalists. Their thesis was that international law is based on law of nature which is above national frontiers and governs relations among States *inter se*. International law, according to them, was based on reason. Prominent among naturalists have been Hugo Grotius, Sameul Pufendorf and Vattel.

Hugo Grotius (1583-1645) was Dutch by birth. An accomplished writer of poems in Greek and Latin in his young days, he studied mathematics, philosophy and law at a very young age and was admitted to the practice of law at the age of sixteen. Known as a prodigy, the University of Orleans had conferred the degree of Doctor of Laws on him. He was consulted in the Dutch-

Spain war while he was only 20 years of age and wrote a book, *De jure Praedae commentarius* in 1605. His another study *Mare Librum*, expounding the theory of freedom of high seas was published in 1609. In 1607, he was appointed Attorney General for some of the provinces of Netherlands. However, due to conflict between Calvinists and Armenions, he was sentenced to life imprisonment. He managed to flee to France where he wrote his famous book, *De jure Belli ac Pacis*, in 1625, and dedicated it to Louis XIII of France as a token of his appreciation for the king had who received him kindly. Later, he shifted to Sweden which gave him the ambassadorial post in France. He was, however, recalled later on. Dejected and shattered, he sailed out of Sweden on a ship which got wrecked. In the process of rescuing himself, he died on 29th, August 1645. Thus ended the life of a great international lawyer.

Grotius was a naturalist. He considered the high seas free for all. He also introduced the doctrine of just war. He expected humane treatment for prisoners of war who were not to be made slaves. He considered the law of reason as governing relations between States.

On the Western continent, he is known as the father of modern law of nations and his book on War and Peace has been extensively translated in local languages. In England, the Grotius Society was found in early twentieth century. It has since been merged in the British Institute of International and Comparative Law.

Sameul Pufendorf (1632-1694) was a German who had studied law, philosophy and history. Among his many assignments, he was also Professor at University of Heidelberg in Germany and University of Lund in Sweden. He wrote a number of books on jurisprudence. His first book was published in 1660 on the "Element of Universal Jurisprudence". In 1672 he published "Law of Nature and of Nations". Essentially, a natural law exponent, he argued that relations between States were regulated by natural law. He insisted that all States were equal irrespective of size or resources. This is the fundamental rule of international law even today.

Emmerich de Vattel (1714-1767) was a Swiss national. He held many diplomatic assignments and although he did not live long, he made an impressive contribution to international law by writing his famous book *Le droit des gens, on principas de la loi naturelle appliques' a' la conduct et aux affaires des nations et des souverains*, in 1758. As the title of the book connotes, he considered that international law means the application of law of nature to relations between nations and sovereigns. For example, he said that perpetrator of unjust war will have to pay for his evil designs. This is nothing else but influence of natural law. He considered God as Super King to whom the earthy king has to account for his evil deeds. Vattel has been considered as a great writer on international law and is often quoted despite the fact that he had no legal background. But having studied humanities and philosophy, he utilised his diplomatic experience in the writing of his book which is considered as one of the classics in international law.

Positivists

The positivists claim that the law of nations is not the creation of natural law. Instead they claim that international law is either customary or conventional. According to them, international law develops through custom or through treaties. At the back of this assertion is the well-entrenched belief that the basis of international law is consent and unless the nations have expressly or impliedly agreed to a given rule of international law, it cannot be considered as binding. They treat customary international law also as based on tacit consent in the continuance of the same. The noted protagonists of this school have been Zouche, Bynkershoek and Martens. Anzilloti is the present century exponent of this school.

Richard Zouche (1590-1660) was Professor of Civil Law at Oxford. He was also judge at the Admiralty Court. His main publication was *juris et judicil fecialis, sive juris inter gentes et quaestion um de eodem explicatio* which came out in 1650, ten years before his death.

According to Zouche, who may well be considered as leader of the Positivist School, international law is either based on custom, which must be reasonable, or on treaty.

Cornelis Van Bynkershoek (1673-1743) was a Dutchman who was appointed as member of the Supreme Court in Hague in 1704, Later, he was elevated as its President in 1724. His first publication on international law was *De domino maris dissertatio*—Dominion of the Seas. Later he published *De foro legatorum*—jurisdiction over Ambassadors. In 1737, he published the famous book, *Quaestionum Juris Publice Libri Duo*—Questions of Public Law.

Like a typical judge, he considered himself to be always right. He did not agree with the Grotian concept of just war. His main contribution was in the field of Neutrality, Prize law, Blockade and Regime of Seas. He was the founder of the three mile rule of territorial waters which was determined by him on the range of a cannon shot during his days. He was also a champion of *Pucta sunt Servanda* regarding sanctity of treaties.

Georg Friedrich Von Martens (1756-1821) was a German from Hamburg. He obtained a Doctor's degree in Law from the University of Gottingen where he subsequently held the position of Professor, and later on its law faculty Dean and President. He also held a number of Government positions, including that of Hanovarian representative to German Parliament (Bundestag). His main publication, *Precis du droit des gens moderne de l' Europe Fonde' sur les traites et l' usage*, was out in 1789. His earlier essay, *Versuch uber die Existenz eines positiven Europaischen Volkerrechts und den Nutzen dieser Wissenchaft*—Existence of positive European law of Nations and the Advantage of this Science, was published in 1787. This showed his inclination towards positivism. Another of his publications was a compilation of treaties known as Martens, *Recueil de traites*.

Appraisal

From the preceding pages, it can be seen that in Western countries, the modern concept of law of nations started in the seventeenth century, particularly with the publication of *De Jure Belli ac Pacis* by Grotius. It was but natural that while international law was in the process of being formulated, it required legs to stand upon. There were not many customary rules governing relations among nations; there was also the lack of conventional law between nations. The publicists, therefore, based international law on natural law and reason.

However, with the growth of relations among nations, customary rules grew with these relations. Nations also entered into treaties between themselves. Consequently, the original basis of international law—reason and natural law—receded in importance. Instead, the positivists gained ground. Therefore, it may be noticed that while in the seventeenth century, naturalists were the leaders in the subsequent centuries the positivist theory became more prominent. This is clear from the fact that consent is now considered to be the basis of international law. Anzillotti, an Italian jurist, is an important positivist of the twentieth century.

It would however be incorrect to champion the cause of one theory to the exclusion of the other. Neither the naturalists nor the positivists can claim to be exclusively correct. As has been said earlier while discussing the basis of international law, consent is not the basis of all international law. Natural law has played and does play, an important role in the development of internatoinal law. The recognition by Article 38 of the Statute of the International Court of Justice that the court shall apply general principles of law as well as teachings of noted publicists goes to prove that customs and treaties are not the exclusive basis of law. The Charter of the United Nations has also recognised the influence of naturalists inasmuch as it recognises equality among nations and inherent right of self defence.

In conclusion one must say that no theory can be said to be correct in its entirety. Both the theories are useful historically as well as otherwise.

Notes

1. Lauterpacht, Oppenheim's International Law (Eighth Edition) Vol.1 pp. 1-2.
2. Singh, Nagendra, India and International Law (1969).
3. Belli, an Italian Jurist, lived from 1502 to 1575. He wrote his book, *De Militari el de Bellori*—On Military and War Matters, in 1563.
4. Gentili, again an Italian jurist, lived from 1552 to 1608. He was appointed Professor of Civil Law at Oxford. He was consulted by the British Government in the Mandoza case in 1584. He wrote several books of International Law, the first being—*De Legationibus*—On Embassies, in 1585. Another book, *Commentationes de Jure Belli*—Commentary on Laws of war—was published in 1598. This book has been rated as a classic.
5. Lauterpacht, Oppenheim's International Law, op cit. vol.1, p. 72.
6. For detailed study of International Law in ancient India, See Vishwanath, S.V. International Law in Ancient India (1925); Bandhyoypadhyay, Pramathanath, International Law and Custom in Ancient India (1920); Singh, Nagendra, India and International Law (1969).
7. Singh, Nagendra, op. cit., pp. 22-23.
8. Adhyaya VII, Sloka 63.

9. Singh, Nagendra, op. cit., p.48.
10. As cited by Nagendra Singh, op. cit., 50,
11. Singh, Nagendra, ibid, pp. 37-39.
12. Ibid, p. 41.
13. Ibid, p. 68.
14. Ibid, p. 70.
15. Ibid, p. 10.

CHAPTER 2

SOURCES OF INTERNATIONAL LAW

Sources here would mean the components of which International law is made up. These components are fairly well known and there is not much controversy over most of them.

Article 38 of the Statute of the International Court of Justice provides that the Court shall apply:

(a) international custom, as evidence of a general practice accepted as law;

(b) international conventions, whether general or particular, establishing rules expressly recognised by the contesting States;

(c) the general principles of law recognised by civilised nations;

(d) judicial decisions; and

(e) teachings of the most highly qualified publicists.

Statute is a form of treaty between various nation-states which are members of the United Nations or otherwise party to it. All these States seem to have accepted the sources as mentioned above. They are discussed below in more detail, along with one other source which has become very important today.

International Custom

Custom is the oldest source of international law in the same way as it is of any other law. Previously, international law developed through practices and usages which were prevalent among nations in their relations *inter se*. When these practices or usages were continuously observed and became stablised they acquired the force of law between nations. In this way, usage should be distinguished from custom; while the former is not binding, the latter is. It often happens that usage assumes the form of custom with the passage of time.

The International Court of Justice had the occasion to define international custom in the Colombian-Peru Asylum Case. Thus it held that the party relying upon custom must make out that particular practice has become binding on the other party and the rule is in accordance with a constant and uniform usage practised by the States in question, and that this usage is the expression of right appertaining to the State granting asylum and a duty incumbent on the territorial State [1]. In the light of the above definition of custom, the court was of the opinion that there was no customary rule of diplomatic asylum on the American continent as claimed by Colombia [2].

Thus, there may have been some practices of grant of diplomatic asylum as in the case of King Tribhuvan of Nepal in the Indian legation in Kathmandu in 1950 and Cardinal Mindszerty at the American Embassy in Budapest in 1956. But these practices have not put a correlative duty on the territorial States to respect diplomatic asylum which may at the most be considered as a usage not having yet matured into binding custom.

It may be asked as to how much time it takes for usage to mature into custom. The question is difficult to answer. It depends upon individual States to accept particular practices as having the force of law. This may take a long while or it may just take very a short time as in the case of the acceptance of the continental shelf. The shelf came into recognition for the first time in the post-World War II period with the Truman Declaration in 1945 and soon it became a customary rule of international law having been accepted by other States in quick succession. It has eventually become a conventional rule of international law by the Geneva Convention on Continental Shelf, 1958. Something may be said in respect of economic resources zone which has also matured into customary rule of international law in the seventies. On the other hand, many usages, including diplomatic asylum, have not yet matured into customary rules of international law despite the long passage of time. Therefore, no time limit can be taken as a yardstick for converting usage into custom. It would all depend upon the general acceptability of a particular usage, whether or not it has been operative continuously and without break and has acquired a legal sanctity conferring rights on one State and correlative duty on other States.

Treaties

Today, treaties form the most important source of international law. However, bilateral or multilateral treaties may be distinguished from general or universal treaties. While the former do not make international law, the latter form part of international law. Bilateral or multilateral treaties bind only two or more States but not all or most of the States as in the case of universal and general treaties. Bilateral treaties may be evidence of customary international law as in the case of extradition which is mostly the product of bilateral treaties. International law made up of treaty law is called conventional international law meaning thereby that international law is based on conventions.

The present tendency in the world community is to convert customary international law into conventional international law. Thus law relating to diplomatic and consular relations which until recently was the product of customs developed through a few countries has now been mostly converted into conventional law by the Vienna Convention of 1961, on Diplomatic Relations and Vienna Convention of 1963 on Consular Relations. Earlier, law relating to regulation of hostilities was codified by the Hague Regulations of 1899 and 1907, and the Geneva Convention relating to Prisoners of War in 1929. The latter was amended by the Geneva Convention of 1949 in the light of the experiences of World War II. This phenomenal rise in so-called international legislation is motivated to make international law more certain and specific. Article 13 of the United Nations Charter authorises the General Assembly "to initiate studies and make recommendations for the purpose of encouraging the progressive development of international law and its codification."

For this purpose, International Law Commission has been established to prepare drafts on various aspects of international law for eventual codification by nation-states in the form of conventions. This is perhaps the best substitute for legislation in the international community, keeping in view the fact that the world community does not have a parliament to legislate for the former as in the case in municipal law.

General Principles of Law [3]

Article 38 of the Statute of the International Court of Justice says that the Court shall apply among other things general principles of law as recognised by civilised States. The phrase is unhappily worded inasmuch as States seem to be divided between civilised and uncivilised States. Better phrasing would have been general principles of law as commonly recognised by most of the States.

Recognition of general principles as a source of international law has been given for the first time specifically by this Statute although international courts did utilise these principles in their decisions. Thus the Permanent Court of International Justice used the doctrine of estoppel against the State of Norway in its dispute with Denmark over the claim relating to Eastern Greenland by declaring that the statement of the foreign minister of Norway precluded the Norwegian Government from claiming ownership over Eastern Greenland later on [4].

What are these general principles as recognised by States? They may comprise of such rules which are commonly used by States in their municipal law. This category may, therefore, include the principles of occupation, rule of presumption, doctrine of estoppel, servitudes and principles of contract. In the Protugo-Indian Case regarding the right of passage through Indian territory, the International Court of Justice held that although the Portuguese Government was given right of collection of revenue only in Dadra and Nagar Haveli enclaves, yet by continuous exercise of sovereignty over these enclaves for a long time, the Portuguese Government had acquired sovereignty over these territories [5]. It used the principle of prescription in the case.

Decisions of International Tribunals [6]

Decisions of International tribunals also form a source of international law. Such decisions may be followed in future transactions between nations. This may be despite the fact that Article 59 of the Statute of the International Court provides that the "decision of the Court has no binding force except between the parties and in respect of that particular case." This would mean that the decision of the International Court may not form a precedent in the common law sense of the word. However, these decisions would demand respect and would normally be observed as in the case of precedent under Continental Law System. This is recognised by Article 38 clause (d) of the Statute of the Court which treats judicial decisions "as subsidiary means for the determination of rules of law."

Practice has shown that courts have frequently depended upon past judicial decisions for the determination of present legal issues. Besides, these decisions have been treated as enunciating existing rules of international law and the same cannot be ignored unless there is some basic defect in the given judgment.

National Judicial Decisions

Decisions of municipal courts also play their part in the development of international law although their role should not be overestimated. The role of the municipal court is essentially to determine the legal position with regard to a particular rule of international law within the precincts of the given State. These courts have, however, a bigger role to play in such fields of international law which are interwoven between international law and municipal law, particularly the ones dealing with diplomatic immunities, law of extradition, nationality and prize law. Determination of any rule of international law by municipal courts in the above fields has a great impact on the development of international law. This is clear from the fact that most of the cases reported in Annual Digests (now called International Law Reports) are those cases which are decided by municipal courts but which are no less an important source of international law. The British Year Book of International Law, American Journal of International Law and in this respect perhaps every national year book of international law gives municipal court decisions relating to interpretation of international law. Castioni's case defining "political offence" for purpose of non-extradition is fairly important [7]. The Sabattino case as decided by the Supreme Court of the United States of America some years back is equally important regarding the Act of State doctrine [8].

Contribution by Jurists

Jurists contribute a lot to the development of international law. Their writings are often quoted with approval by national as well as international courts. Grotius, Vattel, Bynkershoek, Pufendorf are among the frequently mentioned jurists. Calvo Clause is famous and so also the Drago Doctrine and the Tate letter. Anzilloti is famous for his positivism, Oppenheim for his constitutive theory and Brierly for his declaratory theory relating to recognition. Lauterpacht, Philip Jessup and Myres McDougal are frequently quoted for their contribution to various aspects of international law. Kautilya may be considered as the Indian political philosopher who contributed a lot in the field of international law.

International Comity

It consists of acts of politeness extended by one State towards another. These States are not bound to extend such courtesies but nevertheless do so mostly on mutual basis. These acts of courtesy do not form part of international law but by passage of time they become so much engrained in the practice among nations that they acquire the status of customary international law. This would mean that comity of today may become customary international law of tomorrow.

Resolutions of the General Assembly [9]

There has been a recent development of treating resolutions of the General Assembly of the United Nations as a source of law. Consent being the basis of international law, resolutions of the General Assembly adopted unanimously or by a substantial majority is indicative of the consent of all these States which vote for it or abstain from voting on it. The Patna Declaration as adopted by International Law Teachers from India and Nepal in 1970 recommended that any resolution passed by the Assembly by its three-fourth majority should be treated as enunciating a principle of international law [10].

The United Nations having 149 States as its members is indeed the most representative organisation whose resolutions deserve to be treated as quasi-conventional, if not conventional international law. Indeed, there are many resolutions of the General Assembly which have been treated as, or have created, new rules of international law. For example, the Universal Declaration of Human Rights 1948 is the result of the General Assembly resolution of 10th December, 1948. The Convention Against Elimination of Racial Discrimination, 1965 is another example. The two International conventions on Social, Cultural and Civil Rights 1966 are the result of resolutions passed by the General Assembly. Declaration on Decolonisation, Declaration on Territorial Asylum and Declaration on Principles Governing Friendly Relations Among Nations are a few principles of international law, which have been declared as such by resolutions of the General Assembly. The present trend makes the resolution of the General Assembly a very common source of international law.

NOTES

1. Colombian-Peru Asylum Case, 1950 I.C.J. Reports 276-77. The case involved Haya de La Torre, a Peruvian revolutionary who had taken refuge in the Colombian legation after an unsuccessful attempt at a coup d'etat. Later, the Colombian Embassy asked for safe conduct from the Peruvian Government for taking the refugee outside Peru which the Government refused. The case was referred to the international Court of Justice by mutual agreement for determining whether there was any customary rule of diplomatic asylum on the American continent as claimed by Colombia but challenged by Peru.
2. Also the Court said: "there has been so much inconsistency in the rapid succession of Convention on asylum, ratified by some and rejected by others, and the practice has been so much influenced by considerations of political expediency in the various cases that it is not possible to discern in all this any consistent and uniform usage." Ibid as cited by L.C. Green, International Law through the cases, (1959) p. 321.
   Also see the case of United States Nationals in Morocco, 1952 I.C.J. Reports 200.
3. Cheng Bin, General Principles of Law as Applied by International Courts and Tribunals (1958); Schlesinger Rudolf, B. Research on the General Principles of Law Recognised by Civilised Nations, (1957)51 A.J.I.L. 734.
4. Legal Status of Eastern Greenland, decided on April 5, 1933-P C.I.J Series A/B No. 53 at p. 73.
5. Right of Passage over Indian Territory case (Portugal vs India) 1960 I.C.J. Reports p. 42.
6. Lauterpacht H. The Development of International Law by the Court of International Justice (1958).
7. Re Castioni, (1891) I.O.B. 149.
8. Banco Nacional de Cube *vs*. Sabbatino, 376 U.S. 396.
   Also see Pengler, Judicial interpretation of International Law in the United States (1928).
9. Hingorani, R.C., International Law Through United Nations (1972) 193; Higgins Rosylin, Development of International Law Through Political Organs of the United Nations (1963).
10. Hingorani, R.C., op .cit., pp. 201-02.

CHAPTER 3

RELATIONSHIP BETWEEN MUNICIPAL LAW AND INTERNATIONAL LAW

International law regulates relations between States while municipal law is law of the given land. Yet, international law has an impact on municipal law and *vice versa*. Treaties are within the domain of international law but many treaties require national legislation for implementation. Besides, these treaties affect municipal law. Again, in some cases, it is given to municipal law to implement international law within national boundaries. Diplomatic immunities granted by international law would become a sham unless the same are recognised and protected by municipal law. Similarly, customary rules of international law governing extradition are to be interpreted and applied by municipal courts. The state determines rules for conferring its nationality upon certain persons. At the same time, nationality is a link between an individual and international law. All this shows that there is constant interaction between municipal and international law. It is, therefore, necessary to ascertain the relationship between the two and determine how they coexit and what happens if one is in conflict with the other.

Relationship between municipal law and international law has given rise to a number of theories. Five theories are prevalent in this field today; these are monistic, dualistic, transformation, delegation and harmonisation.

Monism

Kelsen, Kunz and Wright are the protagonists of this theory [1]. According to the monistic theory, international law and municipal law are both species of one genus—law. They deny dualist's allegations that international law and municipal law have different sources as well as different subjects. It is asserted by monists that law is a command whether it is the case of international law or municipal law. Similarly, although it may be said that States are subjects of international law while individuals are subject of municipal law, in the ultimate analysis, individuals become subjects of international law. Municipal as well as international law are part of one universal legal system, which is binding on human beings, either collectively or singly. Supporters of the monism theory consider international law as superior to national law.

Dualists

Triepel, Anzilloti, Oppenheim and Lauterpacht have been the exponents of the dualist theory [2]. Their contention is that international law and municipal law are two different systems because of basic points of difference between the two. Dualists contend that while international law regulates relations between States, municipal law regulates relations between individuals. Again, international law develops through the consent of States while municipal law operates by the will of the sovereign. Others doubt the validity of international law without disputing the sanctity of municipal law. Dualists consider municipal law to be superior to international law.

Transformation Theory

Supporters of this theory say that for any rule of international law to be observed under municipal law, it has to be transformed into municipal law. This transformation may be by mere recognition of the customary rules of international law as part of national law or by specific incorporation of conventional law. In both the cases, there has got to be a transformation. The transformation theory is said to have been inspired by dualists, who favour the supremacy of municipal law.

Delegation Theory

Protagonists of this theory contend that practices show that many rules of international law are left to States and national law for implementation. Thus, the problem of implementation is delegated to national law. This leads to the theory of delegation.

Harmonisation Theory

An exponent of this recent theory is professor D.P.O. Connel [3]. He says that international and national law are to be interpreted in such a way that there is harmony between the two laws. This may be considered as a rule of interpretation inasmuch as that rules of municipal and international law which may obviously be in conflict with each other are so interpreted as to be in harmony with each other.

Analysis

While academic discussion may continue regarding the relationship of international law and municipal law, the fact is that international law and municipal law are both species of the common genus—law, and both the branches of law affect the individual whose importance is progressively increasing in the international area. It cannot be denied that for most part of international law, it relies upon municipal courts for implementation of its norms, like recognition, succession, nationality, extradition and diplomatic relations. As to how for international law is accepted by municipal law is a matter of practice by different States and the same is discussed below.

United Kingdom

Customary rules of international law which have been universally recognised are considered as part of the British municipal law [4]. English courts have treated universal international law as part of the law of the land, subject to the condition that it does not conflict with any British statute [5]. However, until these rules are adopted by courts or incorporated into municipal law by legislation, international law so far as its incorporation into municipal law is concerned, remains in a state of uncertainty in a similar way as custom becomes law when the seal of authority is put by courts [6]. But unlike custom, which requires to be proved, courts take judicial notice of customary rules of international law as given in textbooks [7].

Regarding adoption of treaties, the position in the United Kingdom is well given in McNair's latest Treatise on Law of Treaties [8]. It is a common practice there to place the treaty before the two Houses of the Parliament for 21 days before it is ratified [9]. However, it does not mean anything. Treaty does not automatically become part of British municipal law. Legislation has to be passed wherever the treaty seeks to affect the rights of individuals, overrule any statutory or common law, cede any territory as in the case of colonies [10]. In the absence of enabling legislation, a British statute will supersede conflicting treaty [11].

United States Practice [12]

In the United States of America, customary rules of international law and treaties are law of the land insofar as these rules do not conflict with the statutory law of the States [13]. Statutes are so interpreted as not to violate the customary rules of international law. However, if a statute is unambiguously in conflict with any customary rule of international law, the former prevails.

Treaties in the United States are in a better position than customary rules. Article VI clause 2 of the United States Constitution provides that treaties will be the 'supreme law of the land'. Therefore, treaty will prevail over earlier statute also where there is conflict between the two [14]. The fact is that treaty in order to be effective, has to have ratification by two-third majority of the U.S. Senate.

India [15]

Article 51 of the Indian Constitution says that "the State shall endeavour to foster respect for international law and treaty obligations in the dealings of the organised peoples with one another." Although this Article comes in the chapter on Directive Principles, which are not justifiable the above sermon should be considered as an article of faith by the State and its agencies including the judiciary. Article 51 is one of the Directive Principles of State Policy.

The courts would, therefore, treat customary rules of international law as part of the Indian municipal law unless there is such conflict between the two that they cannot be reconciled. In the absence of any such conflict, international law will be enforced by Indian municipal courts. This is in conformity with the British practice where customary international law has been treated as part of British law. This was the practice in the pre-independence era in India. Article 372 of the Indian constitution provides that all law which was in force in India before the commencement of the constitution from 26th January 1950, will continue to be in force unless it has been specifically repealed. Article 13 of the constitution further says that any existing law which may violate fundamental rights will cease to be effective. Therefore, customary rules of international law will continue to be valid in India under Article 372 unless they are repugnant to any of the fundamental rights. Indian judicial opinion is divided between monist and dualist theories.

NOTES

1. Kunz. Joseph, The Vienna School and International Law (1933-34) 11 New York University Law Quarterly Review 370-421; Lauterpacht H. Modern Theroies of Law (1933) pp. 125-9 for Kolsen's views; Jones, J. Walter, The Pure Theory of International Law (1935) 16 B.Y.I.L. 5-20.
2. Anzilloti; *Corso di diritto internationals*, Volume 1 (1928) pp. 29-38; *Triepel Volkerrecht land-es recht* (International and Municipal Law); *Lauterpacht*; Oppenheim's International Law, Volume 1 (Eight Edition) p. 37, footnote 1.
3. D.P.O'. Connel, International Law (1965) Vol. 1 P. 52
4. Blackstone, Commentaries on the Law of England, Volume IV, Chapter 5; West Rand Central Gold Mining Co. *vs* The King (1905) 2 K.B. 391; Felice Morgenstern, Judicial Practice and the Supremacy of International Law, (1950) B.Y.I.L. 42-92.
5. See remarks of Lord Atkin in Chung Chi Cheung *vs* R (1939) A C 160 at p. 168 where he said:
   "The courts acknowledge the existence of a body of rules which nations accept among themselves. On any judicial issue, they seek to ascertain what the relevant rule is, and having found it, they will treat it as incorporated into the domestic law, so far as it is not inconsistent with rules enacted by statutes or finally declared by their tribunals."
6. For contra, See R. *vs* Keyn (The Fran conies) (1876) 2 Ex. D. 63 at p. 202.
7. *Re Piracy Jure Gentium* (1934) A.C. 586.
8. The Law of Treaties (1961) 81-110.
9. Ibid p. 99.
10. For example, the British Parliament had to enact Indian Independence Act 1947 while giving Independence to India and Pakistan.
11. Colleo Deelings Ltd. *vs* Inland Revenue Commissioners (1961) I. All E.R. 762.
12. For details, see Erades and Gould, International Law and Municipal Law; for earlier works, see Quincy Wright, The Enforcement of International Law Through Municipal Law in the United States (1916).
13. The Paquete Habana (1900) 175 U.S. 677. at p. 700.
14. Bank Voor Bandel Scheep-Vart *vs* Kennedy (1961) 288 F. (2d) 375.
15. C.H. Alexandrovitcz, International Law in India, 1952 I.C.L.Q. 289.

CHAPTER 4

SUBJECTS OF INTERNATIONAL LAW

International law regulates relations among States. States are primary subject of international law. But difficulty arises as to the concept of State which is subject of international law because all States are not members of the international community. Only sovereign States enjoy this privilege. Discussion of the concept of State and its different categories, therefore, is considered essential.

Concept of State

State in its generic sense should fulfil the conditions of having: (a) permanent and organised population, (b) some territory, and (c) government to administer that territory.

However, all States having the above requisites do not become subjects of international law. A fourth requirement is necessary to qualify for international personality. That is the requirement of being sovereign. A State therefore, in order to be an international person, should have the following qualities:

(1) Permanent and organised population;
(2) Some territory;
(3) Government to administer that territory; and
(4) Sovereign status.

Article 1 of the Montevideo Convention of 1933 said that "The State as a person of international law should possess the following qualifications: (a) a permanent population, (b) a defined territory, (c) a government, and (d) a capacity to enter into relations with other States."

This writer agrees only partly with the above requirements. For example, permanent population alone will not do. The permanent population must be organised. Again a State may not have defined territory. Israel does not have one. This requirement of the Montevideo Convention is also vague.

Permanent and organised population

A State should have permanent and organised population. The population should be permanently settled in the territory. Any transitory population which has no moorings cannot form a State in the modern sense of the word. Similarly, a population must form itself into an organised society. One cannot conceive of a State consisting of exclusively an unorganised population although a State may have some organised as well as some unorganised population consisting of primitive tribes as was the case of the United States having Red Indians when it was first discovered and colonised.

Territory

There should be some territory attached to the State. One cannot visualise a State without territory which, as far as possible, should be well defined. There may, however, be some rare situations where the State's territory is not fully determined as in the case of Israel whose boundaries have not been fixed since its inception due to a state of war between her and her Arab neighbours. All territory need not be inhabitated. Some territory may remain uninhabitated. In some cases, it may be very thinly inhabitated. As to what constitutes State territory and how it can be acquired in international law is discussed separately.

Government

There must be some government which administers the territory for the welfare of the permanent population. Administration would mean maintenance of law and order within the territory as well as carrying out other duties of government inclusive of passing of law and administering justice to its people.

Sovereign status

This fourth essential is a 'must' for acquiring membership of the world community. Only sovereign States can be the subjects of international law. By sovereign status, it would mean that the government is independent in its internal as well as external activities. Any fetter on its activities may compromise its position in international law. Of course, the word 'sovereignty' has undergone a great dilution since it was initially defined by Bodin and Hobbes. In the original sense of the word, sovereignty was absolute and indivisible. No State is an absolute sovereign today. By passage of time, the State has committed itself to many limitations on its sovereignty. Nevertheless, it maintains its sovereign status in the circumstances to be able to be a member of the world community.

This writer has doubts about the fourth requirement of the Montevideo Convention regarding "capacity to enter into relations with other States." It may be noted that a number of States may have entered into international relations with other States despite the fact that they were not sovereign States. India was a member of the United Nations before it attained independence in 1947. Tibet entered into a number of international agreements although its independent character was doubtful. These and other similar instances only mean to convey that even non-sovereign States may have the capacity to enter into international relations. Capacity does not make them eligible to be members of the world community. In order to become an international person, a political community has to have sovereign status, irrespective of the capacity of that community.

Categories of States

States may be divided into many categories depending upon their status in international law. Well-known categories are: Unitary, Federal, Confederation, Vassal, Protectorate, Trust and Colony.

Unitary States

A State which has a single centralised government responsible for governing its whole territory is known as a unitary type of State. Burma and Sri Lanka are unitary types of States. Singapore is another, so also the State of the United Kingdom although it comprises England, Scotland and Northern Ireland. There is, however, only one government which is responsible for governing the whole territory of the United Kingdom. France is also a unitary State.

Federal States

In a federal State, there is one government at the centre and the other Governments in the provinces. India, the United States of America, Malaysia, Canada, and Australia are examples of a federal State. In such cases, only the central government is considered to be an international person which is entrusted with the task of conducting the external affairs of the State. The provincial governments have no status in international law.

Confederation

The word 'confederation' is a very loosely defined word. In some cases, confederation is nothing else but only a synonym of federal government with little more power given to the provincial government. For example, Switzerland is considered to be a confederation of cantons (provinces) which enjoy comparatively more powers than provinces under a federal system. There is no hard and fast demarcation between federal and confederate States. But so far as international law is concerned, only the Central Swiss Government is an international person.

Confederation may also connote a Union of independent States which may form a Union for some particular purposes but have left individual status of the joining States intact. Such States continue to be international persons individually thus making a union an internal affair. At present, there is no such confederation existing although such attempts have been made in the Arab world, as between Syria, Egypt and Libya from time to time.

Protectorate

A State which is small and weak may enter into an arrangement with another State to take care of its defence and external affairs. In such a situation, the State which seeks protection of the powerful neighbouring State in conduct of its foreign and other affairs as agreed upon between the two States is called a Protectorate. There are no fixed conditions for a protectorate. Each protectorate may have its own terms with the protecting State. Bhutan has one set of terms with India and could become a member of the United Nations despite its being a protectorate. Sikkim had different set of terms when it was India's protectorate before referendum in favour of its merger with India in 1975.

A protectorate State is a State in the making. The terms of arrangement regarding protection are chalked out in mutual consultation with each other between the protectorate and the protecting State. In the case of Tunis Morocco Nationality Decrees, the PCIJ held that relationship between the protectorate and protecting State as well as relations of these two States with rest of the world depend upon the terms of treaty or arrangement which has created the special status. No uniform rules apply; nor is there any uniform practice. Treaty of Protection need not always be between the two concerned countries. A protectorate could be created under an international treaty in respect of a third territory. The Ionian Islands were British protectorates under an international treaty between Great Britain, Russia, Austria and Prussia.

Status of a protectorate State in international law has not been free from controversy. Some say it is an independent State which because of its inherent smallness and weakness has entrusted the job of external and defence affairs to a powerful or neighbouring State. This trust can be revoked at any time. The Ionian Islands were termed as "free and independent State" although they were the protectorate of Great Britain. The Sultan of Johore was given sovereign immunity by the court in 1894 although he was only Head of the British Protectorate [1]. Under the Treaty of February 1912, Morocco remained a sovereign State which authorised France to exercise some of its sovereign powers on behalf of Morocco. In other cases, a protectorate is completely assimilated with the protecting State, thus making the former as good as a colony or federated State as the case may be, depending upon whether the two States are neighbours or not.

Bhutan

Bhutan is a Protectorate State of India, having a population of about eight hundred thousand. It is very strategically situated in the Himalayas. It has common borders with India and Tibet. There is a 1950 Treaty of Protection between Bhutan and India which permits India to govern Bhutan's external relations with other countries. In 1971, India sponsored Bhutan's membership to the United Nations. It was the second State to recognise Bangla Desh in December 1971. Nevertheless, it continues to be Protectorate of India.

Vassal State

The vassal status for any State is yet another instance of a confused state of affairs. There have been different stages of colonisation, varying from an outright colony to other nomenclatures, including a vassal State which is considered to be under the suzerainty of the powerful State. What is the actual relationship between the vassal and suzerain State? A vassal State is definitely not sovereign and independent. The rest depends upon what the suzerain power has delegated to the vassal State towards internal administration. Normally a vassal State has internal autonomy subject to overall control of the suzerain power. But it cannot be called a self-governing territory which also comes between a colony and a sovereign State.

In some cases, vassal States have exercised international and sovereign rights like entering into some treaties and sometimes even sending emissaries to foreign countries. But that does not make the vassal State. At the most, it can be called a quasi-sovereign State. In any case today, the word is of historical importance only as there are no so-called vassal States.

Tibet

Tibet requires special mention here in view of its importance as a buffer State between India and China and also because of its uncertain international status. Tibet was an independent State before it became vassal State of China. Nevertheless, it continued to negotiate treaties with foreign States. In 1842, there was a treaty between Tibet, the Raja of Jammu and China. In 1856, it entered into a treaty with Nepal. In 1904, Tibet signed a separate treaty with Great Britain in which it agreed to carry out the terms of the Sino-British Treaties of 1890 and 1893. Prior to that, Tibet had refused to carry out the terms of the same treaties to which it was not party. This showed the independent character of Tibet even it was a vassal State of China [2]. It is said that Tibet made declaration of independence in 1913 [3]. The Urga Treaty of 29th December, 1912 between Tibet and Mongolia recognised the independence of Tibet. This independence was reiterated by the Tibetan representative at the Simla Conference in 1914 in the following words:

> "It is decided that Tibet is an independent State and that the precious Protector, the Dalai Lama, is the Ruler of Tibet, in all temporal as well as in spiritual affairs". [4]

The Simla Agreement of 1914 recognised Tibetan autonomy under China although the British Political Officer in Sikkim often negotiated with Tibet directly, independently of China. The Chinese suzerainty over Tibet was minimal until the advent of the Peking regime in 1949. Thus, when the Peking Government sought to enforce its rule in 1949, the Dalai Lama, complained to the United Nations. In 1951, the Dalai Lama signed a treaty with China in which China recognised him as spiritual-cum-temporal ruler of Tibet subject to Chinese suzerainty.

Perhaps, the treaty was not liked by both the parties. The Peking regime was not happy with only its suzerain status; nor was the Dalai Lama happy for being subservient to the Peking regime. The simmering discontent erupted in March 1959 when the Dalai Lama had to flee to India with the occupation of Tibet by Chinese troops. Since then, the Dalai Lama has stayed in India hoping to return to Tibet some day.

Trust territory

The "trust" territory system was introduced after World War II under the United Nations Charter. It replaced the earlier "mandate" system which had been created by the Government of the League of Nations. It was thought that the word "trust" was desireable to connote that the administering State should consider this new type of colonial system as a trust to be redeemed as soon as the trust territory becomes fit to govern itself.

Under Article 77 of the United Nations, all mandate territories were to be called trust territories. Territories taken from enemy States after World War II were also treated as trust territories. Besides, colonial powers could convert their colonies into trust territories. Article 76(b) of the Charter aims at promoting "the political, economic, social and educational advancement of the inhabitants of the trust territories, and their progressive development towards self-government or independence as may be appropriate ......" The administering authority, therefore, has to prepare the trust territory for eventual attainment of independence in accordance with its stage of advancement. The administering authority has to submit annual reports regarding progress of the trust territory under her.

South West Africa (*Nambia*)

South West Africa was a mandated territory under the League system with South Africa as the mandatory power. After World War II, when the League of Nations was replaced by the United Nations, the mandatory system also ended. It was replaced by the trusteeship system under the United Nations Charter. The mandated powers were to negotiate new arrangements with the United Nations which is the supervisory body in respect of trust territories.

South Africa refused to negotiate new trusteeship arrangement with the United Nations and tried to incorporate South West Africa within its own Union. According to South Africa, since the League was no more, the mandate had ceased. The General Assembly referred the matter to the International Court of Justice in December, 1949 for advisory opinion on three counts:

(a) Does the Union of South Africa continue to have obligations under the mandate for South West Africa, and, if so, what are these obligations?

(b) Are the provisions of Chapter XII of the Charter applicable to the Territory of South West Africa?

(c) Has South Africa the competence to unilaterally modify the status of South West Africa?

In its opinion dated 11th July, 1950, the International Court of Justice advised that South Africa continued to have obligations with respect to South West Africa. It held that the General Assembly had the supervisory power to which South Africa was under obligation to submit annual reports as well as transmit petitions.

Regarding the second question, the court held that although mandated territory did not automatically become trust territory, Chapter XII applied to South West Africa since South Africa was under obligation to submit annual reports and transmit petitions. However, South Africa was free to accept or reject the terms of draft trusteeship agreement. It did not consider a mandatory State to be under a duty to negotiate and conclude trusteeship agreements.

Regarding the third question, the court held that South Africa cannot unilaterally modify the international status of South West Africa [5].

However, South Africa has persistently defied the United Nations resolutions. This prompted the General Assembly to recommend snapping of diplomatic relations by United Nations members in 1962. In 1963, the Security Council recommended oil embargo to South Africa. In 1966, the General Assembly terminated South Africa's trusteeship over South West Africa [6]. In 1971 the International Court of Justice considered South Africa's presence in South West Africa as illegal and advised her to withdraw from that territory. In 1972, the General Assembly recommended stopping of aid to South Africa. However, the Security Council has not been able to act due to veto by the United States, United Kingdom and France. In 1974, South Africa was not allowed to participate in the General Assembly's 29th Session due to rejection of its credentials. In 1974, the United Nations Commission for Nambia (African name for S.W. Africa) was appointed to negotiate transfer of administration from South Africa to United Nations Council for Nambia. However, Nambian problem has been a stalemate.

Micro or Mini States

Of late, the problem of mini States has been raised in the United Nations forums. Today, the United Nations has the membership of 149 States. All these States are equal and have one vote, irrespective of their size, population and economic viability. Some States are very small having the population of a few hundred thousands which may be less than the population of an average single city of a bigger State. Admission of mini States has tilted the balance in favour of newly independent States and boosted the number of non-aligned States. The United States is very sore about this development which has deprived her of a majority in the General Assembly and consequently in the Security Council. Again, while these States enjoy all the benefits which go with the United Nations membership, they contribute a very small amount towards the budget of the United Nations. This naturally causes a drag on the big States which have to contribute comparatively more than what they benefit. The block voting of these new small States has resulted in unpalatable results insofar as election to different bodies from the General Assembly is concerned. This has caused some bickering among big powers.

It was suggested in some quarters to introduce a new type of membership at the United Nations. The member may be called an associate member of the United Nations. According to these quarters an associate member cannot vote or seek office. Another suggestion was that these small States may themselves volunteer to abstain from voting and seeking office. Former U.N. Secretary-General, U Thant, is also on record having said that a demarcation has to be made somewhere in the admission of States as full members of the United Nations. According to him the right to independence should not be confused with full membership of the United Nations which is onerous [7].

However, small States which have now tasted the advantage of full membership without comparative duties are in no mood to abdicate their voting rights which often bring them some additional advantages in the bargain.

While it may be desirable to draw a line, it is impracticable to do so. The question normally asked is: how small is really small? Besides what should be the criteria for determining the smallness of a State; population, size or gross national product, or all the three combined together. There is no ready reckonor for this. The result is that it is left to the good sense of the new States whether to apply for membership or not. For example, Naura and Anguilla islands, which have the population of a few thousand each, preferred not to apply for U.N. membership. So far Maldive Island, which is a member of the United Nations had the lowest population of 100,000 at the time of admission in 1965.

Holy See (Vatican)

Until 1870, the Pope was the spiritual Head of the Catholic community in the world as well as temporal Head of the Papal States. Italy annexed the Papal States in 1870 but later on by the Treaty of Guarantee, 1871, it recognised the Pope as the spiritual Head along with some guarantees to him and the Holy See. Although, the Pope entered into a number of treaties and a number of ambassadors were accredited to his court, the position of the Pope as a sovereign was uncertain. Of course, he enjoyed privileges and immunities of a sovereign within the confined limits of the Vatican City in the city of Rome. It is said he did not leave his city until 1929.

Relations between the Pope and the Italian Government remained strained till 1929 when both signed the Lateran Treaty by which the Italian Government recognised the Pope as the temporal sovereign of the Vatican City with other paraphernalia of a sovereign country. The Vatican City, by virtue of its religious character, has remained neutral between the temporal claims of States. It does not participate in any conference except in one of a humanitarian nature.

The Vatican is the smallest of the small States and yet it enjoys more prestige because of its religious character. Otherwise it is like a small enclave within the city of Rome with no independent residents except those who are functionaries of the Church Basilica of St. Peter.

Whether the State should be called Holy See or Vatican, it is doubtful. It will, however, be safe to say that the State of Holy See is located in the conclave of the Vatican.

NOTES

1. Mighel vs Sultan of Johore (1894) 10. B. 149
2. Surya P. Sharma, The India-China Border Dispute, An Indian Perspective (1965) 59 A.J.I.L. 16 at pp. 20 and 21 Foot notes 23 and 24.
3. David McCabe, Tibet's Declaration of Independence (1966) 60, A.J.I.L. 370.
4. Ibid, p. 371
5. International Status of South West Africa, 1950 I.C J. Reports, p. 128
6. U.N.G.A. Resolution No 2145 ((XXI) dated 27 October, 1966. The vote was 114-2 (South Africa and Portugal (Voting against) Some people have doubted the legality of this resolution. But if the United Nations is the supervisory body and the administering State is a consistent violator, the only alternative is to revoke the trust, implied or express.
7. U.N.G.A.O.R (22nd session) 1967 Suppl: 14 (O/6701/Add. 1) p. 20.

CHAPTER 5

STATE TERRITORY

State Territory means the territory where the State can exercise exclusive jurisdiction which is a sign of sovereignty. One of the essentials of statehood is the exercise of sovereignty over some territory.

State territory is three dimensional. It consists of land, adjacent sea and air space. Land includes not only the surface but anything under and above the surface, i.e. mines and anything grown or constructed on the surface of the land. Laws relating to sea and air space are discussed after this chapter.

So far as acquisition of land as territory in international law is concerned [1], it can be acquired in a number of ways. Important modes of such acquisition may be summed up as occupation, prescription, annexation, plebiscite, transfer, accession, and accretion. Each one of them is discussed below.

Occupation

The word has a Roman origin. It is derived from 'occupatio' which in Roman Law meant occupation of a *res nullius* a thing owned by none before. In international law, it means that territory can be acquired by occupation if it is not anyone else's property before. Occupation has two essentials: discovery and exercise of sovereignty over it. In international law, *terra nullius* alone can be the object of *occupatio*. Only that 'terra' can be occupied which has not been occupied before. Land which has been occupied before even by aborigines cannot be owned by *occupatio*. Territory which is inhabited by local tribals can only be acquired by conquest and settlement. The United States, Canada, Australia and New Zealand were not discovered. There were settlements by European migrants in these territories which were already inhabited by local tribals who were not considered as civilised and, therefore, did not form part of the world community of nations. In the loose sense, however, *occupatio* has been applied to settlements on territories inhabited by local tribals. This is not a correct use of the word.

Occupation has two essentials: discovery and administration. Mere discovery does not give title to the discovering authority. It must be accompanied by effective administration with an intention to exclude another claimant. Few cases will illustrate the point.

In the Falkland dispute between Great Britain and Argentina, facts proved that the British garrison controlled it until 1774 when it was abandoned after leaving the British flag and a lead plate which contained British claim to the Islands. In 1832, Britain retook possession. It was held that Argentina had done nothing until 1832. The Islands were, therefore, held to be the property of the Great Britain.

The Palma Island Case : The Island was claimed both by the United States and Holland. The United States claimed the island on the basis of discovery as a successor of Spainish rights under a treaty of 1898 which transferred the Philippine Islands to the United States. Holland claimed administration over the island through Dutch East India Company in the seventeenth and eighteenth centuries. Evidence showed that native princes had transferred rights of sovereignty to the company and later to Holland. No act of administration on the part of Spain was shown. The Permanent Court of Arbitration held that Holland had exercised sovereignty over the disputed island [2]. The arbitrator held that "discovery alone, without any subsequent act, cannot at the present time suffice to prove sovereignty." [2] Subsequent action would mean administration depending upon circumstances and situation of each case.

Thus in the Clippertion Island case where the dispute was between France and Mexico, the French claim was based on the proclamation of French sovereignty by its officer in 1838 which was later officially ordered and published. It also granted concession for the exploitation of Guano. The Mexican claim was based on the Spanish discovery and altenatively the ineffectiveness of the French administration. The arbitrator upheld the French claim despite the island's contiguity to Mexico. It further held that acts of sovereignty may not necessarily be continuous. In given circumstances even isolated acts of exercise of sovereignty should be enough [3].

In the Eastern Greenland Case, the dispute was between

Norway and Denmark. Norway proclaimed sovereignty over the disputed territory, treating it as *terra nullius* until then. Denmark disputed it and claimed the disputed territory on the basis of the recognition of Danish sovereignty over it by some powers in addition to Danish enactments which were applied to the territory. The Permanent Court of International Justice, to whom the case had been referred, held that Danish legislation showed its intention and will to exercise sovereignty. It was therefore, declared to be under the sovereignty of Denmark. The Court did not consider active administration of the territory necessary in view of the inaccessible and uninhabited character of the territory [4].

It may be remarked here that in the case of territories with high terrain and inhospitable weather, which mostly remain uninhabited, even cartographical claims may be considered as enough evidence of exercise of sovereignty in the absence of concrete competing claim. Similarly rocky places which do not permit permanent settlement of even a blade of grass to grow may be the object of exercise of sovereignty through survey maps.

Question may arise whether possession of part of a region would amount to possession of the whole region. The question was answered by the King of Italy who gave the award in the arbitration between British Guiana and Brazil in 1904. He said:

> "effective possession of part of region although it may be held to confer a right to the acquisition of the sovereignty of the whole of a region which constitutes a single organic whole cannot confer a right to the acquisition of the whole of a region which, either owing to its size or to its physical configuration cannot be deemed to be a single organic whole *de-facto*" [5].

Therefore, it would all depend upon the character and position of the territory for purposes of determining whether possession of part of a territory would amount to possession of the whole. In my view, if there is a single administrative unit or central administration or if it is under one native ruler, it may be treated as possession of the whole. Similarly, if a nation controls the seacoast of any territory, it owns the territory behind the seacoast.

Prescription

It is the adoption of municipal rule in international law by which a State having possession of a given territory for a long time is said to have acquired title over it. It is a case of adverse possession as is known to municipal lawyers. No show of title is necessary. Long possession and administration of the territory are sufficient.

Prescription is different from occupation. In *occupatio*, *terra nullius* is discovered and administered, not necessarily for a long time. In prescription, it is long possession of someone else's territory. In some cases, prescription may have semblance of occupation when the earlier discoverer of the territory abandons its claim to the territory or when prescription is claimed against the discoverer who has failed to consolidate and administer the discovered territory.

What are the conditions regarding acquisition of a territory in international law by prescription? The Indian municipal law required 12 years' peaceful enjoyment for claiming title by adverse possession. But no fixed time is given in international law; what is requires is a long, peaceful and public exercise of sovereignty. In the Portugo-Indian case regarding Right of Passage through the Indian Territory, the International Court of Justice held although Portugal had only right to collect revenue in Dadra and Nagar Haveli, it acquired sovereignty over these enclaves by long possession and exercise of sovereignty which had evoked no protests from any party [6].

Annexation

It is doubtful today if annexation is a valid mode of acquiring territory in international law. Earlier, the Kellog-Briand Pact of 1928 banned war as an instrument of national policy. Article 2(4) of the U.N. Charter prohibits the use of force against other States. All these rules give rise to an impression that annexation is not permissible in the present world situation. It is in this connection that Israel was asked to vacate the territories occupied by her during the six-day war of June 1967. Annexations or conquests did occur in the past before World War II. After World War II trends are different. They do not permit annexation through use of force. Today, use of force may only be permitted for the purpose of decolonisation. Colonies may become independent through use of force when the colonical power has refused to grant independence to its colonies. Algeria secured independence through use of force and so did Indonesia and French Indo-China although power was transferred to the local population in these territories by voluntary transfer when it was not found feasible to hold on against the wishes of the local population. These are called wars of liberation. India recovered Goa, Daman and Diu by use of force from Portugal because of Salazar's refusal to part with them. Similarly use of force may be permitted to recover a lost territory. Thus if India were to use force for recovery of its territories presently occupied by China since the 1962 war, India's action will not be considered as illegal. When Egypt resorted to force in October 1973 against Israel, no one blamed her.

Plebiscite

Plebiscite is one of the modes of acquiring territory. Indonesia got sovereignty over the territories of West Irian and East Timor through plebiscite. Saar was transferred to Germany through plebiscite. Sikkim, formerly an Indian protectorate, merged with India through plebiscite.

Plebiscite means ascertaining the wishes of the local population regarding their status either as part of a given State or as an independent entity. While plebiscite is an accepted mode of transferring sovereignty, the mode of holding plebiscite is controversial. It is difficult to say what is the proper agency for ascertaining the wishes of the people: Is it referendum on a particular point or general elections resulting in the emergence of pro-merger or a pro-independent party? Should such referendum or general election be on the basis of adult franchise or limited franchise? Is international supervision over referendum or general election necessary? If so, should the international agency be chosen by the interested State or it should be under the U.N. auspices? All these questions make the problem of plebiscite a little difficult.

Transfer

Territory may be transferred by one sovereign to another sovereign in international law. This process is popularly known as cession. Cession may be forced or voluntary; insofar as forced cession is concerned, it may amount to annexation and may thus raise doubts in the present-day world context. However, voluntary cession is an accepted procedure and, perhaps today, the most common procedure.

Voluntary cession may take the form of sale, exchange or gift.

Alaska was sold to the United States by Russia by the Alaskan Cession Treaty of 1867. The city of Bombay was given to the British ruler as a dowry. France transferred her Indian enclaves to India consequent upon her attaining independence in 1947. A State may also cede some portion of its territory and make it a separate independent unit. Cession may be motivated by a number of reasons. It may be based on award by boundary tribunals, just as in the case of Radcliffe award and the Kutch Tribunal Award between India and Pakistan. It may be transferred on the basis of self determination, just as Saar was transferred by France to West Germany. Similarly West Irian had been transferred to Indonesia subject to the ultimate choice of its citizens who later consented to such a transfer. It could also be a matter of exchange which results in cession and acquisition of a territory.

Accession cum Merger

Small territory may accede to or merge with a bigger State. When India became free in 1947, there were a number of princely States which were under the British paramountcy. The British paramountcy lapsed with its withdrawal from the Indian sub-continent. These princely States were allowed to remain separate States or merge with India or Pakistan. There were roughly 500 such States which acceded to either Pakistan or India. None preferred to remain independent. Initially the Maharaja of Kashmir negotiated an agreement with India as well as Pakistan. Soon thereafter, when the Pakistan pressure increased on the Maharaja through clandestine infiltration into Kashmir valley, the Maharaja acceded to India on 26th October, 1947.

Accretion

State gets extra territory when the river changes its course and leaves behind some dry land where it was previously flowing. This becomes the property of the State. Similarly, extra territory may be obtained by the State by reclamation of the adjoining sea. The principle of accretion however applies if there is a gradual change of course. But, if there is sudden and abrupt change of course of the river, no territory is gained and the boundaries will remain as if there is no change of course.

Recent Trends

Recent trends have brought new dimensions to the acquisition of territory in international law. Self determination is one. Colonies have become independent on this principle. However, extension of this principle any further would tend to create complications and threaten disintegration of otherwise single units. The former U.N. Secretary U Thant, has once said that no right of self-determination can be given to constituent units of Member States of the United Nations.

Ethnic affinity has been given as a cause for claiming territory which is inhabited by the given ethnic group in another State. Contiguity is another factor which influences the States to claim adjacent areas. However, contiguity is no recent innovation. The United States claimed the Palmas Island on the basis of it being contiguous to the Philippines which was then U.S. territory [7]. The claim was rejected. But the principle of contiguity was upheld in the Eastern Greenland case by the Permanent Court of International Justice when Denmark had taken that plea. Indonesia claimed West Irian on the basis of ethnic similarity and contiguity. Contiguity has been a determining factor in giving sovereignty over nearby islands beyond territorial waters to the littoral State. In the Anna Case, Lord Stowell held such Island as natural appendages which function as portico to the sea shore [8].

Multinational claims to the Antarctica are based on contiguity, administration or discovery. There have been claims by Argentina, Chile, Norway, Denmark, the Soviet Union, Australia, New Zealand, Canada, the United Kingdom, France over the Antarctic region. Only France lays its claim on discovery and Norway and Denmark for actual administration [9]. The 1959 Treaty for Peaceful Co-operation in the Scientific Exploration of the region does not solve any claims regarding ownership. Future events alone will show the sensitivity of the knotty problem relating to sovereignty in the Antarctica.

Historic reasons have of late been advanced for recovery of territory which once belonged to the State but which was transferred by its functionaries to another State at a time when they were either weak or corrupt. These reasons have some validity.

Nationalism is often nourished by frontier disputes which erupt into war. The post-World War II era has not only witnessed proliferation of States but also proliferation of border disputes.

The Soviet Union has been the worst victim of this nationalism. Romania has border disputes with the Soviet Union over Bessarbia and Bukovina; Japan has border disputes with the Soviet Union regarding a chain of islands stretching over 1000 kilometres from Hokkaido in Japan, to Kamchatka in the Soviet Union; China also claims great chunks of Soviet territory. China claims that the Amur river was known as Heilung Kiang river. It also calls Vladivostok by the Chinese name of Haishenwei and identifies the industrial city of Khabarovk as the ancient city of Poli. According to Chinese sources, these were seized by Czarist Russia under an unequal treaty of 1860. The Soviet Union refutes Chinese claims by saying that the Sino-Soviet border is along natural frontiers which were legalised by three treaties. The Soviets further claim that the Sino-Soviet Agreement of 1924 annulled all inequitable and secret agreements. The three treaties of Aigung, Tiensin and Peking were not considered as inequitable. On the African continent there are border disputes between Algeria and Morocco, Ethiopia and Sudan, Mali and Somalia, Tunisia and Algeria, Dahomey and Niger, Ghana and Ivory Coast, Liberia and Guinea, Uganda and Sudan, Senegal and Gambia, aad Chad, Niger and Libya.

NOTES

1. For detailed study, see Hill, Claims to Territory in International Law and Relations (1945); R. Jennings, Acquisition of Territory in International Law (1963).
2. United Nation Report (1928) Volume II, 829, at p. 846.
3. U.N. Reports (1931) Volume II, p. 1105.
4. P.C.I.J. Series A/B No. 53 (1933).
5. As cited by O' Connel, International Law (1965) Volume I, pp. 476-77.
6. 1960 I.C.J. Reports 42.
7. Jessup, The Palmas Island Arbitration, (1928) 22 A.J.I.L. 735-52.
8. (1805) 5.C. Rob. 373.
9. For vairous writings on the subject, please see, Hayton Robert, The American Antarctic, (1956) 50 A.J.I.L. 583 Toma, Peter A., Soviet Attitude Towards the Acquisition of Territorial Sovereignty in the Antarctic, (1956) 50 A.J.I. L. 611.

CHAPTER 6

AIRSPACE AND OUTER SPACE

Airspace

State territorial sovereignty extends to airspace above its territory. Until the nineteenth century, States did not attach much importance to airspace. However, with the advent of the aircraft invented by Wright brothers, airspace assumed importance in the world community. Initiation of aerial warfare in World War I made the State's security vulnerable through aerial bombing and espionage by the enemy. States, therefore, started exercising sovereignty in airspace above their territory.

Until World War I, a subjacent State exercised sovereignty over airspace above its territory unilaterally. This was confirmed by Article 1 of the Paris Convention of 1919 which gave "complete and exclusive sovereignty" in airspace to the subjacent State over its territory including its territorial waters.

The Paris Convention which dealt with aerial navigation, however, permitted right of innocent passage through a State's airspace during peacetime. Some Latin American States to which the Paris Convention was not applicable preferred to conclude the Havana Convention in 1928.

The Paris and Havana Conventions of 1919 and 1928 were replaced by the overall Chicago Convention of 1944 towards the end of World War II. It reiterated State sovereignty in airspace over its territory. By this time, the States had been embroiled in global war which had given them the horrors of aerial warfare which was fraught with doom and disaster. The final blow came as a parting kick from the United States which used two nuclear bombs on Hiroshima and Nagasaki in 1945.

States have zealously guarded their airspace from unwanted intrusions. They do not brook any interference with it. Aerial intrusions were sternly dealt with when an Indian military canberra was shot down by Pakistan while it was on routine survey flight in 1957. Pakistan claimed that it had intruded into Pakistan airspace [1]. The United States U-2 was shot down by a Soviet rocket in May 1960 [2]. It created a furore in the world community. This was followed by the shooting down of a RB-47 in July, 1960. While the Soviet Union claimed that the RB-47 had intruded into Soviet airspace, the United States denied the charge claiming that it was flying over international waters [3].

While there is right of innocent passage of foreign civil aircraft under Article 5 of the Chicago Convention, 1944, it is not universally acceptable to all States in view of State's vulnerability through airspace. But all aerial intrusions do not meet the same drastic response [4]. It depends upon the nationality of the aircraft and its mission. If it belongs to a friendly State, it does not create much fuss, etc. Similarly, if intrusion is innocent as in the case of distress, mistake or loss of route, it is condoned provided the pilot responds to the orders of the control tower of the territorial State. The subjacent State may permit the intruding aircraft to land or ask it to flyover. Distressed aircraft may be allowed to land if it is short of fuel or has been brought into foreign airspace by hijackers or has developed some mechanical defect which has affected its airworthiness.

The intrusion could also be hostile or from a hostile country. Intrusion is hostile if the motive is attack, reconnaisance, aid to subversive activities, smuggling or calculated defiance of the control tower. If the aircraft is military or belongs to an enemy or potential enemy, it may evoke hostile response.

In all the cases of aerial intrusions, the territorial State has the right to order the aircraft pilot to land at a given point or face the consequences of disobedience. The aircraft must invariably be given warning to land. There should be no instant shooting down of aircraft, particularly of civil commercial aircraft. Any precipitate action of shooting down should be preceded by warning. In extreme cases, when either it is military aircraft or there is calculated disobedience of orders from below, the aircraft may be shot down in the interest of the State's security.

At the Chicago Diplomatic Conference in 1944, some States wanted to incorporate "Five Freedoms of the Air" in the convention. The idea was dropped due to resistance to these freedoms on the part of a number of States to include them in the convention.

Consequently, two separate Agreements were signed in Chicago. The Five Freedoms of the Air relate to:

(a) fly across foreign territory without landing;

(b) land for non-traffic purposes;

(c) disembark in a foreign country traffic originating in the State of origin of the aircraft;

(d) pick-up in a foreign country traffic destined for the State of origin of the aircraft; and

(e) carry traffic between two foreign countries.

While the first two freedoms were brought in International Air Services Transit Agreement, signed on 7th December, 1944, all the five freedoms were brought in another International Air Transport Agreement signed on the same date. From the practices of States, however, it has been found that very few States subscribe to five freedoms. Instead, States have found it convenient to conclude special agreements for the above freedoms. In case of the first two freedoms—fly across and landing for non-traffic purposes, it depends upon the good relations between two countries. For example, India did not allow Pakistan aircraft to fly across Indian territory after the hijacking of an Indian Airlines Fokker Friendship in 1971. Pakistan reciprocated. The 'fly across' permission was reciprocally given in 1976 when diplomatic relations were restored between them. The other three freedoms are subject to negotiations and agreement between any two countries which permit such rights on a reciprocity basis to their respective national airlines.

Outer Space

While the Paris Convention, 1919 and Chicago Convention, 1944 confirmed a subjacent State's sovereignty in airspace, it was never defined. Nor was its height fixed. The common notion of airspace sovereignty was understood to be sovereignty in airspace *ad infinitum*. This was also called *usque ad coelum*. With the experimentation during International Geophysical Year in 1956, jurists and scientists were confronted with the problem of defining airspace and separating it from outer space.

Some defined airspace as that part of space above surface which contains air to lift the aircraft. Others defined it as containing atmospheric gases. Yet others refused to give a restrictive definition of airspace, partly due to practical difficulties in fixing the ceiling of airspace [5]. Resultantly, no boundary line could be fixed between airspace and outer space. Confronted with these difficulties, the jurists just ignored to demarcate between airspace and outer space. Thus while airspace and outer space are freely used in different connotations, no attempt is made at defining and differentiating between them.

This outer space may be defined as space above airspace. The first satellite, sputnik, was launched on 4th October, 1957. Since then outer space has been a fertile ground for many satellites which orbit around the earth for a variety of purposes—from peaceful to reconnaisance and military. The United States and the Soviet Union have been the two pioneering States in the launching of satellites and experimentation in outer space. A satellite has landed on the moon as well as on Mars. India also launched its first satellite, Aryabhatta, in April 1975 from a Soviet Cosmoport with the help of a Soviet rocket. There has also been a unique mass communication experiment through Satellite Instruction Television Experiment with the help of the United States Applied Technology Satellite-ATS 6—from 1st August, 1975 to 31st July, 1976.

Satellites pass through the outer as well as airspace of various countries. States have not objected to the orbiting of satellites through their sovereign zones. Some jurists have considered this as acquiescence [6]. However, this should not be taken as such. For one thing, States have either no means to control space activities of other States or it is costly for them to do so. Besides, space activities are carried out by the two super powers for the common benefit of other States also to whom they transmit part of the scientific data collected by them.

The United Nations General Assembly has been trying to evolve the space law through its Committee on Peaceful Uses of Space. The Committee is assisted by a legal sub-committee which looks after the legal aspects of space exploration. The first important resolution of the General Assembly was 1962 (XVIII) of 13th December, 1963 which had been unanimously adopted. The resolution enunciated some legal principles which are summarised below.

(a) Free exploration and use of outer space for all makind on basis of equality;

(b) No national appropriation of celestial bodies;

(c) Activities relating to exploration and use of outer space in accordance with international law and the U.N. Charter;

(d) States bear responsibility for space activities, whether

State-sponsored or otherwise;

(e) Exercise of jurisdiction over space vehicles by State of registry;

(f) Duty of State to assist and rescue astronauts in distress.

Earlier there was Resolution 1884 (XVIII) of 17th October, 1963 which prohibited placing of nuclear weapons in space vehicles. There was yet another resolution of the General Assembly 2222 (XXI) of 14th December 1966 which commended a Treaty on space as its annexe. The Treaty was signed simultaneously in London, Moscow and Washington on 27th January, 1967. It is better known as the Treaty on Principles Governing the Activities of States in the Exploration and Use of Outer Space, including the Moon and other Celestial Bodies. It is a seventeen article treaty. It reaffirms and elaborates the principles of 1963.

Article 1 of the Treaty declares that exploration and use of outer space will be for the benefit of and in the interests of all countries. It shall be free for exploration and use by all States, irrespective of their economic development. There shall be freedom of scientific research.

Article 2 reiterates that celestial bodies shall not be subject to occupation or national appropriation. Article 3 says that space activities will be in accordance with international law, the U.N. Charter and in the interest of maintaining international peace and security and promoting international cooperation and understanding.

Article 4 reiterates resolution 1884 of 1963 which prohibited the placing of nuclear weapons in space vehicles or stations which are put in orbit. It declares that the moon and other celestial bodies are used exclusively for peaceful purposes.

Article 5 regards astronauts as envoys of mankind in outer space and States undertake to render all possible assistance to astronauts in distress.

Articles 6 and 7 make the launching or a sponsoring State responsible for activities in space as well as any damage caused by such activities.

Article 8 gives jurisdiction over space vehicles to a State of registry irrespective of their position, whether on land, airspace or celestial body.

Article 9 requires mutual cooperation and assistance among launching States which shall not do anything which will interfere with peaceful experimentation by other States.

Article 10 provides that in order to promote international co-operation in space exploration, launching States should give opportunity to other States to observe flight of space objects. Article 11 envisages dissemination of scientific knowledge acquired through space experimentation to the United Nations, international scientific community and to public.

Article 12 gives free access to all States to any space stations, installations, equipment and space objects on the moon or other celestial bodies on the basis of reciprocity.

It is hoped that the principle of reciprocity is applicable to launching States only. In the case of non-launching States, which cannot launch satellites due to paucity of funds and lack of technological know-how, free access to installations may be given.

Notes

1. The Times of India, April, 11, 1959,
2. The Times of India, May 6, 1960.
3. The Times of India, July 13, 1960.
4. Hingorani, R.C., Aerial Intrusions and International Law, 1960 Northernlands International Law Review, 165-169.
5. Hingorani, R.C., An Attempt to determine sovereignty in space, December 1957 Kansas City Law Review 5-12.
6. Starke, J.G., Introduction to International Law (1967), 173.

CHAPTER 7

LAW OF SEA

The sea has been fairly rough in the twentieth century. It had enjoyed comparative peace for three centuries during which period, the Law of Sea remained stabilised. The sea was then divided into three major parts—territorial sea, contiguous zone and high seas. Territorial sea was a considered part of the territory of a coastal State which exercised exclusive jurisdiction over that portion of the sea. It extended up to three nautical miles, the extent of a cannon shot as enunciated by Bynkershoek. This was called the principle of effective exercise of jurisdiction. A coastal State exercised jurisdiction over contiguous zone adjacent to the territorial sea for police purposes. A coastal State advanced grounds of maintaining the health of its people on the mainland, regulating external trade, and to avoid smuggling but these were considered as subsidiary reasons. The contiguous zone extended for an extra three miles besides the three mile territorial sea. Beyond the territorial sea and contiguous zone lay the high seas which were free to all the nations. The doctrine of the high seas as free for all was advocated by Grotius who deprecated the idea of the maritime powers in the seventeenth century to apportion the sea amongst themselves to colonise for purposes of external trade with the African and Asian States and thus creating zones of influence for them. Then the maritime powers were toying with the idea that whosoever controlled the sea controlled the universe. They were, therefore, vying with each other to supervise large chunks of the sea. However, with Grotius' strong plea for the *mare liberum* the concept of freedom of the high seas was well established by mid-seventeenth century. This three-tier compartmentalisation of the whole sea dominated the world scene up to the early twentieth century. Things have began to change during this century. For example, Russia claimed a twelve mile territorial zone in 1909 and the Scandinavian countries claimed four miles. In 1930, the Hague Codification Conference failed to decide on a maximum limit of territorial sea. The stalemate has continued to linger.

In 1945, President Truman of the United States issued a Proclamation on 28th September unilaterally assuming jurisdiction over the continental shelf for purposes of exploitation of petroleum and mineral resources of the sea. The other States, instead of denouncing the unilateral action of the United States, followed its example and assumed similar jurisdiction over their respective continental shelves; India did so in 1951. This new development in the realm of the sea and other allied problems like fishing gave rise to a demand for a diplomatic conference to sort out the Law of Sea. It culminated in the covening of the Diplomatic Conference in 1958 in Geneva. The International Law Commission had done good spadework for this Conference in the form of preparing a draft convention.

The Geneva Diplomatic Conference concluded four Conventions on the Law of Sea. These are the Convention on the Territorial Sea and Contiguous Zone, Convention on High Seas, Convention on Fishing and Conservation of Living Resources of the High Seas and the Convention of the Continental Shelf. However, the Diplomatic Conference was only partly successful. It left a number of issues unsolved particularly the width of the territorial sea and exclusive fishing rights of the littoral States. While the developing and new States claimed 12 miles as territorial sea, the maritime States like the United States and the United Kingdom were in favour of retention of a three-mile limit of territorial sea. At the most, they could accept only six miles as territorial sea in deference to the preponderant wishes of the developing States, besides an additional six miles as fishing zone subject to historial and traditional rights of the fishing nations. But, this did not come through. Reluctance on the part of the maritime States to extend the jurisdiction of littoral States was obvious. These maritime powers did not want to lose their hold on sea manoeuvres for political and economic reasons. The second diplomatic conference on Law of Sea held in 1960 was again a failure due to clash of interests between the developing littoral States and the maritime powers. The United States has large fishing interests near the coasts of the Latin American countries which are rich in tuna fish. A number of fishermen in Britain depend on cod fishing near Iceland for their livelihood. Besides, Britishers have developed a taste for cod fish which is not available anywhere near the British coast. Japan has also vast fishing stakes near the Soviet coast as well as elsewhere. Besides, big powers want freedom of navigation for political and strategical reasons. This is bound to be affected if littoral States appropriate large chunks of sea adjacent to their coasts either as territorial waters or as fishing or economic resources zones.

With the advent of a large number of newly independent States the clamour for extension of territorial waters became persistent. At the Geneva Diplomatic Conference in 1958, maritime States like the United States, the United Kingdom, Australia, France, Japan, and Netherlands were in favour of the three-mile limit. However, they were outnumbered by newly independent States along with the Latin American States which could not assert themselves earlier. The Asian-African States were in favour of twelve miles while most of the Latin-American States were in favour of 200 miles. Maritime States, however, were insistent that States cannot unilaterally alter an established rule of international law. These States were apprehensive that any extension of territorial waters to 12 miles would bring 116 international straits as national waters [1].

Innocent Passage

Maritime powers were reluctant to the extension of territorial waters because it would affect their freedom of navigation on the otherwise high seas. These powers wanted a guaranteed right of passage through territorial waters. As a U.S. spokesman put it:

> "Quite understandably countries that depend on maritime commerce and access to the oceans will only accept the 12-mile rule if they have some objective principle that guarantees continued passage.[2]"

Article 14 of the Geneva Convention on Territorial Sea and Contiguous zone, 1958 does permit the right of innocent passage through territorial waters, but disputes may arise as to what amounts to "innocent passage." Big powers assert that it should not be the discretion of the coastal State to determine the nature of passage [3]. One is at pains to understand as to who else should decide.

One could conceive of three agencies for the purpose—the coastal State, flag State or third party. Gardner had asserted that the coastal state's determination could be unilateral and subjective. If it were so, surely a flag State's determination will not be less biased. The big powers may suggest some neutral agency to determine the nature of passage through territorial waters. But that would not be a practicable suggestion. For one thing, it would be inconsistent with the nation of sovereignty of the territorial waters. In any case, the initial decision has got to be taken by the coastal State. If such a decision is adverse to the flag State, the controversy erupts and becomes time-consuming and purpose-defeating for the latter which would prefer gate-crashing. A coastal State would not be readily agreeable to it.

The controversy centres upon the right of innocent passage by warships as claimed by some and decried by others [4]. Sometimes, even a commercial vessel may just be a camouflage ship. Elsewhere electronic espionage may well be conducted by commercial vessels with sophisticated electronic equipment. This would entail the right of visit and search on the part of the coastal State within its territorial waters to the annoyance of the flag State.

Passage may be considered as innocent if it is not prejudical to the peace, good order and security of the State [5]. Undoubtedly, excessive vessel traffic may increase the chance of pollution through oil leakage, emission of gasses which may affect the healthy growth of fish in coastal waters.

Fishing Rights

Today, fishing has become lucrative and an important exchange earner. Coastal States have become conscious of rich fishing potential near their coasts. At the same time, they have become apprehensive that mechanised and distant-sea fishing fleet may deplete the stock due to over-exploitation. This has resulted in the extension of fishing and conservation zones by coastal States. Iceland has increased its fishing zone three times to 12 miles in 1958, 50 in 1972 and 200 in 1975. The European Economic Community has extended respective fishing zones to 200 miles [6].

At the 1958 Geneva Diplomatic Conference, an agreement on fishing zone was proving to be elusive. Small States wanted a 12 miles exclusive fishing zone. The fishing powers wanted recognition of historical and traditional rights of other States in the outer six miles zone. This was not acceptable to small coastal States.

Fishing has become a highly politicised matter. It involves

political, legal, economic and biological issues. For some States, it is a question of national existence. Fish accounts for 90 per cent of Iceland's total export. On the other hand, deprivation of traditional grounds may render thousands of British, American and Japanese fishermen out of their family business. Two-thirds of total deep-sea catch for the British comes from waters near Iceland.

Fishing resources are not inexhaustable. Mechanised over-fishing may threaten extinction of the fishing industry in some areas. Article 1 of the Convention of Fishing and Conservation of Living Resources 1958 recognises the interests of coastal States in fishing and conservation of living resources on the high seas adjacent to their coasts. There have been conservation agreements relating to closed seasons, no fishing in spawning and breeding areas, maximum catch limit, fixing national quota and prohibition on catch of young fish [7]. A number of States including India have claimed conservation zones.

India has a good fishing zone of about 4,00,000 square kilometres of which only 20 per cent has so far been tapped. It exports fishing products like prawns, squids, cuttle fish, perch and tuna although prawns account for 90 per cent of the fish export. Presently, Indian fishing is confined to its narrow coastal belts. Deep waters have remained untapped. According to data supplied by the Central Marine Fisheries Research Institute, there are extensive stocks of shrimps in 150-160 fathoms off the Southwest Coast. Stocks of oil sardines and mackerel can also be increased substantially if mechanised boats are used during off-season, May to October, when the shoals move further offshore.

There is also a great potential of anchovy fishing which can be found in the southwest and southeast coast. The Gujarat coast is rich in prawns. Squids and cuttle fish can be found along the southwest coast and the Bay of Bengal. Tuna resources of the high seas near the Indian coast have remained unexploited due to want of trawlers capable of remaining at sea for days together. India has not yet taken to deep and distant sea fishing. Nor has it got sophisticated mechanised boats to do fishing in a scientific manner. It is hoped that with technological advances, it may soon take to deep sea and distant sea fishing in a big way. Presently, India's annual marine catch is hardly 2.5 million tonnes. It has a potential of 11 to 20 million tonnes [8].

Some experts bring in biological factors in the regulation of fishing rights of coastal States. These scientists divide fish into three categories:

(a) Coastal fish;

(b) Anadromous fish like salmon upward swimming specie which spawn in fresh water river system and migrate thousand of miles away and return for spawning again in the fresh water river.

(c) Migratory fish, like tuna, which migrates all over the ocean.

While littoral States claim exclusive right over coastal fish, others claim traditional and historical rights over this specie. This had led to a clash of interests between coastal and distant fishing States like the United Kingdom and Japan. The trend seems in favour of coastal states.

In respect of anadromous fish, it is claimed that a State which maintains fresh water and promotes breeding should have a prior claim over the salmon irrespective of the distance from the coast.

With respect to migratory tuna fish, it is suggested to fix a global quota on the basis of maximum sustainable yield and distribute among the States, keeping in view the past fishing practice and interests of new States.

In view of the awakening of new States to the fishing potential, fishing States like Japan and the United Kingdom are feeling the strain. The United States has reduced the Japanese catch by 25 per cent crab and pollack in the Alaskan and East Bearing waters. With the introduction of a 200-mile economic resources zone with effect from 1st March, 1977 Japan is faced with more restrictions. Japan is also fearing restrictions on fish catch near the Siberian coast which is a major supplier of sea food to the Japanese. Resultantly, Japan is contemplating to develop fishing farms near the coast.

The United States is also having difficulties in respect of distant sea fishing in tuna and shrimp near the Latin-American coasts in the light of their claim over 200 miles as territorial waters. Canada has closed its Atlantic ports to Soviet fishing due to excessive fishing in view of acceptance of the 200-mile economic resources zone. The United Kingdom is also having trouble with Iceland over the latter's extension of its fishing zone to 200 miles.

Continental Shelf

The continental shelf is a post-World War II baby. It is a

prolongation of land mass into the sea. It was first proclaimed on 28th September, 1945 by President Truman when he sought unilateral jurisdiction over a continental shelf up to 100 fathoms (200 metres) for purposes of exploitation of sea minerals and petroleum products. Other States followed suit. India claimed jurisdiction over its continental shelf in 1951. In 1953, the International Law Commission recognised this right. By 1958, it had become a conventional rule of international law with the adoption of the Ganeva Convention on Continental Shelf. Article 1 defines the continental shelf as follows :

(a) "The sea bed and subsoil of the submarine area adjacent to the coast but outside the area of the territorial sea, to a depth of 200 metres or beyond that limit to where the depth of the superjacent waters admits of the exploitation of the natural resources of the said areas;

(b) The sea bed and subsoil of similar submarine area adjacent to the coasts of Island."

Omnibus clause of Article 1 has led the nations to interpret the extent of continental shelf to their own advantage. This has resulted in four criteria which are: depth, exploitability, distance from the coast and extent of continental margin. United States practices reveal that while it has permitted drilling up to 4,000-5,000 feet deep on the Atlantic coast, it has been exploring for oil and gas up to 300 miles on the east coast continental slope (Florida Cape Cod). Developed countries have applied the exploitability test. These unilateral extensions have resulted in disputes between Germany, Denmark and the Netherlands. Article 6 of the Convention purports to divide a continental shelf between neighbouring States on the basis of either an agreement or the principle of equidistance. The International Court of Justice had held that delimilation should be on equitable principles [9].

Southeast Asia is rich in continental shelf having 8,00,000 square miles. It has a rich oil potential. India has more than 2,000 miles of sea coast and its continental-shelf extends to several hundred thousand kilometres. It borders with Pakistan in Kutch, with Bangla Desh in the Bay of Bengal, with Thailand, Burma and Indonesia near Andaman and Nicobar Islands, and with Sri Lanka and Maldives in the south.

There is also a tendency to claim jurisdiction over a continental shelf up to the end of the continental margin. The United

States, Canada, Bangla Desh, Australia, India and Pakistan are main protagonists of this theory.

Economic Resources Zone

Technological developments have made the exploitation of sea resources easier than expected. Until recently, only fishing was possible in the sea. Today, it promises rich potential in petroleum and other costly minerals like nickel, cobalt, copper and manganese. All these minerals have remained untapped so far. Littoral States have, therefore, tried to appropriate great chunks of sea adjacent to their coasts and called these chunks as economic resources zone.

Economic resources zone, which is also called patrimonial sea, was visualised at the Geneva meeting of the U.N. Committee on Peaceful Uses of the Sea Bed and Ocean Floor Beyond the Limits of National Jurisdiction in August, 1971. Initially, some 25 States mostly from Latin America and partly from Africa claimed 200 miles as territorial sea. Their idea was to exploit sea resources near their coasts without foreign interference. This was resented by maritime powers which were more developed and whose fishermen specialised in distant-sea fishing. With the realisation of rich potential of sea resources, number of States claiming large chunks of sea gradually increased. Maritime powers also felt that instead of extending the territorial sea limit to 200 miles, formula may be sorted out to satisfy the increasing demands of coastal States for exclusive exploitation of sea bed and fishing resources without interfering with traditional rights of freedom of sea and their historic rights subject to a limit on catch and payment of royalty [10]. This gave rise to the concept of economic resources zone.

Concept of economic resources zone is that the coastal State will have jurisdiction over the given zone in respect of living and non-living, renewable and non-renewable resources within the area. The coastal State will also have the right to protect marine environment for economic exploitation. Economic resources zone was accepted in principle at the Caracas Conference in 1974. At the Sixteenth Session of the Asio-African Legal Consultative Committee held in Tehran in February, 1975, the Committee favoured such sovereign rights which were necessary for the conservation and enjoyment of economic rights [11]. These economic rights would include exploitation of the sea bed and ocean floor within 200 miles. The zone is now labelled as exclusive economic zone.

While economic resources zone has been generally accepted by the world community, there has been difference of emphasis between developed and developing nations. Developed and maritime States would like to treat economic resources zone as part of the high seas with concessions given to the coastal States to exploit the sea resources. As U.S. Ambassador Richardson put it, the developed nations "seek to safeguard traditional high seas freedoms within this zone except for specific resource related rights" [12]. The developing States, while claiming sovereign rights over the zone are ready to give concessions to developed States in respect of navigation, right of overflight and laying of submarine cables. The "Single Negotiating Text" which emerged from the Geneva Meet in 1975 provided that the high seas will start from outside the economic resources zone over which the coastal State would exercise sovereign rights in respect of living and non-living resources [13]. Surprisingly, bipolar powers are united on treating the economic resources zone as part of the high seas subject to the economic rights of coastal States.

There is also a group of landlocked and geographically disadvantaged States. This new pressure group of 52 States wants a 'pound of flesh' for itself. These States back the proposal of freedom of seas in the economic zone. Besides, they want some rights of exploitation in the economic zones of their neighbouring coastal States. The coastal States oppose such proposals. They concede freedom of navigation. Landlocked countries want free transit and other rights at par with coastal States irrespective of the question of sovereignty.

The coastal States' position was explained by Dr. Jorge Castaneda of Mexico, Chairman of the Group, when he said that economic resources zone enjoyed special international status without forming part of either territorial sea or the high seas. He expressed the willingness of his Group to discuss with landlocked countries regarding access to living resources in the economic zone so long as the catch did not exceed a maximum sustainable yield. He, however, ruled out any participation by landlocked countries in the non-renewable mineral resources within the economic zone of coastal States [14].

Every State has sovereignty over its natural resources. The sea coast is also a nature's gift and should be considered as a natural resource whether it comprises of living or non-living resources. The coastal State, therefore, can exercise sovereign rights over the economic resources zone. Landlocked countries can only claim right of access to sea. Beyond that, any additional right can be acquired by the landlocked country through an agreement with the coastal State either on bilateral or regional basis. Besides, if a landlocked State were to be given right in the economic resources zone of the neighbouring States, it may turn out to be better positioned if it has a number of neighbouring coastal States. That will indeed be a funny situation.

Any permanent right claimed by a landlocked State irrespective of the consent of the coastal State would mean an international servitude which no coastal State would accept. There should rather be mutual realisation of the legitimate interests of the other.

Fishing problems are bound to arise when economic zones are delimited. Fishing is no more an unskilled profession. It requires scientific methods to breed, conserve and catch the fish. For some, it serves as a food; for others it becomes a source of living; for States it is an exchange earner. At the same time, fishing resources are not inexhaustible. Excessive fishing threatens extinction of a given specie. Therefore fishing cannot be permitted beyond a maximum sustainable yield. There are conflicting claims of coastal States and other States which had been fishing so far in the newly made economic zone of the other State. These distant States claim right of fishing on historic and economic grounds.

The problem of fishing within an economic zone should be tackled on a matter of fact thinking on the subject. The coastal State has to establish and maintain conservation plans for proper and continuous fishing within the zone. It should have therefore preferential right of fishing within the zone. However, if the maximum sustainable yield exceeds the fishing requirements of the coastal State, the latter can lease out the fishing rights to traditional fishing and nearby landlocked countries.

Some developed countries also claim the right of scientific research within the economic zone of another State. In this connection, while they concede the consent of the coastal State should be obtained, they resent an increasing degree of State control of foreign scientific research. This may pose some difficulties.

There can be no full exploitation of the economic zone without protecting a proper marine environment necessary for breeding, conservation and living of fishes. Pollution of marine environment may threaten breeding or make it inedible. It may cause the extinction of a given type of fish or change the taste. Coastal States should, therefore, regulate undesirable discharges in marine environment of the economic zone. Other States should comply with such regulations

Maritime States claim the right of freedom of navigation through the economic zone. No coastal State would interfere with innocent navigation. But a coastal State has to regulate traffic and ascertain the nature of transit. Both these things are necessary for security purposes as well as for prevention of pollution, conservation and protection of its installations.

There is controversy over the legal status of exclusive economic zone. As has been said above, there has been difference of emphasis between the developed and the developing countries. Undoubtedly, this zone, which is now termed as exclusive economic zone [15], would encompass territorial sea, contiguous zone, continental shelf (unless its margin extends beyond 200 miles) and fisheries zone. The economic rights cannot be exercised without exercising sovereign rights over the zone. In short, the coastal State will exercise quasi-sovereign rights over this zone by legislating and regulating activities in respect of this zone.

Marine Pollution

Protection of the marine environment has become imperative in view of it having been used as a dumping ground for all types of wastes. Nuclear tests and super oil tankers have aggravated the matter. Scientific research also contributes partly to marine pollution. Previously, there was the impression that sea water could well absorb these wastes without a corresponding danger on its living resources. Today, we must check pollution or sea fish may no more be worth eating and they may die because of pollution. Contamination of sea water may affect the atmospheric environment also.

While a coastal State would legislate and regulate sea activities up to 200 miles, there is need for international standards to prevent marine pollution on the high seas. Besides, the coastal States should not spread marine pollution beyond their national borders either to the high seas or other States. There are three conventions on preventing marine pollution. These are the Convention of Prevention of Marine Pollution by Dumping of Wastes and other Matters, signed in London on 10th November, 1972, Convention of Prevention of Pollution from Ships, signed in London on 2nd November, 1973 and Protocol Relating to Intervention on the High Seas in cases of Marine Pollution, also signed in London on 2nd November, 1973.

Deep Sea Mining

Science has made it possible to explore the deep sea and ocean floor. Research has shown that the sea bed and ocean floor are rich in minerals which have remained accumulated there. Some ocean floors are said to be literally paved with multimineral nodules. Metals found in the sea bed are manganese, copper, cobalt and nickel. Manganese helps in steel making; copper is used in electrical plating and telephone servicing; nickel is a component of stainless steel and cobalt is used in magnets, missiles and jet engines.

The big powers were quietly exploiting the minerals of the sea bed with their technological know-how and resources. While the developed nations were colonising the sea bed and ocean floor, small States were basking in their ignorance.

Credit for raising the problem of exploration of the sea bed and ocean floor goes to a newly independent small State of Malta whose United Nations representive, Arbid Pardo, brought the matter before the General Assembly in 1967. He pleaded for an international regime for the sea bed and ocean floor. In 1970 the U.N. General Assembly adopted a Declaration of fifteen Principles covering the peaceful uses of the sea bed and ocean floor. The first Principle declares the sea bed beyond national jurisdiction as common heritage of mankind. The second Principle declares that it shall not be subject to national or private appropriation.

The 1976 and 1977 New York Sessions of the Third Conference on the Law of Sea have been deadlocked on the exploitation of the sea bed beyond national jurisdiction. While it is agreed that there would be an international authority to exploit the sea bed and ocean floor beyond national jurisdiction, developed nations want parallel exploitation by an international sea bed authority as well as by private industrial corporations of the developed countries. The latter is not acceptable to the Third World. This stalemate works in favour of the developed nations. Thus, while diplomats of the developing nations are debating, the developed nations are digging and depleting the resources.

Landlocked States: There are about twenty-four States having no sea coast. So far these States have contented themselves with the right of transit of goods for import and export through neighbouring coastal States. They also enjoy the right of having a maritime flag [16]. Their vessels have the right of innocent passage through territorial waters of other States [17]. Today, these States constitute a powerful pressure group at the Law of Sea Conference, along with about twenty-eight disadvantaged shelflocked States. Landlocked States want some rights in the economic resources zone of the neighbouring States. There is resistance from the coastal States to this demand.

Notes

1. Bowett, Second U.N. Conference on the Law of Sea, (1960) 9 I.C.L. Q., 417.
2. Richard Gardner, The Politics of Oceans, Summer 1974, American Review, 90.
3. Ibid.
4. Akehurst Michael, Modern Introduction to International Law (1971) 210. Also see Sri Lanka's Declaration on Maritime Zone dated 15th January, 1977. It declares: "Foreign warships and Foreign military aircraft, however, require prior consent of the Minister of Defence and Foreign Affairs. The Minister also retains the right to suspend innocent passage for a specific area if it were necessary to do so to safeguard peace, order and security of the Republic." The Statesman, 17th January, 1977.
5. Article 14 (4) of the Geneva Convention of 1958 on Territorial Sea.
6. The Statesman, 3rd January, 1977.
7. Akehurst, op. cit., p. 209.
8. The Searchlight, 1st March, 1977.
9. North Sea Continental Shelf Case, 1969, I.C.J. Reports 1.
10. The International Herald Tribune (Paris), 30th August 1971.
11. The Times of India, 11th February, 1975.
12. The United States Information Service Bulletin (India) dated 22nd July, 1977.
13. The Statesman, 22nd April, 1976.
14. U.N. Weekly Newsletter (India), 13th August, 1976.
15. India's notification of 15th January, 1977 called it exclusive economic zone. Notification empowers the Government to exercise sovereign rights for exploring and exploiting living and non-living resources and exclusive jurisdiction to authorise, regulate conduct and control

scientific research and take measures to preserve and protect marine environment. —The Hindustan Times, 16th January, 1977.

16. Barcelona Declaration of 20th April, 1921.
17. Article 14(1) of the Geneva Convention of 1958 on Territorial Sea.

Chapter 8

RECOGNITION

Recognition may be defined as an acknowledgement of existence of the entity so recognised. The recognised State may be a new State which was not an international person before; it may be a new government which has come into power in an already existing State by replacing the earlier government; in other cases, it may be the recognition of belligerency within a warring State which may thus give some rights and some duties as well to the insurgents.

Recognition is an important aspect for any new entity in the world community. In the absence of such recognition, the emerging entity may find itself handicapped in its relations with the outside world. Therefore, recognition is absolutely necessary for a new entity particularly if it has come into existence by revolt or unconstitutional means. Entities which have sprung through constitutional process or peaceful means do not face much of a problem. The world community is a close-knit community which does not admit new entrants to it except by consent in the form of recognising the new entrant. This consent goes to the farthest limit which almost amounts to vetoing at least insofar as relations between the new entrant and non-recognising State are concerned. The new entity may have been recognised by many States. Yet a recalcitrant State may withhold recognition from the new entity with the result that the latter does not get any kind of facilities, privileges or status within the territory of the former State or while dealing with it. This was obvious during the period Bangla Desh was not recognised by Pakistan or the Peking regime was not recognised by the United States.

Perhaps, the foremost task which a new entity faces while emerging on the international horizon is that of recognition. It is no wonder that the members of the world community are least obliging to a new aspirant who desperately seeks their blessings.

The irony, indeed, is that while recognition may be given to most of the new entrants to the world community, the case may be quite reverse in case of a few entrants who chase the pre-existing members of the world community, seeking their recognition.

It is said that recognition is granted when some conditions are fulfilled [1]. Nothing can be farther from the truth than this statement. It must be admitted that there are no illusions as to that. Undoubtedly in most cases, recognition follows when the new State fulfils the conditions of statehood as given elsewhere. Similarly, a new government is recognised when it fulfils the conditions which are being discussed in subsequent pages. But the fallacy of the above statement lies in a few important cases where despite the fact that new aspirants fulfil the conditions of recognition, they are, nevertheless, denied that privilege due to political motivations. No one can doubt the statehood of Southern Rhodesia after its unilateral Declaration of Independence in November 1965. But not many States have recognised it as member of the international community. The State of Israel has not been recognised by the Arab States despite its existence as an international person for more than a generation. Similarly, no one could challenge the existence of the Communist government of China on the legal plane. Yet it has remained unrecognised so far by the United States of America. The Union of Socialist Soviet Republics was established in 1917. Yet it was only recognised by the United States of America in as late as 1932. India has not recognised the Nationalist government of China in Formosa, although it fulfils the requirements of recognition. Bangla Desh remained unrecognised for more than two years by Pakistan and Peking regimes. Outer Mongolia was not recognised as a State for a number of years due to the fear that it was not fully independent inasmuch as it was thought to be a Soviet protege. Conversely, a number of States have been recognised before they actually came into existence. For example, Czechoslovakia and Poland were recognised as States by a number of Western Powers during the First World War even before they were christened as States. Recognition and symbolic functioning of governments in exile of overthrown countries in London during World War II are examples of political manifestations of recognition. In recent history, the Algerian Rebel government was recognised by many Arab and other States before it was given formal independence by France. All these practices go to prove that it is not obligatory to recognise a State or government if it fulfils the legal requirements as suggested by Lauterpacht.

These practices may lead us to the conclusion that the process of recognition is more political than legal. But one must hasten to emphasise here that recognition is neither entirely political nor entirely legal. In most cases, it is a combination of both. Definitely, political considerations do weigh in granting recognition, including the time taken but this should not prejudice the legal aspect of recognition. In most cases of recognition, States have followed the normal process by which they have accorded recognition on the basis of that State having fulfilled the requirements necessary for the purpose. In only a few cases, the States have departed from this practice due to political motivations and have thus withheld recognition where it is deserving. The result is that these few instances have obsessed the legal nature of recognition. With this little background, we will study the process of recognition at different levels.

Recognition of a State

Problem of recognition of a State arises when a hitherto dependent community matures into a sovereign independent State or part of an already sovereign State breaks from the parent State and secures a separate independent status. Poland became independent by separating from Austria. So did Hungary from Austria, Greece from Turkey, Iceland from Denmark. Bangla Desh became a separate State after seceding from Pakistan.

The bulk of dependent communities which were colonies until World War II became independent in the post-World War period. India, Ceylon, Burma, Indonesia, Malaysia, Singapore, Laos, Cambodia, and many African States have all become sovereign independent States after World War II.

Recognition of these new States was not difficult. They were mostly recognised as soon as they became independent. They fulfilled all the four requirements for being recognised as States. These four requirements are, as has been mentioned earlier, territory, permanent people, organised government which must be sovereign without having any superior, and willingness and capacity to carry out international obligations. There was no difficulty as to their recognition partly because of the fact that there was a peaceful changeover by agreement between colonial power and the colony's representatives from a colonial status to an independent status.

The problem of recognition arises wherever a change has been sought to be brought about by force as in the case of Algeria, Indonesia, Bangla Desh, Vietnam. These States were not universally recognised until the changeover was agreed to by France in the case of Algeria, and the Netherlands in the case of Indonesia. Bangla Desh took some time to be recognised by Pakistan and China. This delayed its entry into the family of the United Nations. Vietnam's entry into the United Nations was vetoed by the Ford regime of the United States. Some States are cautious in granting recognition in such cases because any indiscretion in their act may offend the parent State and may be construed as intervention. Bangla Desh State was not recognised before 6th December 1971 although there were pressures on the Indian Goverment to do so immediately after 25th March 1971 when the Pakistan Government interned political leaders for revolting in erstwhile East Pakistan. The political situation also in such cases is very uncertain and the States do not propose to precipitate a crisis by granting premature recognition. They prefer to wait and see the final outcome of a revolt which would determine their action in granting or refusing recognition. The Swedish Prime Minister rightly said that they recognise a new State when it has full control over its territory, is established and does not have foreign troops on its soil [2].

Recognition of Governments

It is but natural that there is continual change of governments in the world community. All these changes do not require recognition from other States. In most cases, recognition is taken for granted and is implied. This is specially so when the change in government is by a constitutional process. If the government is replaced by the Labour party in England due to general elections, no problem of recognition arises. Nor when the Republican President is replaced by a Democratic Party President or *vice versa* in the United States. If Mr. Nehru was succeeded by Lal Bahadur Shastri or Indira Gandhi by Morarji Desai, no question of recognition arose. Similarly when Nasser was succeeded by Sadat in Egypt.

The question of recognition arises when there is change of

government through a *coup d'etat* or when two opposing parties claim government control in a given country. Naturally recognition of the government would be necessary in such a situation. When President Ayub took over the reigns of the Pakistan government or Nasser overthrew King Farouk in Egypt or when Ben Bella was overthrown by military regime in Algiers—in such cases, if there is a complete takeover of administration by the new regime and there is no imminent force opposing the new regime, recognition is granted to the new regime without much waiting although in the earlier part of the century, one opinion was that government which has overthrown a lawful government by extra constitutional means should not be recognised. This was termed as the Tobar Doctrine. In 1907, Dr. Tobar of Equador propounded that a revolutionary government which has assumed power through a *coup d'etat* should not be recognised. The doctrine was embodied in the five power treaty between the Central American States in 1907 [3]. The doctrine was strengthened by the practice of the United States of America in the succeeding years. Thus, President Wilson applied the doctrine to Nicaragua, in 1912, Mexico and Equador in 1913, Costa Rica and Cuba in 1917 [4]. In 1923 the Tobar Doctrine was further extended by a provision in the new treaty that year that if an initially revolutionary government converts, itself into a constitutionally backed government, such a government shall not be recognised if the President happens to be from the revolutionary *Junta* [5]. This treaty was, however, denounced by Costa Rica in 1932 and Salvador in 1933 [6]. The Tobar doctrine was never accepted as a general rule of international law. Some jurists have rightly deprecated the practice of States passing judgment over the legitimacy of a revolutionary regime in a given country.

The Estrada Doctrine stands in direct opposition to the Tobar Doctrine. The doctrine was enunciated by the Mexican Foreign Minister Senor Estrada, who said in 1930 that States should continue with their diplomatic relations in a given country despite the fact that there has been a *coup d'etat* in that country. His argument was that States should continue relations with whatever regime is in power and any refusal or grant of recognition to a new regime was tantamount to passing a judgment over the legitimacy of a regime of a foreign State and may amount to interference in the internal affairs of that country [7].

Both these doctrines represent two extreme viewpoints. But if one were to accept the principle of right of self-determination, every State has a right to decide for itself what type of government its people want. If the people want a military *Junta* in preference to constitutional government, it is their right and foreign States have no right to sit in judgment over another country's government. The Estrada Doctrine seems to follow the right of self determination. To that extent, this Doctrine is good. Nevertheless, it is said that before a government is recognised, it should have a full grip over the country with reasonable prospects of control for an indefinite period. Besides, it should have the express or implicit consent of the people of the territory and it should be willing to carry out international obligations. The Anglo-American practice with regard to granting of recognition to a government is whether the government is effective within the territory or not [8]. Of late, there has been a distinct shift in the United States policy of recognition. Previously, the U.S. government insisted upon approval of the new regime by its people in some overt manner [9]. But there is no more insistence upon the rule of overt approval. Instead, if there is acquiesced approval and the absence of resistance to the regime which has *de facto* control over the territory, it is considered to be sufficient [10]. Previously, constitutionality of the government was a weighty consideration for granting recognition. However, today, it is no more such an important consideration. *De facto* control is more necessary, irrespective of the mode of acquiring control whether by constitutional means or by *coup d'etat*. In the post-World War II era, it has almost become a fashion to stage a *coup d'etat* to acquire State control. It should, therefore, be no surprise to find that there are more governments in Asia, Africa, and Latin America which have assumed power through *coup d'etat* than through constitutional means.

There have been some cases, however, where political considerations have outweighed legal considerations in granting recognition or withholding the same. Thus, if it is found necessary to boost the morale of the given regime, it is granted recognition where it does not deserve. For example during World War II, recognition was granted to *emigre* governments of occupied territories in Europe in order to boost the morale of the residents of these territories. These governments had no legal basis for recognition.

They were recognised for political purposes. Conversely, recognition has been withheld from deserving governments for political reasons. The Union of Soviet Socialist Republics was not recognised for a number of years until 1932 by the United States of America despite the fact that the U.S.S.R. government assumed control over Russian territory in 1917. The obvious reason for non-recognition was the fear of the socialist policies of the Soviet government and nationalisation of banks, including foreign American banks [11]. The U.S. government wanted to use the process of recognition as a lever to extract concessions from the Soviet government. Same is the policy of the United States government with regard to the Chinese government at Peking which remains formally unrecognised until today although it assumed control over the Chinese mainland in 1949. Use of recognition as a lever for bargaining concessions from the harassed unrecognised government has been the regular practice among nations. The Pakistan Government did not recognise Bangla Desh until understanding was reached for non-trial of prisoners of war for alleged war crimes.

There is Stimson Doctrine named after the Secretary of State of the United States. In 1931, when Japan occupied Manchuria, then part of China, Stimson said that world community should not recognise any territorial developments brought about by use of force. This was okayed by the League of Nations. The United Nations also does not approve of or recognise new frontiers acquired through the use of force.

Recognition of Belligerency

Where a rebel group within a given territory has risen against the government in power, State of a belligerency may be recognised by other States if the rebel group controls some territory, runs an orderly government within that territory, observes rules of warfare and is able and willing to secure protection to foreigners and foreign property. A State of belligerency is recognised by foreign States partly to acknowledge the existing state of affairs within the given State and partly to protect its interests within the territory occupied by rebels who may not afford protection unless they are recognised as the government in control of some territory side by side with the *de jure* government as in the case of Vietcong in South Vietnam sometime back. Recognition of belligerency becomes necessary for States to declare their attitude of neutrality in an internal conflict. But any precipitate recognition of the rebel government and State of belligerency may put the recognising State in a position where it can be charged with interfering in the affairs of another State.

Recognition of belligerency may likewise be done in a situation when a colony rises against colonial power to gain independence as happened in the case of Algeria where rebels fought under the label of the National Liberation Front, in Angola and Mozambique against Portugal.

With the recognition of belligerency in a particular situation, States are supposed to observe their neutrality towards the warring groups and the rules of warfare apply to such hostilities.

It is said that there can be State of insurgency before State of belligerency when the rebel group is not under the command of organised authorities or when the rebels do not observe the rules of warfare [12]. In this writer's opinion, there is no such thing as recognition of insurgency which does not amount to State of belligerency. If the insurgents control some territory, form an organised authority, and are ready to observe rules of warfare, State of belligerency should be recognised. Failing that, no State of belligerency can be recognised because either they are insurgents entitled to belligerent status or they are not insurgents and, therefore, not entitled to any privileged status. It is possible that third States may maintain some contacts with insurgents in order to protect their nationals and their property but this does not mean anything like recognition of insurgency not amounting to belligerency. Whenever insurgency is recognised, it would amount to recognition of belligerency thus making the phrase, recognition of insurgency, as superfluous and sometimes confusing.

Recognition of Acquired Territory by Force

There is a modern tendency not to recognise the sovereignty over newly acquired territory which has been obtained through use of force. This principle was first enunciated by the Stimson Doctrine in early 1932. Mr. Stimson was U.S. Secretary of State. While declaring the U.S. State policy on acquisition of Manchuria by Japan by conquering from China, he said that the U.S. Government "does not intend to recognise any situation......brought about by means contrary to the covenants and obligations of the Treaty of Paris of August 27, 1928." The Treaty of Paris related to renunciation of war as an instrument of national policy.

The Stimson doctrine of 1932 was reiterated by an Assembly Resolution of the League soon thereafter in March, 1932. The U.N. Charter also bans use of force under Article 2 class 4. In 1967 when Israel occupied some Arab territories, the U.N. Security Council called upon her to vacate the occupied territories. Declaration on Principles Governing Friendly Relations among Nations proclaimed in 1970 that "No territorial acquisition resulting from the threat or use of force shall be recognised as legal." This has been reiterated by a number of resolutions of the U.N. General Assembly.

Modes of Recognition

It is said that there are two modes of recognition. They are: (i) express, and (ii) implied.

(i) *Express Recognition*

Recognition is said to be express when a pre-existing State recognises the new State or government in express words which may be contained in an *aide-memoire*. This is, however, seldom done except in case of State of belligerency when the States have to declare their neutrality. At other times, new States or rebel regimes, request the States to grant recognition to them. In such cases, express recognition may be granted.

(ii) *Implied Recognition*

Recognition may be implied when there is no formal declaration of acknowledgement but there are enough indications which reflect the mind of the pre-existing government as to the acknowledgement of a new emerging State, government or regime. Such indications should be unequivocal leaving no doubt in the mind of the new entity regarding its recognition by the pre-existing State.

Actions implying recognition may be sending of the greetings message to the Head of the new State or regime, sending any representatives to attend the inaugural function or swearing-in ceremony of the new government, correspondence for the exchange of diplomatic or consular agents, continuance of diplomatic relations, voting for the admission of the new government to the United Nations and such other international organisation [13] or entering into treaty relations.

Initiation of diplomatic relations between China and the United States in 1973 and between the two Germanys in 1974 has been unique insofar as recognition is concerned. Whereas the United States was equivocal regarding recognition while establishing a Liaison Office with Peking, the West German Government denied having recognised the East German Government while establishing Permanent Representation with her. Such refutation has little significance because it is only a face-saving device. Otherwise establishment of such relations means implicit recognition for all practical purposes. In any case, this may be considered as quasi-recognition. No recognition can be inferred if the new regime and the government of an already existing State participate in some international conference or even enter into bilateral talks or arrangements. For example, the United States of America and the Communist Chinese regime were party to the Geneva Protocol on French Indo-China in 1954 and 1962. Such participation did not mean that the United States Government recognised the Communist Chinese Government in Peking. Nor can such an inference be drawn when Israel and the Arab States, including the Palestine Liberation Organisation participated in the Geneva Conference to settle the Middle East question.

De Facto Recognition [14]

It is said that *de facto* recognition is factual recognition of the state of things as they exist in a given territory. A new regime or State is granted *de facto* recognition in view of its fulfilling the requirements of government-cum-State, although it may not have attained the stability that is desired of it. On the other hand, it may convey the state of indecisiveness on the part of the recognising State inasmuch as it has not yet decided whether to grant *de jure* recognition to the new regime. A number of States granted *de facto* recognition to the Soviet Union for a number of years. The ostensible plea was that it was unwilling to carry out international obligations [15]. The real reason could have been that the Western powers had not reconciled to the presence of a socialistic State in their midst. Hence it was granted *de facto* recognition by some and still no recognition by others.

De facto recognition may be considered as a preliminary step towards *de jure* recognition though the latter may take some time to materialise. The period between the time of *de facto* recognition and *de jure* recognition may be treated as a stabilising phase which matures into *de jure* recognition of government, already recognised as *de facto.*

It may be of interest to note that the problem of a *de facto* recognition arises in situations where there is no smooth or constitutional changeover. It is the sign of abruptness. Such situations are compact with controversies. Thus, it may happen that a rebel group has come up with the semblance of government in *de facto* control of some territory which it governs and controls; or a colony rises in revolt against the imperial power and forms a rebel government of the colony just as it was done in Algeria by the National Liberation Front. It may also be that a warring nation may occupy the other State's territory thus requiring *de facto* recognition in respect of that territory as happened with Italy occupying Ethiopia in 1939. The British government initially accorded *de facto* recognition to Italy [16]. In such situations, while one regime may enjoy the *de facto* recognition the other party may already have the *de jure* recognition on its side. Thus, there may be a clash between fact and law.

De Jure Recognition

De jure recognition is the final seal of recognition granted to a new regime or State. This type of recognition is a matter of course in case of constitutional changeover. However, in the absence of legal changeover, *de jure* recognition is generally preceded by *de facto* recognition.

Since *de jure* recognition is a final word insofar as recognition is considered, great caution is exercised in the grant of the same. *De jure* recognition is granted on the basis of assessment of factual as well as legal factors.

Quasi-Recognition

Developments in Sino-American relations and between the two Germanys have given rise to the coining of the term of quasi-recognition. There has been no recognition of the Peking regime by the United States because of the dispute over the status of Formosa. In the meantime, however, the two countries have entered into diplomatic relations which due to non-recognition have been labelled as Liaison offices. The functions of such Liaison offices are equivalent to those of embassies and the personnel enjoy diplomatic privileges and immunities.

Similarly the States of Federal Republic of Germany (representing West Germany) and Democratic Peoples Republic of Germany (representing East Germany) have entered into treaty and established Permanent Representatives in the respective capitals. These Permanent Representatives enjoy diplomatic privileges and immunities like ambassadors. The term has been borrowed from the nomenclature given to national representatives assigned to the United Nations.

A similar kind of relationship was developed between Egypt and Israel when President Sadat visited Israel in November, 1977 and the visit was returned by Israeli Prime Minister Begin, to Ismaila in December, 1977.

Such a relationship is nothing else but recognition. But the Statss deny the process of recognition. It may thus be observed that establishment of such relations may amount to quasi-recognition which means as good as recognition, like quasi-contract without formalities.

Ad Hoc Recognition

This type of recognition, as the term may itself convey, occurs when the given State or regime lacks *de facto* as well as *de jure* recognition. Nevertheless, there is some kind of correspondence or negotiations with the regime giving rise to an *ad hoc* arrangement with the regime. Such a diplomatic exchange may be considered as *ad hoc* recognition of the regime for a specific purpose and no more. It is purely temporary. It is this writer's opinion, that participation by the United States of America and the Peking regime at the Geneva Conference on French Indo-China in 1954 and 1962, amounted to an *ad hoc* recognition of Communist China on the part of the United States of America. However, until *de facto* or *de jure* recognition is accorded, *ad hoc* recognition has no wide ranging consequences. *Ad hoc* recognition serves only a particular specific purpose, nothing more. It has no legal impact.

Difference between de facto and de jure recognition

So far as the recognised regime is considered, it is not affected by any difference between *de facto* and *de jure* recognition. A government or State, once recognised, enjoys all the privileges and immunities irrespective of the fact whether it is recognised *de facto* or *de jure* [17]. Its internal laws cannot be questioned nor its instrumentalities denied privileges and immunities within the territory of the recognising State.

Some controversy, however, may be erupted if there are two governments, one recognised as *de facto* and the other recognised as *de jure* with respect to the same territory. Here the problem may arise as to whose writ should prevail within the territory of the recognising State. One view is that the writ of the *de jure* recognised government should prevail over the writ of the *de facto* recognised government if there is coniflict between the two laws. The reasoning behind this is that while the *de jure* government is the lawful government of the territory, the *de facto* government may eventually prove to be a usurper. However the other view is that the writ of the *de facto* recognised government should prevail with regard to territory occupied by it [18]. The reason is that the *de facto* government controls the territory whereas the *de jure* government has been displaced.

Insofar as jurisdictional immunity is concerned, both the governments will enjoy the same within the territory of the recognising State. It was, therefore, natural that it was held by the British Court in the Arantzatzu Mendi case that the *de facto* government of Spain enjoyed jurisdictional immunity in Britain against the action sought by the *de jure* government of Spain [19]. Although, the decision in the case has been criticised by Lauterpacht [20] and Briggs [21], this writer finds no cogent argument in such criticism and considers the decision as sound.

It is also not fair to say that *de facto* recognition is provisional and temporary while *de jure* recognition is final and permanent. The fact is that both types of recognition continue to be valid so long as the circumstances, which impelled the grant of a particular type of recognition, continue to exist. With the disappearance of the circumstances, it is not only *de facto* recognition which can be withdrawn but even *de jure* recognition can be withdrawn. British withdrawal of *de jure* recognition from Haile Selassie government of Ethiopia consequent upon the occupation of the territory by Italy and reversal of the above act by Britain sometime after that makes it clear that there is no sanctity of permanency attached to *de jure* recognition. With the above background, some differences between the two types of recognition are stated as follows:

(a) *de facto* recognition may be said to be provisional and partial acknowledgement of the given State or government; *de jure* recognition is said to be full acknowledgement.

(b) In the case or any claim and counter-claim over any local property within the territory of the recognising State, *de jure* government may get precedence over *de facto* government.

Starke gives two other points of difference between the two types: (a) *de jure* government may espouse the cause of its nationals which may be a breach of international law, and (b) *de facto* government's representatives do not get full diplomatic immunities [22]. Since Starke considers the second difference as doubtful, this writer does not feel the necessity to comment upon it except by saying that no such difference exists in international law. As regards the first point of difference, it may be said that the *de jure* government alone does not have the monopoly to espouse the claim of its nationals. Even the *de facto* government can do so if the national comes from the territory controlled by that government. So it depends more upon the fact as to which government controls the territory and not as to which government is recognised *de jure*. Perhaps the question of effective nationality of the aggrieved person may crop up, but not the difference between *de facto* and *de jure* governments.

Different Theories Regarding Recognition

There are two important theories relating to recognition: Constitutive, and Declaratory.

Constitutive theory

Protagonists of constitutive theory assert that a State becomes an international person through recognition only. It has three active supporters in Oppenheim, Anzilloti and Kelson. Students of international law are familiar with Oppenheim's famous saying: "A State is, and becomes, an international person through recognition only and exclusively" [23]. Judge Lauterpacht was also charmed by this theory.

Their arguments are twofold. If consent is the basis of international law no State or government can have the advantage of being treated as an international person without the consent of pre-existing States. Their second argument is that an unrecognised State or government has no legal status insofar as its relations with non-recognising States are concerned.

Declaratory theory

Supporters of the declaratory theory treat recognition only as an evidential value inasmuch as they claim that a State or government exists even prior to recognition whose function is to put an evidenciary seal on the State or government as to its earlier existence. Brierly is one of the supporters of this theory.

Constitutive and declaratory theories represent two sides of the same coin. To say that one theory is true to the exclusion of the other theory will be hardly correct. Both the theories have some valid arguments but both of them are true to a certain extent and no more. A State or government does not acquire legal status within the territory of the other State unless it is recognised by the latter. But that does not mean a State or government does not exist at all. As has been aptly said by Briggs: "Nascent States, however, indeterminate their status politically or legally, do not exist in vacuum" [24]. All the States do not recognise the new entrant in their community simultaneously. One recognition is followed by another. Do the supporters of the constitutive theory mean to say that a given State exists for one set of States which have recognised it and does not exist for another set of States which have not so far recognised it? That will indeed be an anamoly. The fact is that the State exists irrespective of recognition but it can enter into relations with the other State only when that other State has recognised it. The Chinese regine did exist despite its non-recognition by the United States of America. But it could not enter into diplomatic relations with the United States without the latter recognising it.

Again, as is well known, recognition once given, works retrospectively from the date of its establishment. Therefore, if the constituent theory were to be interpreted to its logical end, how can that entity be given retroactive effect prior to its existence? It only means that the State or government does exist even before its recognition.

Besides, when recognition takes place it is naturally an acknowledgement of prior existence of some entity. Otherwise what is sought to be acknowledged through recognition?

Article 9 of the Charter of the Organisation of American States signed at Bogota in 1948 provides: "The political existence of

State is independent of recognition by other States."

Prior existence of State or government can well be understood by the statement of the Department of State of the United States of America in 1933, in New York Court of Appeals where it said:

> "The Department of State is cognisant of the fact that the Soviet regime is exercising control and power in territory of the former Russian Empire and the Department of State has no disposition to ignore that fact". [25]

From the above discussion, it is clear that the Declaratory theory is more correct than the Constitutive theory which is also partly correct.

Withdrawal of Recognition

Can recognition, once granted, be withdrawn? It is said that while *de facto* recognition may be withdrawn, *de jure* recognition cannot be withdrawn. This is said to be one of the points of difference as between *de facto* and *de jure* recognition. The Institute of International Law also adopted a resolution in 1936 to the effect that *de jure* recognition of State is irrevocable. But this is oversimplifying the difference.

In fact, there is no absolute sanctity regarding recognition, irrespective of the fact whether it is *de facto* or *de jure*. Both types of recognition are granted on assumption of some basic factors. If those very factors cease to exist, there is nothing wrong if the recognition is withdrawn. Pakistan was initially granted *de jure* recognition with regard to the two wings of Pakistan—East and West. East Pakistan having seceded and become Bangla Desh, *de jure* recognition of Pakistan control over Bangla Desh was impliedly withdrawn by those States which recognised Bangla Desh subsequently. Similarly, if South Vietnam was given *de jure* recognition by the United States, it became obsolete with the merger of the two Vietnams.

But while recognition is motivated by political considerations, withdrawal is dictated by factual conditions. Thus Britain withdrew recognition of Naples when it was annexed by the Kingdom of Italy in 1861. Similarly the United States of America withdrew recognition of Montenegro in 1921. France withdrew recognition of Finland in 1918. Britain withdrew *de jure* recognition of Ethiopia and granted the same to Italy in 1939. It withdrew recognition of the Kuomantang Nationalist Government of China in 1950, consequent upon the recognition of the Communist Chinese regime. India did the same thing when it recognised the Peking regime.

Withdrawal, however, should not be confused with severence of diplomatic relations. The latter only means that due to rupture of relations, the two nations, or even one State unilaterally, cease to have any relations with one another. This does not mean withdrawal of recognition of that State. Recognition continues notwithstanding severence of diplomatic relations as between Portugal and India during Salazar's period; or between India and South Africa.

Effects of Recognition

Recognition of a State or government confers upon the recognised entity a number of rights vis-a-vis the recognising State. These rights are consequent upon the recognition of the given State or government as the case may be. These rights are:

(i) The recognised State may enter into diplomatic relations with the recognising State. But it is not always necessary to have diplomatic relations with all States which have been recognised. For example although India recognises Israel, it has not so far exchanged diplomats with Israel except at Consular level. But this is a rare practice.

(ii) It enjoys diplomatic immunity within the territory of the recognising State.

(iii) It can sue in the territory of the recognising State. As was aptly said in an American case:

> "A foreign power brings an action in our courts not as a matter of right. Its power to do so is the creature of comity. Until such government is recognised by the United States, no such comity exists." [26]

(iv) It can succeed to the property of the former regime from which recognition may have since been withdrawn [27].

(v) Acts of the recognised State will be treated as legal and their validity cannot be challenged [28].

(vi) Some treaties with former government are revived.

Effects of Non-Recognition [29]

State or government which has not been recognised suffers some disabilities which may be summarised as follows:

(i) It cannot sue within the territory of a State which has not so far recognised it.

(ii) It cannot succeed to the property of the government which it has overthrown within the territory of the non-recognising state.

(iii) It cannot enter into permanent diplomatic relations with the non-recognising State.

(iv) Its nationals cannot enter the territory of the non-recognising State on the passport of the non-recognised government or State, exceptions apart.

(v) Treaties with former government of that territory remain suspended.

Despite these disabilities of the non-recognised governments they may enjoy international status inasmuch as,

(i) They may enter into *ad hoc* diplomatic relations with the non-recognising States just as Communist China and United States did at the Geneva Conferences in 1954 and 1962 or as Israel and Eygpt did in post-1973 October War.

(ii) The legislation of non-recognised government may not always be treated as invalid. Thus in Solimaff and Co. versus Standard Oil Company of New York, the New York Court of Appeals considered the Nationalisation Decrees of the Soviet Government, not yet recognised by the United States, as valid [30].

NOTES

1. C.H. Alexandrowitcz, The Quasi Judicial Function in Recognition of States and Governments (1952) 46 A.J.I.L. 46. Also see what Oppenheim has said: "Recognition of States, is, of course, a political function in the meaning that it is within the province of the Executive and not of the Judiciary, but, it will be noted, the executive organs within the State are often charged with the function of ascertaining and applying the law." Lauterpacht, Oppenheim's International Law, (Eight Edition vol. I, p. 128 footnote 1).
2. The Hindustan Times, January 4, 1974 vide statement of Swedish, Prime Minister, Olof Palme, in connection with Swedish recognition of the State of Bangla Desh.
3. (1908) 2 A.J.I.L. (Suppl.), 229.
4. Hackworth, Digest of International Law, vol. I, p. 187.
5. (1923) 17 A.J.I.L. (Suppl.), p. 118.
6. Lauterpacht, Oppenheim's, International Law, op. cit. vol. I, p. 132.
7. (1931) 25 A.J.I.L. (Suppl.) 203; For comments on the Doctrine, see Phillip Jessup, The Estrado Doctrine, (1931) 25 A.J.I.L., 719-29.

8. Lauterpacht, op cit. vol. I, p. 131.
9. Goebel, The Recognition Policy of the United States (1915); Cole, Recognition Policy of the United States since 1901 (1928).
10. MacMohan, Recent Changes in the Recognition Policy of the United States (1934).
11. Dickinson, Edwin D., The Recognition of Russia (1931-32) 30 Michigan Law Review. 181-96; Korovin, Eugene A., The Problems of International Recognition of the Union of Socialist Soviet Republics in Practice, (1933-34) 19 Iowa Law Review 259-71.
12. Lauterpacht, op. cit. vol. I, p. 140-41; Lauterpacht, Recognition in International Law (1947) pp. 270-310; Wilson 'George Grafton, Insurgency and International Maritime Law (1907)' I.A.J.I.L. 46-60.
13. Union of Soviet Socialist Republics vs. Luxembourg and Saar Company, 1935-37, Annual Digest case No. 34. In this case, the Commercial Tribunal of Luxembourg held in 1935 that the admission of the Soviet Union to the League of Nations amounted to the recognition of the Soviet Government by Luxembourg.
14. For *de facto* recognition, see Dickinson Edwin D. The Unrecognised Government or State in English and American Law (1923-24) 22 Michigan Law Review 29; Baty, Thomas, So-called *De facto* Recognition, (1922) 31 Yale Law Journal 469-88;H.Lauterpacht, *De facto* Recognition, Withdrawal of Recognition and Conditional Recognition, (1945) 22, B.Y.I.L. 164-90.
15. H. Lauterpacht, Oppenheim's International Law, op. cit. vol. I, p. 136; Andla, Chandla, R, Recognition of Russia, (1934) 28 A.J.I.L. 90-97.
16. Haile Selassie vs Cable and wireless Ltd., (1939) Ch. 182.
17. Luther vs Sagor (1921) 3 K.B.532. Also see Bank of Ethiopia vs National Bank of Egypt and Ligouri, 1937, Ch. 513.
18. Bank of Ethiopia vs National Bank of Egypt and Ligouri, ibid.
19. 1939 A.C. 216.
20. Lauterpacht H., Recognition of Insurgents as a *de facto* Government (1939-40) 3 Modern Law Review. 1-20.
21. Briggs, Hubert, W. *De Facto* and *De Jure* Recognition; The Arantzatzu Mendi case. (1939) 33 A.J.I.L.669-99.
22. Starke, op. cit. p. 158-59.
23. Lauterpacht, Oppenheim's International Law, vol. I, p. 125.
24. Briggs, H. Law of Nations (1953) 144.
25. Solimaff Co. vs Standard Oil Company of New York (1933) 262 N.Y. 220.
26. Russian Socialist Federated Soviet Republic vs Cibrraio (1923) 235 N.Y. 255 (New York Court of Appeals).
27. Bank of Ethiopia vs National Bank of Egypt and Ligouri, 1937 Ch. 513.
28. Luthor vs Sagor (1921) 3 K.B. 532.
29. Regarding Status of unrecognised government, Kallis Millton A. The Legal Effects of Non-Recognition of Russia (1933-34) 20 Virginia Law Review 1-36; Dickinson Edwin D., The Unrecognised Government or State in English and American Law, (1923) 22 Michigan Law Review 29-45 and 118-34.

30. (1933) 262 N.Y.220. For comments thereon, see Dickinson, Edwin D. The case of Solimaff and Co., (1933) 27 A.J.I.L. 743-47 In Haasner vs. Banque Internationale de Commerce de Petrograd, the Swizz Federal Tribunal held in 1924 : "The non-recognition of the Soviet Government has the sole consequence that, in the field of international law, this government has no qualification for representing Russia in Switzerland, either in matters or public law or in those of private law. But this circumstance does not prevent the Russ ian Law, from existing or from having its effects" (1925-26) A.D. 97.

CHAPTER 9

STATE SUCCESSION

In the realm of international law, there is no other topic more controversial than the one being presently discussed. Just as in private law, succession takes place on the death of one person, similarly succession takes place in international law also when one Government succeeds another or a colony or trust territory becomes a sovereign State and succeeds the erstwhile imperial or administering power. This can be said with certainty and without fear of being contradicted. Beyond this, one has to tread the path of uncertainty because the practices so far witnessed do not reflect a uniform policy or law. In some cases, the practices are too rarified to have the semblance of law. The law of succession in international law should have priority for codification at the hands of the International Law Commission which, of course, did consider this problem at its Fourteenth Session in 1962. In the 1972 Session, it prepared a draft on Succession of Treaties by New States. The International Law Association also considered the problem of Succession of new States to Treaties at the Helsinki Session in 1966. But it requires a closer study of the subject.

With this background, it may be desirable to divide the subject broadly into two subheads: Succession by States; and Succession by Government.

Succession by States

Succession by a State may arise when a colony or trust territory acquires independence and becomes an international person. Similarly, a quasi-independent or self-governing State may acquire full sovereignty and thus become an international person. The cases of India, Burma, Ceylon and Indonesia, to mention only a few, are relevant. It is also possible that a part of a sovereign State may secede from the latter, just as Iceland seceded from Denmark or Bangla Desh seceded from Pakistan, and became separate independent States. A new international person may also come up by the amalgamation or merger of two or more sovereign States. All these changes may bring forth the problem of State Succession.

Practices reveal that wherever there has been a peaceful changeover, there have been inheritance agreements between the new emerging States and colonial power regarding succession. The British Government entered into such agreements with Iraq in 1930, Transjordan in 1946, India and Pakistan in 1947, Ghana in 1957, Sierra Leone in 1961 and Jamaica in 1962. The Netherlands entered into such an agreement with Indonesia in 1949 and France did the same thing with Tunisia and Morocco in 1955 and 1956 respectively. These inheritance agreements simplified the problem of succession.

A State which comes into existence through revolt does not enter into an inheritance agreement. Its succession, therefore, is to be governed by the customary rules of international law. Some such rules are as follows :

Succession to Treaties [1]

Do the States succeed to treaties which were applicable to their territories prior to their becoming an international person ? No one reply can be given to this question. There are a number of issues involved in this question. One reply may be that a new State starts with a clean slate, having no treaty obligations [2]. The reasoning for such a stand is the bringing of private law analogy in the domain of international law. The contention is that personality of parties is an important element for continuing validity of a contract, in this case a treaty. Protagonists of this theory apply the doctrine of *res inter alios* [3] and assert that the personality of a State is pivotal for State succession [4]. Others challenge the assignability of treaties [5]. Some seek to apply the doctrine of *rebus sic stantibus* (vital change of circumstances). Yet others do not consider it as a matter of State succession but a matter of treaty interpretation [6].

Despite all these adverse arguments, practices reveal that new States have felt themselves bound by at least 50 per cent treaties, originally concluded by imperial or parent State [7]. Therefore, to say that new States start with a clean slate could not be wholly correct.

The fact is that States have either felt themselves bound or have adopted some treaties in the interest of self-existence. It is but natural that on the emergence of a new international person, it wants to have some kind of treaty relations with other States. Besides, it does not want to give any impression that it will not respect the obligations undertaken by the colonial power in respect of the new State's territory. Therefore, as far as possible, it desires to be bound by at least some of the treaties which are not unequal or inconsistent with its new status as a sovereign State [8]. There is no automatic devolution of treaties on the new State, which becomes discriminative and chooses as to which treaties will bind her or otherwise. This was made amply clear by the Irish Prime Minister in 1935 when he said:

> "When a new State comes into existence, which formerly formed part of an older State, its acceptance or otherwise of the treaty relationship of the older State is a matter for the new State to determine by express declaration or by conduct as considerations of policy may require." [9]

The Israeli Prime Minister just echoed what the Irish Prime Minister had said earlier when he observed:

> "On the basis of generally recognised Principles of international law, Israel which was a new international personality was not automatically bound by the treaties to which Palestine had been a party." [10]

Keeping the above thing in view, devolution of treaties on a new State may be analysed as follows :

Bilateral treaties

Bilateral treaties may be divided into political or personal, local, commercial, or administrative. Regarding political treaties which are often the result of personal relations between the two States, they do not bind the new State. Personality of participants is pivotal here and the doctrine of *res inter alios acts* applies in such cases. The new State, therefore does not succeed to political treaties like that of alliance, mutual assistance and amity, neutrality including neutralisation and settlement of international disputes. One may confess here that dispute may arise whether a particular treaty is political or otherwise.

So far as local treaties are concerned, they are problematic. Local treaties are those treaties which have created rights in them within the new State's territory. Such rights may relate to frontier fixation or creation of international servitudes. Professor O' Connel is of the view that such treaties devolve upon the new States. He says:

> "Treaties which create real rights are described as dispositive. Their legal effect is to impress upon a territory a status which is intended to be permanent, and which is independent of the personality of the State exercising sovereignty." [11]

The argument of Prof. O' Connel and like thinkers is that the new State can takeover only what its predecessor possessed [12].

This writer, however, has partial reservation to what O' Connel and others may have said. The writer feels that insofar as frontier agreements are concerned there should be some sanctity about them. Sometime back, the International Court of Justice held likewise in the case of Temple of Preah Vihear between Cambodia and Thailand. As it held:

> "In general, when two countries establish frontier between them, one of the primary objects is to achieve stability and finality. This is impossible if the line, so established can at any moment, and on the basis of continuously available process, be called in question, and its rectification claimed." [13]

There could, however, be no such sanctity regarding agreements which seek to create servitudes within foreign territory. No automatic devolution is witnessed in State practices [14]. Nor are publicists unanimous on this point [15]. It will also be negation of territorial sovereignty if the new State were to feel itself bound by a permanent scar on its sovereignty.

It may, therefore, be said that while a new State should feel itself bound by frontier agreement, it cannot be bound by servitudes created on its territory. It may, of course, adopt such servitudes which may be consistent with its dignity and new status as an international person. It is on this basis that the Government of India did not consider itself bound by provision in the Treaty of Poona by which the Maratha ruler had given right of access to the Portuguese authorities through the Indian territory to the former Portuguese enclaves of Dadra and Nagar Haveli.

Commercial treaties could be of two kinds—one may be a commercial treaty, pure and simple but the other may be a commercial treaty with political undertones. While a new State is bound by purely commercial treaties, it cannot feel itself bound by the other type of commercial treaty because of its political bias.

The new State should be bound by administrative treaties, which may relate to extradition, enforcement of foreign judgments, avoidance of double taxation, etc. Some publicists, like Oppenheim, have treated extradition treaties as political [16]. But it may be submitted that these treaties are mostly motivated by the desire of bringing the fugitive at the altar of law and in the interests of administration of justice. State practices also go to prove that States consider such treaties as non-political and, therefore, bound by them. For example, India considers itself bound by extradition treaties entered into by the British Government for the territory of India.

Multilateral treaties

Multilateral treaties can likewise be divided into political or personal, local, commercial, or administrative.

It is said that political or personal treaties, whether bilateral or multilateral, are normally entered into due to personal and political considerations on the part of the signatories. The NATO or Warsaw treaties may be labelled as multilateral political treaties. Such treaties do not bind the new State despite the fact that its territory was within the sphere of the multilateral treaty.

Multilateral treaties creating local rights like frontier fixation or creation of servitude may by considered as binding on the succeeding new State. As has been said above, frontier-fixation agreements should be permanent in nature. Otherwise, frontier disputes which are often the points of conflict between the neighbouring States will be a continual source of tension between States thus endangering international peace and security. The Indo-Pakistan and Indo-Chinese disputes are the result of not adhering to the above formula. There must be some sanctity to frontier fixation agreements. Therefore, if there is any multilateral treaty relating to frontier fixation, it has more sanctity than the bilateral treaty inasmuch as there is less chance of political exploitation of a weak nation, although the possibility of such exploitation cannot be ruled out.

Something may be said here about the creation of a servitude by a multilateral treaty. In such treaties there would be less element of exploitation and in most cases, the servitude would be a servitude of necessity. Such a servitude may be considered as binding on the new State.

So far as multilateral commercial treaties are concerned, this writer has come across only such treaties in which the signatory States also form an organisation. There is normally no succession to such treaties except when the new State also becomes a member of the organisation. Factually, therefore, there is no succession in such cases but only adherence by the new State.

Multilateral administrative treaties devolve upon the succeeding new State because such treaties are of mutual interest and the new States would not feel the pinch of inequality in such treaties. Practices reveal that a number of new States have considered themselves bound by multilateral administrative treaties [17].

General or universal treaties

General or universal treaties are those to which almost all the States are party. They may also be called law-making treaties. New States feel bound by these treaties in which the personality of the State is not an essential factor. Such treaties may be like the four Geneva Conventions of 1949 on Protection of War Victims, Vienna Convention of 1961 on Diplomatic Relations, or the Chicago Convention of 1944 on Civil Aviation. New States succeed to such treaties.

Succession to International Organisations

International Organisations are open to States through membership. In fact the membership is personal. Therefore, unless the new State was already a member of a given organisation, it does not become a member because the metropolitan power was its member. Thus, India continued to be a member of the United Nations because it was already its member even before 1947. Pakistan had to seek fresh membership despite the fact that it was formerly part of India, nor could it claim membership because the United Kingdom was a member of the United Nations. In fact, Pakistan claimed automatic membership of the United Nations on the basis of its being a former part of India, which was already a member of the United Nations, but its claim was rejected by the Legal division of the organisation [18]. Similarly Bangla Desh had to seek a fresh membership of the United Nations. Curiously, what was asserted by Pakistan in 1947 was challenged by her in 1972 when Bangla Desh sought membership.

Financial Arrangements

A New State succeeds to financial arrangements as were prevalent at the time of exit of the foreign power. It succeeds to currency arrangements and agreements which the former government may have had with International Monetary Bodies.

Question may arise as to how far a new State is bound by public debts which the colonial government had incurred? Here, the inquiry may be held whether the debts were incurred for the welfare of the people of that State or otherwise. If they were taken for the welfare of the people, the new State should be bound by it. Otherwise, it may denounce any such debts. Any general principle of taking "burden with benefits"[19] cannot be made applicable here because it may cause a drag on national economy of the new country.

Bangla Desh was confronted with the problem of accepting liability of one-third of foreign debts of Pakistan on the ground that the amount was invested within the territory. There was also some pressure exercised by creditor nations, including the World Bank, on the new State.

While it may be argued that Bangla Desh should be responsible on equitable grounds if the money was invested within the territory, it has also to be ascertained as to how much money was pumped in and whether it remained intact at the time of the changeover. Because if nothing was left at the time of changeover or if more money was pumped out than pumped in, the equity will be on the side of the new State. Besides, a new State should not be compelled to accept foreign liability at the risk of being involved in national bankruptcy, particularly when the State has suffered from a war-torn economy. In any case, succession should be overall and not piecemeal.

International Contracts

International contract may mean any contract to which the other party is a national of some foreign State. The new State is not bound by such contract automatically. The nature of the contract may be scrutinised by the new Government which may disown the same if it contains political, concessionary or unequal element. Otherwise it may accept the contract.

Internal Contracts

A new State is bound by such contracts because the other party is its own national, and there is little chance of such a contract being an instance of exploitation. However, if the new State finds a given contract as palpably inequitable, it may disown the contract by municipal legislation or otherwise as the occasion may require.

Torts

The new State is not responsible for any torts which the former colonial power or parent State may have committed [20]. The Brown Claim [21] and Hawaiian claim cases of 1925-26 [22] amply prove that successor State is not liable for the torts committed by the prior administration.

Local Laws and Property

A new State succeeds to local laws and property within its territory. Local laws continue to be valid, unless repealed, even though some laws may be inconsistent with the newly acquired status of the State [23].

Succession by State which has Annexed another State

When an already existing State absorbs another State through conquest or annexation, it assumes sovereignty over the annexed territory. Absorption may also occur through voluntary, though prompted, merger. In such cases, the absorbing State does not succeed to any treaty unless it is renegotiated. Nor is the absorbing State liable for any pecuniary outstandings against the absorbed or merged State. The Americo-German controversy consequent upon the taking over of Austria by Germany in 1938 is famous in this connection. The German Government denied any legal liability for the foreign public debts of the erstwhile Austrian Government. But when it negotiated with the creditors of the former State, it was more out of comity than out of legal obligation. Rightly enough, the German Government had informed the U.S. Government on 16th May, 1938 that it "was of the opinion that it was not under any legal obligation to assume the foreign debts of the former Austrian Federal Government" [24]. However, the U.S. Government claimed indemnification under international law and dictates of equity and justice [25].

Legally, neither Germany was liable for Austrian debts nor was

Japan liable for Korean debts when Germany absorbed Austria in 1938 and Korea merged with Japan in 1910. However, the devolution of liabilities of the absorbed or merged State can be the subject of negotiation and agreement between the absorbing State and the absorbed State when absorption is voluntary and between the absorbing State and the erstwhile State's creditors when there is forced liquidation of the State. In its absence, there is no legal liability [26]. Normally, the absorbing State negotiates a settlement of debts of the former State in order to get recognition of its action from the creditor States. But this is only international policy.

Regarding private rights, the absorbing State shall be bound by such rights. The position of private rights was aptly put by Chief Justice Marshall when he said :

> "It may not be unworthy of remark that it is very unusual even in cases of conquest, for the conqueror to do more than to displace the sovereign and assume dominion over the country. The modern usage of nations, which has become law, would be violated; that sense of justice and of right which is acknowledged and felt by the whole civilized world would be outraged, if private property should be generally confiscated, and private rights annulled. The people change their allegiance; their relations to their ancient sovereign are dissolved; but their relations to each other and their rights of property remain undisturbed." [27]

However, if the absorbing State or new State desires to bring some change or reforms in private rights, there is no check upon the sovereignty of the State to do so. It can, therefore, pass any legislation giving effect to its desired change [28]. But it is possible that there may be such check upon the powers of the absorbing or new State if there is any such ban envisaged in the terms of transfer, merger or whatever the case may be.

Succession by Government

No problem of succession arises if one government is succeeded by another government by peaceful and constitutional means in the same country. It succeeds to all the rights and liabilities of the State even though the succeeding Government may have policies different from the earlier government, and therefore, it may not like some of the actions of the former government. Thus, no problem of succession really arose when the Janata Government headed by Morarji Desai replaced the Congress Government of Indira Gandhi in March, 1977. At the most political treaties may require review by the new government which may accept on reject the political treaty. Thus, the Janata Government in India could have rejected the Indo-Soviet treaty of 1971. But it preferred to abide by it. At the same time, the Soviet Government could have also terminated it with the change of the Government in India. But it preferred to continue with it. However, difficulties may arise if one government is overthrown by a *coup d'etat* and a new government takes over. In such cases also if there is not much difference of policies and ideologies between the outgoing and incoming governments, no difficulty regarding succession may arise. The incoming government may undertake, as it does often undertake in the Latin-American countries, to respect all the commitments of the former government. It feels bound by such transactions.

But if there is a clash of ideology and difference of outlook, the real problem crops up. This happened when in 1917, the Imperial Russian Government was overthrown by the Communist regime which is better known now as the Union of the Soviet Socialist Republics. This gave rise to the problem of succession. The matter was further complicated by non-recognition of the Soviet regime for quite some time by major powers. No succession was, therefore, permitted in the case of Lehigh Valley Railroad Co. versus State of Russia [29].

In case where the new Government is recognised, it succeeds to the liabilities and assets of the former government. In the award of Laussane, the Franco-Chilean Arbitral Tribunal held in July, 1901 that the new Government cannot escape its liability for the acts of the former government, whatever be the character of that government so long as it exercised power in the country. It was held, therefore, that the Peruvian Government was responsible for the transaction which the earlier government had entered into with foreigners [30].

In 1917, when the new Soviet Government overthrew the Czarist regime in Russia, it repudiated the foreign public debts incurred by the former government. Number of governments challenged this repudiation but the Soviet government pleaded the analogy of *force majeure* and asserted that the revolutionary governments are not bound by the obligations of the fallen government [31]. In the post-World War II era when a number of governments were replaced in Europe by Socialist regimes, the latter disowned the liabilities as well as treaties of the previous governments. This was repeated when the Nationalist Government was replaced by the Communist regime in China in 1949. In 1972, the Ghanian Government repudiated a 92 million dollar obligation to Britain.

How far could these governments be held responsible for the liabilities of the fallen government is a moot point devoid of any legal authority or precedent. It was for the first time in 1917 that the government was guided by ideology, which held different views on a number of points which were considered as settled by some States. The post-World War II period witnessed another phase of international law when the erstwhile colonies of the Western countries became sovereign States and claimed equal status with the Western powers which had so far dominated in the making of international law. Naturally, there is bound to be difference of opinion as to succession in the circumstances. The situation is far from settled today.

Notes

1. Hingorani, R.C., Succession of New States to Treaties, 1971 Journal of the All India Law Teachers' Association, p. 5.
2. Lester, State Succession of Treaties in the Commonwealth, 1963 International and Comparative Law Quarterly 477, McNair Arnold, Law of Treaties (1961) 601; O'Connel, D.P., The Law of State Succession (1956) 32.
3. Lester, ibid, 526.
4. Hall, International Law (Eighth Edition) 1926, 114.
5. Mann, F.A. The Assignability of Treaty Rights, 1953, B.Y.I.L. 475.
6. O 'Connel, D.P., State Succession and Problem of Treaty Interpretation, (1964) 58 A.J.I.L. 41.
7. Keith and O'Connel, State Succession to Treaties in the Commonwealth: Two Aspects, 1964 I.C.L.Q. 1444.
8. For example see Tanganyikan Prime Minister's statement as cited by D.G. Valentine, Problems of State Succession in Africa : Statement of the Prime Minister of Tanganyika, 1962. I.C.L.Q. 1212.
9. As reported by Lester, Supra, 478.
10. Ibid 479.
11. O'Connel. D.P. op. cit. 49.
12. Ibid 50.
13. Case concerning the Temple of Preah Vihear-Cambodia vs Thailand

(Merits) 1962, I.C.J. Reports 34.

14. O'Connel, op. cit. 52 footnote, 3.
15. See in particular Dr. Strupp in Hague Recueil vol. XLVII (1934) 487.
16. Lauterpacht, Oppenheim's International Law, vol. I (1955) p. 159.
17. Keith and O' Connel, supra, 1443.
18. Schacter, Qsar, The Development of International Law Through the Legal Opinions of the U.N. Secretariat (1948) 25. B.Y.I.L. 101-09, Liang, Lionel H., Admission of Indian States (1949) 43 A.J.I.L. 144-54.
19. For example, see Hyde, C.C., International Law, vol. I pp. 418-19.
20. O'Connel, International Law, vol. I p., 448, Lauterpacht op. cit. 162, also see Hurt, State Succession in Matters of Torts, 1924 B.Y.I.L.
21. (1925) 19 A.J.I.L. 193-206.
22. (1926) 20 A.J.I.L. 381.
23. Peter Pazimany's case (1933) PCIJ Series A/B No. 61, p. 237.
24. As reported by Briggs. Herbert, Law of Nation, 235.
25. Garner J.W., Questions of State Succession Raised by the German Annexation of Austria (1938) 32 A.J-I.L. 421-28, Garner, Germany's responsibility for Austria's Debts, (1938) 32 A.J.I.L. 766-75.
26. Cook vs Sprigg (1899) A.C. 572.
27. United States in Percheman (1833) 7 Peters 51, 86-88 as given in Briggs, op. cit., 237. Also see F.B. Sayre, Change of Sovereignty and Private Ownership of land (1918) 12 A.J.I.L. 475, 481, 495-97.
28. Also see, Georges Kaeckenbeck, The Protection of Vested Rights in International Law (1936) B.Y.I.L. 17.
29. 21. F. 2nd. 396.
30. As reported by Briggs, op. cit. 211.
31. T.A. Taraconzio, The Soviet Union and International Law (1935) 21.

SECTION II

FUNDAMENTAL RIGHTS AND STATE RESPONSIBILITY

CHAPTER 10

FUNDAMENTAL RIGHTS OF STATES—SOVEREIGNTY

As member of the world community, each State has a number of fundamental rights in the same way in which an individual has in municipal law. In this writer's opinion, a State has two basic rights—sovereignty [1] and self preservation. But these rights are inseparable from each other inasmuch as one cannot exist in the absence of the other. Besides, if these rights disappear, a State as an international person also disappears. Of course, they in turn give birth to a number of other rights which derive their strength from them.

In the realm of political theory, no word has been so evasive in its meaning and scope as the word "sovereignty". Known as the pet child of Bodin, a French political philosopher, he introduced this word into the political science vocabulary in his famous classic *De La Republique*, published in 1577. As a person is a slave of his circumstances, Bodin was greatly influenced by the policy of absolutism which was reigning high in France since its initiation by Louis XI who was considered the founder of French absolutism. Bodin defined sovereignty as absolute, indivisible and perpetual. Bodin thought a monarch was supreme in his land and he knew of no restrictions, except the law of nature and God's commandment. In the seventeenth century, Hobbes surpassed Bodin by denying that sovereign was subject to law of nature or God's commandment. However, Pufendorf thought that while a sovereign was supreme, he did not wield absolute power.

The eighteenth century witnessed the recognition of divisibility of sovereignty with the emergence of hundreds of reigning princes who constituted the German empire. They did exercise some independent powers although they were not fully sovereign. Their position was akin to that of the Indian princely States under British paramountcy. This gave rise to the idea of a full sovereign State and quasi-sovereign State. The emergence of the Federal State of the United States of America in 1787 reflected the divisibility of sovereignty. The nineteenth century debated the divisible nature of sovereignty despite the emergence of Germany and Switzerland as federal States. However, the nature of sovereignty as a concept of absolute power was not much disputed [2].

The twentieth century has been the real challenge to Hobbe's concept of absolute sovereignty. Until the end of the nineteenth century, States were considered as real sovereign not being answerable to international law and this remained the position until the beginning of the Hague Conferences in 1899 and 1907. It was realised then that absolute sovereignty was inconsistent with the concept of international law and world community. Therefore, it was argued that although States were sovereign they should feel themselves bound by what they have expressly agreed to or what has been tacitly agreed by them. Although this kind of self-restraint has brought some sort of rule of law in the domain of international relations, it is yet far from satisfactory. States have been very much conscious of their sovereignty which has jeopardised the reference of disputes to the International Court of Justice and the establishment of unified legislative and enforcing agencies. Nevertheless, there is also an awakening among the States that in the age of interdependence, it is idle to stick to Hobbe's concept of sovereignty.

Sovereignty is an important concept of international law and an equally important aspect of statehood. A State derives many of its rights through exercise of sovereignty. Right of equality, exercise of territorial jurisdiction, right to determine nationality within its territory, right of regulating entry into and exit from its territory and the right of nationalisation are some of the aspects of exercising sovereignty.

(a) Equality [3]

All States being sovereign, and therefore subordinate to none, are equal in status irrespective of their size, population, power or resources. No State can claim superiority over an other State The principle of equality of States was recognised as early as 1648 in Article 5 of the Treaty of Osnabruch. The concept of equality of States was pronounced by Chief Justice Marshall of the United States Supreme Court in following terms:

"No general principle of law is more universally acknowledged than the perfect equality of nations.........no one can rightfully impose a rule on another. Each legislates for itself, but its legislation can operate on itself alone" [4].

Article 2 (1) of the United Nations Charter says that "The Organisation is based on the principle of the sovereign equality of all its Members." Article 18 of the Charter gives one vote to each of the States. No weightage has been given to any State in the voting system of the General Assembly. All States enjoy jurisdictional immunity in another State on the ground that all states being sovereign and equal, none shall be subject to the jurisdiction of another State, nor shall any State exercise jurisdiction over another State except in cases when it has been subjugated in which case it ceases to be a real State.

Equality of States is an old concept. It has its roots in the Naturalist school. Equality of men and analogically equality of States is a well recognised principle of natural law. Today, of course, the concept has been strengthened by the Positivist school also inasmuch as unanimity is the basic rule of international conferences unless the rule is specifically waived by States.

It is a well-known principle of international law that no State can challenge the acts of another State. This is known as the Act of State doctrine [5]. The doctrine is based on the twin principles of sovereignty and equality of States.

While discussing the principle of equality of States, I am reminded of Dicey's concept of the rule of law and Article 14 of the Indian Constitution both of which guarantee equal protection of laws and equality before the law. In my opinion, this legal concept equally applies to States which also enjoy the equal protection of laws and equality before the law. This means that the rights of States, particularly those of small States, shall be recognised and protected and that every State will be subject to international law irrespective of its size or strength. Therefore, if a State has committed an international tort, it shall be responsible for it in law without making any exception in favour of the big powers.

Equality of States is nowhere more visible than in the corridors of the U.N. General Assembly where all States, big or small, have one vote and the vote of small nation has same value as that of the large State. But it is a place of contrast also if one looks at the functioning of the Security Council where five big powers have been given veto power. No resolution of the Security Council can be valid and binding unless the five big powers concur amongst themselves [6].

It must be admitted that the principle of equality of States is more publicised than practised. Undoubtedly, a small State is equal in status with the big nation. But practices reveal the opposite story. If the United States votes in a particular way in the General Assembly, that vote carries more weight than that of a small nation. A big power can escape more easily with impunity, for violating international law than a small nation. The United States toppled the Allende regime in Chile because it was not pro-American. The Soviet Union intervened in Hungary and Czechoslavakia for similar reasons. Examples of violations of international law on the part of big powers are innumerable. There lies the difference between precept and practice. Already, there is an undercurrent in the United States as well as elsewhere which clamours for weightage in voting based on other grounds. Some small States are sought to be labelled, although unsuccessfully, as micro States not deserving equal rights. Oppenheim distinguishes between legal equality and political equality [7]. According to him, while States enjoy legal equality, small States cannot be political equals of big powers. This differentiation cannot be denied absolutely in view of the factuality of the situation where powerful States wield economic or military control over some of the small nations.

(b) **Jurisdiction** [8]

Sovereignty of State implies exercise of jurisdiction by the State within its territory. A State's law reigns supreme there except insofar as its powers are restricted by international commitments or by customary international law. As judge Huber said in the Island of the *Palmas Arbitration* Case: "Territorial sovereignty...involves the exclusive right to display the activities of a State" [9]. It was aptly said by Chief Justice Marshall in the Schooner Exchange case that "The Jurisdiction of the nation within its own territory is necessarily exclusive and absolute" [10]. Local municipal law in some cases supersedes even customary or conventional international law if the latter is in conflict with the former. Jurisdiction is an attribute of territorial independence [11].

Exercise of jurisdiction means that all persons who are living within the territorial limits of a given State are subject to the laws of that State irrespective of whether they are residing there temporarily or permanently. The principle was well enunciated by Lord MacMillan in 1938 when he said:

"It is an essential attribute of sovereignty..., as of all sovereign independent States, that it should possess jurisdiction over all persons and things within its territorial limits and in all causes, civil and criminal arising within these limits."[12]

Jurisdiction includes control over foreign vessels within territorial water. But some categories of personnel like diplomatic staff of foreign States as well as foreign men-of-war are not subject to territorial jurisdiction of the local State unless there has been waiver of immunity by their government. By virtue of customary and conventional international law, they enjoy the privilege of ex-territoriality which means that they are supposed to be living outside the territory of the local government by means of a fiction of law. In some cases, the armed forces personnel of foreign government are exempted from local jurisdiction as were the U.S. armed personnel during World War II and sometimes after the end of war also in Europe [13]. Prior to that, some Afro-Asian States were subjected to the restrictions of not exercising jurisdiction over nationals of the Western States on the basis of unequal treaties which Oppenheim called as a treaty obligation and customary law. This practice no more exists and was never a part of international law.

Jurisdiction over open seas

States exercise jurisdiction over occurrence on the open seas also in some cases. Thus, a State exercises jurisdiction on merchant vessels registered with the State and even over foreign commercial vessels if any of the acts or ommissions committed overboard cast a shadow on its territory, transitory or floating. In the famous Lotus case [14], the Permanent Court held that the Turkish Government had not violated any rule of international law by exercising jurisdiction over the French officers of the vessel 'Lotus' due to whose negligence, there was a collision on the open seas between the French vessel and a Turkish vessel resulting in the death of eight Turks. The jurisdiction was exercised when the French vessel entered Constantinople. The rule has since been reversed by the Convention for the Unification of Certain Rules relating to Penal Jurisdiction in Matters of Collisions and other Incidents of Navigation held in 1952. Article 11 of the Geneva Convention on High Seas of 1958 gives exclusive jurisdiction to the flag State in respect of penal and disciplinary matters arising out of collisions at sea, unless the accused is a national of the State assuming jurisdiction.

Customary international law also permits States to exercise jurisdiction over piratical acts committed by persons who have since then come under the control of the government. Piracy is treated as an international crime and the perpetrator may be tried and punished by any State where he is found. Aerial hijackers and terrorists are also liable to be tried by any State where the culprits are found as in the case of pirates.

Article 23 of the Convention on the High Seas, signed at Geneva on 29th April, 1958 gives the right of 'hot pursuit' to the coastal State if a foreign vessel has in its view violated any of its laws while it was within the territorial sea limits of the State. In these circumstances, the territorial State may pursue the defying vessel even on the high seas and apprehend it there and bring it to its port. This could have happened when the two Taiwanese trawlers were seized off the Kerala coast in 1976 [15].

In time of war, belligerent States have the right of visiting and searching foreign vessels on the high seas if the given vessel is suspected of carrying contraband goods to the enemy State or is engaged in unneutral service.

Personal jurisdiction

As distinguished from territorial jurisdiction, a State does also exercise personal jurisdiction over its nationals who have committed crimes abroad as well as over its men-of-war and merchant vessels flying its flag. Sections 3 and 4 of the Indian Penal Code vest such powers in the magistrate if the person is found within his jurisdiction limit after having committed a crime in foreign territory or on the high seas. The United States also exercises jurisdiction over its nationals abroad [16].

(c) Sovereign Immunity [17]

One State enjoys immunity from jurisdiction in another State. This is called sovereign immunity. This immunisation from local jurisdiction is based on a number of factors. Primarily, it flows from the doctrine of sovereignty of States. All States being sovereign, one sovereign State cannot exercise jurisdiction over another sovereign State. Equality of State is another determining factor. States enjoy equality in status. Therefore, there can be no exercise of jurisdiction by one equal over another [18]. Jurisdiction can be exercised only by a superior over its inferior and since there is no superior in international law, there is lack of jurisdiction. Subsidiary reasons for jurisdictional immunity of sovereign States are the theories of dignity and comity. Thus, it is said that it may compromise the dignity of a sovereign State if it were to be subjected to the local jurisdiction of another State. Comity requires extension of courtesy by one State to another. Exercise of any jurisdiction would be contrary to that comity.

The Schooner Exchange case is the leading authority on the doctrine of sovereign immunity. The facts of this case were that the "Exchange" was on its way to Spain from Baltimore in 1809. In December 1810, it was seized under a Napoleon decree. On her re-entry into the United States, it was claimed by its former owners on the ground that no seizure order of the vessel was passed by any competent court. The U.S. Attorney opposed any such restitution because the vessel had entered Philadelphia as a French public armed vessel and, therefore, not liable to local jurisdiction. The U.S. contention was upheld by the District Court, but reversed by the Circuit Court, although restored by the Supreme Court. Chief Justice Marshall who delivered the judgment said :

> "Perfect equality and absolute independence of sovereigns..... have given rise to a class of cases in which every sovereign is understood to waive the exercise of a part of that complete exclusive territorial jurisdiction, which has been stated to be the attribute of every nation.... It seems then to be principle of public law that national ships of war are to be considered exempted by the consent of the power from its jurisdiction." [19]

The Parlement Belge is the famous British case on jurisdiction a immunity. In this case, Parlement Belge was a Belgian postal packet which was treated as a man-of-war under the Anglo-Belgian Postal Convention, 1876. Having been involved in a collision, it was sought to be attached in the British courts. The British Attorney General claimed that British Court had no jurisdiction over men-of-war belonging to a friendly sovereign. The lower court, presided over by Sir Robert Phillimore, overruled the Attorney General's contention. The Attorney General appealed to the Court of Appeals. L.J. Brett, who delivered the judgment, said:

> "The principle...is that as a consequence of the absolute independence of every sovereign authority, and of the inter-

national comity which induces every sovereign to respect the independence and dignity of every other sovereign State, each and every one declines to exercise by means of its courts any of its territorial jurisdictions over the person of any sovereign or over the public property of any State which is destined to public use...." [20]

In the Christina case, Lord Wright gave several grounds of jurisdictional immunity of foreign sovereign. According to him, it flows from international comity or courtesy; it is also based on the principle *per in parem non habet imperium* (no State can claim jurisdiction over another sovereign); any exercise of jurisdiction may be considered as an unfriendly act; or an exercise of auto limitation on one's own powers on basis of reciprocity [21]. More recently, it was held in the case of Juan Ysmael & Co. versus, Indonesian Government that "it is beneath the dignity of a foreign sovereign Government to submit to the jurisdiction of an alien court" [22]. Grant of jurisdictional immunity to a foreign sovereign is also an instrument of foreign policy [23].

The Indian position on jurisdictional immunity in the post-independent era was considered in the case of re-Commissioner for Workmen's Compensation by the Madras High Court. The facts of the case were that the applicant, who was employed by the Admiralty Civil Engineer, was injured while unloading the girders. He claimed compensation from his employers, the British Crown, under the Indian Workmen's Compensation Act, 1923. It was contended on behalf of the Crown that it could not be sued in the Indian Courts on account of jurisdictional immunity of a foreign State under international law. This contention was upheld by the High Court which observed:

> "One of the cardinal principles of International Law is that every sovereign State respects the independence of every other sovereign State and as a consequence of this absolute independence of the International comity which underlines the relation between sovereign States, each State declines to exercise by means of any of its courts jurisdiction over the person of any Sovereign or Ambassador or over the public property of any State .. A sovereign State cannot be sued in the courts of a foreign State, unless of course it voluntarily submits to the jurisdiction of the court." [24]

In a later case, Royal Nepalese Airline Corporation versus Manorama, the Calcutta High Court held that a foreign sovereign cannot be sued even when he is not directly involved in the suit. The facts of the case were that a wife of the pilot in the employment of the Royal Nepalese Airlines claimed damages against the Airlines for the death of her husband due to negligence of the defendant. The Court held that there are two basic principles of international law giving jurisditional immunity to a foreign sovereign and they are:

> "The first is that the courts of a country will not implead a foreign sovereign, that is, they will not by their process make him against his will a party to legal proceedings whether the proceedings involved process against his person or seek to recover from him specific property or damages. The second is that they will not by their process, whether the sovereign is a party to the proceedings or not, seize or detain any property which is his or of which he is in possession or control. There has been some difference in the practice of nations as to possible limitations of this second principle as to whether it extends to properties only used for the commercial purposes of the sovereign or to personal private. In this country it is, in my opinion, well settled that it applied to both." [25]

In addition to jurisdictional immunity of a foreign State in India, there is an additional privilege given by the Indian Civil Procedure Code. Section 86 of the Code says that no foreign sovereign can be sued in the Indian Courts without the permission of the Government of India.

Extent of sovereign immunity

While sovereign immunity is an accepted principle of international law, its extent is doubtful. Up to the nineteenth century, the matter was fairly settled that the sovereign State enjoyed absolute immunity from the jurisdiction of another sovereign State. This was due to the impression then that sovereignty was indivisible. However, the bubble of indivisibility of sovereignty has been pricked and exposed to encroachment; hence the doubts relating to the extent of sovereign immunity. Today, there are two schools prevailing in the arena. One advocates for the continuation of absolute and unlimited sovereign immunity. The other purports to limit the immunity to *jure imperii*—sovereign acts—as distinguished from *jure gestionis*—non-sovereign acts—of the State. The Anglo-American System, which India also seems to be following, supports the former school [26]. The Continental system supports the latter school [27]. However, it may not be wrong to say that there is re-thinking even in the Anglo-American System over the absolutism of sovereign immunity.

The result is that there is appreciable dilution of the doctrine of absolute sovereign immunity [28]. This only means that the practices are veering around restricted sovereign immunity. Indian Courts in the post-independence era have also cast doubts on the doctrine of absolute immunity although some courts have also upheld the principle. Thus in the case of Dulerai and Co. versus Pokerdas where the Maharaja of Baroda was sued as a partner of the defendant business firm, the High Court of Bombay held that the immunity is absolute and it is not limited to any particular class of suits or in respect of his public dealings [29]. The Court was interpreting the connotation of Section 86 of the Civil Procedure Code which states:

> "No Rule of a foreign State may be sued in any court otherwise competent to try a suit except with the consent of the Central Government certified in writing by a Secretary to that Government."

In the Mirza Akbar versus United Arab Republic case, the Calcutta High Court held that "there is no principle of absolute immunity" and besides, transaction of commercial nature "is not entitled to immunity" [30]. In this case, the High Court of Calcutta had held that the U.A.R. Government was not entitled to jurisdictional immunity for its commercial transactions like the agreement for purchase of tea from the petitioner.

There seems to be a growing tendency to apply the doctrine of jurisdictional immunity to only *jure imperii* acts or the legislative, executive and administrative acts of foreign governments [31]. Similarly, foreign States are also entitled to immunity in respect of title deeds [32]. But as the court held: "mere assertion of a claim by a foreign State to a property which is not admittedly vested in him or which is not in his possession cannot attract the principle of immunity from the legal processes of the Municipal Court of the country."[33]

According to the English practice, a foreign sovereign is not supposed to prove title to the property in suit although courts must be satisfied that the claim of the foreign government is not merely illusory nor is it manifestly defective. This was held by the Privy Council in the case of Juan Ysmael versus Indonesian

Government [34]. Earlier, it was held by Lord Wright and Lord Maughan that the mere assertion as to the right to possession is not enough. There must be some substance in the assertion [35].

Waiver of Immunity [36]

While a foreign sovereign enjoys jurisdictional immunity, it may as well be waived by the sovereign who may therefore submit to the local jurisdiction. This is called waiver of immunity. Since such a step is a departure from the customary rule of international law, waiver, in order to be effective must be clear [37]. Mere putting in of appearance to bring one's status to the notice of the court cannot be considered as submission to the jurisdiction of the Court and, therefore, waiver. In the famous case of Mighel versus Sultan of Johore, where the Sultan pleaded in a suit against him for breach of promise that the Court had no jurisdiction as he was a sovereign foreign ruler, it was not considered as his submission to Court's jurisdiction [38]. It was, therefore, wrong to construe, it is submitted, on the part of Calcutta High Court in the case of Mirza Akbar versus United Arab Republic that because the U.A.R. Government challenged the suit of the plaintiff on the ground of want of sanction under Section 86 of the Civil Procedure Code and sovereign immunity, it would be treated as submission to court's jurisdiction [39]. However, if the sovereign State applies for issue of letters of requests to examine witnesses and deposit money as per orders of the court, the Calcutta High Court rightly held that this may be construed as submission to the court's jurisdiction [40].

As to when a State can consent to its submitting to jurisdiction of foreign court is a controversial issue. While Continental law permits such waiver any time even before the initiation of proceedings or as part of contract [41], English law requires such consent when the proceedings have really been started. No earlier waiver is valid even though it is specific. Thus was held in the case of Kahan versus Government of Pakistan [42]. The case arose out of alleged breach of contract on the part of the Pakistan Government which had entered into the contract with the plaintiff for the supply of Sherman tanks. The relevant portion of the contract was as follows: "The Government agrees to submit for the purpose of this agreement to the jurisdiction of the English Courts." However, the Court of Appeals held that mere agreement by a foreign sovereign to submit to the jurisdiction of the courts of this country is wholly ineffective if later on the foreign sovereign chooses to resile from it. Nothing short of actual submission to the jurisdiction will suffice [43]. Equity demands that declaration of waiver, if it is specific, should be binding irrespective of its timing.

Institution of proceedings by foreign sovereign is considered as waiver of immunity. This has been held by the Privy Council in the case of Sultan of Johore versus Abubakar Tunku Bendahar [44]. In this case, the Sultan of Johore had secured a judgment in his favour from the Japanese Occupation Court during World War II. After the Japanese withdrawal, the judgment was sought to be set aside but the Sultan raised the plea of sovereign immunity. The Singapore Judge rejected the plea on the ground that the Sultan had himself initiated the proceedings. The Judge's order was upheld by the Singapore Court of Appeal and the Privy Council. The National City Bank versus Republic of China case represents the U.S. viewpoint [45].

NOTES

1. For some literature on sovereignty, see Harold Laski, Studies in the Problem of Sovereignty (1917), same author, Foundations of Sovereignty (1920); Mattern, Concepts of State Sovereignty and International Law (1928); Merriam, History of the Theory of Sovereignty since Rousseau (1900).
2. For History of the concept of sovereignty from the days of Bodin till nineteenth century, see Lauterpacht, Oppenheim's International Law (Eight Edition) vol. 1. pp. 120-22.
3. Barker, The Doctrine of Legal Equality of States, (1923-24) 4.B.Y.I.L.1-20; McNair, Equality in International Law, (1927), 26 Michigan Law Review 131-52; Kelson, Hans, The Principle of Sovereign Equality as a basis for International Organisation (1944) 53 Y.L.J. 207-20; in International Law. Thomas A.J. and Wynen Annvan, Equality of States: Fact or Fiction, (1951) 37 Virginia Law Review 791-823; Weinschel, The Doctrine of the Equality of States and its Recent Modifications (1951) 45 A.J.I.L. 417-22; O'Connel, International Law, vol. 1, pp. 344-48. Oppenheim, op. cit. vol. 1 pp. 263-67; Dickinson, Equality of States in International Law (1920). According to Oppenheim, there are four advantages attached to the doctrine of equality. They are that every State has a right to vote, vote of every State has equal value irrespective of its size on development of State, no State is subject to the jurisdiction of another State nor can one State challenge the official act of another State, 263-67.
4. The Antelope 10 Wheaton 66 at p. 122 (1825).

5. Sabbatino Case, 376 U.S. 396.
6. Article 27 (3) of the U.N. Charter.
7. Oppenheim, op. cit., vol. 1 pp. 275-77.
8. Beckett, W.E., The Exercise of Criminal Jurisdiction over Foreigners, 1925 B.Y.I.L. 4460; same author, Criminal Jurisdiction over Foreigners—The Franconia and the Lotus, 1927 B.Y.I.L. 108-28; Beale, The Jurisdiction of a Sovereign State, (1923) 36 Harvard Law Review 241-62.
9. As reported in Green L.C., op. cit, p. 351.
10. Schooner Exchange vs McFadden, 7 Cranch 116 as reported by Herbert Briggs, Cases and Materials on Law of Nations, p. 414.
11. Sardar Gurdiyal Singh vs The Raja of Faridkot, 1894, A.C. 670 at p. 683.
12. Compania Naviera Vascongado vs Christina S.S., 1938 A.C. 485 at pp. 496-97.
13. See the United States of America (Visiting Forces) Act, 1942; King Archibold, Jurisdiction over Friendly Foreign Armed Forces, (1942) 36 A.J.I.L. 536-67, McNair Edwin C., United States Army, Courts in Brikuir (1944) 60 L.Q.R. 356-60.
14. P.C.I.J. (1927) Series A. No. 10 and Series C, No. 13 (ii).
15. Times of India, April 22, 1976. Two Taiwanese trawlers were spotted off Kerala coast ostensibly for fishing purposes. These trawlers were seized by Indian navy and later on it was found that the trawlers carried sophisticated electronic equipment not meant for fishing but for espionage.
16. Harry, M. Blackmar vs United States of America (1932) 284 U.S. Reports 421.
17. F.A. Mann, Immunity of Sovereign States, (1938-39) 2 Modern Law Review, 57 Baty, *T. De Facto* States, Sovereign Immunities, (1951) 45 A.J.I.L. 166-70, Carter, Immunity of Foreign Sovereigns From Jurisdiction, (1950) 3 I.L.Q. 78, Gracia Mora, The Doctrine of Sovereign Immunity of Foreign States and its Recent Modifications, (1956) 42 Virginia Law Review 335-59, Lauterpacht, The Problem of Jurisdictional Immunities of Foreign States, 1951 B.Y.I.L. 20, Fitzmaurice, State Immunity from Proceedings in Foreign Courts, (1933) 14 B.Y.I.L. 101 and 124, Notes—Sovereign Immunity—Waiver and Execution—Arguments from Continental Jurisprudence, 1965 Y.L.J. 887.
18. Lauterpacht, Oppenheim's International Law, vol. 1. 264.
19. The Schooner Exchange vs Mc Fadden, (1812) 7 Cranch 116 (Supreme Court of the United States of America) as given by L.C. Green, International Law Through Cases (1959) pp. 195, 198.
20. The Parlement Belge, (1880) 5 P.D. 197 as given by L.C. Green, ibid., 192 at p. 200.
21. (1938) A.C. 485. It was a House of Lords decision purporting to uphold the Spanish Government's claim that the owners of the vessel Christina, could not claim the vessel which had been requisitioned by the Govərnment.
22. (1955) A.C. 72. In this case, vessel, S. S. Tasikmalaja belonging to

the Indonesian Government was attached in an action in rem and remained in the custody of the bailliff of the Supreme Court of Hong Kong. Indonesian Government put in an appearance through Indonesian Consul General under protest and claimed sovereign immunity. The Supreme Court held against the Indonesian Government which appealed. The Appealate Court allowed the Indonesian appeal. The claimants appealed to the Privy Council which upheld the doctrine of sovereign immunity.

23. (AIR) 1951 Madras 880 at 881.
24. (AIR) 1966 Calcutta 319 at 325.
25. Abel Paul, Immunity of Foreign States Engaged in Commercial Operations, (1951) 45 A.J.I.L. 354-57, Fensterwald Bernard, Sovereign Immunity and Soviet State Trading, (1950) 63 H.L.R. 614-42.
26. Hanbury, The Position of Foreign Sovereigns Before English Courts' (1950) Current Legal Problems. Sweeny, Policy Research Study, International Law of Sovereign Immunity, (1963) 38-39.
27. Also see Allen, The Position of Foreign States Before National Courts, (1933) 221-29. Vattel also gave Immunity to Foreign States in respect of their official acts—Le Droit Des Gens, Book IV, Chapter VIII, Sections 110-15; Note, Sovereign Immunity, Supra, 1965, Y.L.J. 89.
28. For example, see the Tate letter in which Mr. Jack B. Tate, Acting Legal Adviser to the U.S. Department of State said:
"The reasons which obviously motivate State trading countries in adhering to the (absolute) theory with increasing rigidity are most persuasive that the United States should change its policy. The Department feels that the widespread practice on the part of governments of engaging in commercial activities makes necessary a practice which will enablé persons doing business with them to have their rights determined in the Courts." (1952) 26 D.S.B. 984 at p. 985.
29. (AIR) 1952 Bombay, 335.
30. (AIR) 1960 Calcutta 768 at p. 775 para 31.
31. Ibid, p. 774 at para 27.
32. Indian National Steamship vs Mawx Faul-baum (AIR) 1955 Calcutta 491.
33. Ibid, para 23 at p. 495.
34. 1955 A.C. 72.
35. The Christina—1938 A.C. 485 at pp. 506 and 516.
36. Cohn E.J. Waiver of Immunity, (1958) 38 B.Y.I.L. 260-73.
37. Duff Development Co. Ltd. vs Government of Kelantan, 1924 A.C. 797 as per Viscount Finlay.
38. (1894) 1. Q.B. 149.
39. (AIR) 1960 Calcutta 768 at para 32.
40. (AIR) 1955 Calcutta 491 at p. 493.
41. Cohn, Supra, 263-64.
42. (1951) 2 K.B. 1003.
43. Ibid, p. 1012.
44. 1952 A.C. 318 as per Lord Simon.
45. (1955) 348 U.S. 356.

Chapter 11

NATIONALITY

Definition

Nationality [1] may be defined as a symbol of belonging to a particular State. It is a bond of relationship between an individual and the State which gives rise to some benefits to the individual and imposes some obligations upon him. Oppenheim defines the word as "his quality of being a subject of a certain State, and therefore its citizen" [2]. Harvard Research Draft defines the word as the "status of a natural person who is attached to a State by the tie of allegiance" [3]. The concept of nationality was well defined in the case of Re Lynch by the British-Mexican Claims Commission in the following words:

> "A man's nationality is a continuing legal relationship between the sovereign State on the one hand and citizen on the other. The fundamental basis of a man's nationality is his membership of an independent political community. This legal relationship involves rights and corresponding duties upon both on the part of the citizen no less than on the part of the State." [4]

In Nottebohm case, the International Court of Justice defined nationality as follows:

> "Nationality is a legal bond having as its legal basis a social fact of attachment, a genuine connection of existence, interests and sentiments, together with the existence of reciprocal rights and duties." [5]

In fact, nationality, whatever its definition, connotes that a given individual is the national of a particular State. Article 15(1) of the Universal Declaration of Human Rights says that everyone "has the right to a nationality."

Difference between Nationality and Citizenship

Here some confusion needs to be cleared with regard to intermixing or interchangeability of the words, nationality and citizenship. It has often been noticed that these two words are used interchangeably without attributing any difference between them. Whether there is any difference between them is for the municipal law of a particular State to decide. Some States seek to differentiate between the two as in the case of the United States and the United Kingdom [6]. These nations consider citizenship as a superior right to that of nationality. But most of the countries do not make this kind of artificial distinction between the two words. Therefore, there is no basic difference between the two words insofar as international law is concerned. India uses the word 'citizen' only in the Indian Constitution as well as in the Indian Citizenship Act.

Functions

Nationality or citizenship is a symbol of the identification of an individual with a particular State in the realm of international law. Whenever a national of a State has relations with foreign countries, his nationality may come handy to him. If he has to go out of his State, he has to secure a passport from his State for going abroad, as well as to facilitate his return from abroad. The passport is said to be evidence of his nationality [7]. There is a rule of diplomatic protection of nationals abroad by which a State takes up the cause of its aggrieved national with another State which is alleged to have committed international tort against him or any such thing [8]. There have been numerous occasions in the past where States have intervened in the affairs of a foreign State on the plea of protecting their nationals. If the national is stranded in a foreign territory, his State seeks to rescue him through its diplomatic mission there. Similarly, if a person dies in a foreign country and has no one there to look after his burial or cremation, his State normally takes care of these rites. A State is also bound to receive back its nationals who are deported from foreign territories. Some States exercise personal jurisdiction over their nationals even when they are abroad inasmuch as they may be held liable in their own country for the crimes committed by them in a foreign territory. India is one of such countries.

Acquisition of Nationality

Nationality of a State can be acquired in a number of ways. Oppenheim mentions five modes for acquiring nationality. They are through birth, nationalisation, reintegration, subjugation and cession [9]. The Indian Citizenship Act, 1955 provides six modes for acquiring Indian citizenship. They are birth, descent, registration, naturalisation, incorporation of territory and resumption or reintegration [10].

Birth

Many countries recognise that any child born within their territorial limits will acquire the nationality of that State. The United Kingdom, the United States and India come in this category. Section 3 of the Indian Citizenship Act confers such a right. The right is also called *Jus soli* and is the main mode of acquiring nationality. Argentina is one of such countries which recognises *Jus soli* exclusively. This means that the place of birth is the sole criterion for determining the nationality of person. Thus, if a child is born in Argentina, he acquires Argentinean nationality irrespective of the fact whether his parents were Argentineans or not. At the same time, a child born outside Argentina does not acquire Argentinean nationality although the parents may be Argentinean.

Descent

Some countries confer their nationality on such children only whose parents enjoy that country's nationality. Germany grants nationality on this criterion. India, the United States and the United Kingdom also recognise this additional criterion for giving their respective nationality. Thus children born of Indian parents abroad will be treated as Indians. Section 4 of the Indian Citizenship recognises this rule which is called *Jus sanguinis*. A majority of States recognise the principles of *Jus soli* as well as *Jus sanguinis*.

Naturalisation

A person acquires his first nationality at birth. However, if he wants to change that nationality subsequently, he may acquire it by naturalisation. Article 15(2) of the Universal Declaration of Human Rights says that no one shall be "denied the right to change his nationality." Oppenheim gives six modes of acquiring nationality through naturalisation. These are through marriage, legitimation, option, acquisition of domicile, appointment as Government official and grant on application [11]. State practices, however, are not uniform. Some State laws accord the woman the nationality of her husband on marriage. Other States do not. Some laws leave the option to the woman to retain her original nationality or acquire her husband's nationality. Some States permit the woman to retain her own nationality as well as acquire the nationality of her husband also. Legitimation may give the hitherto illegitimate child the nationality of his father. Domicile does not necessarily give right of naturalisation to the person although acquisition of domicile may be an important factor while determining the application for naturalisation. There is an outmoded practice to consider that if a person accepts an appointment with a foreign government, he becomes naturalised.

The only valid way of naturalisation accepted by international law as well as by municipal law is an application to the local government expressing an intention to seek nationality of that State. The applicant has to fulfil a number of requirements depending upon the relevant municipal law of that country. India has prescribed the following conditions to be fulfilled by a foreign applicant for naturalisation.

(a) He is not a citizen of the country which refuses naturalisation to Indians;
(b) Either he is stateless or he has validly renounced the former citizenship;
(c) He has been in India or in the service of the Government of India for one year continuously at the time of his application for naturalisation;
(d) He has been in India or in service of the Government of India for an aggregate of four years out of a total period of seven years preceding the earlier one year;
(e) He is of good character;
(f) He knows one of the regional languages as recognised under the Indian Constitution;
(g) He has the intention to settle down permanently in India [12].

Reintegration

Persons who have lost their original nationality may regain it on fulfilment of some conditions. The process is called reintegration which means restoration. Section 8 (2) of the Indian Citizenship Act, 1955 permits the minors, who lost Indian citizenship due to their parents, to be restored as Indian citizens by making such a choice within one year from the date of attaining age of majority. The procedure for restoration is given in Section 20 of the Citizens Rules 1956 [13]. The Indian Citizenship Act does not provide for reintegration for adults. Reintegration of adults, who once were Indian citizens, will, therefore, be regulated through the process of naturalisation.

The difference between reintegration and naturalisation is that reintegration can only be with regard to such persons who were citizens of the State at one time but had lost the same, while naturalisation relates mainly to foreign applicants. Besides, reintegration may be by a simple procedure while naturalisation may be a cumbersome procedure.

Subjugation, Incorporation or Cession

A person may acquire new nationality through subjugation or incorporation. This occurs when a State is subjugated by another State and incorporated within its territory. When Germany absorbed Austria, all Austrians became German nationals. All Puerto Ricans have become American citizens with the incorporation of Puerto Rico with the United States of America.

Hitherto an independent State may merge with another State. Resultantly, the nationals of a merged State may acquire the citizenship of a new State. This happened when Sikkim became a part of India. Consequently, all Sikkimese became Indian citizens.

A similar result is achieved when a State cedes part of its territory to another State resulting in the acquisition of a new nationality by the residents of the ceded territory.

The difference between subjugation and cession is that while subjugation is through use of force, cession may be voluntary but in some cases it may also be through threat or use of force.

Option

It has been of late found that in case of voluntary partition, cession or exchange of territories, an option is given to the inhabitants to opt for any of the two nationalities. On the partition of India into two independent States, India and Pakistan, the residents were given the option to opt for Indian or Pakistani citizenship. Similarly, when the French ceded its possessions in India to the latter, the option was given to the residents of French territories to opt for either French or Indian citizenship. Similarly, India gave the right of option to the residents of the erstwhile Portuguese possessions to opt for either Portugese or Indian citizenship. In the case of exchange of Berubari, the residents were given the option to choose Indian or Pakistani citizenship. When Britain left from its erstwhile African colonies, the non-Africans were given the choice to opt for either the citizenship of the new State or to maintain their British nationality.

The option may also be exercised by a woman married to foreigner. She may make the choice between retaining her own nationality or accepting the nationality of her husband if it is available to her.

Registration

Registration is an offshoot of the principle of option. Section 5 of the Indian Citizenship Act, 1955 provides for acquiring Indian Citizenship through registration. It permits following categories of persons who can benefit under this provision:

(a) Persons of Indian origin who have been in India for at least six months preceding their application for registration;

(b) Persons of Indian origin residing outside undivided India;

(c) Foreign women married to Indian citizens;

(d) Minor children of Indian citizens if they are not already Indian citizens. This will indeed be a very rare case because children born to Indian citizens in India or outside automatically acquire Indian citizenship;

(e) Citizens of any Commonwealth country including the Republic of Ireland;

(f) Any minor under special circumstances [14].

Legislation

It is now a well-established rule of international law that although it is within the domain of a sovereign State to enact the law relating to acquisition or loss of its nationality, it cannot impose its nationality upon unwilling foreigners who happen to be within its territory [15].

The Hague Convention on Certain Questions Relating to the Conflict of National Laws of 1930 to which India is a party does confer the right upon a State "to determine under its own law who are its nationals." But such a law should be "consistent with international conventions, international customs and the principles of law generally recognised with regard to nationality" [16]. Article 2 of the Convention provides that any "question as to whether a person possesses the nationality of a particular State shall be determined in accordance with the law of the State." A State may, however, confer its own citizenship upon willing foreigners, whether within its territory or elsewhere [17]. There is also the practice of conferring honorary citizenship on foreign dignitaries.

Loss of Nationality

There are some recognised modes of losing citizenship like renunciation, deprivation, termination, lapse and substitution [18].

Renunciation

A person who is a national of a particular State may renounce the nationality of that State by a procedure fixed for the purpose by that State. This may happen either when the person is seeking another nationality, or when he is disgusted with the conditions or policies of the State or when he has to make an option between choosing one nationality and renouncing the other in case of his enjoying dual nationality. The Indian Citizenship Act envisages renunciation only in case of persons enjoying dual nationality [19]. It is considered to be a person's inherent right to change his nationality according to his choice although some States insist that persons cannot renounce their nationality without the permission of the former State. Today, this stand looks archaic.

Deprivation

Some State laws provide for depriving its nationals of their nationality in case of their committing some crimes against the security of the State or such other indiscretions which are not palatable to the State [20]. Thus, a person may be deprived of his nationality if he takes up arms against his own State and sides with its enemy. Also if he spies for enemy country or commits treasonable act [21].

The Indian Citizenship Act provides for deprivation in the following cases:

(a) If naturalisation or registration has been obtained fraudulently or by concealing any material fact;

(b) If he has been disloyal or dis-affected to the Union of India;

(c) If he has done any prejudicial act or traded with enemy while India is at war with that country;

(d) If a naturalised or registered citizen has been sentenced to a term of two years within the five years from the date of his registration or naturalisation;

(e) If he has continuously resided in a foreign country for seven years or more without being a student, Central Government employee or international civil servant in any organisation recognised by India and has also not registered himself at an Indian Consulate [22].

Article 15(2) of the Universal Declaration of Human Rights prohibits arbitrary deprivation of nationality. This means that the citizen should not be deprived of his nationality arbitrarily without being given a chance to explain his case. Although the Declaration does not have the sanctity of law, it may work as a guideline inasmuch as there should be a valid ground for depriving any person of his nationality.

Termination

Some States prescribe that if any of its citizens acquired nationality of another State, he ceases to be the citizen of the former State. India is one of such countries. Section 9 of the citizenship Act provides that if an Indian citizen has voluntarily acquired foreign citizenship either through naturalisation, registration or otherwise he shall cease to be a citizen of India.

Lapse

Nationality may be lost by continuous stay outside the country of his nationality. The U.S. Nationality Law of 1952 provides that a naturalised citizen of the United States loses his citizenship if he has continuously stayed for three years in the place of his birth or former nationality or by continuous residence for five years in a foreign country. The Indian Citizenship Act likewise provides that if a citizen has remained continuously for seven years in a foreign territory except for purposes of study, employment with Indian Government or International Organisation and he has not chosen to register himself at the Indian Consulate, he will lose his Indian citizenship [23].

Substitution

Nationality is sometimes lost when a particular person acquires the nationality of another State as a consequence of which he loses his earlier nationality. This may happen in case of annexation by way of merger of his former territory with the State of his new nationality. Thus, when people in Bangla Desh got Bangla citizenship, they lost Pakistani citizenship. Similarly, when non-Africans opted for the citizenship of Kenya, Uganda or Zambia, they lost their British or Indian nationality.

Again, some persons may get naturalisation in a foreign country. Such naturalisation may have the effect of that person losing his former nationality. The U.S. Nationality Law of 1952 and the Indian Citizenship Act of 1955 provide that the U.S. and Indian citizens shall lose their American or Indian nationality, as the case may be, if they acquire any foreign nationality.

Double Nationality [24]

Some persons may be nationals of two States at the same time. This may happen in the case of a person who is not born in the country of his parents but in some foreign country. The result is that he may acquire the nationality of the country where he is born on the basis of *Jus soli* and he also acquires the nationality of his own country on the basis of *Jus sanguinis*—nationality of his parents. Thus, he acquires two nationalities. Or it may also happen that a person may get himself naturalised in a foreign country without simultaneously losing his former citizenship. This gives double nationality. A woman may acquire double nationality by marrying a foreigner whose State awards its nationality to wives of its nationals without the wife losing her original nationality.

Double nationality gives some benefits but at the same time it puts the person in an awkward situation. Both the States expect his allegiance to them separately and simultaneously. The situation becomes complicated if both States are at war with each other. This is exactly what happened in the case of Tomoya Kwatika versus the United States [25]. In this case, the accused enjoyed American and Japanese nationalities. He went to Japan on a U.S. passport before the initiation of hostilities between the two countries during World War II. While in Japan, he was asked to look after American prisoners-of-war camps. After the cessation of hostilities, he returned to the United States and was charged with treasonable activities and inflicting brutalities on American prisoners. While upholding the judgment of the Lower Court, the U.S. Supreme Court held that "one who has a dual nationality will be subject to claims from both nations, claims which at times may be competing or conflicting" [26]. A person having double nationality may be subject to military service in both the States. They are rightly called as *sujets mixtes* meaning thereby that they are mixed subjects.

Articles 3-6 of the Hague Convention of 1930 deal with problems of dual nationality. Article 3 is declaratory inasmuch as each State shall treat the person as its own national. Article 4 debars the person from seeking diplomatic protection of one State against the second State of his nationality. This is also the Anglo-American practice [27]. The International Court of Justice considered this is to be the general practice [28]. Article 5 provides that insofar as a third State is concerned, a person having double or more nationalities will be treated as if he has one nationality depending upon his habitual and principal residence in the State or the one with which he is most closely connected. Article 6 permits him to renounce any one of the two nationalities with the permission of the State whose nationality he proposes to surrender.

Effective Nationality [29]

In case of double or multiple nationality, the question sometime arises as to which is the person's effective nationality. If a person has an American as well as an Indian nationality, a question may be asked as to which is his effective nationality. This will depend upon the nature of his residence or closer association. Article 5 of the Hague Convention accepts the principle of effective nationality inasmuch as the third State will treat him as a national of that State where the permanently and habitually resides or with which he is in fact closely connected. India follows this rule. This may be evident from Section 8 of the Foreigners' Act, 1946 which speaks that "foreigner may be treated as the national of the country with which he appears to be most closely connected for the time being in interest or sympathy." This may be clear from the fact that he has contested for any political post in one State or from the issue of passport to him by a particular State. But if he has passports from both the States, complications may arise.

Statelessness [30]

A person who does not enjoy the nationality of any State is said to be a stateless person. This may be the consequence of municipal law which may deprive a person of one nationality without that person getting the nationality of any other State. Refugees fleeing from their country may become stateless.

Grant of nationality is said to be one of the sovereign rights of a State. And although Article 15(2) of the Universal Declaration of Human Rights prohibits arbitrary deprivation of nationality, it is not binding as law. Therefore, a State considers it within its sovereign power to deprive any person of its nationality. It remains oblivious of its consequences upon the affected person. The result is appalling. Overnight, persons become stateless by a stroke of a pen by hostile authorities of the State. In some cases, the national of one country loses his nationality because of his long domicile or stay in a foreign country. A person may have been born as stateless if he is born in a country which recognises *Jus sanguinis* and the State of his parents recognises *Jus soli.* Statelessness may be caused by conflict of nationality laws [31].

Nationality, as has been said above, is the link between the individual and international law. A national of any State is assured of his State's protection if he suffers any injustice at the hands of a foreign State. There is no such protection in case of stateless person who has no State to sponsor his cause. Besides, being a foreigner in his own State of birth or residence, he may suffer many other handicaps which are faced by aliens.

International elites have been conscious of the difficulties of stateless persons. Article 15(1) of the Universal Declaration of Human Rights says that everyone has a right to nationality. The problem has been discussed at the U.N. forum and its allied bodies. There has been 1954 Convention on Stateless Persons which has been in effect from 6th June, 1960 and there have been 28 ratifications so far. There has been another Convention of 28th August, 1961 on Reduction of Statelessness which has come into effect from December, 1975 two years after the sixth ratification by Australia. However, the ratifications have been much too few.

Notes

1. Hanna, Nationality and War Claims (1945) 45 Columbia Law Review, 301-44, Koesler, Subject, Citizen and Permanent Allegiance, (1947)

56 Yale Law Journal 58-76; Bischop, Nationality in International Law (1943) 37 A.J.I.L. 320-325.

2. Lauterpacht, Oppenheim's International Law, vol. 1 pp. 642-43.
3. Harvard Draft Convention on Nationality, 1929 A.J.I.L. (Special Supplement) p. 13.
4. 1929-30 A.D. 221 at p. 223.
5. 1955 I.C.J. Reports p. 23.
6. Oppenheim, op. cit. vol. 1 pp. 644-45.
7. Passport is defined as "a document of Identity and Nationality." Hackworth's Digest of International Law, vol. III, p. 435.

   Clause 3 of Schedule III of the Citizenship (India) Rules, 1956, says: "The fact that a citizen of India has obtained passport on any date from the Government of any other country shall be conclusive of his having voluntarily acquired the citizenship of that country before that date."
8. Borchard, Diplomatic Protection of Citizens Abroad (1915); Mavrommatis Case decided by the Permanent Court of International Justice—Series A. No. 2,(1924). In this case, the Court held that it is "elementary principle of international law that a State is entitled to protect its subjects, when injured by acts contrary to international law committed by another State, from whom they have been unable to obtain satisfaction through ordinary channel." p. 12.

   Also see the Nottebohm case, 1955 I.C.J. Reports 1. The case was based on Leichtenstein's right to protect interests of its national although the Court dismissed the case on the ground that the person did not enjoy effective nationality of Leichtenstein in order to entitle the State to champion his cause.
9. Oppenheim, op. cit. vol. 1, p. 650.
10. Sections 3-8 of the Act.
11. Oppenheim, op. cit., pp. 655-56.
12. Schedule III, attached to the Indian Citizenship Act, 1955 read with Section 6 of the Act.
13. See Gazetee of India, Extraodinary, Part II, Section III, No. 204 dated 7 July, 1956.
14. Rules 3 to 15 of the Citizenship Rules, 1956 deal with Procedure for registration.
15. J. Mervyn Jones, British Nationality Law and Practice (1947) p. 15.
16. Article 1 of the Convention.
17. However see Nottebohm's case where the International Court of Justice rejected the plea of Leichtenstein that the aggrieved person, who had been granted nationality by that country was its effective national-1955 I.C.J. Reports 1.
18. Also see Oppenheim, op. cit., 657.
19. See Section 8 of the Act. Rule 21 of the Citizenship Rules, 1956 prescribes the procedure for renouncing Indian nationality in case of the person enjoying double nationality.
20. Preuss, International Law and Deprivation of Nationality (1934) 22 Georgetown Law Review 250-76; Abel Paul, Denationalisation (1942)

6 Modern Law Review 57-68.

21. For example, see United States Nationality Act of 1952; Strause Edgar, A. Constitutional law—Denationalisation under the Immigration and Nationality Act 1952 (1952-53) 51, Michigan Law Review 881-913.

22. Section 10 of the Citizenship Act and Rules 22-25 of the Citizenship Rules, 1956.
Somewhere it has been argued that the provision of 'deprivation' under the Act is not desirable. The protagonist of this view cites some countries whose nationality laws do not contain such provisions. He also says that there is discrimination between two types of citizens. Further, he considers the words—disloyal and disaffected—as too vague. See S.K. Aggrawala, International Law—Indian Courts and Legislature (1965) pp. 173-74. It is submitted that it is on the contrary good to have such provision in the Act as it would forewarn the citizens, particularly of foreign origin, that they would stand the risk of being deprived of their nationality in the above circumstances. The words—disloyal—and disaffected are commonly used words and the people should know which acts would be considered as disloyal. Surely, the courts would interpret the words in case of any such situation. The distinction between born Indian citizen and Indian citizen of foreign origin is also well founded because born citizen will have sentimental attachment with India while citizens of foreign State may lack that emotional attachment with the country. This writer is sure that distinction will withstand the rigours of Article 14 of the Constitution guaranteeing equality before law. The Indian provision on deprivation is akin to Section 20 of the British Nationality Act, 1948.

23. Section 10 of the Indian Citizenship Act, 1955.

24. Bar-Yaacov, Dual Nationality (1961).

25. (1952) 343 U.S. 717.

26. Ibid, p. 733.

27. For American Practice, see Hackworth, Digest of International Law, vol. III. p. 353. For British Practice, see Sinclair I.M. Nationality of claims (1950) 27. B.Y.I.L. 125-44.

28. In the Reparation for Injuries suffered in the Service of the United Nations, the Court held that general practice is that the "State does not exercise protection on behalf of its own nationals against a State which regards him as its own national." 1949 I.C.J. Reports 174. Also see Conevaro case between Italy and Peru as given by Briggs, op. cit., p. 512.

29. Rode Zvanksr, Dual Nationals and the Doctrine of Dominant Nationality (1959) 53 A.J.I.L. 139-44.

30. Weiss, The Problem of Statelessness (1944); Samore, Statelessness as a Consequence of the Conflict of Nationality Laws (1951) 45 A.J.I.L. 476; Erwin Locwenfeld, Status of Stateless persons (1942) 27 G.S 59-112.

31. W. Samore, Ibid; George Ginsburg, Soviet Citizenship Legislation and Statelessness as a Consequence of the Conflict of Laws, 1965, I.C.L.Q. 1.

CHAPTER 12

ALIENS

State enjoys territorial supremacy. This right confers a consequential right upon the State by which it regulates entry into and exit of aliens [1] from within its territory. No alien can claim a right to enter any foreign territory. Nor is a State under a duty to accept aliens [2]. Almost all States have by now resorted to practice of issuing visas to aliens aspiring to visit a particular foreign country. Some States have waived the visa system vis-a-vis each other on reciprocity basis. Until recently, citizens of the Commonwealth countries did not require visa for entering the United Kingdom. Of late however, the entry rules have been tightened at least with regard to coloured immigrants. Similarly, many European States have waived the visa system in respect of each other's nationals on reciprocity basis. Some States like the Scandinavian countries and the Federal Republic of Germany have waived the visa system for such foreigners who are on a brief halt in their territory. Nepal and India do not require visa for entry into each other's territory by its nationals. All these practices show that the permission of a territorial State, express or implied, is necessary for effecting entry into its territory.

With the growth of air travel, increase in international trade and tourist traffic, entry of aliens has been liberalised by many countries due to the self-interest of promoting international goodwill and at the same time earning foreign exchange. Notwithstanding all this, a State reserves the right to refuse entry into its territory to any foreigner whom it does not feel inclined to grant visa for whatever reason [3]. However, barring a few States like the Soviet Union, the United States of America and the Socialist countries, visa for travel purposes is given as a matter of course while the above said States are strict on the observance of some formalities before the issue of even a travel visa. The Indian Foreigners Act of 1946 empowers the Central Government to make provisions regarding entry into and expulsion of foreigners from India [4].

Alien and the Law

When an alien enters a foreign territory for whatever duration, be it in transit, short, long or indefinite he, becomes subject to the municipal law of the country [5] unless he enters the territory as a diplomat or recognised official of the foreign government. He does not, however, owe temporary allegiance to the local government as has been said by Oppenheim or Starke and others [6]. Allegiance is a sentimental attachment to the State of one's nationality and is a synonym of loyalty. The alien does not owe any such sentiment to a foreign country which is his temporary abode. A person owes allegiance to only one State of which he is a national. Any duality of allegiance may create complications as has been witnessed in the case of holders of dual nationality. Of course he has to abide by the law of the land and should not do anything prejudicial against that country thus prompting the State to deport the alien in public interest. Nor can the alien be permitted to do anything which may jeopardise the cordial relations between the country of his temporary residence and any other foreign country. Aliens are sometimes subjected to restrictions on their movement in public interest or on the basis of reciprocity. Section 3-2 (e) of the Foreigners Act, 1946 empowers the Indian Government to put any restriction on foreigners during their stay in India. But the Government may also exempt any category or categories of foreigners on the basis of reciprocity or otherwise. Section 3A of the Foreigners Act provides for exemption, if so ordered, in the case of citizens of any Commonwealth country or individual foreigner or class of foreigners from the rigours of the Act.

In many respects, aliens are treated at par with local citizens. They are subject to taxes and territorial jurisdiction as the local resident may be. Today no foreigner enjoys ex-territoriality as a Westerner used to enjoy in some of the Afro-Asian countries some time back. Similarly, aliens are entitled to most of the rights which may be available to local citizens. The Indian Constitution guarantees aliens a number of fundamental rights. They are assured of equal protection of laws and equality before the law, protection against unlawful detention and free access to courts. How far are foreigners liable to conscription in police or military service without their consent is a debatable point although practices show that the United States conscripted foreigners residing in the United States under an Act of Congress in 1941. The U.S. Immigration and Nationality Act, 1952 disqualifies any alien from naturalisation if he had sought exemption from military service while he was an alien. The British Government used the aliens in military and allied services with the consent of the related States [7]. Better opinion will, however, be against using aliens in military or allied services without their consent. Such a practice of employing aliens in military assignments is against the customary rule of international law and is a violation of personal sovereignty enjoyed by States over their nationals abroad. The High Court of Australia has held in the case of In Politis versus the Commonwealth [8] that compelling aliens to serve in the Australian armed forces is against international law. India does employ Gorkhas from Nepal in the Indian army but it is with the consent of the personnel as well as the Government of Nepal.

Extent of rights and disabilities of an alien has no uniformity. There are different practices in different countries. In some countries, aliens cannot own land as is provided in the Afghan Constitution of 1931. In England, an alien cannot be issued a pilotage certificate under the Alliens Restriction (Amendment) Act of 1919. Article 19 of the Indian Constitution guarantees right to acquire, hold, and dispose off property to its citizens only. But there is no specific restriction on aliens to acquire property in India although they cannot do it as of right. An alien, therefore, can own property in India. There are many business concerns owned by foreigners in India. Of late, India has launched a liberal investment policy for foreigners. The Uragvayan Constitution of 1934 even permits aliens, who have stayed in the country for more than 15 years, to exercise suffrage.

Expulsion

A State's territorial supremacy implies the right to permit entry of aliens and to expel them also. The power is generally exercised by the Home Ministry in each State. The power, however, is sparingly exercised in compelling circumstances on the basis of adverse reports received from the police. Any arbitrary expulsion is likely to cause straining of relations between the territorial State and the alien's State which may take up the matter if th expulsion is not justified by circumstances and it has involved him in unnecessary loss. This may happen if the alien has been staying in that State for a good period and had started some business. In Beffolo's case [9], it was held by the umpire that although the State had a right to expel an alien, the power should be exercised only in extreme cases with least deprivation to the person and property of the alien. The umpire further held that the expelling State should be able to justify the expulsion order before any arbitrator. Thus, although the right of expulsion by the territorial State cannot be challenged, its arbitrary nature either in the issue of the order or its execution may be challenged whenever the occasion demands. It was on this account that when Uganda's President Amin ordered expulsion of Asians of non-Ugandan nationality, his action could not be challenged although criticised for the arbitrary nature of his order. Eventually, the Governments of Uganda and India agreed on the quantum of compensation to be given for the loss incurred by the Indian nationals in the process.

Section 3(1) of the Foreigners Act, 1946 empowers the Central Government of India to make provisions regulating departure or deportation of aliens from within its territory.

NOTES

1. Henriques, The Law of Aliens (1906); Bonne, A Treatise on the Laws Governing the Exclusion and Expulsion of Aliens in the United States (1912); Foreigners' Act (India) 1946.
2. However, see O'Connel, op. cit. vol. II, p. 753, wherein he says: "there is a widespread consensus of opinion, particularly on the continent, favouring a general duty in international law to receive aliens." This writer regrets to disagree with O'Connel that there is any such duty in international law to admit aliens.
3. Musgrove vs Chun Teeong (1891) A.C. 272; Fong Yue Ting vs United States (1893) 149 U.S. 698.
4. Section 3(1) of Act 31 of 1946.
5. Fraser, Control of Alien in the British Commonwealth of Nations (1940); Wheeler, Everett P., The Relation of the Citizen Domiciled in a Foreign Country to his Home Government, (1909) 3 Proceedings of the A.S.I.L. 869-84.
6. Oppenheim, op. cit., vol. I p. 680; Starke, op. cit., 290,
7. Huprtmann, Pavel, The Allied Powers (war service) Act (1942) 6 Modern Law Review 72.75; Oppenheim, op. cit. vol. 1, 681.

8. 1945 Commonwealth aw Reports 60-1943-5, A.D. Case No. 61.
9. U.N. Reports, vol. X, p. 528. This was a case where Italy had complained against Venezuela for expelling an Italian who had written an article criticising the local administration.

CHAPTER 13

NATIONALISATION OF FOREIGN PROPERTY

The twentieth century has witnessed a swing from private ownership to public ownership of capital goods and means of production. States have embarked upon social welfare activities which require lot of finances. All these finances cannot be had through taxation which may put undue pressure upon its people. In some cases, foreign enterprises have been considered as last vestiges of colonialism. Elsewhere, some foreign enterprises and multinational corporations have been citadels of intrigues and subversion. This has prompted States to nationalise private enterprise wholly or partially [1]. Majority of States have resorted to this practice although in varying degrees [2]. This may involve nationalisation of business which may be owned by its own nationals or by foreigners. Insofar as nationalisation of property of its nationals is concerned, no question of international law would arise, but it may arise when any foreign business is nationalised.

The word 'nationalisation' has been purposely used. Some writers use the word 'expropriation' or even 'confiscation'. Both these words are misnomers because the normal purport of takingover property is not to deprive the owner of the same but to utilise it for the good of the country. The word 'nationalisation' is therefore, more appropriate. The other two words smell of stigma on the nationalising State which many a time may not be warranted by law or facts.

Undoubtedly, a sovereign State has an inherent right to deal with property or business situated within its territory subject to its laws on the point [3]. This equally applies to properties owned by its nationals or foreigners. However, if the local government has entered into any agreement with the foreign investor or his government or given any public assurance with regard to foreign investments, its actions may be circumscribed by such agreement or assurance. In its absence, the State has a free hand to nationalise any foreign property.

The pace of nationalisation was started by the Soviet Union in 1918-19 and it was followed by Mexico in 1938-40. Post-World War II period witnessed nationalisation on a mass scale on the European continent. Then came the newly independent States which resorted to nationalisation of foreign business mainly on three grounds: firstly, because they are suspicious of the activities of the foreign business through which the colonial powers got their foothold in their erstwhile colonies; secondly, it is a drain on the foreign exchange because of repatriation of profits by the foreign investor to his parent State; thirdly, it may be in the interests of their national economy or declared policy of the State to do so. In some cases, it may be to remove the last vestiges of colonial rule. Whatever the motivation [4] nationalisation is an attribute of territorial sovereignty and, therefore, quite legal in the realm of international law [5]. But there must be some compensation for acquisition of foreign property [6].

The question, however, hinges on the quantum of compensation which may be awarded for nationalising foreign property [7]. Practices vary with regard to fixing of compensation for acquired property. Some States give the market price of the nationalised enterprise. Others give nominal compensation. Sometimes, there is sham compensation amounting to confiscation. At other times, there is a worked out compensation depending upon the capital invested, profits earned since the establishment of the business and book value of the business according to income tax returns after giving due allowance for depreciation [8]. The state of economy of the territorial government also determines the quantum of compensation. In normal circumstances, there is negotiated takeover of foreign business as in the case of Burmah Shell and Caltex in India.

Of course, compensation on the basis of market value of the business would be ideal [9] but no hard and fast rule can be fixed to determine quantum of compensation because in the ultimate analysis it depends upon the condition of economy of the State concerned. There is no rule of customary international law which may have fixed the procedure for determining compensation. Nor is there any decision of an international tribunal which may have fixed rules regulating compensation. Municipal courts of some capital exporting countries and *ad hoc* international tribunals may have fixed some rules but such rules cannot give any guidelines because they may have national or developed nations bias. In other cases, words used are so vague that no fixed rules can emanate therefrom. For example, in the Anglo-Iranian Oil Company case, the Supreme Court of Aden Protectorate said that the Iranian legislation of 1951 purporting to nationalise the Anglo-Iranian Oil Company was illegal because it did not provide for just, adequate and effective compensation [10]. Incidentally, the court had a British bias. The real position, as representing the conflicting views, was well summed up by the U.S. Supreme Court 1964 in the Sabbatino case when it said:

> "There are few if any issue in international law today on which opinion seems to be so divided as the limitations on a State's power to expropriate the property of aliens. There is, of course, authority in international judicial and arbitral decisions, in the expression of national governments and among commentators for the view that taking is improper under international law if it is not for a public purpose, is discriminatory, or is without provision for prompt, adequate and effective compensation. However, Communist countries, although they have in fact provided a degree of compensation after diplomatic efforts, commonly recognise no obligation on the part of the taking country. Certain representatives of the newly independent and undeveloped countries have questioned whether the rules of State responsibility towards aliens can bind nations that have not consented to them and it is argued that the traditionally articulated standards governing expropriation of property reflect 'imperialist' interests and are inappropriate to the circumstances of emergent States." [11]

So far as India is concerned, takingover of property is governed by Article 31 of the Indian Constitution which runs as follows:

> "(1) No person shall be deprived of his property save by authority of law.
>
> (2) No property shall be compulsorily acquired or requisitioned save for public purpose and save by authority of a law which provides for acquisition requisitioning of the property for an amount which may be fixed by such law of which may be determined in accordance with such principles or given in such a manner as may be specified in such law; and no such law shall be called in question in any court on the ground that the amount so fixed or determined is not adequate or that the whole or any part of such amount is to be given otherwise than in cash."

Unless the municipal law provides otherwise, foreign property can be acquired lawfully irrespective of the fact whether or not adequate compensation has been given. Where, of course, no adequate compensation has been given, the matter can be negotiated through diplomatic channels between the nationalising State and the State whose national's property has been takenover. This was done in the case of takeover of property of Indian nationals by Uganda. India and Uganda negotiated and Uganda agreed to pay compensation to the Indian Government. Same was repeated by Sri Lanka when it nationalised some British industries [12]. It will not, therefore, be correct to say that nationalisation becomes unlawful because of non-payment of adequate compensation as has been asserted in some quarters [13].

While determining the compensation for the nationalised property, particularly when the nationalisation affects nationals of the State as well as some foreigners, the question may arise whether there can be two standards for determining the quantum of compensation, one for its nationals and the other for foreigners. One view is that the nationalising State does not incur international responsibility if it treats nationals and foreigners at par while fixing compensation. It is said on their behalf that foreigners cannot be treated preferentially. This is a Latin-American practice also [14]. The other view is that whatever compensation may be given to its nationals, the State incurs international responsibility if the compensation awarded to aliens is not adequate, prompt and effective [15]. The argument advanced for the latter view is that it is not the business of international law as to how the State treats its nationals. Therefore, if no compensation or only illusory compensation is given to its own nationals, international law is not concerned. But it is definitely the concern of international law if foreigner's property is taken without providing for payment of adequate compensation.

It does not appeal to reason that foreigners should be treated more liberally then one's own nationals, unless, of course, there is some obligation undertaken by the State in this regard. In some States, like India, any preferential treatment given to foreigners may violate the rule of equality before the law and equal protection of the laws. Article 14 of the Indian Constitution guarantees "equality before the law or the equal protection of the laws within the territory of India." Hence, any difference between the compensation given to its nationals and to a foreigner may land the government in litigation and may further cause heartburn among its nationals. The Government may, therefore, be ill-advised to fix two standards of compensation, one for its nationals and the other for aliens. Compensation should be the same for both. There cannot be two different yardsticks.

Practices reveal that in almost all cases of nationalisation of foreign property, the State whose nationals are affected by such decrees steps in to see that some compensation is paid to its nationals. Here comes the duty, or the right, of the State to protect its nationals abroad. The nationalising State also succumbs to pressures from other States in one way or another. The U.S. Supreme Court has rightly assessed the situation when it said in the Sabbatino case:

> "The newly independent States are in need of continuing foreign investment; the creation of climate unfavourable to such investment by wholesale confiscations may well work to their long-run economic disadvantage. Foreign aid given to many of these countries provides a powerful lever in the hands of the political branches to ensure fair treatment of United States nationals. Ultimately the sanctions of economic embargo and the freezing of assets in this country may be employed." [16]

And we witnessed the suspension of the U.S. aid to Sri Lanka consequent upon the nationalisation of petroleum companies by Sri Lanka in 1963 [17], although it did not dispute Sri Lanka's right to nationalise the same.

In conclusion, it may be said that nationalisation of foreign property by a sovereign State is quite lawful unless it has agreed not to do so for a fixed period of time. Normally a State should negotiate takeover of foreign concerns as India did in the case of Burmah Shell in 1975. Whenever any foreign property is nationalised, some compensation should be paid. Such compensation should be fair, if not adequate, depending upon the total investment, profits earned, book value of the enterprise and condition of economy of the nationalising State. As far as possible, compensation should be given in the currency in which it has invested and unless the condition of the State's economy warrants otherwise, payment should not be too much deferred.

Notes

1. For detailed study of the problem of nationalisation and international law, see W. Friedman, Expropriation in International Law (1953); Isi Foigel, Nationalisation: A study in the Protection of Alien Property in International Law (1957); B.A. Wortley, Expropriation in Public International Law (1951); Gillian White, Nationalisation of Foreign Property (1961); Fauchiri Alexander Expropriation and International Law, (1925) B.Y.I.L. 159-171.
2. Regarding nationalisation practices, see Doman, Post-war Nationalisation of Foreign Property in Europe (1948) 48 C.L.R. 1125 J. Gutteridge, Expropriation and Nationalisation in Hungary, Bulgaria and Romania, (1952) I.C.L.Q 14; Ford, The Anglo-Iranian Oil Dispute of 1951-52 (1954).
3. In a statement by the United States Government regarding Ceylonese (now Sri Lanka) nationalisation of oil companies, it said: "The Government of the United States did not then and does not now contest the right of Ceylon as a sovereign State to nationalise private property." The Times of Ceylon, February, 9, 1963.
4. See however, D.P. O.' Connel, International Law, vol. II, pp. 853-54 wherein he says that bad motive may vitiate the act of nationalisation. In this writer's opinion, this is hardly correct statement of law.
5. Also see Katzarov, Validity of the Act of Nationalisation and International Law (1959) 22 Modern Law Review 639-48 Upper Silesia Case-P.C.I.J. Series A, No. 7. p. 22.
6. Brussels Conference on Russia in 1921 said: "Nationalisation without any compensation or remuoneration of property in which foreigners are interested is totally at variance with practice of civilised states. When such expropriation has taken place, a claim arises for compensation against the Government of the country." Arnold McNair, Opinions, vol. 1 p. 9. It may be submitted here that motivated assertion by so called aggrieved State does not mature into practice.
7. C.C. Hyde, Compensation for Expropriations (1939) 33 A.J.I.L. 108-114; Bin Cheng, The Rationale of Compensation, (1958-59) 44 G.S. 267; Drucken, Alfred, Compensation for Nationalised Property; the British Practice (1955) 49 A J.I.L. 477-486. Regarding International Settlements for nationalisation, see D.P. O.'Connel, op. cit., vol. II 841-42; also see O'Connel, Ibid, 863.
8. Section 47 of the Ceylon (now Sri Lanka) Petroleum Corporation Act of May 29, 1962 fixed the amount of compensation at the rate of purchase price of property and any additions made after making allowance for depreciation and in case of failure to ascertain the price on above basis, the market value of the enterprise at the time of taking over. C. Amarsinghe, Ceylon Oil Expropriation, (1964) 58 A.J.I.L. 445 at p. 447.
9. In Charzov Factory case, the P.C.I.J. held that the value of the undertaking at the time of expropriation plus interest in case of

deferred payment will be treated as an adequate compensation—P.C.I.J. Series A. No. 17 (1928).

10. Anglo-Iranian Oil Co. Ltd. vs Jaffrata (1953) I.W.L.R. 246. Also see U.S. Memorandum to Mexico in 1940 regarding Mexican nationalisation of oil industry when it said that compensation should be adequate, effective and prompt, 1940 D.S.B. p. 381.
11. Banco National De Cuba vs Sabbatino, 376 U.S. 398 as reported in (1964) 58 A.J.I.L. 779 at p. 792.
12. Sri Lanka agreed to pay 5·3 millions to owners of ten coconut and rubber plantations which were nationalised in October, 1975—The Statesman 29 Map, 1976.
13. D.P. O.'Connel, op. cit, Vol. II, p. 861.
14. Ibid, p. 854.
15. See the U.S. Government view on compensation for expropriation in its statement on Ceylonese Nationalisation of Petroleum Companies. It said "when such property belongs to a citizen of a company of a foreign country, the payment of prompt, adequate and effective compensation is required by international law." Times of Ceylon, 9 February, 1963.
16. Banco National De Cuba vs Sabbatino, 376 U.S. 398 as reported in (1964) 56 A.J.I.L. 779 at p. 795.
17. C. Amar Singhe, Supra, (1964) 58 A.J.I.L. 446.

CHAPTER 14

ASYLUM

In the present world torn into conflicting ideologies where the loyalty of person is predetermined by his birth in a particular country, asylum is the only ray of hope for a self-determining person. It is a unique phenomenon of life, and indeed of the world power process, that the majority of the world population is doomed to a particular political philosophy not by their own volition but by virtue of the fact that they happen to be born citizens of a given country. They cannot possibly disown the ideology of their State while living there. Consequently, dissenting citizens have to seek asylum in some other country if they wish to subscribe to the philosophy of their own conviction. Totalitarian tendencies witnessed in a number of countries discourage opposition to the ruling group. This results in the seeking of asylum by dissentors in some other country. Discrimination on grounds of race, religion or linguistic minority may also prompt the aggrieved person to find its new abode somewhere else.

Asylum may be defined as sanctuary granted by one State to the national(s) of another State [1]. Normally, it is granted to the person of foreign origin for his fear of being persecuted in his own State because of his race, religion, political belief or activities. In 1971, ten million people had to seek asylum in India from the erstwhile East Pakistan (now Bangla Desh) because of rule of repression let loose by the Pakistani authorities to suppress secessionist tendencies among the Bengalis. In another case, a person may be seeking asylum for his having committed some political offence for which his custody may have been sought by the parent State. State of asylum, therefore, grants protection to the refugee who has sought asylum in the given State. Once asylum has been given, the refugee cannot be sent back to the persecuting State on the basis of the principle of *non-refoulement* as recognised in the Geneva

Convention of 1951 on refugees. He may be allowed to go to some other State which is willing to admit him to its territory.

The history of asylum is as old as humanity. It was practised in ancient India and Greece as well as during the Roman period. Then sanctuary was sought in temples which were considered as inviolable. The Christian period witnessed the seeking of asylum in churches. Even today, some people seek sanctuary in religious places and the local government exercises self-restraint by not interfering with their asylum. The Mosque of Oman was recognised as a place of refuge for the Grand Mufti of Jerusalem. But the practice of treating religious places as sancturies is dying.

Right of Asylum

There is quite a controversy whether the "right of asylum" is vested in the individual seeking it or in the State which is approached by the individual for granting it. The phrase is so unhappily worded that refugees have a feeling that they have the right to seek and get asylum in the place of their choice. Nothing could be farther from truth than this impression. States have resolutely resisted this impression and have categorically said that it is in exercise of their territorial sovereignty to grant or refuse asylum to any individual. Any other interpretation would abridge the State's right of territorial sovereignty. Therefore, the right of asylum vests in the territorial State. The refugee is only given the right to seek asylum and enjoy the same when it is granted. The refugee has no right to be given asylum by a particular country nor has that State any corresponding duty to grant asylum within its territory without its consent. So the "right of asylum" is that of the State and not that of the individual [2]. This is also borne out by Article 14(1) of the Universal Declaration of Human Rights which says that everyone "has the right to seek and to enjoy in other countries asylum from persecution." This means that the individual may ask for asylum but the State which has been so requested may not grant it. Attempts to confer "right of asylum" on an individual was not accepted by the General Assembly in 1948. The individual was only given the right to leave any country, including his own and seek asylum, elsewhere.

The misconception regarding right of asylum as being vested in the individual arises from the fact that it is considered as a supreme humanitarian duty to see that an individual who is likely to be persecuted in his home State in case of his return to that country is granted asylum somewhere. But this does not impose any specific obligation upon a particular State to grant asylum to the individual against its wishes. States have, however, risen to the occasion by granting asylum wherever it is absolutely necessary. This position was made clear by the Under Secretary of State for Home Affairs in the British Parliament in 1958 when he said:

> "Applications for political asylum are dealt with on their merits in the light of the facts of the particular case. If it is reasonable to suppose the result of refusing admission to a foreigner would be his return to a country in which, on grounds of political opinion, race, or religion, he would face danger to life or liberty, or persecution of such a kind and extent as to render life insupportable, he would normally be admitted unless there were positive grounds for considering him undesirable [3].

This position represents the State practices. In 1971, India had to give refuge to ten million Bengalis from the East Pakistan on grounds of humanity at the risk of being misunderstood by the Pakistani authorities and in spite of the fact that it caused a great economic strain on her.

Grant of asylum is motivated by a number of considerations, political as well as humanitarian. In the case of a request for asylum, the State has to consider the implications arising out of the grant of asylum. It is possible that the grant of asylum may strain otherwise cordial relations, which were subsisting before, between the granting State and the State to which the asylee belonged. For example, relations between Nepal and India became slightly strained when India granted asylum to a number of Congress leaders from Nepal consequent upon the dismissal of the Koirala Government by the King of Nepal. Similarly, India's relations with China became more strained when India granted asylum to the Dalai Lama and other Tibetans. It also took the displeasure of Pakistan when it admitted millions of refugees from erstwhile East Pakistan in 1971. This was labelled as intervention by Pakistan despite the mandate by the U.N. Declaration on Territorial Asylum that grant of asylum shall not be considered as an unfriendly act.

Grant of asylum may be fraught with other problems. If the number of refugees seeking asylum is great, it may create economic and political problems for the granting State. It may affect the national economy of State because most of the refugees may have to be fed by the local State. The State may have to arrange for their employment which may cause bickerings between the local and refugee labour. Idle refugees may create law and order problems because an idle mind is the devil's workshop. A large number of refugees may tilt the balance in favour of one community to the prejudice of another community. In a small State, a large number of refugees may swamp the local population. Asylum should be differentiated from planned immigration through governmental agencies. Some States promote planned immigration to fill vacancies of skilled labour and technical experts. Planned immigration does not create problems which are inherent in the grant of asylum which occurs suddenly and abruptly.

Territorial Asylum

Asylum may be granted by a State either within its territory or in its legations abroad or on men-of-war. Asylum granted within its own territory is known as territorial asylum. It is in exercise of its territorial sovereignty which cannot be questioned unless such a grant is a violation of any treaty obligation. Thus, a State may grant asylum to any foreigner in order to protect him from persecution or even otherwise. But if there is a treaty obligation upon the State to extradite persons of his category, the State surrenders the custody of the person to the requesting State. Of course, political offenders are not extradited today. They are given asylum. Formerely, political offenders were extradited while the custody of criminals was not demanded. The reason was that the political offenders were considered to be the personal enemies of the monarch and monarchs used to oblige each other in their self-interest. With the advent of democracy, the wind has been blowing the other way.

Territorial asylum is the normal and recognised institution. It is an established rule of international law that a State has a sovereign right to give or refuse asylum to any foreigner. The U.N. Declaration on Territorial Asylum 1967 says that asylum granted by a State shall be respected by all other States [4].

Ex-Territorial Asylum

Asylum granted by a State beyond its territory is called ex-territorial. Such asylum may be granted either in Chanceries of a State in foreign countries or on its men-of-war whether they are on high seas or within the territorial waters of any foreign State.

How far such asylum is recognised is yet a moot point insofar as its legality is concerned although such practices are not wanting.

Diplomatic Asylum

States have sometimes granted asylum to refugees within their embassy premises abroad in order to protect them from the local mob or official fury. Such kind of protection is called diplomatic asylum. The embassy premises are deemed to be outside the jurisdiction of the territorial State and, therefore, inviolable. No entry is made in the chancery premises by the local functionaries except when requisitioned by the head of the legation. This concept of ex-territoriality is granted to foreign embassies in order to facilitate their official functioning. But it is sometimes used for granting diplomatic asylum.

In the history of nations, most of the States have resorted to this type of practice at one time or another. In the sixteenth and seventeenth centuries, France was the champion of diplomatic asylum. India is against diplomatic asylum [5] but it did give diplomatic asylum to late King Tribhuvan of Nepal when he sought asylum at the height of the Rana revolt against him. Britain has done the same thing. The Ripperda episode of 1726 is famous inasmuch as the British Embassy in Spain give asylum to the Duke of Ripperda although later on he was forcibly removed from the embassy premises despite British protests and demand for reparation. The United States practices also reveal that asylum has been granted by its diplomatic personnel abroad. Cardinal Mindszenty's sojourn in the U.S. embassy premises in Budapest for a number of years has been perhaps the longest period of stay in the history of diplomatic asylum. The U.S. Embassy in India gave diplomatic asylum to Mr. Zade temporarily after which he was surrendered to the Indian authorities. The surrender was perhaps a gesture towards India, and no less towards the Soviet Union. At the same time, it did give asylum to Svetlana, Stalin's daughter. Diplomatic asylum is more in vogue in the Latin American countries where change of government by revolt or *coup d'etat* is a normal feature. The rulers of today may become refugees and targets of public wrath tomorrow. Consequently, they seek refuge in one of the foreign legations soon after their dethronement. The Latin American countries have taken cognizance of this situation realistically and have concluded a number of conventions on this aspect. The

Havana Convention of 1928 on asylum was the first in the series. The Convention was supposed to bring customary law of diplomatic asylum in Latin America into conventional law. It was a declaratory convention of existing practice. This convention was followed by the Montevideo Convention of 1933 on Political Asylum and it substituted Article 1 of the Havana Convention. Article 3 of the Convention called political asylum as an institution of humanitarian character. There was yet another Montevideo Convention of 1939 on Political Asylum and Refuge, Article 2 of which reiterates the practice of granting asylum in embassies. The last Convention in the series is the Caracas Convention of 1954 on Diplomatic Asylum.

Despite the fact that asylum in legations is sometimes granted, its legality is doubted in the realm of international law. The Vienna Convention of 1961 on Diplomatic Relations does not say anything like the right of a State to grant asylum in its legations abroad. Bland, who has edited Satow's book on Diplomatic Practice, has said "it is now an established doctrine in Europe that no right to give asylum to political refugees in the house of diplomatic agent exists" [6]. The United States does not accept the concept of diplomatic asylum as having the force of law. It considers the practice as motivated by humanitarian consideration. Political considerations cannot be wholly ruled out. Territorial States do not interfere with these practices in most of the cases because they do not intend to strain relations with the foreign State over the question of custody of an individual. However, in some cases, States have protested against the practice diplomatically and at other times through the use of force [7].

Even in the Latin American countries where diplomatic asylum is more practised and recognised as a customary rule of international law, the law was upset by the decision of the International Court of Justice in the Asylum case, a dispute between Colombia and Peru over the grant of diplomatic asylum to Victor Paul Haya de la Torre by the Colombian Embassy in Peru. Torre was a leftist leader who was involved in an abortive military revolt on 3rd October, 1948. The revolt having failed, he sought and got asylum in the Colombian embassy in Lima, Peru. The Colombian ambassador informed the Peruvian authorities of having granted asylum to Torre under Article 2(2) of the Havana Convention, 1928. He further asked for safe conduct for him to leave Peru on the basis of his being a political refugee. The Peruvian Government challenged the asylum granted to Torre as well as the unilateral determination of the refugee as political by the Colombian ambassedor. The dispute having been referred to the International Court of Justice, it held that the institution of diplomatic asylum owes its devolopment in Latin America to extra-legal factors. As the Court put it: "considerations of convenience of simple political expediency seem to have led the territorial State to recognise asylum without that decision being dictated by any feeling of legal obligation" [8]. Later on, in the Haya de la Torre case, the same Court held that diplomatic asylum is "a provisional measure for the temporary protection of political refugee" [9]. Therefore, it looks that practice and precept do not tally here. It may, however, be mentioned here that the International Law Association has prepared a Draft Convention on Asylum including Diplomatic Asylum at its 1972 Session in New York.

Asylum in consulates however is discouraged by governments and it does not enjoy that much sanctity as diplomatic asylum. Nevertheless, some people do take asylum in consulates and they are not disturbed because of comity. Sometime back, a Russian Engineer working in India, who was wanted in connection with the murder of his wife, took asylum in the Soviet Consulate in Calcutta [10].

Asylum on Men-of-War

The men-of-war enjoys immunity from local jurisdiction in the same way as legation. It does not, however, mean that the captain of the warship should abuse the privilege by granting asylum on board. Asylum, however, has been sought and given on a warship, although not frequently. In 1849, Lord Palmerston said that while it "would not be right to receive and harbour on board of a British ship-of-war any person fleeing from justice on a criminal charge or who was escaping from the sentence of a court of law, yet it can always give refuge to a person fleeing from persecution on account of their political conduct or opinion" [11].

Asylum on Merchantmen

Merchantmen cannot give asylum to political refugees and even if they give, the political refugees can be withdrawn from the vessel while it is within territorial waters. Eisler was removed from the Polish vessel, Batory, by the British authorities while the ship was in a British port.

Duties of the State of Asylum and Asylees

While the refugee remains within the territory of any State, it is as much the duty of the State of asylum as that of the asylee to see that he does not abuse the hospitality of the territorial State. The refugee should not forget that the State of asylum has already earned the wrath of the refugee's State by granting him asylum. Therefore, he should not do anything which may further aggrevate the bad relations between the two States. He cannot make the territory as a base for his activities which are prejudicial to the interests of the foreign Government. Nor should he do anything against the interests of the local government. This was the reason that the Nepalese government warned the Khampas to surrender their arms and planned to move them from the Tibetan border to the interior of Nepal for resettlement purposes. According to Nepalese sources, the Khampa activities near the Tibetan border were embarassing the Nepalese government because they were carrying on guerilla attacks against the Chinese administration in Tibet. Besides being heavily armed, the Khampas were creating law and order problem for the local administration. Same can be said about the Palestinian refugees stationed in Lebanon who were causing lot of embarassment to the government vis-a-vis its relations with Israel. Lebanon has been subjected to many reprisal attacks by Israel because of the Palestinians using Lebanese territory for launching sabotage and terrorist activities against Israel. It is also the duty of the local State to see that political refugees who have been given protection by it do not abuse the facility by propagating against their parent State which may or may not be on friendly relations with the local State. The Indian Government does not permit the Nepalese refugees to propagate against the King of Nepal. Similarly, India does not permit the Dalai Lama to propagate against the Chinese Government.

NOTES

1. For readings on the Law of Asylum, see R.B. Greenburg, Recent Developments in the Law of Asylum, 41 G.S. 103; Arnold McNair,

Extradition and Exterritorial Asylum (1951) B.Y.I.L. 172; Felice Morgenstern, the Right of Asylum (1949) B.Y.I.L. 327.

2. In Chandler vs United States, the U.S. Circuit Court held that the "right of asylum is that of the State voluntarily to offer asylum, not that of the fugitive to insist upon it." 171 F (2nd.) 921.
3. March 6, 1958, 583 Hansard, written Answer, Col. 153.
4. Article 1 of the U.N. Declaration on Territorial Asylum adopted by the General Assembly vide its Resolution 2312 (XXII) dated December 14, 1967.
5. Government of India issued a circular to chanceries in India on 30th December, 1967 which reads as follows:

No. 6297/JSP/67 30th December, 1967

The Ministry of External Affairs present their compliments to the Foreign and Commonwealth Diplomatic Missions in India and have the honour to state as follows:

The Government of India wish to draw the attention of Foreign and Commonwealth Diplomatic Missions in India to the fact that the Government of India does not recognise the right of such Missions to give asylum to any person or persons within their premises. Immunity from local jurisdiction is granted to Diplomatic Missions and Legations to enable the representatives and members of the Missions concerned to enjoy fully the opportunity to represent the interests of their States and to promote friendly relations between India and their countries. Every Diplomatic Mission is expected to respectfully the exclusive jurisdiction of the Government of India in all matters which do not come within the purposes of the Mission in India. It is well established that the affording of asylum is not within the purposes of Diplomatic Mission. The Government of India expects the Foreign Missions in India to respect this well-established international practice.

It is requested that if such Missions receive any request for asylum, or temporary shelter, or refuge, such request should not be granted and the Chief of Protocol of the Ministry of External Affairs should be immediately informed.

The Ministry avail themselves of this opportunity to renew to the Foreign and Commonwealth Diplomatic Missions the assurances of their highest consideration.

All Foreign and Commonwealth Diplomatic Missions in New Delhi.

6. Satow, Guide to Diplomatic Practice (1957) Edited by Bland p. 219, Moore, Digest of International Law, vol. II, p. 766.
7. International Law Association Report of Committee on Legal Aspects of the Problem of Asylum (1964) pp. 15-16.
8. (1950) I.C.J. Reports as reported by L.C. Green op. cit., p. 325.
9. (1951) International Court of Justice Reports, p. 71 and reported by L.C. Green, ibid p. 328.
10. One Vlacinier Koutcha, Engineer working in Bokaro Steel Plant was wanted by police in connection with murder of his wife. He took

asylum in the Soviet Consulate General in Calcutta.—The Times of India, June 27, 1974.

11. Moore, op. cit., 849, Regarding practices of granting asylum on men-of-war, see pp. 849-55.

CHAPTER 15

EXTRADITION

In the fast-shrinking world of today, where interdependence of States is but natural and very essential, problems of extraditions are bound to increase. Air traffic has made the flight of a criminal easier than before, and if law has to take its course and pursue the fleeing offender, extradition proceedings are a necessary instrument to secure the return of the fugitive at the altar of law. In recent times, we secured the custody of Sucha Singh, Dr. Teja and the Narang brothers through the process of extradition. No one should be given any impression that he can treat the arms of law with contempt. Any laxity in the extradition efforts would only whet the offender's appetite to commit crime with impunity by fleeing to a foreign territory where he cannot be touched except by the instrumentality of extradition.

Extradition may be defined as surrender of an accused or convict by the territorial State, where the above person is found, to the requesting State where he is alleged to have either committed the crime or has been convicted of the same [1]. Although, the word 'extradition' has received universal recognition by now, its use has been relatively recent. It was first used in a French Decree in 1791 and later again by France in a treaty in 1828 after which the word has been uniformly used [2].

Extradition is practised among nations mainly due to two reasons. Firstly, to warm the criminals that they cannot escape from the clutches of law by fleeing to a foreign territory. The Congress of Comparative Law held at the Hague in 1932 said that the States should treat extradition as an obligation "resulting from the international solidarity in the fight against crime". Earlier, Lord Russell had aptly said that:

> "the law of extradition is...founded upon the broad principle that it is in the interest of civilized communities that crimes... should not go unpunished, and it is part of the comity of nations that one State should afford to another every assistance towards bringing persons guilty of such crimes to justice." [3]

Therefore, extradition works as a deterrent. Secondly, it is in the interest of the territorial State to get rid of the criminal who has taken refuge within its territory. The prospect of reciprocity is yet another motivation [4]. Maintenance of cordial relations, as part of its foreign policy, is a contributory factor which assists in the surrender of the fugitive.

Grotius was of the opinion that it is duty of State to extradite fugitive criminal [5]. Vattel was another international lawyer who considered it as the duty of a State to surrender fugitive criminals [6]. However, it has never been recognised that States are under any duty to surrender criminals. There is no general obligation under international law to extradite fugitives except under treaty [7]. Instead, in some States, no extradition is permitted in the absence of an extradition treaty [8]. Even in cases, where fugitives are extradited without treaty obligation, it is more out of international polity than due to any international duty. In fact, extradition is an exercise of sovereignty on the part of a territorial State and any supposed duty of extradition would be negation of such sovereignty.

Law of extradition is a dual law. It is ostensibly a municipal law; yet it is part of international law inasmuch as it governs relations between two sovereign nations over the question whether or not a given person should be handed over by one sovereign nation to another sovereign nation. Extradition, or not, is determined by national courts or decision-makers but on the basis of international commitments as well as the rules of international law on the subject which have been incorporated in, or recognised by, municipal law.

Realising the necessity of extradition as part of international cooperation, a number of attempts have been made regionally as well as otherwise to conclude a multilateral convention which would regulate extradition requests among nations. The treaty of Amiens in 1802 was the first successful attempt at multipartite convention on extradition [9]. The American continent has witnessed a number of conferences to conclude a regional convention governing extradition among the Latin American States. The Second Pan-American Conference of 1902 produced a treaty of extradition signed by twelve States but the same was not ratified. In December 1933, the Seventh Pan-American Conference concluded an Extradition Convention which was ratified by a number of States, including the United States of America [10]. Earlier, the League Codification Committee had doubted the feasibility of a general convention on extradition [11]. In 1935, the Harvard Law School brought out a draft convention on the subject after a good deal of research but it has not been made use of despite general feelings about its utility [12]. In 1960, the Asio-African Legal Consultative Body prepared a draft convention on extradition at its Colombo session. In September 1965, the Commonwealth Conference of Law Ministers and Chief Justices expressed the desire of having a Commonwealth code of extradition [13]. In March, 1966, the Commonwealth Law Ministers reached an accord in London for speedy extradition of fugitives between the Commonwealth countries [14].

Nations, however, have not waited for the multilateral convention on extradition. In its absence, they have resorted to bilateral arrangements by which they agree to surrender fugitive criminals to each other under certain conditions. France has greatly helped in the development of bilateral treaties on extradition. Practices reveal that it had entered into treaty as early as in 1371 with Savoy and later with Austria and Spain in 1612. By 1868, France had extradition treaties with 53 States.

Bilateral treaties on international level are supplemented by national laws at municipal level. Belgium, which may be considered as the pioneer in extradition law, was the first country to bring out a national legislation on the subject in 1833. These national laws purport to implement the obligations undertaken by the nation under extradition treaties. Besides, they prescribe the procedure to be followed in case of any request for surrender of a fugitive.

India had its first Extradition Act in 1903 which worked as a supplement to the British Extradition Act of 1870, as modified from time to time, and the Fugitive Offenders Act, 1881. The recent Extradition Act of 1962 is the result of the advent of independence on the Indian sub-continent.

Extradition treaties between nations, draft conventions and national laws and practices have revealed that some customary rules of international law, discussed below, have developed in the process.

Doctrine of Double Criminality

By this doctrine, the offence attributed to the fugitive must be indictable within the State of asylum as well as within the requesting State's territory. In its absence, no extradition can take place. It is but natural that it will offend the conscience of the territorial State if it were to extradite the man whom its law does not consider as a criminal. And of course, the demanding State would not demand the custody of a person if he were not accused of any act or omission which is not a crime within its territory.

States, therefore, prepare a list of extraditable offences as part of their extradition law. The United Kingdom is one of such countries. The list of extraditable crimes in the United Kingdom is given in the Extradition Act of 1870 as amended from time to time in 1870, 1906 and 1932. All British extradition treaties must conform with this list. The Indian Extradition Act of 1962 has evolved a double procedure regarding extraditable crimes. With regard to non-treaty and Commonwealth countries, the list of extraditable offences is given in the Second Schedule attached to the Act. However, so far as treaty States are concerned, the list is compiled by treaty. The Indian practice is an improvement on the English practice inasmuch as the treaty list has nothing to do with the list given in the Second Schedule, while in England, the treaty list is restricted by the list given in the Acts.

There is, of course, scope for improvement even in the Indian Act which has followed the practice of denominating crimes. It would perhaps be better to resort to the "test of sentence" by which States may undertake to surrender a fugitive who is accused of having committed a crime which carries sentence of one year or more. The British Fugitive Offenders Act of 1881 has adopted this rule [15]; so also the French Extradition Act of 1927 [16]. The Harvard Draft on Extradition has preferred this rule [17]. More recently, a Draft Convention as prepared by the Council of Europe in 1954]18] and a similar document prepared in 1960 by the Asio-African Legal Consultative [19] Committee have adopted this formula. The Irish Extradition Act of 1965 has also preferred this system [19A].

This new formula would be more appropriate in view of the fact that sooner or later the State will have either a general convention on extradition or there will be increase in bilateral treaties with the proliferation of States, advent of jet travel and consequent easy flight of the fugitive. There is also a demand for an ever-in creasing list of extraditable offences which cannot otherwise be done except through a fresh treaty and this is not an easy task. The number of independent States has also increased and it is possible that many States may have different and confusing names for the same crime. The controversy which the international lawyers witnessed over the Insull [20] and Eisler [21] cases could have been avoided if the "sentence" formula had guided the requests for extradition.

Extradition of Political Offenders

It may be of interest to note that there has been a swing from extradition of political offenders to their non-extradition [22]. Gone are those days when monarchs preferred to extradite political offenders because it suited their convenience and selfish interest. Paradoxically enough, in those days, the extradition of ordinary criminals was not much pressed for and they were not extradited. Instead, there was a clamour for the surrender of political offenders who were considered as the monarch's personal enemies and, therefore, the territorial monarch extradited such offenders in the interest of mutuality [23]. With the diminishing of monarchies and the development of democracies, the rules as to extradition of political offenders has been reversed since the nineteenth century. Presently, while the ordinary criminals are extradited the political offenders are not extradited.

Reasons for non-extradition of political offenders are manifold. Firstly, rebels of today may be the rulers of tomorrow; secondly, there is fear on the part of the territorial State that if it were to extradite these offenders, they may not get a fair trial at the hands of their adversaries. It is also an attempt at avoiding interference in the foreign State's affairs [24]. Besides, political offenders are not dangerous and undesirable elements as may be the case with regard to ordinary offenders. The constitutions of France and Italy and the Basic Law of the Federal Republic of Germany guarantee right of asylum to political fugitives.

Prohibition on surrender of political offenders has sometimes resulted in the abuse of the same. The first attempt at checking such abuse was the introduction of *attentat* clause by Belgium in 1856 in its national extradition law. This clause permits the extradition of a political offender if he is charged with the murder of the Head of the foreign government or any of his family members. This Belgian action was the outcome of an attempt in 1854 on the part of Celestin Jacquin who tried to blow off the railway track between Lille and Calais with the intention to murder Emperor Napoleon III who was to pass that way.

Some European States have followed the Belgian practice by incorporating the *attentat* clause in their national legislations but the same has not been generally accepted as a customary rule of international law. The reason for the failure of this clause is probably due to the fact that in the present context of different forms of governments operating in the world, the Head of the State may just be titular not enjoying much power and importance. For instance, the Queen of England or the President of India may not be as powerful as the Prime Minister. It will, therefore, be indeed ridiculous that while the murderer of the Head of the State may be extradited under the *attentat* clause, the murderer of Prime Minister cannot be extradited under the clause. Perhaps, the clause was meaningful during the monarchical era only.

There was an attempt on the part of Russia to convene a conference of powers in Brussels in 1881, following the murder of Alexander II in that year. It purported to exclude murder or attempt to murder from the ambit of political offence. The conference, however, never took place.

In 1934, King Alexander of Yugoslavia was murdered in France. This prompted France to propose at the League of Nations to bring out a Convention for Prevention and Punishment of Acts of Political Terrorism. The Convention was concluded in Geneva on November 16, 1937 and signed by 23 States, including India. The Convention purported to treat acts of political terrorism as ordinary crimes, perpetrators of which would not benefit by the rule of non-extradition of political offenders. By another Convention signed on the same day in Geneva by 10 States, including India, the parties agreed to the establishment of the International Criminal Court which would try such persons who were not extradited or tried by the territorial State [25]. The Conventions, however, never came into force and the law remains as it was before. Perhaps, any enthusiasm for cooling down the rule of non-extradition of political offenders has subsided in view of the growth of authoritarian regimes in a number of countries where there is no other media for expressing dissatisfaction with the regime except through acts of terrorism.

Although, political offence is not generally an extraditable offence [26], it has defied all attempts at its definition [27]. Publicists, judges and national decision-makers have failed to define it. Some say that political motive is important; others consider political purpose as more important. Some stress upon both, motive as well as purpose. Yet others consider crimes against the State as political, i.e. treason, sabotage, espionage and subversion [28]. Nevertheless, some offences may be obviously political and, therefore, non-extraditable. The difficulty arises only with respect to such crimes which are ostensibly common crimes but have political undertones. Such offences are called relative political crimes or *delits complexes* [29]. Controversy hangs around them.

Number of courts from different parts of the world have dwelt upon such cases. In the famous English case, Ex-parte Castioni [30], the accused had taken part in a revolutionary movement in the Canton of Ticino and incidentally shot a member of the Government. His extradition was refused on the ground that it was a political offence. The court defined the political offence as:

> "It must at least be shown that the act is done in furtherance of, done with the intention of assistance as a sort of overt act, in course of acting in a political matter, a political rising or dispute between two parties in the State as to which is to have the Government in its hands." [31].

In another case, however, the same court permitted the extradition of a French anarchist who was charged with causing two explosions in Paris one of which resulted in the death of two individuals. The Court held:

> "In order to constitute an offence of political character, there must be two or more parties in the State each acting to impose the Government of their choice on the other... if the offence is committed by one side or the other in pursuance of that object it is a political offence, otherwise not." [32]

In the same year, the Federal Court of the United States held that in order "to bring an offence within the meaning of the words of 'political character' it must be incidental to, and form part of political disturbance." [33]

The Swiss Extradition Law of 22nd January 1892 provides that:

> "Extradition is not granted for political offences. It is granted, however, even when the guilty person alleges political motive or end, if the act for which it has been requested constitutes primarily a common offence. The Federal Tribunal decides liberally in each particular instance upon the character of infraction according to the facts of the case". [34]

In re Kavic, Bjelanovic and Arsenijevic, the Swiss Federal Court refused extradition of the accused charged with exercising constraint on the crew of aircraft. The Court held that the offences "were means to effectuate their escape abroad and coincided completely with that escape." The court further held that in countries where "political opposition is suppressed and a fight for power is, if not impossible from the start, at least practically without any chance of success," the only alternative for the dissidents is to escape abroad [35].

The Chilean Supreme Court has defined the political offence in following words:

> "Generally accepted principles are in agreement that a political offence is that which is directed against political organization of the State or against the civil rights of its citizens and that the legally protected rights which the offence damages is the constitutional normality of the country affected. Also included in the concept are acts which have as their end the alteration of established political or social order in the State." [36].

The Indian courts have not so far defined the scope of political offence despite the fact that they did have some opportunity to define the same in the cases of Babu Ram Saxena [37] and G.C. Menon [38]. These cases were disposed off on other grounds.

It is, therefore, difficult to determine as to what would be the scope of relative political offence. In many a case, the accused just raises the plea of political offence on the slightest pretext in order to invite the sympathy of the territorial government and its people and thus escape from the arms of the law. Nor can a single definition hold good for all situations. Judge Cassels has, therefore, rightly said that the political offence "must always be considered according to the circumstances existing at the time when they have to be considered" [39]. Perhaps, this was the echo of what Moore had said earlier in his book on extradition [40].

Despite these handicaps and knowing fully well the limitations, one may humbly venture to give the scope of political offence as under.

Whenever an offence is committed, it may be considered as a political offence if it were to be in the series of attempts to overthrow or influence the government. Similarly, any common crime may be considered as political if it was done as a means of expression of disappointment or dissatifaction with the policy or policies of the government [41]. It may also include terrorist activities in watertight countries where freedom of expression is frozen and open opposition not tolerated.

The scope of political offence may be utilised as a guideline and should not be considered as exhaustive. It is just exploratory. Predominance of political motive may make the common crime as a political one although there may have been personal motivation of vengeance also during the course of the commission of the crime. Again, while the main participant may be guilty of common crime, the abetter may still be a political offender inasmuch as the latter may have hired the former to execute his political plans.

Whether Extradition Demand Has Ulterior Motive

Sometimes, the requesting State, fearing that the fugitive may not be extradited for political offences, seeks surrender of the fugitive on charge of some common crime. The fugitive, however, raises the plea that the surrender has been demanded for an ulterior motive. If it is so, the territorial government does not surrender the fugitive. Article 31 of the Indian Act provides a safeguard against such veiled requests. Section 31(a) provides that the fugitive shall not be surrendered:

> "If he proves to the satisfaction of the magistrate or court before whom he may be produced...that the requisition or warrant for his surrender has, in fact, been made with a view to try or punish him for an offence of political character."

In C.G. Menon's case, the Menons had contended that their surrender was demanded by the Singapore Government for ulterior political reasons [42]. In Tarasov's case, which came on the heels of the Indian Act, the accused alleged that the charge of theft was fabricated against him in order to secure his custody and then punish him for refusing to return to his home country which was an offence of political character.

Despite general recognition in international law that extradition would be refused if the same is demanded for an ulterior purpose, it is very difficult to prove the ulterior purpose of the requesting State. This will amount to attributing malafide to the requesting State and any such determination is likely to strain relations betwern the otherwise friendly States. A fugitive's claim alone will be too subjective unless there is corroboration of his claim. This was exactly said by the inquiring magistrate in Tarasov's case when he held:

> "The statement of the fugitive alone cannot amount to evidence and it cannot be taken as proved that he is actually required for the offence of political character." [43]

However, much will depend upon the circumstantial evidence in the case. If it goes to raise a doubt in the mind of the magistrate that it is very likely that the fugitive may be required for an offence of political character and the present charge is only a cover, then the fugitive may be given the benefit of the doubt and released. However, it should better be left to the executive wing of the Government to determine an ulterior motive of a request.

Rule of Specialty

It is a universally recognised rule of international law that a fugitive whose extradition has been obtained in connection with some given crime cannot later on be tried for any other offence, committed before his extradition, unless he is given opportunity to return to the extraditing State [44]. This is a safeguard against fraudulent extradition and is an extension of the above rule that no person should be extradited on the pretext of one crime while the ulterior motive was either to try or/and punish him for an offence of political character or some other non-extraditable crime.

Section 3(c) of the Indian Act provides for the rule of specialty inasmuch as the extradition will be refused:

> "Unless provision is made by the law of the foreign State or Commonwealth counrty or in the extradition treaty with the foreign State or extradition arrangement with the Commonwealth country, that the fugitive criminal shall not, until he has been restored or has had an opportunity to return to India, be detained or tried in the State or country for any offence

> committed prior to his surrender or return, other than the extradition offence proved by the facts on which his surrender or return is based."

The Section purports to make it obligatory that the inhibition of trial, for an offence other than for which he has been extradited, should either be incorporated in a treaty or arrangement with the foreign government or Commonwealth country respectively or the same should find place in the national legislation of a foreign State if the extradition is sought in the absence of any treaty relations with India. It may be of interest here to mention that Section 21 of the Indian Act bars the Indian Government from violating the rule of specialty with respect to fugitive criminals extradited to India. It was on this account that Sucha Singh's extradition from Nepal was sought on two charges.

Rule of specialty was invoked in Tarasov's case. The magistrate had asked the representative of the Soviet Embassy to produce a Soviet legislation in order to comply with Section 31(c). As the magistrate put it:

> "the court has to be satisfied that the extradition treaty or according to the provisions of the law of the foreign State, the requirements of Section 31(c) are in existence. It has been brought on record that no extradition treaty exists between the Soviet Government and the Central Government of India, and therefore, it was decided that the laws of the Soviet Union be produced to meet the requirements of Section 31(c) of the Indian Extradition Act" [45].

The magistrate's order was upheld by the Punjab High Court when its Chief Justice held:

> "Quite evidently, in the absence of treaty between India and country concerned, containing such provisions, it is absolutely necessary before the requisition may be granted and the alleged criminal surrendered that there should be provisions in the laws of the foreign country concerned which have the effect of making it irresponsible to obtain his surrender for the purpose of dealing with him for other offences which he may be alleged to have committed." [46]

While the reasoning and conclusions of the magistrate and the learned Chief Justice are sound, it is felt that in some genuine cases, extradition may be withheld on account of the rule of specialty even though there may be *prima facie* evidence against the fugitive criminal. Resultantly, the fugitive may escape from the clutches of law because there is no provision as to the rule of specialty in the treaty or in the demanding state's national law.

It is conceded here that the fugitive should not be extradited fraudulently on the pretext of one crime and later on tried and punished for another crime which may sometimes turn out to be of political character. However, this does not always happen. The fugitive may at most times be required for that crime only. In such a case, the technicality of this rule may come in the way of extradition of the fugitive.

Therefore, it is desirable that when any *prima facie* case is made out against the fugitive criminal with regard to some extraditable offence some via media may be evolved so that the fugitive does not profit by technicalities and at the same time the rule of specialty is also not violated.

This can be achieved by passing conditional order of surrender in which case the demanding State may have to give an undertaking in writing to the effect that the rule of specialty will not be violated and the fugitive will not be tried and punished for any offence for which he has not been extradited. This may be considered as an *ad hoc* observance of the rule of specialty.

The question may arise whether an accused can raise the plea of specialty. Higgins is of the view that he can [47]. However, a better position would be that the accused may raise the plea of specialty if it is part of a treaty or national legislation where the accused is being tried after extradition. But if there is no such provision in the treaty or national legislation, the plea cannot be entertained.

Other Offence

Rule of specialty bars trial of the fugitive for any offence for which he has not been extradited. This would mean that he can be tried for only such offence(s) for which he has been extradited and for no other offence. The difficulty arises as to the scope of "other offence".

Common experience has shown that it is very likely that the person may be accused of one offence but eventually convicted of another offence. For example, a person may be accused of murder but he may later on be punished for culpable homicide not amounting to murder, grevious hurt or such other allied crime. Would the rule of specialty permit the trial and punishment of the fugitive for grevious hurt although he may have been extradited for an offence of murder?

There are two views on this point. One is the strict interpretation of the rule of specialty, thus barring trial of the fugitive for any offence other than the one for which he has been extradited. The United States of America is of this view [48]. This was held in the case of United States versus Rauscher [49]. In this case, the accused was extradited on a charge of murder but was convicted for causing cruel and unusual punishment on member of crew. The conviction was quashed by majority on the basis that this was not the offence for which he was extradited.

The other view is represented by the British courts [50]. King versus Corrigan [51] is an example of this viewpoint. In this case, Corrigan had obtained money from various persons on the understanding that he would purchase oil shares on their behalf. He, however, misappropriated the amounts for which he could be charged with two offences in England—fraudulant conversion of money entrusted to him under Section 20 of the Larceny Act of 1916 or obtaining money entrusted to him under Section 37 of the same Act. He was, however, convicted under the charge of fraudulant conversion. This was challenged by the accused on the ground that he was extradited by France to England on the charge of false pretences. His plea was rejected by the court which held that what was required was not the specific charge but the substance of matter which would mean the facts on the basis of which his extradition was requested and granted. This is also consonant with Section 19 of the British Extradition Act of 1870 which provides that the extradited person may not be tried for any offence other than the one which may be proved by the facts on which surrender was granted.

As between the two opposite views, the British viewpoint appears to be more amenable to reason. Section 31(c) of the Indian Act accepts the British viewpoint when it says that the fugitive shall not be tried or detained for any offence "other than the extradition offence proved by the facts on which his surrender or return is based." Therefore, hopefully, there should be no controversy as to the scope of 'other offence'. Trial and conviction will be unassailable if on the basis of the same facts as given in the requisition for surrender, the fugitive is convicted for some other crime and not necessarily for the crime for which he was extradited, provided, of course, the offence for which he has been convicted is also an extraditable offence.

Prima facie case

No fugitive is extradited without proof of *prime facie* evidence against him with regard to extraditable crime which he is alleged to have committed. Bilateral treaties often contain a clause to that effect [52]. This is supplemented by national legislations. Section 7(4) of the Indian Extradition Act provides that the magistrate may commit the fugitive to prison if "*prima facie* case is made out in support of the requisition...." Earlier, Justice Rajagopalan of the Madras High Court had held:

> "The need for offering evidence to show that *prima facie* the offender is guilty of the crime with which he has been charged by the country asking for his extradition has been wellrecognized. Though it may not be an integral part of the law of extradition of every State in relation to every other State, it is certainly a normal feature, and we can say, almost a universal feature of extradition law." [53]

The reason for requirement of *prima facie* case against the fugitive is obvious. He is not an offender in the State of asylum. Another State demands his custody by attributing commission of some crime to him. If he is to be arrested and extradited to that State, there must be some basis for his surrender. The State of asylam is to ensure that the demand is not frivolous or for any political reasons. This works as a check against abuse of the extradition facilities.

While there is almost unanimity [54] that a *prima facie* case must be established against the fugitive before the order for his surrender is passed, the quantum of evidence required for the purpose and the extent of powers of the inquiring magistrate are often the subject-matter of controversy. Two schools of thought operate in this area.

One school expects that the magistrate has to be satisfied that *prima facie* evidence exists against the accused and the evidence laid before him is enough to cause conviction of the fugitive. In the absence of such evidence, the magistrate must discharge the fugitive [55].

Another school claims that extradition proceedings are not criminal proceedings; nor is the magistrate an adjudicator. Magisterial inquiry is just a hearing "to determine whether adequate grounds exist to warrant returning the fugitive to the custody of the requesting State." [56]

Actually, there is a hairline difference between the two schools as it is only a question of degree as to how much evidence would be considered adequate to support extradition. There is no denial of the fact that evidence must be weighed to ascertain whether there are fair chances of the fugitive being convicted by the trying magistrate. The inquiring magistrate cannot function as a trying magistrate. His functions are similar to those of a committing magistrate under Section 209 and 210 of the Criminal Procedure Code. Section 7(1) of the Indian Extradition Act clearly provides that the nominated magistrate "shall have the same jurisdiction and powers, as nearly as may be, as if the case were one triable by a Court of Sessions or High Court." Section 209 of the Criminal Procedure Code empowers the magistrate to discharge the accused if "there are not sufficient grounds for committing the accused person for trial...." Section 210 permits the framing of charge if "the magistrate is satisfied that there are sufficient grounds for committing the accused for trial."

The Supreme Court of India was seized of the matter in connection with the powers of the committing magistrate under Sections 209 and 210. It aptly said:

> "An examination of the large number of rulings cited before us...shows that though it is not easy to say that a magistrate should commit the accused for trial if he is satisfied that sufficient grounds for doing so have been made out, it is difficult to apply those crucial words "sufficient ground" to individual cases. Apparently, conflicting observations about the powers of a committing magistrate have been made in reported cases, but these observations have to be read in the light of the facts and circumstances disclosed in the case then before the court." [57]

Thus, while no hard and fast rule can be formulated so as to work as a guide in future cases, it is necessary to understand the purpose of magisterial inquiry in extradition cases.

Admittedly the purpose of such inquiry is to ascertain whether the fugitive is really involved in the offence which is attributed to him. If he is, he should be extradited. If he is not, he should not be extradited. The magistrate can reach one of these conclusions only when he can weigh the evidence of the prosecution as well as that of the accused and ascertain whether he is likely to be convicted on the basis of evidence laid before him. Any other conclusion would make a sham of a magisterial inquiry [58]

Non bis in idem

It is a general principle recognised by all members of the international community that a person should not be subjected to repeated trials for the same act. This is commonly known as a rule against double jeopardy. It may as well be called as a rule of natural justice. States normally refuse to extradite the fugitive if he has been once tried or is undergoing trial in the territory of the requested State for the same act for which his surrender has been demanded [59].

There is no such specific provision in the Indian Extradition Act. But a rule against double jeopardy is incorporated in Section 403 of the Criminal Procedure Code. Besides Article 20(2) of the Constitution guarantees that "No person shall be prosecuted and punished for the same offence more than once." The word 'person' signifies that this fundamental right is not confined to Indian citizens alone. It applies to all persons in India, irrespective of the fact whether they are citizens of India or otherwise.

This kind of protection by national legislation is in many cases supplemented by bilateral treaties. For example. Article 6 of the Indo-Nepalese Treaty of 1953 provides that "Extradition shall not take place if the person whose extradition is claimed by one of the Governments has already been tried and discharged or punished or is still under trial in the territory of the other Government for the crime for which extradition is demanded." Similar provision is found in Article 4 of the Anglo-German Treaty which is also binding on India under Section 2(J) of the Indian Act.

In view of the recognition of protection against double jeopardy, national courts will be entitled to go into the question whether the fugitive has already been tried or is undergoing trial for the same offence, irrespective of the place of such trial. However, the rule against double jeopardy is confined to the trial or punishment of the fugitive for the crime attributed to him. It does not apply to extradition proceedings which do not amount to a trial. Consequently, rejection of request for extradition does not prevent the requesting Government from making another request for the surrender of the same fugitive for the same offence for which the request was turned down earlier [60]. This happened in the case of Stallman who was discharged in extradition proceedings in India [61] but was extradited by a British Court to Germany [62].

Time-Barred Crimes

It has been noticed that nations are presently withholding extradition of such fugitives who have obtained immnuity from prosecution for the crime(s) they have committed. This has been the result of some national legislations which give immunity to fugitives from being prosecuted after a lapse of some time. Article 4 of the Harvard Research Draft on Extradition had recommended that a fugitive may not be extradited if he has obtained immunity from prosecution under the law of the requesting State or that of the territorial State where the fugitive has taken refuge [63]. Section 31(b) of the Indian Act, however, provides that extradition may be refused if prosecution is barred by a lapse of time under the law of the requesting State. On its own part, India does not recognise immunity from prosecution through lapse of time.

While there can be no controversy over the non-extradition of fugitives who cannot be tried due to a lapse of time, controversy may, however, arise with respect to effective date which may determine whether or not the prosecution is time barred. There may be a number of dates which may be relevant for determining this question, e.g.

(1) the date of request for extradition;

(2) the date of receipt of such request by the territorial Government;

(3) the date on which the magistrate decides on the preliminary issue;

(4) when the magistrate submits his report to the Government recommending the fugitive's extradition;

(5) 15 days from the date of submission of magistrate's report which is the normal period before which the fugitive cannot be extradited in a number of countries [64]; or

(6) when the Government orders extradition

However, the date on which the Government passes the order of surrendering the fugitive is the crucial date. If the fugitive can be prosecuted on this date, he may be extradited. But if he has acquired exemption from prosecution by this time, he may be discharged.

An interesting case arose in England on this point. A fugitive who had been convicted in Belgium managed to flee to England. Belgium asked for his extradition. However, his extradition was delayed because he was to undergo sentence for the crime he had committed in England. When he completed his term of imprisonment, he challenged his extradition on the plea that the Anglo-Belgian Treaty provided limitation on surrender if the fugitive had acquired exemption under the English Law [65]. The Court, of course, rejected the plea on the ground that the commital order was passed before the exemption was acquired [66].

In fairness, the period of sentence which the fugitive may undergo in the State of refuge should not be computed towards determining the period of limitation, irrespective of the fact whether the order of committal was passed before or after. Besides, the rule of time bar should be applied to prosecution alone; it should not be applied to cases where the person has been convicted but has managed to escape from the custody of the requesting State.

Surrender of Nationals

It has been practice of a number of Continental States not to extradite their nationals. Italy, Germany and France are a few among such States. Bar on such extradition is sometimes witnessed in bilateral treaties [67]. In other cases, States show their inability to extradite their nationals in view of the ban to that effect by national legislation [68]. There are other States like the United States of America, United Kingdom and India which do permit extradition of their nationals if there is no such bar under a treaty. This is despite the fact that Sections 3 and 4 of Indian Penal Code authorise the Indian judiciary to take cognizance of offences committed by Indians in foreign countries. Nationals may, therefore, be extradited if there is no national or treaty bar. Article 2 of the Indo-Nepal Treaty of 1953 goes further than modern practice when it provides that only nationals of the requesting State can be extradited [69]. This is a new development in international practice on extradition.

Executive Discretion

There is always an invisible hand of the Ministry of External Affairs or State Department in deciding to extradite (or not) the fugitive offender. After all formalities and magisterial inquiries are over, the magistrate recommends to the Government that extradition would be in order. The Government has to decide whether to surrender the fugitive or refuse surrender because of extra legal considerations. This is clear from the fact that while the British Government agreed to the surrender of Enahoro to Nigeria, it refused the surrender of Zakaria to Cyprus. This was despite the fact that Enahoro was essentially a political opponent of the then Nigerian Government while Zakaria cooperated with the British Government during the independence struggle in Cyprus. More recently, when Jerath exhausted all legal avenues in the United States to prevent his extradition to India from the United States, he succeeded in convincing Kissinger in December 1976 that he had better not extradited. So he was not extradited even though the charge against him was that of embezzlement of Government funds while he was Judge Advocate General of the Indian Navy. There was no political charge against him.

Conclusions

Law relating to extradition has been discussed above in its broader perspectives. In the process, one may have noticed that extradition is not an easy exercise as one may have imagined or desired. It is packed with many complications and pitfalls. Nations have, therefore, resorted to means which have the semblance or effect of extradition minus its handicaps. Kidnapping from a foreign country is one process of getting the custody of the desired fugitive. We have known in recent history how Eichmann was kidnapped by Israel, agents from Argentina to face trial in Israel; the Indian police party pursued Sucha Singh in Nepalese territory.

There is also the procedure of expulsion or deportation of the required fugitive if he is wanted in the State of his nationality. The territorial State may oblige a friendly State by deporting the national of the latter country if there is any hitch in his extradition. This may sometimes be intentional and many a time coincidental. We witnessed this in the deportation of Hans Muller by India to Germany [70] and the attempted deportation of Soblen by the British Government to the United States of America [71].

A fugitive may be surrendered by mistake as it happened in the case of Savarkar [72]. He had escaped from the mail steamer, Morea, to the French shore in Marseilles where the steamer was then anchoring. The French Police handed over Savarkar's custody by mistake, without knowing that political offenders are not to be surrendered.

Mention of the above practices is to remind the international elites that the process of extradition should not be cumbersome and time-consuming. Of course, one should see that the liberty of an individual is not bargained for on the international chess-board. Enahoro's case is a pointer to us that the territorial Government may sometimes be selective and hand over custody of such persons who should not normally be extradited, in order to please the rulers of friendly country. But at the same time, a fugitive should not escape from the clutches of law by taking advantage of the stringency of the extradition law. Some suggestions follow:

1. In case of border States, where there is more likelihood of fugitive's flight, fugitive should be extradited without proof of *prima facie* evidence but on the production of an authenticated warrant;

2. While it is desirable to incorporate the rule of specialty in extradition treaties, fugitive may nevertheless be extradited even in the absence of such a provision in treaty or national legislation, provided there is an *ad hoc* assurance in writing given by the requesting State to the effect that the rule of specialty will be scrupulously observed;

3. Extradition offences should be determined on the basis of the term of sentence provided, of course, the rule of double criminality is not violated;

4. Nationals who are not extradited must be tried by their own States;

5. With respect to convicted fugitives, evidence as to their conviction and identity should be required unless he has been convicted in absencia in which case *prima facie* evidence may also be required; and

6. Rule of time bar should not be applied to convicted fugitives.

Notes

1. For example, see definition of extradition in Oppenheim, International Law, vol. I (Eighth Edition) p. 696
2. Harvard Research Draft on Extradition, (1935) 29 A.J.I.L (Supplement) p. 66.
3. Re Arton. (1896) 1 Q. B 108 at p. 111.
4. Harvard Research Draft, op. cit. (1935) A.J.I.L. (Suppl.) p. 41.

5. *De jure Belli* ac Pacis (1625) Book ii, chapter 21 and section 4.
6. The Law of Nations (1760) vol. 1-Book II-Section 76.
7. Oppenheim says: "In the absence of extradition treaties stipulating to the contrary no State is by international law obliged, to expel or deliver him up to the prosecuting State" op. cit, 677. Also see Arnold McNair, Extradition and Ex-territorial Asylum, 1950. B.Y.I.L. II, 174-7 Felice Morgenstern. The Right of Asylum. 1949 B.Y.I.L. 327: Factor vs Laubenheimer, 290. U.S. Reports 276 at p. 283.
8. Felice Morgenstern, supra, 1949 B.Y.I.L. p. 344; Factor vs Laubenheimer. 290 U.S. 276. p. 283.
9. Harvard Research Draft, (1935) 29 A.J.I.L. (Supl) pp. 41-2. It was a treaty between Great Britain, France, Spain and Holland for extradition between parties. The treaty did not come into effect on account of war.
10. As reported by Oppenheim, op. cit. p. 697
11. Brierly-de Visscher Report on Extradition-League Doc. 1926 vol. 8 8
12. For other attempts at bringing out international code on Extradition see Harvard Research Draft, (1935) 29 A.J.I.L. (Suppl) 47-8.
13. Canberra Times, September 4, 1965.
14. The London Times, March 27, 1966.
15. Section 9.
16. Article 4.
17. Article 2.
18. Article 1.
19. Article 2.
19A. Section 10.
20. 1933 Annual Digest, Case No. 146.
21. The London Times, May 28, 1949.
22. Oppenheim, op. cit. 696, 704-05.
23. J. Menalco Solis R. Private International Law.—Extradition-Political Offences (1960) 24 Tulane Law Review 848.
24. R.V. Enahoro, 1963 Modern Law Review 555 at p. 557.
25. Oppenheim op. cit., 710
26. However, see the four Geneva Conventions of 1949 relating to protection of war victims which permit the extradition of political offenders. Convention for the Amelioration of the Condition of the Wounded and Sick in Armed Forces in the Field (Article 49), Convention for the Amelioration of the Condition of the Wounded, Sick, Shipwrecked Members of Armed Forces (Article 50). Convention Relating to Protection of Civilians During War (Article 146).
27. See Amarsinghe, The Schtraks Case-Defining Political Offences and Extradition, 1965 Modern Law Review 27; Same author. Political Offences in the Law of Extradition, 1961 The University of Ceylon Review 195.
28. Oppenheim. op. cit., vol I, p. 707.
29. Nature and Definition of Political Offences in International Extradition, (1909) 3 Proceedings of the American Society of International Law

Discussion by Messrs Clark, Coundert and Mack.

30. (1891) 1 Q. B. 149
31. Ibid p. 158, see Comments on the case by Piggot, Extradition (1910) pp. 50-56. The case confirmed the definition of Sir Fitzjames Stephen in his History of the Criminal Law of England. According to him, fugitive criminals are not to be surrendered for extradition crimes, if those crimes were incidental to and formed part of political disturbances. Coincidentally, Justice Stephens was one of the Judges who decided the Castioni Case. This Court, however, rejected part of Sir John Stuart Mill's definition of political crime given in the Parliament (House of Commons) in 1866 to the effect that the political offence may be "Any offence committed in the course of or furtherance of civil war, insurrection or political commotion "
32. Re Meunier (1894) 2. Q.B. 415 at p. 419.
33. Re Ezra (1894) 62 F. 972 at p. 999.
34. Article 10.
35. 1952 International Law Reports Case No. 80.
36. Hector Jose Compora and others in the Matter of Extradition decided by the Supreme Court of Chile or September 24, 1957 as given in (1959) 53A.J.I.L. 963.
37. (AIR) 1950 Supreme Court 155.
38. (AIR) 1953 Madras 729.
39. Ex-Partes Kolizynski and others (1955) 1 All England Reports 31 at p. 35.
40. Moore, Extradition (1891) vol. 1 p. 308 wherein he has said: "The question whether a particular act comes within that category is predominantly circumstantial.
41. In Schtrak's case, the Divisional Court defined political offence as under:

    "A crime of political charactor is a crime committed as a part of political movement with the object of influencing the policy of the governing party of state" (1962)2 Weekly Law Reports 976 at p. 997.
42. (AIR) 1953 Madras 729.
43. Judgement of N. L. Kakkar, First Class Magistrate, New Delhi, who inquired into the case of Tarasov and who delivered his judgment on 29th March, 1963.
44. Oppenheim, op. cit., 702 and Foot Note 3 on that page. Also see Extradition Case (Germany and Czechoslovakia) 1919-22, Annual Digest Case No. 182 where the German Reichgerecht in criminal matters acquitted the petitioner on the ground that in the absence of a treaty, the accused's trial after extradition was governed by customary rules of international law which stipulate that the accused can only be tried for the offence for which his extradition has been granted.
45. See Magistrate's order dated 13. 2. 1963; also see the Statesman (India) of 19. 2. 1963.
46. See his Judgment dated March 7, 1963.

47. Paul O'Higgins, Unlawful Seizure or Irregular Extradition 1961 B.Y.I.L. 279 at p. 318.
48. Arnold Mc Nair, supra, 1951 B.Y.I.L. 191.
49. (1886) 116 US. Reports 407; also see People exarel Young vs Street 30 New York Suppl. 898. In this case, the United Slates-Great Britain Treaty provided extradition of person "charged with crime of murder or assault with intent to commit murder." Therefore, it was held in this case, that a person extradited on charge of assault with intent to commit murder cannot be convicted for assault with intent to cause bodily harm.
50. Arnold McNair, Supra, 1951 B.Y.I.L. 192
51. (1931) 1 K.B. 327.
52. For example, see Article 10 of the Anglo-German Treaty of 1871, Article 2 of the Anglo-Danish Treaty of 1873, Article 12 of the Anglo-Iraqian Treaty of 1932 and Anglo-America Treaty of 1931.
53. C.G. Menon vs State of Madras, AIR 1953 Madras 763.
54. India does not require proof of *prima facie* evidence with regard to requests from such Commonwealth countries which have extradition arrangement with India-see Section 17 of the Indian Extradition Act 1962. Also see Article 17 of the Harvard Research Draft on Extradition which disfavours practice of proof of *prima facie* case. In this writer's opinion, proof of *prima facie* case in extradition proceedings is a safeguard against frivolous applications. India seems to have abondoned the idea of having special arrangement with the Commonwealth countries which waives requirement of *prima facie* evidence.
55. See the extradition proceedings of Samuel Insull (1934) A.J.I.L. 362. Also see Madras High Court decision in C.G. Menon vs State of Madras (AIR) 1953. Madras 739 wherein the High Court has said: "To surrender a fugitive offender without a *prima facie* case being made out is opposed to principle of natural justice" column 60.
56. Alona E. Evans, Reflections Upon Political Offences in International Practice. (1963) 57 A.J.I.L., 21, also see Editorial comment, The Extradition Case of Samuel Insul, Sr in Relation to Greece. (1934) 28 A.J.I.L. 307 at p. 309.
57. R.G. Ruia vs State of Bombay (AIR) 1958 Supreme Court 106 para 20.
58. Hyde has said that evidence in the case should be such as would "according to the law of the place where the accused might be found, justify his apprehension and commitment for trial." Hyde, Notes on the Extradition Treaties of the United States, 1914 A.J.I.L. 487. Also see the case of C.G. Collinn vs Victor Loisel where the United States Supreme Court has held. "It was not the function of the committing magistrate to determine whether Collins was guilty but merely whether there was competent legal evidence which according to the law of Louisiana, would justify his apprehension and commitment for trial if the crime had been committed in that State," 259 U.S. Reports 309 at pp. 314-15.

59. For example, see Article 3(b) of Montivedeo Convention of 1933 and Article 2(5) of the Central American Convention of 1934 which provide protection against double jeopardy. However, see Harvard Research Draft on Extradition which makes the protection against double jeopardy only permissive and not mandatory—Article 9 of the Draft in (1935) 29 A.J.I.L. (Suppl).
60. Note: Executive Discretion in Extradition, 1962 Columbia Law Review 1314.
61. Rudolf Stallman vs Emperor (ILR) 38 Calcutta 547: in Re Rudolf Stallman (ILR) 39 Calcutta 164.
62. Rex. vs Governor of Brixton Prison, Ex-parte Stallman (1912) 3.K.B. 424 at p 444 as per Lord Alevstone.
63. Also see Article 10 of the Draft Convention as prepared by the Asio-African Legal Consultative Committee at its Colombo Session in 1960; also see Article 7 of the Draft Convention on Extradition as prepared by the Consultative Assembly of the Council of Europe in 1954.
64. See Section 31 (e) of the Indian Act, 1962; also see Section 3(4) of the British Extradition Act of 1870.
65. Article IX of the Anglo-Belgian Treaty of October 29, 1901 says : "The surrender of fugitive shall not take place if since the commission of the acts charged, the accusation or conviction exemption from prosecution or punishment has been acquired by lapse of time, according to the laws of the country where the accused shall have taken refuge." See Piggot, op. cit., Appendix II, p. 47; also see article V of the Anglo-German Treaty of 1872 and Article VI of the Anglo-Italian Treaty of 1873.
66. Rex vs Governor of Brixton Prison (1908) 96 Times Law Reports 821.
67. For example, see Article III of the Anglo-German Treaty of 1872 as well as of the Anglo-Italian Treaty of 1873.
68. For example, see the Italian Penal Code.
69. "Neither Government shall be bound in any case to surrender any person who is not a national of the country by the Government of which the requisition has been made..."
70. Hans Muller of Nurenburg vs Superintendent, Presidency Jail, Calcutta, 1955 Supreme Court Journal 324.
71. Rex vs Governor of Brixton Prison, Ex-parte Soblen (1963) 2 Q.B. 243.
72. The Savarkar Case—France vs Great Britain, decided by the Hague Court of Arbitration in 1911,

CHAPTER 16

DIPLOMATIC RELATIONS

Functions

A diplomat is an important instrument for maintaining a link between his country and the host country to which he has been assigned. It is also a sign of sovereignty of a State to send diplomatic agents to another sovereign State. It is an old institution and diplomats were sent in ancient days also. In the ancient Hindu period, he was called "*Doota.*" Diplomats may broadly be divided in two categories—*ad hoc* and resident. *Ad hoc* diplomats may be assigned for a particular purpose. This category may include even a Head of State, Prime Minister, Minister or any other official functionary who visits another country on a good will mission or for any other specific purpose. Diplomats are sent to attend an Independence Day celebration, coronation, burial or cremation of a Head of State, Prime Minister or any other high dignitary. Representatives attending particular Congress or Conference are categorised as *ad hoc* diplomats. So also a person who visits another country as his country's representative to fulfill a given mission. Countries appoint ambassadors at large who are not assigned to a particular country but who are considered as trouble-shooters. They are directed by their Government to go to any country to offer good office, mediation or any other such assignment. The importance and number of *ad hoc* diplomats has increased in present times. But it is the resident diplomat who represents his country in the host country and has important functions to perform.

The main functions of a resident diplomat may be summarised as promotion of friendly relations, negotiations, observation and protection [1]. Article 3(1) of the Vienna Convention, 1961 enumerates the functions of diplomats as follows:

(1) Representing the sending state:

(2) Protecting the interests of the sending state and its nationals;

(3) Negotiating with the host state;

(4) Promoting friendly relations between the parent State and the host State;

(5) Ascertaining by lawful means conditions and developments in the host country and despatching the same to his own country.

The most important function of a diplomat is to promote friendly relations or improve relations, where they are bad between the two countries. He normally presents his State's point of view before the host Government. If there is any difference of opinion between the two Governments, his job is to either decrease the differences to the minimum or maintain friendly relations despite points of difference between the two countries. In modern days, a diplomat also tries to put his country's viewpoint on current international and bilateral issues before people from different walks of life of the host country. Today, diplomats have come in very handy for discussing voting patterns and planning voting strategy at various bodies of the United Nations and other international diplomatic conferences with a host government.

A diplomat also negotiates with the host government on behalf of his own government on a number of commercial and aid deals which may be struck between the two countries. Nowadays, States enter into many bilateral arrangements varying from entering into an extradition treaty or protection from double taxation to a mutual waiver of visas or entering into a treaty for supply of any commodity or financial assistance or even cultural exchange. It is the resident diplomat who negotiates all these sorts of bilateral arrangements although in some cases *ad hoc* diplomats may also do the same job.

Kinds of Diplomats

The Vienna Congress of 19th March, 1815 established three types of diplomatic agents in order of preference—Ambassador, Minister Plenipotentiary and Charge d'affaire. The Congress of Aixla-Chapelle which assembled in 1818 added a fourth category of 'Minister Resident' between Minister Plenipotentiary and Charge d' affaires. The Vienna Diplomatic Conference of 1961 has reverted to the three tier system thus restoring the decisions of the Vienna Congress of 1815. Thus the three categories today in order of preference are:

(1) Ambassadors or *nuncios*;
(2) Envoys, ministers or inter-*nuncios*;
(3) Charge d' affaires.

In the Commonwealth countries, an ambassador sent from one Commonwealth country to another Commonwealth country is designated as a High Commissioner. But for different nomenclature, there is no difference between an ambassador and a High Commissioner.

The exigency of a situation may require a different nomenclature for diplomatic agent, although for practical purposes there may be no difference between the ambassador and the incumbent having a different name. This happened between the United States of America and the Peoples Republic of China when they established diplomatic relations between them in 1972. Their embassies are called Liaison Office and the ambassador as Head of the Liaison Office.

Difference Between Various Categories

An ambassadorial post is the highest diplomatic post; next comes the post of an envoy and after that the post of a Charge d'affaires.

Ambassadors and envoys are accredited to the Head of the State while the charge d'affaires is accredited to the Foreign Minister of the receiving State.

An ambassador has the right to be called as His Excellency. The others are not called as such although envoy may be called His Excellency by courtesy.

Previously, only the big powers used to exchange ambassadors. Today the sending of an ambassador to a country has become a symbol of sovereignty, status, dignity and friendship. Friendly States often open legations at the embassy level.

An ambassador has direct access to the Head of the State although examples will not be lacking where ambassadors had been refused interviews by the Head of State. But that is a discourtesy not only to the ambassador but also to the country he represents. Sometimes, it is a reflection upon the acceptability of the given ambassador. A State should change its ambassador if he has become *persona non grata* impliedly although not expressly.

An ambassador has a general right to negotiate with his host country. There is lack of this general power in the case of envoys and charge d'affaires.

The ambassador of any country has the right to fly the flag of his country at his residence as well as on his car while he is in it. Envoy or charge d'affaires has no such right unless he is officiating as the Head of the Mission. Article 20 of the Vienna Convention gives such right only to the Head of the Mission.

The importance of diplomatic agents has gradually decreased due to frequent diplomatic talks between countries at the level of Heads of States, Prime Ministers, Foreign Ministers or *ad hoc* emissaries.

Appointment of Diplomats

Article 2 of the Vienna Convention says that States can establish diplomatic relations with other States by mutual consent. It is within the sovereign right of each State to establish or refuse to establish diplomatic relations with another State. For example, India has not established diplomatic relations with Israel so far. It has only consular relations with Israel. It is also the sovereign right of the State to determine the level of representation in a foreign country. The level of representation depends upon the relations between the two States, importance and size of a State and quantum of workload. From 1961 to 1976. India and China had reduced the level of their embassies to that of a charge d' affaires because of low-key relations between them. Some small States send ambassadors to a few important States. Elsewhere, they are represented by charge d'affaires. In far-off countries, they do not send any diplomats at all.

If the States have agreed to establish diplomatic relations at whatever level, the receiving State must consent to the choice of the Head of the Mission. This is called *Agre'ment* under Article 4(1) of the Vienna Convention. Under Article 4(2), the host country need not give reason for *Agre'ment* as to the proposed Head of the Mission. Article 9 of the Convention permits the withdrawal of *Agre'ment* (consent of the receiving State) or declaration of the incoming diplomat as *persona non grata* even before his arrival.

The size of mission is also to be determined by the receiving State unless it has been mutually agreed to between the receiving and the sending State. This is provided for under Article 11 of the Convention. In many instances, the host country has asked for reduction of diplomatic staff and mostly it is on the basis of reciprocity. The host country may ask for reduction of diplomatic staff of a given mission because of the suspicion that the staff is disproportionate to the workload or because of the unfounded fear or otherwise, that some of the diplomatic personnel are involved in espionage.

No particular qualifications are fixed for appointing diplomatic staff. Every State has the right to appoint anyone on the diplomatic staff provided the host State has no objection to such an appointment. Nevertheless, a State uses its discretion to appoint such a person as the Head of the Mission who can represent his country well. Although no State will specifically agree, yet it has been found that the appointment of the Head of the Mission is a matter of patronage distributed by the powers that exist in any State. India has appointed ambassadors from politicians, career diplomats, retired army officers, lawyers, journalists, retired judges, princes, women and all sorts of other categories. But they have been mostly from careerists and politicians. In other countries, a sizeable number of ambassadors are appointed from professors.

Ambassadors are appointed by a Letter of Credence which the ambassador has to present to the Head of the host country. Officially, he functions as ambassador only after presentation of the Letter of Credence to the Head of the State. Unofficially, he is the ambassador from the moment he arrives in the State. The Letter of Credence of the ambassador is signed by the Head of the sending State while the Letters of Credence of other diplomatic agents are signed by the Foreign Minister.

Sometimes the same ambassador may be accredited to two States. For example, India's High Commissioner to the United Kingdom is also accredited as the ambassador to the Republic of Ireland. So also the Indian Ambassador to the United States of America who is accredited to some Latin American countries.

Rights and Privileges of Diplomatic Staff

It may be made clear at the outset that whatever rights and privileges the diplomats enjoy in a foreign host country, they are in fact the rights and privileges of the State whom they represent [2] Because they enjoy these rights as representatives of their country, these rights and privileges are attributed to them. They cease to enjoy these rights if they do not represent their State. With this clarification, rights and privileges of diplomats may be given as follows.

(2) *Inviolability of person*

A diplomat is immune from arrest. There will be no constraint of a diplomat except in his own interest. In cases when a diplomat is arrested inadvertently, he is let out as soon as his identity as diplomat is established [3]. In some countries there has been flagrant violation of this privilege although ultimately diplomats are let out after the lodging of protests. Article 29 provides that the "person of a diplomatic agent shall be inviolable."

(2) *Inviolability of premises*

The Embassy premises as well as the residence of a diplomat are inviolable [4]. It is due to this fact that such premises enjoy the right of exterritoriality. According to this principle, the premises are supposed to be outside the territorial jurisdiction of the host State. Diplomatic asylum is granted by the Head of the Mission in exercise of this right. Although diplomatic asylum has not yet developed into a customary rule of international law, the host state is averse to entering into the diplomatic premises. Thus, when the American Embassy in India gave asylum to a Russian scholar Arzade, in December, 1967, the Indian Government protested against this practice although it did not enter the American Embassy. The local police may, however, enter the premises if the Head of the Mission invites it [5].

A host state also discourages hostile demonstrations before diplomatic missions. Special protection is accorded to the mission against which a demonstration is staged and in almost all cases the police prohibits entry of demonstrators within a prescribed radius from the premises. In some cases, peaceful demonstrations are permitted. Host states normally regret the occurrence of any violent demonstration against any diplomatic mission. In some cases, the local State compensates any damage caused by demonstrators. Chancery premises as well as residences of the ambassador are normally given police protection for security and political purposes. In modern days, there is more tightening of security arrangements due to terrorist activities against some embassies.

(3) *Exemption from local criminal jurisdiction*

No criminal proceedings can be initiated against any foreign diplomat whose name appears in the Government's Diplomatic List. However, this does not mean that diplomats are at liberty to violate the local laws. They are expected to observe the local laws and whenever a diplomat commits a crime, he is either recalled by this State or the latter waives the immunity in order to enable the local State to proceed against him. Thus, one Latin American ambassador accredited to India was once recalled because of his unbecoming behaviour in an Indian Hotel. Similarly, the Burmese ambassador to Sri Lanka (then Ceylon), Mr. Boonawat was recalled by his government because he was suspected to be involved in the murder of his wife. The Ceylonese police was handicapped in its investigations because they could not enter the ambassador's house nor could they examine him because of his diplomatic immunity. In 1976 three diplomats from an African country were involved in smuggling in India. They were recalled by their government when their activities were detected and reported to their governments.

Of late, there has been lot of criticism in the papers regarding the diplomats' exemption from criminal jurisdiction. Diplomats have been frequently involved in traffic offences and some are suspected to be involved in selling duty-free goods. The number of diplomats has also grown enormously and this has resulted in a comparative increase of violations on the part of the diplomatic society. Nevertheless, diplomats continue to enjoy exemption from criminal jurisdiction under Article 31 (1) of the Vienna Convention.

(4) *Exemption from civil jurisdiction*

Diplomat enjoys exemption from civil liability. However, the extent of exemption from civil liability is disputable. The English Courts provide complete exemption from civil liability. So also the Soviet practices. In India, no diplomat can be sued without the permission of the Union Government [6]. The position is unsettled in some countries like Holland, Sweden and South America [7]. But Courts in West Germany, Italy, Belgium, Switzerland, Austria, France, Greece, Egypt and Jordan recognise only qualified privilege with regard to prerogative acts as distinguished from commercial acts [8]. The American practices also recognise only restricted sovereign immunity. Article 31 (1) of the Vienna Convention exempts the diplomat from civil liability except in cases of:

(a) a real action relating to private immovable property situated in the territory of the receiving State, unless he holds it on behalf of the sending State for the purposes of the mission;

(b) an action relating to succession in which the diplomatic agent is involved as executor, administrator, heir or legatee as private person and not on behalf of the sending State; and

(c) an action relating to any professional or commercial activity exercised by the diplomatic agent in the receiving State outside his official function."

This shows that there is a tendency towards limiting diplomatic immunity only in respect of official acts. Local courts may also exercise jurisdiction over a diplomatic agent in case he defends the proceedings against him without asserting diplomatic immunity or when he initiates the proceedings himself.

(5) *Exemption from service of summons*

Diplomats are immune from being served with any summons. This is borne out by the Musurus Bey versus Gadban case decided in 1894 [9]. Any service of summons may violate Article 29, the latter portion of which says that "the receiving State shall treat him with due respect and shall take appropriate steps to prevent any attack on his person, freedom and dignity." This has been the opinion of the U.S. Department of State when it said that service of summons can be an impairment in the performance of duties by the diplomatic agent [10]. The Court upheld the State Department's assertion that any service of summons may prejudice the friendly relations between the territorial State and the diplomatic agent's State [11].

(6) *Exemption from being called witness*

Article 31 (2) provides that no diplomatic agent may be obliged to give evidence as witness.

(7) *Exemption from local taxes*

Diplomats are exempted from paying local taxes. Article 34 of the Convention exempts the diplomat from paying local taxes. Article 36 exempts the diplomat from payment of customs duties.

Subordinate Staff [12]

Practices vary in the grant of privileges and immunities to subordinate diplomatic staff. While the Common Law countries do not much differentiate between the superior and subordinate diplomatic staff, the Continental practices reveal that there is some difference in the privileges and immunities of the two groups [13]. As late as in 1958, the International Law Commission remarked that there was no "uniformity in the practice of States" as to "which member of the staff of a mission shall enjoy privileges and immunities" [14]. Article 37 of the Vienna Convention, however, grants same facilities to the subordinate administrative and technical staff of the mission as are given to the diplomats. These facilities include exemption from custom duties at the time of first installation, but not later on. Their immunity from civil and administrative jurisdiction as given under Article 31(1) will not extend to acts performed outside the course of their duties. Law and practices seem to favour the Continental viewpoint.

Privileges and Immunities of Families of Diplomatic Staff

The wife and children of a diplomat enjoy the same rights and immunities which the diplomat himself enjoys [15]. The word "family" would include unmarried children of the diplomat. Married children who either live with the diplomat or have come for a sojourn with their parents cannot technically be termed as family members of the diplomat for the purpose of invoking diplomatic immunities and privileges. A married child of the diplomat forms a separate family of his own and is therefore not entitled to diplomatic privileges and immunities. However, divorced or separated daughter of the diplomat may be entitled to privileges if she stays permanently with her parents.

Some States are liberal in their grant of immunities to the dependants of a diplomatic agent. For example, Hyde, exponent of the U.S. policies on international law, says that family could include not only wife and children but parents and other near relations who live with the diplomat [16]. The British practice is not that liberal. Thus the brother of the Portugese ambassador to the St. James Court in London, while staying with him, was arrested, tried and executed on a charge of killing an English man in 1653 [17]. The Soviet Union is more liberal like the United States and it extends privileges to relatives of the diplomat also if they are staying under the same roof and are dependent upon him [18]. On the other hand, while privileges and immunities are attributed to the family members of the Head of the Mission, the same are not attributed to the family members of lesser diplomatic, administrative and technical officers attached to the mission [19]. This is, however, not a correct assessment of the situation. Article 37(1) does not make any such distinction. What is required is the entry of the name of the diplomat and his family members in the diplomatic list as maintained by the territorial State.

Retinue

Article 37(3) of the Convention gives immunity to service staff of diplomats provided they are not nationals of the territorial State. Practices reveals that personal servants, who are not nationals of the local State, are immune from local jurisdiction. Only sometime back, the Ministry of External Affairs of the Government of India communicated to the various legations located in India that Indian drivers attached to the various embassies are not entitled to any immunity and that they would be tried if they are found violating traffic rules. This would imply that if the servants were non-Indians, they would be exempted from liability.

Review of Diplomatic Privileges and Immunities

Diplomats are given privileges and immunities on two grounds: exterritoriality and proper functioning on their post. They are, therefore, not to pay local taxes and are immune from local jurisdiction. The doctrine of sovereign equality of States prevents one State from assuming jurisdiction over the functionaries of another State.

This does not mean that they are at liberty to violate local laws with impunity; far from it. They are under an obligation to observe the laws of the land. Article 41(1) of the Convention provides that diplomats are under a duty to observe laws of the receiving State. If any diplomat violates any laws, he can be declared *persona non grata* and packed home at a very short notice depending upon the gravity of his violation. Instances are not lacking in diplomatic circles when diplomats have been asked to leave or recalled when they have been involved in indiscretionary acts. Cases have also occurred when a diplomat has eventually left if his wife or any of his wards has violated any law. Mrs. Sommerlatte, wife of the Second Secretary at the U.S. Embassy in Moscow, left because of Russian allegation of hooliganism against her. Similarly, an Italian Minister had to leave Peking because his wife was involved in attacking another Italian lady [20]. The Burmese ambassador to Ceylon, Boonawat was recalled by his Government because he was suspected of the murder of his wife in Ceylon.

Waiver of Immunity [21]

Article 32 of the Convention provides for waiver of immunity from jurisdiction of diplomats and their families by the sending State. Waiver must be express except in cases where the diplomat initiates proceedings in which case he will be deemed to have impliedly waived immunity in respect of any counterclaim connected with the principal claim. Two separate waivers are required, one for the suit and one for execution thereof [22]. However, it would look illogical to withhold waiver for execution when waiver has been given earlier with respect to the main proceedings. Perhaps, the purpose for requiring specific waiver for execution is to avoid an ugly situation of attachment of a diplomat's property in execution of decree passed by the local court. It would, therefore, be desirable for the diplomat to satisfy the decree outside court. Otherwise, the local Ministry of External Affairs may put pressure on the Head of the Mission, to which the diplomat belongs, to send him back.

Since immunity is enjoyed on behalf of the State which he represents, it is the State alone which can waive the immunity from jurisdiction [23]. Normally, it is expressed by the Head of the Mission in the name of the State [24]. However, if the Head of the Mission is himself involved, waiver is conveyed by the Ministry of External Affairs of the Government, which he represents, to the Ministry of External Affairs of the receiving State. Waiver cannot be given retrospectively [25]. Appearance under protest in order to claim immunity does not amount to waiver. Waiver by the diplomat himself is not valid. It must be given by the Head of the Mission. Once waiver has been given it should not be withdrawn [26]. In one case, the Canadian Government having once waived immunity in respect of its diplomat in Argentina withdrew its waiver. The Argentina Supreme Court upheld such a withdrawal [27]. Such a practice is not desirable although the Vienna Convention is silent on this issue.

Although, diplomats enjoy immunity from jurisdiction, they are also expected to observe the laws of the land. In case of violation of any local law or any outstanding claim against the diplomat, immunity is either waived or the matter is settled through private arbitration. In the absence of the two remedies, the diplomat is declared *persona non grata* and asked to leave the country. Instances of compromises outside court by diplomats involved in motor accidents are many and they go to show that diplomats are as anxious to observe laws as any other individual.

Duration of Immunity

Article 39 of the Convention deals with the duration of a diplomat's immunity. It says that the diplomat enjoys immunity from the moment he enters the territory of the receiving State where he has come to take up his duties. If he is already within the territory, his immunity will start when he has been appointed by his government which also sends notification of his appointment to the Ministry of External Affairs of the receiving country.

Article 39(2) says that immunity will continue even after the end of the mission of the diplomat until he leaves the country or on expiry of reasonable time during which he should wind up his establishment. A diplomat does not enjoy immunity after expiry of this time. As to what is reasonable time can be determined by the Court unless the Ministry of External Affairs has already withdrawn immunity from the diplomat because of overstay beyond reasonable period. This withdrawal of immunity or end of diplomatic immunity is only with relation to private acts of the diplomat. His immunity is permanent insofar as his official acts are concerned.

In case of death of a diplomat, his family will continue to enjoy immunity until such reasonable time when the family is able to leave the country [28].

Diplomat and Third State

Articie 40 of the Convention gives inviolability and such other immunities at the hands of a third State through which the diplomat is passing en route to takingover charge or returning after completion of his mission. Prior to this, some claimed immunity as of right [29] but others gave it as a matter of diplomatic discretion [30]. Normally, the practice is that a diplomat passes through third State by means of a diplomatic visa granted to him for the purpose.

If such a visa is granted, there is little difficulty in according him right of inviolability and other immunities. The difficulty arises where visa is not required by a particular State and the diplomat enters that State. In such cases also, he is given the right of innocent passage through the third State. A diplomat on holiday in the third State has, however, no right of inviolability or other immunities. It is on this ground that the Pakistan ambassador to Tunisia, Prince Haroon-al-Resbid Ab-basi, was arrested by the Italian police on the charge of involvement in hashish smuggling [31].

NOTES

1. Oppenheim, International Law, vol. 1 pp. 785-86.
2. In re Suarez, Suarez, vs Suarez (1918) 1. Ch. 176.
3. Thus, in 1935, Iranian minister accredited to the United States was arrested for exceeding the prescribed speed limit and offering resistence, when apprehended. He was later on released when his identity was established. On protest being lodged with the U.S. authorities, the latter regretted the incident but emphasised that diplomats must observe the law of the land. For comment on this incident, see Reeves. The Elktou Incident (1936) 30 A.J.I.L. 95-96
4. Article 22(1) of the Convention provides : "The premises of the Mission shall be inviolable."

   Article 30(1) of the Convention says: "The private residence of a diplomatic agent shall enjoy the same inviolability and protection as the premises of the mission."
5. In Fatimi vs United States, 1922 At. 2nd 525 (D.C.Ct. A. July 12, 1963). When 14 Iranians had forcibly entered the Iranian embassy, the Minister of the Irani embassy, invited the police to remove the demonstrators who had earlier refused to leave the premises. The court held that it was part of the law of land that "(1) a foreign embassy is not to be considered the territory of the sending State: (2) that local police have the authority and responsibility to enter a foreign embassy if the privilege of diplomatic inviolability is not invoked when an offence is committed there in violation of local law" as reported in (1964) 58 A.J.I.L. 192.
6. Section 86 of the Civil Procedure Code.
7. As given by F.A. Mann, Sovereign Immunity, 1964 Morden Law Review 81 at p. 82.
8. Ibid.
9. (1894) 2. Q.B. 352.
10. See letter of Leonard C. Meeker, Acting Legal Advisor of the Department of State to the U.S. Court of Appeal for District of Columbia Circuit, January 13, 1965 as given in (1965) 59 A.J.I.L. 928.
11. Hellenic Lines Limited vs Moore, 345 F. 2nd 927, U.S. Court of Appeals, District of Columbia Circuit, March 25, 1965.
12. Joyce A.C. Gutteridge, Immunities of the Subordinate Diplomatic

Staff, (1947) 24. B.Y.I.L. 155.

13. Also see Harvard Draft Research in International Law: Diplomatic Privileges and Immunities, 1932 A.J.I.L. (Suppl.) 119.
14. (1958) 11 International Law Commission, Year Book, 101.
15. Article 37(1) of the Convention-En-gelke vs Mussman (1928) A.C. 433.
16. C.C. Hyle, International Law, Chiefly as Interpreted and Applied by the United States, (1945) Vol. II. p. 1273.
17. Oppenheim, International Law, vol. 1, p. 812.
18. Chifton E. Wilson, Diplomatic Privileges and Immunities: The Retinue and Families of the Diplomatic Staff, 1965, I.C.L.Q. 1282.
19. Ibid, p. 1294.
20. Ibid, p. 1285.
21. Hingorani R.C., Waiver of Immunity, 1963 Supreme Court Journal 1.
22. In re Suarez (1918) I Ch. 176, Article 32(4) of the Convention.
23. Engelke V Musman (1928) A.C. 433.
    Montwid vs Ivaldi, 1925-26 A.D. Case No. 245.
24. R.V. Madan (1961)2. Q.B. 1.
25. Ibid.
26. For Contra, see D.P.O.' Connel, International Law, vo'. II, 991.
27. Re Hillhouse, 1955, I.L.R. 533.
28. Article 39(3) of the Convention.
29. Bergman vs de Sieyes, 71 F. Suppl. 334 (1946).
30. New Chile Gold Mining Co. vs Blanco, (1888) 4. T.L.R. 346.
31. The Statesman, April 21, 1970.

CHAPTER 17

CONSULAR RELATIONS

Consuls

Consuls are yet another set of diplomatic agents who represent their State in a foreign country. As to how they differ from diplomatic agents is difficult to discern. In earlier centuries, the main functions of the consul were to look after trade interests of the country he represented and exercise jurisdiction over his conationals in case of their having committed any offence within the so-called less civilised country. Today, of course, there is no uncivilised State in international law dichotomy. Therefore, no consul exercises exterritorial jurisdiction over his conationals within the country where he represents a foreign country. The only function which remains to be done by the consular agent is to look after the trade interests of his country. Even looking after trade interests has become a diplomatic affair with the result that in many cases consular functions hardly differ from diplomatic functions. In some cases, there is a complete fusion of diplomatic and consular functions. This has been noticed in number of State practices. For example, there is no separate cadre of consular agents in many countries, including India. Consuls are selected from the cadre of Foreign Service Personnel who are posted abroad sometimes as diplomatic agents and at other times as consular agents. In some cases, they discharge the dual functions of diplomats as well as consuls. Sometime back India's consul general in New York was also India's representative at the United Nations. The practice has also been developing where a less recognised State, as distinguished from a fully recognised State, is permitted to station only a Consul in a foreign country where he is supposed to represent his State. For example, quasi-recognised States like North and South Korea and Israel were each represented at one time in India, by a Consul-General who represented his country's interests in India.

The establishment of legation or consulate is a political discretion of the State.

Today, there are two main functions of consuls: one, promotion of import trade from their country into the country where they are stationed and issue of visas for entry into their country. Side by side, they also represent their country in the absence of a senior diplomatic agent.

Article 5 of the Vienna Convention of Consular Relations, 1963, however, details 13 functions of consul. They are:

1. Protection of interests of the sending State and its nationals, both individuals and corporate bodies;
2. Furtherance of the development of commercial, economic, cultural and scientific relations between the two States and promotion of friendly relations between the two;
3. Ascertain conditions and developments in the commercial, economic, cultural and scientific life of the receiving State and reporting thereon to his own government and giving information to interested persons;
4. Issue of passports and travel documents to his conationals and visas to persons wishing to visit his country;
5. Helping and assisting his conationals;
6. Acting as notary and civil registrar and in capacities of a similar kind, and performing certain functions of an administrative nature;
7. Safeguarding the interests of nationals in case of succession *mortis causa*;
8. Safeguarding the interests of minors and other persons lacking full capacity;
9. Representing or arranging appropriate representation for conationals before tribunals and other authorities of the receiving State;
10. Transmitting judicial and extrajudicial documents or executing letters rogatory or commissions to take evidence for the courts of the sending State;
11. Exercising of rights of supervision and inspection in respect of vessel and aircraft of the sending State and their crew;
12. Extending assistance to vessels and aircraft registered in the sending State; and
13. Performing any other functions entrusted to him.

Classification of Consuls

Article 9 of the Vienna Convention divides consular staff into four categories: (a) Consul-General; (b) Consul; (c) Vice-Consul; and (d) Consular agent.

Customary international law also has the same four types of consuls.

Appointment of Consular Posts

Consuls are appointed by the sending State by means of a document, known as Commission, which gives the name of the appointee, his category and class, the Consular district and seat of the Consular post [1]. The copy of the Commission is transmitted to the receiving State through diplomatic or other appropriate channel. Two or more States may appoint the same person as their respective consul with the consent of the receiving State [2].

The Exequatur

The head of a consular office can start functioning only on receipt of letter of authorisation from the receiving State known as *exequatur* [3]. The receiving State may refuse to grant *exequatur* and it need not give reasons thereof. The head of a consular post may in some cases start functioning pending receipt of *exequatur* [4].

Although, *exequatur* is necessary only for the Head of a Consular post, local laws of the receiving State may require the issue of *exequatur* for a Consular Officer also [5]. In that case, it may be issued to all Consular Officers.

Precedence as between Consular Heads

Heads of Consular posts shall rank in each class according to the grant of *exequatur* unless he is admitted provisionally to the exercise of functions in which case his precedence shall be determined from the date of his provisional admission [6].

Declaration of Persona non grata

The receiving State may at any time declare any consular officer as *persona non grata*. In that event, the sending State would recall the person or terminate his functions as consular officer. However, if the officer is not withdrawn within reasonable time, the receiving State may withdraw *exequatur* from the officer or may stop recognising him as such [7].

Privileges and Immunities of Consular Officers

Chapter II of the Vienna Convention deals with the facilities, privileges and immunities of the consular posts and officers. These are given below.

Facilities

(1) The receiving State has to accord full facilities for the performance of the functions of the Consular post [8].

(2) The receiving State shall facilitate the requisition of premises necessary for the consular posts, stationed within its territory with its consent [9].

Privileges and immunities [10]

(1) Right of use of national flag.

(2) Inviolability of Consular premises [11]. Consular premises are inviolable. No local police can enter that part of a premises which is exclusively used for official purposes, except with the prior consent of the consular Head or his designee. Great controversy erupted in 1948 over the detention of a Soviet citizen in the Soviet Consulate in New York [12]. The consent of the Head may be presumed in case of fire or other disaster requiring prompt protective action. This rule of inviolability is extended to consular archives, documents and communications [13]. For the latter purpose, even the courier carrying consular mail enjoys personal inviolability and he cannot be arrested or detained [14].

(3) Protection of Consular premises—The receiving State is under a duty to take all appropriate action to protect the consular premises against any intrusion or damage. However, it has been noticed that demonstrations are organised or connived at by local governments against foreign Consular premises. This is a violation of customary as well as conventional international law.

(4) Exemption from taxation of Consular premises—Consular premises are exempt from all national, regional or municipal taxes whatsoever, other than those which represent payment for specific services rendered. This shall not, however, apply to such taxes which are payable by the owner of the premises under the law of the receiving State.

(5) Consuls have freedom to move throughout the territory of the receiving subject to laws and regulations concerning national

security [15]. Besides, some restrictions may be imposed on the basis of reciprocity.

Consular officers have the right to visit a national of the sending State who is in prison and to converse and correspond with him and arrange for his legal defence.

(6) Freedom of Communication: The receiving State shall permit and protect freedom of communication of the consular officer. The consular officer is empowered to use the diplomatic bag for the purpose. This freedom of communication extends not only to correspondence with the sending State but with nationals of the sending State who need to communicate with the consuls [16].

(7) Personal inviolability of Consular Officers: Consular officers will not be liable to arrest or detention pending trial, except in the case of a grave crime and persuant to a decision by competent judicial authority [17]. Any detention, arrest or prosecution shall be notified to consulur Head or his State [18].

(8) Consular officers are not amenable to local jurisdiction in respect of acts performed in the exercise of consular functions [19]. In this connection, it may be said that prosecution of German Consul in England in 1915 for his encouraging German nationals of military age to return to Germany, was not right [20]. Similarly issue of a press statement in clarification of refusal of visa to the plaintiff was definitely in his official capacity. Therefore, the process against the consul by a French Court was not justified [21]. However he may be liable in civil action if the suit is in respect of any contract concluded by the consular officer in which he has not shown himself as an agent of the sending State expressly or impliedly. Similarly, an action by third party may lie in respect of damage arising from an accident in the receiving State caused by a vehicle, vessel or aircraft [19].

(9) Members of a Consular post may be called upon to give evidence before judicial or administrative tribunal. Consular officer may, however, decline to give evidence concerning matters connected with the exercise of his functions and decline to produce official documents. He may also decline to give evidence as an expert witness with regard to laws of his State [22]. While taking evidence from the consular officer, it should be seen that it does not interfere with the performance of his official functions. In order to facilitate the taking of evidence by the consular officer,

it may be taken at his residence or at the residence of inquiring authority or he may be asked to give his statement in writing which may have the value of evidence.

(10) Consular officers as well as other staff are exempted from registration as aliens as may otherwise be required by the local law of the receiving State [23].

(11) Members of the Consular post shall be exempt from obtaining a work permit which may otherwise be necessary for, foreigners seeking employment [24]. They shall be equally exempted from local social security provisions [25].

(12) Consular officers shall be exempt from all local dues and taxes except—

(a) indirect taxes;

(b) dues or taxes on private immovable property within the territory of the receiving State;

(c) estate, succession or inheritance duties;

(d) dues and taxes on private income arising out of investments made in commercial or financial undertakings in the receiving State;

(e) charges levied for specific services rendered;

(f) registration, court fees, mortgage dues and stamp duties.

(13) Consular officers and their families shall be exempt from payment of custom duties on articles meant for official or personal purposes [26].

(14) Consular Officers and their families will be exempt from personal services and contributions [27].

All these privileges and immunities are given to consular officers with the understanding that they are responsible officers of a foreign Government whom they would not like to embarrass. Therefore, the consular officers are required to respect of the law of the receiving State [28]. They shall also insure themselves against third party risks arising out of use of vessel, vehicle or aircraft [29]. They will also not carry out any profitable profession [30].

Duration of privileges and immunities

Consular officer will enjoy privileges and immunities from the time he enters the country of his assignment for joining the post or if he is already there, from the moment he enters on his duties.

These privileges and immunities will come to an end when the officer leaves the territory of the receiving country or on the expiry of reasonable time for leaving the receiving State on completion of his assignment there, whichever is earlier. These privileges will continue irrespective of the fact that there is an armed conflict between the two countries.

In case of death of a consular officer, his family members will enjoy the privileges until the expiry of reasonable time for leaving the receiving country.

Consular officer and his families will enjoy similar privileges and immunities in third State when they are in transit either en-route to joining his post or on the way back after completion of assignment.

Honorary Consuls

The Vienna Convention has also recognised the existing practice of some countries appointing citizens of receiving State as their honorary consuls to carry out consular functions and duties on behalf of the appointing country. Although the practice of appointing such honorary consuls is decreasing, some countries do appoint honorary consuls because of less workload and far-off distance between the appointing State and the country where the honorary consul is appointed. In India, number of Latin American and small European Countries have appointed honorary consuls. Chapter III of the Vienna Convention specifically deals with such categories of consuls.

Privileges and immunities of honorary consul

(1) The territorial State shall accord facilities for the performance of functions by the consuls [31].

(2) He shall be entitled to the right of use of the national flag of the country which he represents.

(3) The receiving State shall facilitate in getting accommodation to the consul.

(4) The honorary consul shall have freedom of movement and communication with the appointing State and its nationals within the territorial State. He shall have the freedom of communication with the territorial State.

(5) The consular premises will be exempt from taxation and the territorial State will take steps to protect the consular premises against any intrusion, damage or disturbance of peace.

(6) The territorial State shall ensure inviolability of consular

archives and documents.

(7) Articles required for official purposes shall be exempted from custom duties.

(8) Any criminal proceedings against an honorary consul shall be conducted with respect due to him by reason of his official position.

(9) The territorial State is under a duty to accord adequate protection to the honorary consul [32].

(10) The consul will be exempt from income-tax on money received from the appointing State as his honorarium for working as such [33].

(11) He will also be exempt from all personal and public services, including military obligations.

Notes

1. Article 11 of the Vienna Convention on Consular Relations, 1963.
2. Article 18.
3. Article 12.
4. Article 13.
5. Article 19.
6. Article 16.
7. Article 23.
8. Article 28.
9. Article 30.
10. Stewart, Consular Privileges and Immunities (1926); Becket, Consular Immunities, (1944) 21 B. Y.I.L. 34-50.
11. Article 31.
12. For particulars, see, Preuss, Consular Immunities : Kasenkina Case, (1949) 43 A.J.I.L. 37-56.
13. Article 33.
14. Article 35.
15. Article 34.
16. Article 36.
17. Article 41.
18. Article 42.
19. Article 43.
20. R.V. Ahlers (1915) 1. K.B. 616.
21. Princess Ziaganoff vs Kahn and Bigloo 1927-28 A.D. case No. 266.
22. Article 44.
23. Article 46.
24. Article 47.
25. Article 48.
26. Article 50.
27. Article 52.

28. Article 55.
29. Article 56.
30. Article 57.
31. Article 28 read with Article 58.
32. Article 64.
33. Article 66.

CHAPTER 18

TREATIES

There are two important sources of international law. One is customary international law; the other is conventional international law. Until very recently, international law consisted mainly of customary international law. However, the trend is towards the development of conventional international law. The main defect of customary international law has been its uncertainty sometimes bordering on controversy. States used to take its advantage and violate it with impunity. There is no such defect with conventional international law—It is certain. As a result, customary international law is being codified and made conventional.

Codification

There have been many attempts at codification of international law. It was advocated by Bentham in the eighteenth century. But it materialised in the late nineteenth century with the establishment of the Institute of International Law, and International Law Association. Both the Associations are devoted to the development of international law and were born in 1873, coincidently in Belgium. Declaration of Brussels regarding the code of war was produced in the succeeding year in 1874. The first concrete attempt at codification was the first Hague Peace Conference in 1899 which was convened at the invitation of the Russian Emperor, Nicholas II. It produced two important Conventions; one on Peaceful Settlement of International Disputes and the second on Law of War. Indeed, the Permanent Court of Arbitration at the Hague owes its existence to this Conference. The Second Hague Conference in 1907 devoted itself to codification of laws and customs of war. Declaration of London of 1909 dealing with laws of naval warfare remained unratified.

The post-World War I period witnessed the signing of four

important documents, namely ban on bacteriological and chemical weapons in the Geneva Protocol of 1925, General Act for Peaceful Settlement of Disputes and Renunciation of War Treaty in 1928 and Prisoners of War Convention in 1929.

The post-World War II era witnessed the passing of Resolution number 174(II) by the United Nations General Assembly on 21st November 1947 to create International Law Commission in pursuance of Article 13 of the U.N. Charter which exhorts for "progressive development of international law and its codification."

Attempts at codification have been gratifying. In 1949, four Geneva Conventions were concluded on the protection of victims during war. This was followed by the Geneva Convention on the Law of Sea—particularly on Continental Shelf and Fisheries in 1958. In 1961, Vienna Convention on Diplomatic Relations codified customary rules on the subject. This was followed by another Vienna Convention of Consular Relations in 1963 again incorporating most of the customary rules on the subject. In 1969, yet another Vienna Convention was concluded on Law of Treaties. Indeed, all these Conventions have been the outcome of the reports and drafts prepared by the International Law Commission.

Kinds of Treaties

Treaties have different nomenclatures—Protocol, Declaration, Convention, Charter, Covenant—but without any differentiation. They are of four kinds—universal, general, multilateral and bilateral. Universal treaties are those which are binding on all States of the world community. There are hardly any such treaties which may be binding on all States, although four Geneva Conventions of 1949 on Protection of War Victims and Vienna Convention on Diplomatic Relations, 1961 may be considered as near universal treaties. Then there is general treaty which is binding on almost all the States. Vienna Conventions on Consular Relations, 1963 and on Law of Treaties, 1969 could be considered as general treaties. Multilateral treaties bind a number of States, while bilateral treaty only binds the two States party to the treaty.

While universal and general treaties form part of conventional international law and constitute law by themselves, same is not the case with multilateral and bilateral treaties. The latter do not constitute conventional international law. At the most, they are evidence of State practices which may give rise to the development of customary international law. Law of extradition is mainly based on bilateral treaties entered into by a number of States between themselves.

Who can Enter into A Treaty

Only sovereign States can enter into a treaty. A colony, trust territory or a federated State cannot enter into a treaty. As a matter of fact, the capacity to enter into a treaty is one of the attributes of a sovereign State [1]. A State does not get divested of treaty-making power because it has become neutralised as in the case of Switzerland, nor does it lose the power to make treaty only because some third States have guaranteed its sovereignty and territorial integrity as in the case of Cyprus. Similarly, Vatican City State has an equal right of entering into treaty which is called concordat.

Question may arise as to a protectorate State whose foreign relations are conducted by another State. Such a State cannot enter into a treaty; so also a vassal State. Only metropolitan States can enter into treaty on behalf of a colony, trust territory, protectorate and vassal State.

Tibet, which is known as an autonomous part of China, has claimed independent status because of its ruler having entered into a treaty on some occasions. This has made the status of Tibet debatable.

However, there may be cases when federated States may be empowered to enter into a treaty with foreign States. For example, federated States of the Federal Republic of Germany and Cantons of Switzerland have been empowered to enter into treaties with respect to certain categories [2]. This does not make them independent.

International Organisations

Treaty making is normally the monopoly of sovereign States. However, of late even international organisations have been endowed with international personality and, therefore, with the capacity to enter into agreements. The United Nations [3] and its specialised agencies enjoy this privilege of entering into treaties for effective exercise of their functions. For example, there is Headquarters Agreement between the United Nations and the Government of the United States of America. Article 43 of the Charter authorises the United Nations to negotiate with States in respect of their commitment of military contingents required under Chapter VII. Similarly, UNESCO, WHO, ILO, World Bank have the right to enter into treaties for effective discharge of their functions.

Procedure for Entering into Treaty

Treaty is concluded through negotiations. Negotiations may take place either between plenipotentiaries or between Heads of States or Governments or between Foreign Ministers. No letter of authorisation is necessary in case of the Head of State, Head of Government or Foreign Minister. They have the inherent right of negotiation and conclusion of agreement by virtue of their office [4]. In case of other representatives, letter of authority is required. Such letter of authority is called "full powers".

After each representative's authority is scrutinised, negotiations take place and agreement concluded. There is no particular form of reaching an agreement. The agreement may be signed or initialled. Both forms are valid so long as there is clear intention of parties to conclude the agreement either through signature or initialling. Sometimes, initialling may only be a prelude to signature. But this is not necessarily so. It entirely depends upon the intention of parties. The Polish-German Treaty normalising relations between the two countries, after a lapse of a quarter century, was initialled by plenipotentiaries on 18th November, 1970. Similarly, an agreement between the two Germanys was initialled on 8th November, 1972 [5]. Earlier, the agreement of 27th April, 1914 fixing the boundary between India and China was only initialled by the plenipotentiaries of Great Britain, Tibet and China. The then British diplomat attached to China had informed the Chinese Government that Britain considered the treaty as binding [6]. In 1923, the Hungarian delegate had initialled the statement of Conference with Romania, called by the League of Nations for settlement of the land nationalisation dispute. It was considered as a breach of faith when the Hungarians disavowed it [7]. However, O'Connel is of the opinion that initialling "is merely an indication of approval of the text for subsequent signature" [8]. This is only a half truth.

There are three functions of initialling. Rectification of mistake may just be initialled. It may be an approval of text by one of the members of the delegation for purposes of subsequent signature by the plenipotentiary or leader of the delegation. Initialling may be a substitute for signature. O'Connel refers to only one function of initialling. As a matter of fact, it has been found that many a time, the President, Prime Minister or Foreign Minister only initials with a full sense of committing his country [9]. This is what happened when the German-Polish Agreement and two German Agreements were only initialled. The intention of parties is the main determining factor whether initialling has been used as a substitute for a signature or for any other purpose [10].

Ultra vires signature

Question of *ultra vires* signature may arise in two situations. In one case, there may be want of authority on the part of the signing delegate or lack of competence on the part of the authorising agency. Secondly, there may be an excessive exercise of authority by plenipotentiary.

So far as the first situation is concerned, nowadays credentials or "full powers" are scrutinised by the Credentials Committee before negotiations start, particularly in multipartite diplomatic conferences. Therefore, there is less chance of occurrence of such a situation. Nevertheless, instances have occurred when there has been want of authority. Thus in 1908, the United States Minister to Romania signed a Convention without having the authority to do so [18]. In 1951, a convention was signed at Stressa by a delegate on behalf of both Norway and Sweden while he had no authority in respect of Sweden [12]. In one instance recently, a person participated in a diplomatic conference on behalf of the State of Ghana without having any such authority. But occurrence of such events is not a common practice.

Instances of excessive exercise of powers would not be lacking. Such instances may broadly be divided into two categories. One category of treaties involving excessive exercise of authority by the plenipotentiary may require ratification. The other category of such treaty may not require ratification and may be valid from the date of signature. The first situation does not present much difficulty. Excessive use of authority may be rectified at the time of ratification by either nonratification or ratification with reservation or by simple ratification.

But treaty not requiring ratification does present some difficulty in such a situation. Treaty concluded by an authorised representative will be binding his State even if there has been excessive exercise of authority. This is clear from the wording of Article 47 of the Vienna Convention which says:

> "If the authority of a representative to express the consent of a State to be bound by a particular treaty has been made subject to a specific restriction, his omission to observe that restriction may not be invoked as invalidating the consent expressed by him unless the restriction was notified to the other negotiating States prior to his expressing such consent."

This would mean that unless the restriction so imposed forms part of the "full powers" granted to him or there is collusion between the negotiating representatives, the consent given by the authorised agent will bind his State even if he has transgressed his authority.

Ratification

McNair defines ratification as an "act of appropriate organ of the State which signifies willingness of a State to be bound by a treaty" [13]. Ratification is an act of approval of treaty by a State whose agent has earlier concluded the same. Ratification may be made even in respect of such treaties which have been unauthorisedly signed or signed in excess of power of the representative. Ratification makes the treaty binding on the ratifying State unless it is a multilateral treaty in which case it becomes binding only when it has been ratified by a requisite number of States under the treaty.

Normally there is no time limit fixed for ratification. But if it is bilateral or tripartite, it is expected that an early ratification will be made. In case of multilateral treaties, however, ratification may take years.

Today, ratification occupies an important position in the realm of law of treaties. Previously, signature was more important than ratification which was just an obligatory formality. Since the late eighteenth century, there has been swing from the importance of signature to that of ratification. Nowadays, a State is not bound to ratify a treaty which has been signed by its duly authorised agent. It is entirely within the discretion of a State to ratify or refuse ratification. Almost all treaties require ratification unless provided otherwise in the treaty. In some cases, full powers provide that the authorised agent does not have power to bind his State without ratification by the latter. Article 14 (1) of the Convention provides as under:

> "The consent of a State to be bound by treaty is expressed by ratification when:
> (a) the treaty provides for such consent to be expressed by ratification;
> (b) it is otherwise established that the negotiating States were agreed that ratification should be required;
> (c) the representative of the State has signed the treaty subject to ratification; or
> (d) the intention of the State to sign the treaty subject to ratification appears from the full powers of its representatives or was expressed during the negotiation."

Ratification is a process which gives time to State functionaries to think over the pros and cons of the effect of treaty on the country. The Government also uses this period to gauge the reaction of political leaders and public opinion on the treaty. The Government may itself have second thoughts on its own or due to reaction of public opinion. The treaty is thus ratified or not, depending upon the rethinking in the Government in the light of public and political reaction. Public reaction may not always be favourable and ratification may be done despite adverse reaction just as it happened in the case of transfer of the islet of Kachhativu by the Government of India to Sri Lanka in 1974.

Procedure of ratification varies from State to State, depending upon constitutional provisions and practices. In the United States of America, a treaty must be ratified by two-third majority in the Senate. In the United Kingdom, ratification is done by the Crown on the advice of the minister concerned. In India, the President ratifies the treaty on the advice of the Central Cabinet.

Legal Nature of Treaties not yet Ratified

Treaty without ratification has no legal validity. Lord Stowell had rightly observed in the Eliza Ann Case in 1813 that treaty "is incomplete till it has been reciprocally ratified" [14]. In the case of Armstrong versus Bidwell, the American Judge Ray said, "Until the ratifications were exchanged, it was competent for either power, or both, to recede and rescind its action." [15]

The Permanent Court of International Justice had the occasion to consider the legal effect of an unratified treaty in the cases of Certain German Interests in the Polish Upper Silesia and Jurisdiction of Oder Commission. In the former case, it did not consider disposal of property between the date of signature and ratification as breach of good faith [16]. In the latter case, it considered the Convention as valid only when it is ratified [17].

However, it would be wrong to say that an unratified treaty is just a scrap of paper; far from it. It is an agreement which the parties have solemnly signed subject to ratification. Therefore, in between the period of signature and ratification, the signatory States should not do anything contrary to provisions of the treaty. In the Iloila Claims case, it was held that a territory once ceded under a treaty cannot be ceded again while the earlier treaty was pending for ratification [18]. This was also recognised in the case of Certain German Interests in Polish Upper Silesia [19]. Article 18 of the Convention reinforces this stand when it says:

> "A State is obliged to refrain from acts which would defeat the object and purpose of a treaty when:
> (a) it has signed the treaty or has exchanged instruments constituting the treaty subject to ratification, acceptance or approval, until it shall have made its intention clear not to become party to the treaty; or
> (b) it has expressed it consent to be bound by the treaty, pending the entry into force of the treaty and provided that such entry into force is not unduly delayed."

In some cases, a treaty may itself enjoin upon parties not to do anything during pendency of ratification which may jeopardise the interests of parties after ratification.

Retroactivity of Ratified Treaties

Does the treaty, when ratified, date back to the time of signature? Previously, private law analogy was applied to treaties with the result that the ratified treaty was to be effective from the date of signature. The private law maxim—*ratihabitio ratrotrabitur ad initium*—was also applicable to the law of treaties [20]. The reason was that ratification was a formality then. With the change of emphasis on ratification instead of on signature, treaties also lost retroactivity despite ratification.

In the nineteenth century, France pursued the path of non-retroactivity, while the United States of America and Great Britain subscribed to the theory of retroactivity. As late as 1939, Lord Wright said: "a treaty is concluded as soon as the mutual consent is manifest from acts of duly authorised representatives, although its binding force is, as a rule, suspended till ratification is given" [21]. In an American case, the District Court of Alaska held that the Soviet Union could not grant title to land between the date of signature of Alaska Cession Treaty and its ratification [22]. Surprisingly, the United States disclaimed responsibility for disturbances in the Philippines and the consequent loss of British property despite the fact that things happened during the interval between signature and ratification of the Treaty of Paris, 1898 [23].

In Civil Law countries, no question of retroactivity arises because treaties become valid there from the date of internal act of promulgation [24]. Parties are, of course, at liberty to give retrospective effect to their agreement after ratification.

Accession and Adhesion

Accession is an act of acceptance of a treaty as binding on it by a State which had not signed the treaty earlier. Accession, therefore, has the combined function of signature and ratification. The only difference between ratification and accession is that while the signing State can ratify the treaty, accession is done by a State which has not signed the treaty at the time of its conclusion.

Accession is a process by which the non-signing and non-participating State may be allowed to be party to the treaty. There was some controversy regarding timing of accession which previously could only be done after the treaty had come into effect. However, the trend has changed. A State may ratify or accede to the treaty depending upon whether it has signed or not signed the treaty. Many treaties provide that a treaty shall come into effect after so many ratifications or accessions. This equates ratification with accession. Article XIII of the Genocide Convention, 1948 provided that it shall come into effect after twenty ratifications or accessions. In other cases, some resolutions of the General Assembly have been turned into Conventions by accession only. For example, the General Act of 1928 for the Pacific Settlement of International Disputes, an Assembly resolution of the League of Nations, came into effect by accession only. So also the Convention on Privileges and Immunities of the U.N. which came into force by resolution of the General Assembly in 1946 through accession only.

All treaties are not open for accession. Only multilateral treaties having provision for accession can be acceded to. The treaty may provide as to which category of States are eligible for accession. Accession cannot be made without consent of parties or signatories to the treaty.

Instrument of Accession, like ratification, is to be filed with the depository designated in the treaty. The same has to be communicated to the parties to the treaty. Once the accession has been validly done, the acceding State is at par with the ratifying State. There is no difference in rights and duties of the ratifying and acceding State.

Reservations

Article 2-1 (d) defines reservation as a "unilateral statement made by a State, when signing, ratifying, accepting, approving or acceding to a treaty, whereby it purports to exclude or to modify the legal effect of certain provisions of the treaty in their application to that State."

Reservation is an acceptance of a treaty subject to certain conditions or assumed form of interpretation. A State may accept a treaty as a whole or in part depending upon whether it has ratified the treaty without or with reservations.

In case of a bilateral treaty, reservation amounts to a new proposal which must be accepted by the other State before the treaty comes into effect. In case of multilateral treaty, however, any reservation would not affect the effectivity of the treaty but the treaty shall be applicable to the State concerned subject to reservations made by it. In effect it would mean that other States, party to the treaty, should accept such reservations expressly or tacitly.

Article 19 permits reservations unless they are specifically prohibited or they are incompatible with the object of the treaty or are not from amongst the permissible reservations. Prior to 1951, any such reservation was to be acceptable to other parties. But when the Soviet Union ratified the Genocide Convention of 1948, it made a number of reservations which were not acceptable to others. When the matter was referred to the International Court of Justice for Advisory opinion, the Court, by its majority, advised that reservations so made may not be acceptable to other States [25]. The sum total of the reservations will be that for the State making reservations, only the accepted portion of the treaty will be binding on it so long as the reservations are compatible with the object of the treaty.

Western opinion was in favour of integrity of a treaty while the Latin American countries, the Socialist block and the newly independent States were in favour of flexibility, permiting reservations which may not be acceptable to some States party to the treaty, provided the reservations were compatible with the object and purposes of the treaty.

Article 20 deals with the acceptance of or objection to reservations made. It may be summarised as under:

1. No acceptance is required to a reservation authorised by the treaty itself;

2. When the parties are limited and it is intended that the treaty should be applicable in its entirety acceptance of all other States is essential;

3. When a treaty is a constituent instrument of an international organisation, reservation requires the acceptance of the competent organ of the organisation;

4. Apart from above cases:

(a) If a State accepts the reservation by State, both the States become party to the treaty in relation to each other;

(b) Even if the State objects to the reservation by another State, this does not prevent the treaty from coming into force in relation to each other unless the objecting State intends otherwise and it has made its intention clear;

(c) Acceptance of treaty with reservation does not become effective unless at least one State has accepted the reservation.

5. State must signify its objection to reservation within 12 months from date of notification of reservation or by a date when it has expressed its consent to be bound, whichever is later. If no such objection is made, it will be presumed to have been accepted.

Commencement of the Treaty

In case of a bilateral treaty, it becomes effective when both the parties have exchanged their documents of ratification. In some cases, States may waive the process of ratification in which case, a treaty becomes effective immediately after it has been signed. However, any waiver of the process of ratification should be specific and unequivocal. In some cases, despite ratification, a treaty may be effective from a particular date given in the treaty. An agreement regarding resumption of air and rail traffic between Pakistan and India required the implementation between 17th and 24th July, 1976.

In case of a multilateral treaty, it becomes effective from the date when the prescribed number of ratifications are deposited unless it is intended to make the treaty effective after a lapse of some period from the date of last required ratification. In some treaties, it is required that a treaty will come into effect one year after a prescribed number of ratifications are deposited.

Basis of Validity of Treaty

Pucta Sunt Servanda is the basis of validity of treaty, and indeed of international law. This has been sanctified by Article 26 which says: "Every treaty in force is binding upon the parties and must be performed by them in good faith." In international law, there is no agency to enforce the obligation. It is left to the good faith of the States to carry out their mutual obligations. Treaties involve some rights and duties. The contracting parties must carry out their duties while insisting on the enjoyment of their rights. If the parties become conscious of their rights only without corresponding consciousness of their obligations, the whole fabric of a treaty as a source of law will collapse. States, therefore, must fulfil their part of an obligation in the given treaty. This is one of the principles of the United N itions as given in Article 2 Clause 2 of the Charter.

Treaty and Third States

Normally, treaties bind the contracting parties only. No State is bound by a treaty to which it is not a party. Article 34 states that treaty "does not create either obligations or rights for a third State without its consent." Article 35 says that if an obligation is imposed on a third State by a treaty, the third State may accept the obligation in writing However, rights may be given to a third State and these rights may be valid.

Article 2 Clause 6 of the U.N. Charter states that "Organisation shall ensure that States which are not members of the United Nations act in accordance with these principles so far as may be necessary for the maintenance of international peace and security." How far the principle enunciated by the U.N. Charter is binding upon third States is questionable. It is possible, though, that the United Nations may take an enforcing action against a non-member State if it threatens or causes breach of international peace and security. This is what the United Nations did in 1950 when it took action against the invasion of South Korea by North Korean forces. However, this is an incident which may not be considered as precedent for creating obligations on a State which is not party to a treaty. No State can be bound by a treaty to which it has not consented, unless it reflects customary international law.

Invalidity of Treaty

Treaty may be invalidated by a number of situations which are given below:

(1) *Lack of authority of the representative*

The representative of a given country which is supposed to be party to the treaty may not have authority to bind his State.

It may also happen that while the representative was a plenipotentiary, restrictions had been imposed on his authority or extent of authority and the representative did not observe those restrictions or exceeded his authority. However, if the full powers did not indicate restrictions which could be known to representatives of other States, the State cannot invoke restricted authority for invalidating the treaty. Article 47 says that the treaty may be invalidated if there were specific restrictions on the authority of the representative given in his "full powers."

(2) *Error*

Under Article 48, a State may invoke "error" for invalidating a treaty if it concerned a fact or situation which the State assumed as existing while it was not, provided such fact or situation was an essential basis for its consent. However, if the State was negligent in its own conduct or if the circumstances were such as to put that State on notice of a possible error, the State cannot plead error to invalidate an otherwise valid treaty. An error as to wording only does not invalidate the treaty.

(3) *Fraud*

If one State has played fraud on another State and this has induced the latter State to enter into a treaty, the treaty becomes invalid under Article 49.

(4) *Corruption of the representative*

If the representative's consent has been obtained through corrupting him, the treaty will be considered as invalid under Article 50.

(5) *Coercion*

If the representative has been coerced, the treaty is invalid under Article 51.

If the State has been threatened with use of force in contravention of principles of international law as embodied in the U.N. Charter, the treaty will be invalid under Article 52.

(6) *Jus cogens* [26]

The treaty will be considered as invalid if it is in contravention of peremptory norm of international law.

This new principle of *Jus cogens* has been introduced for the first time in the law of treaties. Article 53 says that *Jus cogens* is a norm which has been accepted and recognised by the international community and from which no derogation is permitted. While Article 53 deals with the existing peremptory norm which makes the treaty invalid if it contravenes the *Jus cogens*, Article 64 states that the existing treaty will be invalid if it contravenes a peremptory norm which has just emerged.

This clause has been the most controversial clause. France voted against the adoption of this clause at the Vienna Conference in 1969. Others who were enthusiastic about the introduction of this new clause were not sure about its scope and content. Anzilotti was the first exponent of this doctrine in the early twentieth century.

While there may be near unanimity that there are some basic principles of international law which cannot be fiddled with by even multilateral treaty, no State can say it for sure as to what these norms are [27]. For some sovereignty may be the *Jus cogens*; for others, non-intervention may be the *Jus cogens*. For developing nations, unequal treaty is *Jus cogens*. Non-use of force may be *Jus cogens* for many but not for those communities which are striving for independence. For some, economic exploitation by developed nations may be against *jus cogens.* For developed nations, price rise of petroleum products may be against *jus cogens.* So no one is sure as to what it exactly means; nor is there any centralised agency which can adjudicate between conflicting claims regarding *jus cogens.*

In the circumstances, it is difficult to say with absolute certainty as to the content of *jus cogens.* Nevertheless, it may be safe to say that principles of the U.N. Charter, as are given in Article 2, could be considered as *jus cogens.* So also the principles enunciated in the General Assembly's Resolution 2625 (XXV) of 1970 on Principles Governing Friendly Relations Among Nations. So also Ban on Genocide and Racial Discrimination; Self Determination and Sovereignty over Natural Resources could also be now categorised as *jus cogens.*

Termination of Treaty

A treaty may come to an end in a number of ways; some are as follows:

(1) *Fulfilment of object*

A treaty comes to an end when its object has been attained and there is nothing more to be done with regard to it.

(2) *Lapse of time*

Treaty may be valid for a number of years. It will, therefore, cease to be effective if the period stipulated in the treaty has expired.

(3) *By agreement*

Treaty may be terminated by mutual agreement of the contracting parties. Since treaty is the product of mutual consent, it is natural that the treaty may also be terminated by mutual consent.

(4) *By denunciation*

Treaty may be terminated by denunciation of treaty by the contracting State. Denunciation may be in accordance with the provision of the treaty or inherent right of the State to withdraw its consent. Article 56 says that when a treaty has no provision for denunciation or withdrawal, it cannot be denounced unless the parties intended to admit the possibility of denunciation or withdrawal or it is implied from the nature of the treaty. However, it may be submitted that since consent in the basis of a treaty, a State has the sovereign right to withdraw its consent subject to the principle of *Pucta Sunt Servanda.* Provision or no provision, a State has an inherent right to withdraw from the treaty. No treaty is permanent.

(5) *By novation*

An earlier treaty may be considered as terminated if a new treaty has been concluded superseding the earlier treaty. This is the basic contractual rule and is given in Article 59.

(6) *Material breach*

Treaty may be terminated by the contracting State if there is material breach of the treaty by the other contracting State. This is another basic contractual rule given in Article 60.

However, there may be difference of opinion as to what is material breach. Material breach should be in respect of essential part of the treaty. In that case, the other State may terminate the treaty as well as ask for compensation for material breach of the treaty.

(7) *Supervening impossibility*

The contracting State may invoke supervening impossibility as reason for terminating the treaty. This may happen when the essential part to be executed has ceased to exist or has been destroyed. For example, if Pakistan had given concessionary contracts in respect of erstwhile East Pakistan (now Bangla Desh), such a contract will be deemed to have been terminated because Pakistan has no more domain over that part.

Supervening impossibility is a common factor for terminating agreements in municipal as well as international law. Section 39 of the Indian Contract Act is identical with Article 61 of the Vienna Convention. However, impossibility should not be the act of the party taking benefit of it.

(8) *Fundamental change of circumstances* (*rebus sic stantibus*)

A treaty may be terminated if there is fundamental change of circumstances with the result that either execution of the treaty becomes too onerous or it would affect the pleading State basically if it were to carry out the treaty obligations. This principle is called *Rebus sic stantibus*. Article 62 which deals with this principle states as under:

> "1. A fundamental change of circumstances which has occurred with regard to those existing at the time of the conclusion of a treaty, and which was not foreseen by the parties, may not be invoked as a ground for terminating or withdrawing from the treaty unless:
> (a) the existence of those circumstances constituted an essential basis of the consent of the parties to be bound by the treaty; and
> (b) the effect of the change is radically to transform the extent of obligations still to be performed under the treaty.
>
> 2. A fundamental change of circumstances may not be invoked as a ground for terminating or withdrawing from a treaty,
> (a) if the treaty establishes a boundary; or
> (b) if the fundamental change is the the result of a breach by the party invoking it either of an obligation under the treaty or of any other international obligation owed to any other party to the treaty."

The principle of *rebus sic stantibus* is recognised by jurists and courts alike. Now it has been legislated. Municipal law also recognises this principles which one can find in frustration of contract or Section 56 of the Indian Contract Act.

However, there is controversy as to what would constitute fundamental change of circumstances and whether it should depend upon the party seeking it or objectively. The Permanent Court of International Justice recognised the principle in Free Zones Case but did not go into the situations which would justify invoking of this principle [28].

There is also an opinion that a State seeking termination of treaty cannot invoke it unilaterally. It can plead the doctrine but can terminate the treaty only by mutual agreement in the sense that other parties should be satisfied about the bonafides of the State pleading the doctrine. Thus when Russia denounced the Treaty of Paris, 1856, it was argued by other powers in 1870 that while Russia could invoke the doctrine, it could not unilaterally revoke the treaty. In another example, when Turkey sought to terminate the Treaty of Lausanne, 1923 relating to the Strait of Dardanelles and Bosphorous in view of the changed political situation in Europe, a conference was held in Montreux in 1936 where the earlier treaty was terminated and another adopted. This procedure may be possible in the case of a multilateral treaty but it may not operate well in cases of bilateral treaties.

India could invoke this doctrine regarding its international commitments in respect of Kashmir on the ground of changed circumstances, like long lapse of time, various general elections resulting in emergence of promerger governments and insistent violation of its commitments by Pakistan.

Sometimes it is said that *Pucta sunt servanda* and *Rebus sic stantibus* stand opposed to each other. This is a wrong misconception. Both are supplementary to each other. *Pacta sunt servanda* says that treaties should be observed in good faith. *Rebus sic stantibus* says that a State may withdraw from treaty if there is a vital change of circumstances. Read together, it could mean that normally, treaties should be acted upon unless there is a fundamental change of circumstances in which case the treaty may be denounced. Therefore, there is no conflict between them. They are in fact complimentary to each other.

War

War terminates some of the treaties, particularly bilateral treaties, between the warring States. In the case of Le Louis [29], the Judge had remarked: "Treaties are perishable things, and their obligations are dissipated at the first hostility." But that is an old view. All treaties do not come to an end with the commencement of hostility. The effect of war on treaties was best explained by Justice Cardozo when he said:

> "International law today does not preserve treaties or annul them regardless of the effects produced. It deals with such problems pragmatically, preserving or annulling them as the necessities of war exact. Provisions compatiable with a state of hostilities unless expressly terminated, will be enforced and, those incompatible rejected." [30]

From this, it can well be inferred that all treaties do not come to an end. Treaties which are compatible with a state of war continue to be effective. Treaties which are incompatible with a state of war are suspended or terminated depending upon the nature of treaty. Some rules may follow:

(1) Bilateral treaties between belligerents presupposing normal relations come to an end.

(2) Bilateral treaties which have been executed and are of a permanent nature in the form of boundary fixation continue to be effective, despite war.

(3) Multilateral treaties to which both the warring nations are parties may continue to be effective if the given treaty is compatible with the state of war.

(4) General law-making treaties continue to be effective.

(5) Treaties which deal with or regulate war become operative with the commencement of hostilities.

(6) Some multilateral treaties which are incompatible with the state of war may be suspended or terminated depending upon nature of the treaty.

Treaty Interpretation [31]

While a treaty has been concluded and has come into force, it may still face some problems in the domain of its interpretation. Since there is no authentic mode or agency of interpretation, parties try to interpret each treaty according to its convenience, wherever possible. This causes disputes and difficulties in the implementation of the treaty.

There are said to be three schools of interpretation—textual, intentions or subjective and teleological. Their import is discussed below.

(1) *Textual*

Protagonists of this school say that a treaty should be interpreted according to the natural and ordinary meaning of the text of the treaty. As far as possible, they try to avoid to know the intentions of treaty makers or objects or purposes of the treaty. They insist on contextual interpretation.

(2) *Intentions or subjective*

Exponents of this school state that any interpretation of a treaty will be incomplete without knowing the intentions of the treaty makers. According to them, the text of the treaty cannot be isolated from the intentions of the parties. Therefore, a treaty must be interpreted by knowing the intentions of the parties. For this, reference to *travaux preparationes* (preparatory work) is necessary. *Travaux preparationes* means that notice should be taken of debates, discussions and correspondence which have preceded the conclusion of the treaty. These may be necessary to discover the intentions of the party.

(3) *Teleological*

Teleological school insists that a treaty can best be interpreted by knowing the objects and purposes of the treaty. It is said by this school that every treaty is concluded for a definite purpose. It is, therefore, the duty of the interpretors to interpret the treaty in the context of purposes and objects of the treaty.

No one theory can be said to be self-contained. All these three theories have some advantages and some disadvantages. None of them is exclusive, rather, they could be complimentary to each other. The Vienna Convention prefers the combination of textual and teleogical schools when it provides a general rule of interpretation in its Article 31 which reads as follows:

(1) A treaty shall be interpreted in good faith in accordance with the ordinary meaning to be given to the term of the treaty in their context and the light of its object and purpose.

(2) The context for the purpose of the interpretation of treaty shall comprise, in addition to the text, including its preamble and annexe :
  (a) any agreement relating to the treaty which was made between parties in connection with the conclusion of the treaty;
  (b) any instrument which was made by one or more parties in connection with the conclusion of the treaty and accepted by the other parties as an instrument related to the treaty.

(3) There shall be taken into account, together with the context:
  (a) any subsequent agreement between the parties regarding the interpretation of the treaty or the application of its provisions;
  (b) any subsequent practice in the application of the treaty which establishes the agreement of the parties regarding its interpretation;
  (c) any relevant rules of international law applicable in the relations between the parties.

(4) A special meaning shall be given to a term if it is established that the parties so intended.

Recourse to *travaux preparationes* could be had as a supplementary means of interpretation as given in Article 32. It runs as under:

"Recourse may be had to supplementary means of interpretation, including the preparatory work of the treaty and circumstances of its conclusion, in order to confirm the meaning resulting from the application of Article 31, or to determine the meaning when the interpretation according to Article 31:
(a) leaves the meaning ambiguous or obscure; or
(b) leads to a result which is manifestly absurd or unreasonable."

This would mean that the main plank of interpretation is textual. But one may take the aid of preparatory work and intentions of the parties in order to confirm the meaning as drawn Article 31 or determine the meaning when its ordinary meaning is ambiguous or obscure and looks absurd or unreasonable. International Court of Justice also favours textual form of interpretation. At the Vienna Diplomatic Conference, the United States wanted the merger of two Articles (31 and 32) so as to avoid primary and supplementary means of interpretation. While it did not receive much support, it was desired that there should be no rigidity in demarcating primary and supplementary rules of interpretation and both should work together.

NOTES

1. Also see Sorenson, Max, Manual of International Law, p. 181.
2. Ibid.
3. Parry Clive, The Treaty-Making Power of the United Nations, (1949) 26 B.Y.I.L. 108.
4. Article 7 (2) of the Vienna Convention, 1969.
5. German News (India) December 1, 1970 and November 15, 1972 respectively.
6. Bell, Tibet: Past and Present (1924) p. 156.
7. Mervyn Jones, Full Powers and Ratification (1946), p. 36.
8. D P. O'Connel International Law (1965), vol. 1, p. 230.
9. 1967 A.J.I.L. 305.
10. Article 12-2 (a) says: "the initialling of a text constitutes a signature when it is established that the negotiating states so agreed."
11. Hackworth, Digest of International Law, vol. IV, p. 467.
12. 1967 A.J.I.L. 300.
13. McNair, Law of Treaties (1961) 129.
14. As reported by McNair, op. cit., 131.
15. (1903) 124 Fed 690 at p. 692
16. (1926) Series A No. 7, p. 39.
17. (1929) Series A No. 23, p. 20.
18. As cited by O'Connel, op. cit., vol. 1, p. 244.

19. (1926) Series A No. 7, p. 30.
20. D.P. O'Connel, op. cit., p. 246.
21. Phillipson vs Imperial Airways, 1939 A.C. 332.
22. United State vs City of Kadiak, 1955 I.L.R. 562.
23. The Iloilo Claims—Great Britain vs United States, U.N. Reports vol. VI p. 158 (1925).
24. D.P. O'Connel, op. cit., 249.
25. Advisory Opinion on the Reservation to the Genocide Convention Case, 1951, I.C.J. Report 51.
26. R.P. Dhokalia, Problems Relating to Jus Cogens in the Law of Treaties, as published in S.K. Agrawala's Essays in the Law of Treaties, 149-77.
27. Ibid, p. 164-65.
28. (1932) P.C.I.J. Series A/B No. 46 pp. 156-58.
29. (1817) 2. Dod. 210, 258.
30. Techt vs Hughes, (1920) 229 N.Y. 222.
31. For interpretation of treaties, see learned articles by Dharma Pratap. Schwarzenberger and Falk, in Agrawala, op. cit., 55-139.

CHAPTER 19

SELF-PRESERVATION

As has been said earlier, a State has two fundamental rights—sovereignty and self-preservation. While sovereignty and its various aspects have been discussed in preceding chapters, an attempt is being made here to discuss the right of self-preservation in international law.

Concept of Self-preservation

Every State has an inherent right to preserve its identity and entity. The U.N. Charter puts a ban on violation of a State's territorial integrity and political sovereignty. It is in exercise of self-preservation that it has been stated under Article 51 of the Charter that every State has an inherent right of self-defence. It is on this account that the phrases, self-preservation and self-defence are commonly used to mean the same thing. Right of angary exercised by warring nations is in exercise of the right of self-preservation.

Right of self-preservation is a natural right in the same way a person has a right of existence. Man has right of private defence which can be adjudicated upon. However, what is permissible under the right of self-preservation is highly debatable and controversial. National publicists have tried to justify the actions of their governments on the pretext of self-preservation. Great Britain tried to justify its action of shelling Copenhagen and seizing the Danish Fleet in 1807 on the ground of self-preservation in the sense that it did not want the fleet to fall in the hands of France and thus augment its gun power. Similarly, it justified its action in the Caroline incident in 1837 when it violated from Canada the United States territory and destroyed the "Caroline" vessel which was suspected of supplying arms etc. to Canadian insurgents. The U.S. authorities, while protesting against the violation of American territory, had conceded the right of self-preservation if it was "instant, overwhelming, leaving no choice of means and no moment for deliberations." Similarly, while Germany justified its occupation of Luxembourg and Belgium—two neutralised States in 1914—in order to forestall similar moves by France, it was criticised by the allied powers as a violation. The drama was repeated by Germany in 1940 when it occupied Norway, Belgium, Holland and Luxembourg. The United Kingdom occupied Iceland as a countermeasure. Earlier, the Soviet Union had occupied Finland in 1939 on the pretext of self-preservation. While the German action was condemned by the allied powers, they tried to justify the Russo-British occupation of Iran in 1941. The United Kingdom repeated its Danish fleet performance in Oran in 1940 when it destroyed the French fleet there. It justified the action on the ground that it feared that after occupation of France by Germany, the French fleet may fall in the hands of Germany. The United States sought to justify its actions of transferring destroyers to Great Britain in 1940 and the Land-lease Act of 1941 on the ground of right of self-preservation. China intervened in the Korean war in 1950 on the ground that the crossing of 38th parallel by the U.N. Force would threaten its security. Cuban quarantine by the United States in 1962 was sought to be justified on grounds of self-preservation and Monroe Doctrine.

Since there is no centralised adjudicating body, all these above instances of self-preservation have been bones of contention between the warring nations. In this writer's view, it is difficult to justify the action of one State while condemning the actions of another State, particularly when the actions taken by the contenders are identical, if not similar.

The important question that may be posed is whether self-preservation could be an anticipatory action or it should wait until something has been done against the territorial integrity of the State. It is difficult to answer the question straightaway. No uniform or single reply would suit all the situations. It is possible that an unscrupulous State may take advantage of the right of self-preservation and disturb the territorial integrity of another State as has been noticed above.

Thus, although the right of self-preservation has been recognised, its scope has remained undefined. In most cases, the principle has been abused under false pretexts. The question is as to how to channelise the principle so that it may be invoked for the purpose for which it is meant. The principle is not for self-aggrandisement. It is for self-protection. The tragedy occurs when the right of self-preservation becomes a casualty at the altar of self-aggrandisement.

CHAPTER 20

STATE RESPONSIBILITY

Although a State is sovereign, it is not absolved of all responsibility. By dint of sheer necessity for world order and through the process of auto-limitation, a State is responsible for some of its acts and omissions. No individual State can enjoy its rights without recognising and respecting the rights of other States. This brings in the concept of State responsibility in the realm of international law. However, there are no fixed rules regarding State responsibility which are in the process of formulation. International Law Commision is seized of the problem of determining it. Nevertheless, a State may incur liability essentially under two heads: tortious or contractual. Besides, it may be responsible for quasi-criminal acts.

Tortious Liability

It may arise out of any international wrong or negligent act or omission on the part of a State agency towards foreigners within a State's jurisdiction or foreign territory. This is also called delictual liability. It may occur in a number of situations.

(*a*) *Space exploration*

A satellite-launching State would incur liability for any damage caused by its satellite to any object in a foreign territory. This was initially advocated by this writer way back in 1962 [1]. Subsequently, it was brought in a treaty form through a U.N. General Assembly Resolution [2]. Launching State incurs absolute liability in case of damage caused by satellites in view of its dangerous nature. No intention or negligence on part of the launching State is required.

(*b*) *Nuclear exploration*

State should be responsible for whatever damage is caused by nuclear exploration. It is immaterial whether all necessary precautions have been taken and yet damage caused. Nuclear activity is a highly hazardous activity and it should be accompanied by absolute liability. So long as cause and effect are established, there should be no difficulty in fixing the responsibility on the nuclear exploring State. Equally, it is irrelevant whether the victim is human, living resources of the sea, property or pollution of atmosphere.

There can be accidental or experimental fall out which may or may not cause damage. But once the link is established, the liability ensues. There have been some instances of nuclear guided satellites having disintegrated while entering atmosphere. In 1964, the radioisotope unit of U.S. transit satellite disintegrated while entering the atmosphere. In April, 1970, Apollo 13 which was jettisoned into the Pacific also contained radioisotope powered apparatus. In January, 1978, Soviet Cosmos 954 containing power plant fuelled by radioactive uranium 235, disintegrated while plunging into the atmosphere over Northern Canada. Although no damage was reported but any such incident could be catastrophic. Nevertheless, Canada claimed compensation for extricating the parts of the ill-fated sputnik from the frozen parts of North Canada [3]. The launching State should be responsible for any damage suffered and expense incurred by another State.

(*c*) *Activities transcending national borders*

A territorial State should control and regulate any activities, private or public, within its territory if the same have the potentiality of crossing national boundaries and cause damage in foreign territory. Nature of liability would depend on type of activity. If the activity is inherently dangerous, the territorial State where the activity is undertaken, may incur absolute or strict liability. If the activity is normal, the territorial State may incur simple liability, depending upon negligence or intention on the part of the wrongdoing agency. In this connection, it is difficult to agree with Eagleton when he says a State "owes at all times a duty to protect other States against injurious acts by individuals from within its jurisdiction" [4]. It is also difficult to accept what the American-Canadian Tribunal held in the Trail Smelter Arbitration case where it said that under principles of international law, "No State has the right to use or permit the use of its territory in such a manner as to cause injury by fumes in or to the territory of another or the properties or persons therein, when the case is of serious consequence" [5]. Unless an activity is inherently hazardous, a State does not incur liability for any activity which causes damage in a foreign territory provided there is no negligence nor intentional wrong on the part of individual or his State. It would become a case of *damnum sine injuria.*

Damage in Riot

A State is not normally responsible for any damage caused to a foreigner during local riots. Foreigner should take this risk while visiting any country. However, if the riot is directed against foreigners, it is the duty of the territorial State to take reasonable care to protect the foreigners from the rioting mob. In this case, if there is culpable negligence on the part of the territorial State machinery to take reasonable steps to protect the foreigners from the rioting mob, the State may be held responsible in damages for any loss of life and property of foreigners. This does not absolve the foreigner from his duty to be discreet in his behavior in a foreign territory and not do anything which may offend the sentiments of the local population. In case of his failure to do so, the foreigner may forfeit the right of being compensated for any mishap to him or his property.

A foreigner should be distinguished from foreign diplomatic mission. While the local State machinery is under an obligation to protect the life and property of diplomatic agent, both being inviolable, it is not the same kind of compulsion in respect of foreigners. A State Government would be responsible for damage to a foreign mission or injury to a diplomat at the hands of the local population even if the State was not negligent. A territorial State is equally under a duty to facilitate the smooth functioning of foreign embassies. Thus, if any one causes obstacles in the functioning of any foreign mission the same should be removed. In case of injury to a foreigner, a State would be responsible if it remained negligent and did not provide enough protection to him from local rioters.

While a State is not responsible for acts of individuals to foreigners, it is definitely responsible for any damage caused by State functionaries whether on the promptings of the higher-ups or in violation of orders to the contrary. If a territorial State deputes a sentry for protection of an embassy and he turns his gun on the diplomat, the State is liable [6]. In such a situation, it makes no difference whether the damage is caused to a foreign mission or a foreigner. The State is responsible either way.

As to what is a State functionary may sometimes be controversial. While there may be no difficulty to label formal enforcing agencies as State functionaries, the question may arise regarding para-functionaries and ruling party activists. In my opinion, they should be treated at par with State functionaries because in any case they enjoy government patronage and they cannot be separated from the government.

Killings, Maltreatment and Arrest

A State is liable for killing, maltreatment or arrest of a foreigner in the same way in which it could be liable for similar things to its own nationals. There is no extra liability of a State in the case of foreigners. Any person, including a foreigner, may bring an action for his maltreatment or wrongful arrest. Similarly, a legal representative may bring a tortious or criminal action against a State government for the death of a person. There is only one additional right in the case of a foreigner who can approach his own State to champion his cause if he is not satisfied with the decision of the judicial machinery of the territorial State. But that does not make the local State extra liable.

A local State may be responsible for any damage to a foreigner if the State has instigated such damage to him. A State is responsible for all damage prompted by it.

Civil war: Things may be different in case of civil war where the *de jure* government is not in a position to protect the foreigners. In such a case, foreigners may not visit that State for security reasons. Else they visit that State at their own risk. A foreign government may recognise the revolting group as the *de facto* government in respect of the territory occupied by it in order to ensure safety and protection of its nationals within that territory. As a matter of fact, recognition of a rebel group is partly motivated by the fact that it secures the rebel government's cooperation to protect the lives and properties of the nationals of the recognising State.

Contractual Liability

Apart from tortious liability, a State may incur contractual liability in international law. Contractual liability may be incurred by a State when it commits a breach of contract whether it be with another State or a foreign citizen. Thus, contractual responsibility arises out of a breach of treaty or contract, as the case may be.

Breach of treaty

A State may commit breach of treaty with another State. In that case, it has to make good the loss which the other State may have suffered. As it was held in the Charzow Factory case, "breach of an engagement involves an obligation to make reparation" [7]. The nature and extent of reparation for the breach of an international obligation may be determined by the International Court of Justice, some other court, arbitral tribunal or through negotiations. Breach of treaty is a very serious default on the part of a State. It shakes the confidence of nation States in the sanctity of the treaty and doctrine of *Pucta sunt servanda.* States will be ill-advised to commit breach of any treaty.

Breach of contract

A State may have entered into contracts with foreigners for a variety of purposes. A breach may be committed in respect of any of such contracts. It may occur wherever there is violation of the terms of a contract by the State machinery. However, there are some limitations on the part of an individual foreigner or foreign company to get redress for breach of contract by a State. These are discussed below.

Exhaustion of Local Remedies

Foreign national must move the local machinery for redressal of his grievances against the territorial State. Most of the States put the Calvo Clause in international contracts. This enjoins upon foreign nationals and companies to first seek local remedies within the foreign territory before approaching their respective governments for sponsoring their cases diplomatically and otherwise.

Calvo Clause is good to the extent that a foreign investor must seek local remedies for any breach of contract with a foreign State. He may seek his State's diplomatic protection only after his exhaustion of local remedies. Thus in the North American Dredging Case, it was held that as per Calvo Clause, the petitioner should have sought local remedies before invoking diplomatic protection of his State [8]. However, if the clause seeks to absolutely bar the other State from protecting its nationals' interests, the clause is not valid. No individual can bargain away the right of a State to protect the interests of its nationals diplomatically or otherwise as the case may be. Calvo Clause works as a break against precipitate action sometimes taken by big States against weak States.

The exhaustion of the local remedies doctrine means that the so-called aggrieved party should sincerely litigate within the territorial State. Mock or haphazard presentation of his claim to complete the formality will not entitle the foreign State to champion the cause of its nationals. On the contrary, any such attempt may mar his chances of getting justice even through diplomatic channels. In Ambatielo's Case, it was held by Arbitral Tribunal that the Greek company had not exhausted the local English remedies before seeking the diplomatic protection of its State [9].

In an ordinary state of affairs also, a foreign national or company must exhaust all local remedies before seeking his State's protection. It is irrespective of Calvo Clause. It would not be correct to say that exhaustion of local remedies has any exceptions as claimed by Starke [10]. Nor is it correct to say that an injured foreign national need not exhaust all local remedies. A foreign State steps in only when the local State machinery refuses to hear the grievance of the foreigner.

Minimum International Standard

Some States have injected the bogey of minimum international standards. This idea is mostly Western-oriented, particularly by big States which claim that a State must observe some minimum international standard while dealing with foreigners. Else, international responsibility will accrue. It is like calling some States as sub-civilised.

It must be made clear that there is no such thing as minimum international standard. If a State treats a foreigner at par with its nationals, it is absolved from any international liability. A foreigner cannot be given better treatment than its nationals. If an individual has chosen to go to a given country on his own free will he should refrain from condemning it as to have imparted him sub-standard treatment. One has yet to know of modern times where a State may be held liable for imparting sub-standard treatment to a foreigner. As a matter of fact, it was sometime back, big States claimed jurisdiction over their nationals abroad for the reason that they did not expect standard treatment on the part of the so-called backward States. The practice has been stopped in the post-World War II era ever since the advent of the Afro-Asian States in the world community, and their rejection of the doctrine of dual sovereignty within some of their territories.

Nationalisation

A State has the sovereign right to nationalise any business within its territory whether it belongs to its own nationals or foreigners. Whatever reservations may be there earlier, there is no controversy as to that now. Surprisingly, some publicists still consider it as expropriation which is not a proper word for nationalisation. However, a State should give a fair compensation for the nationalised business. It need not be prompt, adequate and effective compensation as is claimed by the Western governments. If the State fails to give fair compensation, it incurs international liability in respect of foreign business.

There can be some dispute where a State has nationalised foreign business in violation of its undertaking that it would not nationalise a given business for a given number of years. This can give rise to an international liability unless there has been violation on the part of a foreign concern also which has prompted early nationalisation. In that case, a State does not incur any liability.

However, nationalisation in violation of a treaty obligation must be treated differently if the treaty is sought to be revoked by the nationalising State on the basis of its being inconsistent with its sovereign status or being labelled as unequal treaty. In both the cases, the nationalising state needs to give only fair compensation without incurring the extra liability for violation of treaty. Thus, when Egypt nationalised the Suez Canal in violation of the Constantinople Treaty of 1888, Egypt was only asserting its sovereignty over the Suez Zone within its territory and thus was responsible for making only fair compensation to the share holders.

Foreign Investment Disputes

Disputes could also arise between a sovereign State and foreign concerns regarding investments. In such a case, a Centre has been established under the auspices of the World Bank to deal with such cases. The Centre is called International Centre for Settlement of Investmant Disputes under the Convention on Settlement of Investment Disputes. There is also the United States guarantee for American business-making investments in approved foreign countries. Thus it works as an insurer against investment risks in developing countries.

Quasi-Criminal Acts

A State may be liable for some additional acts which may make her internationally liable. These acts may comprise crimes against peace, crimes against humanity and war crimes. The Nuremberg principles uphold State responsibility for such acts. However, the difficulty arises as to who will determine the commission of such acts. So far only defeated nations of World War II have been indicted on that account. This does not create a precedent. If it does, it is indeed a bad precedent to try only defeated nations for war crimes as if they are the only perpetrators of such crimes. International elites have to think over these problems.

Border Clashes

A State may be responsible for causing deaths in unprovoked border clashes. In such a case, the State responsible for such deaths either expresses its sorrow over the incident or makes reparation for the loss of lives, besides being sorry.

Violation of Territorial Sovereignty

A State may be made responsible for violating territorial sovereignty as the United Kingdom did in the Corfu Channel Case. In such a case, the United Kingdom should have been held responsible for violating the Alabanian territorial sovereignty. It was indeed surprising that while Albania was asked to pay damages for causing deaths, the United Kingdom was only held as having violated territorial sovereignty. International law should not allow such judicial discrimination. It may perhaps be explained that it was due to absence of Albania from the court or predominance of Western-oriented judges at that time in the International Court of Justice.

Notes

1. Hingorani, R.C., Damage by Satellite, 1962 Kansas City Law Review (Summer Issue) p. 216.
2. U.N.G.A. Resolution 2600 (XXIV) of 1969.
3. The Indian Express, 7 February, 1978.
4. Eagleton Clyde, Responsibility of States in International Law (1928) p. 80.
5. As reported in L.C. Green, International Law Through Cases (1959) pp. 786-87.
6. Youman's Case, 1925-26 A.D. 223. In this case, the Mexican Government had sent troops to protect Americans against rioting demonstrators. The contingent instead of protecting the Americans fired at them. Mexico was held liable in such a situation.
7. 1928 P.C.I.J. series A. No. 17 at p. 29.
8. 1925-26 A.D. Case No. 218.
9. 1956 International Law Reports 306.
10. Introduction to International Law (Eighth edition, 1977) p. 338.
11. As of January 1978, the Convention has been ratified by sixty-eight States.

SECTION III

RECENT TRENDS

CHAPTER 21

INDIVIDUAL, HUMAN RIGHTS AND SELF DETERMINATION

Individual

In the traditional sense, States are the only subjects of international law. Individuals have never been considered as its subjects. This does not mean that there is no role of an individual in the world community. Individuals have played an important role in international law. They are the functionaries of Statecraft. A State being an abstract body, it is represented by individuals as diplomats at world conferences. They negotiate and conclude conventions. But individuals have had no independent status in the world community. They have been known as representing a given State. This is the case whether as a diplomat or as a national.

Of course, an individual has been an object of international law. While he had some duties in international law, he did not have rights, except through the State. A State confers nationality on him. If he has committed some crime, he is liable to extradition subject to some conditions as provided by international law. Similarly, he is also liable for committing war crimes. A State wages war through him. He may commit crimes for his State but he is liable for the crimes he has committed. The plea of "respondent superior" will not be available to him except for determining quantum of sentence. He could also be punished as a pirate or terrorist.

A few rights which an individual could claim in international law are the rights of aliens in a foreign territory, right of asylum which means right to seek and enjoy asylum and as a prisoner of war. Besides, some rights may be specifically conferred upon him under a treaty. In the Danzig Railway Officials' case, the Permanent Court of International Justice held that treaty can confer specific rights on individuals. It was held in that case that Danzing Railway Officials could have direct claim against Polish Government under a treaty which transferred Danzig to Poland [1].

As an alien, individual is entitled to freedom of person. He cannot be arrested unless he has committed some crime. He is free from arbitrary arrest. He is also entitled to protection of his property which can only be taken over with some formalities. The World Bank has opened a Centre for Settlement of Investment Disputes between States and aliens. As a refugee, he cannot be turned back to his country where he fears danger to his life or persecution. Right of asylum, of course, vests in the State and not in the individual who has only the right to seek asylum and enjoy if he gets it. As a prisoner of war, he is entitled to a few basic necessities like shelter, food and some protection measures. But in all these cases when there are violations of the rights of individual, he has no remedy against the defaulting State, except through his own State.

Post-World War II period has been heralded as the enunciator of recognition of an individual's status in world community. To begin with, the U.N. Charter was sworn in the name of "peoples" of the United Nations. The Charter reaffirms faith "in the dignity and worth of the human person." One of the purposes of the United Nations, as given in Article 1 of the Charter, is to promote and encourage respect for human rights and fundamental freedoms.

All these proclamations certify that an individual's position has improved in international law. He has been an object of prevention of injustice to him. The European Convention of Human Rights even gives him the right to move the European Human Rights Commission for any injustice done to him by his State. But when some foreign State does some injustice to him, he has to channelise his complaint through his parent State. International Law does not give him *locus standii* beyond the point of recognition of his rights as a man. Nor does the future hold any better prospect for him. It may be a little crude to say that municipal law passes laws for the prevention of cruelty to animals while international law concludes some conventions for prevention of cruelty to man. Some such international conventions are discussed herewith.

Human Rights

The first document which recognised certain rights of man was the Universal Declaration of Human Rights. It was passed by the General Assembly of the United Nations at its Paris Session on

10th December, 1948. Article 3 declares that everyone has the right to life, liberty and security of person. Article 7 gives equality before the law. Article 9 prohibits arbitrary arrest, detention or exile. Article 10 allows a fair and impartial trial. Article 11 declares that no person shall be prosecuted for *ex post facto* laws. Article 12 gives him the right of privacy. Article 13 gives him the right to leave or return to his country. Article 14 gives him the right to seek and enjoy asylum. Article 15 gives him the right to nationality. No one shall be arbitrarily deprived of nationality or denied the right to change his nationality. Article 17 gives the right to property. Article 18 gives him the freedom of thought, religion and belief. Article 19 gives him the freedom of opinion and expression. Article 20 gives freedom of assembly and association. Article 21 gives right to participate in his government.

The two other important documents which recognise human rights are two covenants passed by the General Assembly in 1966. They are International Covenant on Economic, Social and Cultural Rights and International Covenant on Civil and Political Rights.

International Covenant on Economic and Social Rights ensures certain economic and social rights. Article 3 ensures equality of man and woman. Article 6 recognises the right to work. Article 8 gives the right to form trade union. Article 9 recognises the right to social security. Article 10 emphasises on the rights of family. Article 13 ensures primary education to all and makes it compulsory. It came into force from 3rd January 1976 after 35 ratifications.

International Covenant on Political and Civil Rights ensures some political and civil rights. Article 6 recognises the inherent right to life; he cannot be arbitrarily deprived thereof. Article 7 prohibits torture, cruel, inhuman or degrading treatment. Article 8 banishes slavery and forced labour. Article 9 guarantees freedom of person. Arbitrary arrests are prohibited. Article 12 gives freedom to leave or return to his country. Article 14 guarantees equality before law. Article 17 protects privacy of individual. Article 18 gives him freedom of thought, conscience and religion. Article 21 gives freedom of assembly and Article 22 gives freedom of association. Article 23 recognises family rights. It came into force from 23rd March 1976 after 35 ratifications.

There is an important International Convention on the Elimination of All Forms of Racial Discrimination which was adopted by the General Assembly in 1965 [2]. Article 2 condemns racial discrimination and High Contracting Parties undertake "not to sponsor, defend or support racial discrimination." Article 1 defines racial discrimination as "any distinction exclusion, restriction or preference based on race, colour, descent or national or ethnic origin..."

There has been Geneva Convention of 1951 on the Status of Refugees which came into force from 22nd April, 1954. It recognises some rights of refugees who were uprooted before 1st January, 1951. Article 32 enjoins upon the States not to expel refugees except on ground of national security or public order. Article 33 enjoins upon the State not to return the refugee to the frontier of territory where his life or freedom would be threatened. This refugee convention has been supplemented by Protocol recommended by the General Assembly vide its resolution 2198 (XXI) of 16 December, 1966. The Protocol became effective from 4th October, 1967. The Protocol benefits the persons who have become refugees after 1st January, 1951.

Rights of women

Even since the United Nations has been established, it has strived to better the lot of women. Traditionally, women have been confined to the kitchen and other domestic duties. The U.N. Charter promises equality of man and woman and protection of human dignity. In the second year of its functioning, 1946, it appointed a Commission on the Status of Women. The Commission has sought not only to recognise the rights of women but also to bring about a change in traditional mental attitudes which limit the exercise of such rights. Women are still the prisoners of past prejudices and there is a great difference between rhetoric and reality.

In 1948, the Universal Declaration of Human Rights was adopted by the U.N. General Assembly. Article 2 recognised the equality of sexes. In 1952, the U.N. General Assembly passed Resolution 640 (VII) of 20th December, 1952 which is now better known as the Convention on the Political Rights of Women. It came into force on 7th July, 1954. It gives the right to women to vote, contest election and hold public office.

On 29th January, 1957, the U.N. General Assembly passed another resolution 1040 (XI) which has come to be known as Convention on Nationality of Married Women. It came into effect from 11th August, 1958. Article 1 of the Convention bars automatic loss or gain of nationality by woman on marriage or dissolution of marriage. Nor can the change of nationality of her husband automatically affect her own nationality. Article 3 permits the wife to seek her husband's nationality after marriage if she so desires. The Convention seeks to dispel the traditional role of wife as a sheep which must follow the husband. It gives her an independent individuality which permits her to either retain her premarital nationality or adopt the nationality of her husband of her own free will.

There is third Convention on Consent to Marriage, Minimum Age for Marriage and Registration of Marriage. This Convention was adopted by the General Assembly in its resolution 1763 A (XVII) of 7th November, 1962 and it come into effect on 9th December, 1964. Article 1 requires consent of woman for valid marriage. Article 2 requires the State to fix the minimum age for marriage. Article 3 requires registration of all marriages. Registration of marriages is a very sound requirement in order to keep evidential value of marriage. Some men deny any earlier marriage in order to marry a second time while first marriage is subsisting and manage to evade the charge of bigamy.

In 1967, the General Assembly passed a unanimous Declaration on Elimination of Discrimination against Women. In 1972, the General Assembly commended through its resolution 3010 (XXVII) of 18th December, 1972 to celebrate 1975 as International Women's Year. Accordingly it was observed, and had three slogans—equality, development and peace.

Self-Determination

The post-United Nations era has witnessed the development of the doctrine of self-determination into a full blossom. The doctrine was first enunciated in the U.N. Charter as one of its purposes. Article 1(2) of the U.N. Charter says that one of the four purposes of the organisation is to develop friendly relations among nations based on respect for the principle of equal rights and self-determination of peoples. The same thing is reiterated in Article 55 of the Charter.

In the initial years of the functioning of the United Nations, only lip sympathy was paid to the doctrine and not much was done to promote self-determination. It was perhaps thought that it was just a hangover from the pious declarations made during World War II, particularly the Atlantic Charter of 1941. President Wilson had also raised this slogan in twenties after World War I. Nothing much came out of it. The slogan died with Wilson. It was thought that it would meet the same fate in the post-Charter era. However, it received its impetus from newly independent States, particularly from Asia and Africa, which championed the cause of self-determination.

The U.N. General Assembly passed a resolution—637 A (XII) on 16th December, 1952—in which it impressed upon member States of the United Nations to "uphold the principle of self-determination of all peoples and nations." Some colonial powers raised the bogey of Article 2(7) but it was rejected. It may not be wrong to say that Resolution 637 A transformed the principle of self-determination into a right. This was followed by reaffirmation of the doctrine in the Bandung Declaration of 1955 at the Non-Aligned Conference. In 1960 came the memorable Declaration of the General Assembly in its resolution 1514 (XV) of 14th December, 1960. Its clause 2 declared that "All peoples have the right to self determination." This resolution is also called the Declaration of Decolonisation. Indeed a historic Declaration which hastened the emergence of former colonies into sovereign independent States. A Committee of 24 was appointed to implement the above resolution.

Non-aligned nations have been very vocal in the sponsoring of right of self-determination. This has also been considered as fundamental right which has been reproduced in Article 1 of both the Covenants on Social, Civil and Political Rights as passed by the U.N. General Assembly in 1966. Article 1 declares that "All peoples have the right of self-determination."

While by now, right of self-determination has been accepted as an established principle of international law, its exact scope has remained undefined. Of course, it is now agreed that a colony has a right to be independent. The difficulty sometimes arises when a colony is called an oversea province of the metropolitan State. At other times, it is merged with the State and it is difficult to assess its exact status. For example, the status of the commonwealth of Puerto Rico has raised some eyebrows. There is also a doubt as to the status of Tibet. Similar examples can be given with respect to some other territories. Have these territories the right to independence?

It is said that only colonies have the right of self-determination. An integral part of State has no such right because it may result in secession. The United Nations is against any right to be given to a revolting part to secede from the parent State. Katanga's effort to secede from the erstwhile State, Congo—now Zaire—was resisted by the United Nations on this account. The Bangla Desh struggle was not encouraged in 1971 because then it was part of the State of Pakistan. But the Bangla Desh problem had its own peculiarities. There the majority was not allowed to rule. Besides both the wings were separated by 1200 miles which has no parallel in history. But once Bangla Desh succeeded in its independent establishment, it was accepted.

What is the right of a minority section to claim secession from the State run by majority section If the State is independent, the minority section has no right to seek secession. A majority rule is natural in Democracy. In every society, and for that reason in every State, there is bound to be a minority section. And if every minority section were to demand secession each State runs the risk of being divided into fragments. The best solution in such a situation would be that the majority section should win the confidence of the minority section; besides, the minority section may be guaranteed some rights. President Marcos of the Philippines is now following policy of winning over Muslim rebels.

Right of self-determination includes the right to freely determine its political status as well as its economic, social and cultural structure. This would mean that each nation has a sovereign right to decide for itself its political structure whether it will be a republic, parliamentary or presidential form, democratic or dictatorship, capitalist or socialist, religious or secular. It has also a right to determine its relationship with other countries. A former colony, now an independent State, may like to retain some kind of relationship with its former ruling country just as a British colony may choose to remain in Commonwealth of Nations. But there is no question of hegemony; nor the principle of limited sovereignty. Concepts of hegemony and limited sovereignty are opposed to the doctrine of self-determination and are imperialist-oriented. They cannot be justified on any account.

Right of self-determination may be extended to the right of State to exercise sovereignty over natural resources within its territory. This would include the right of State to fix the prices of commodities manufactured or tapped within its territory. No State or group of States has any right to dictate the level of price which the territorial State may charge for commodities produced by it. Apart from the rule of demand and supply, the State is free to fix prices of its commodities. Equally, other States are free to purchase their requirements from any quarter.

The right of price-fixation was heightened by the hike in petrol prices by Arab countries after the Arab-Israeli war in October 1973. There were subtle challenges to the above hike and the U.S. Secretary of State, Kissinger, threatened to take regulatory action if the Western economy was strangulated by the hike in oil prices. This bore reminiscence of the imperialist stand or gun-boat diplomacy of the war which is hardly tenable in present days.

On an individual level, individuals may exercise equally the right of self-determination. Thus every individual has the right to leave, or return to, his country under Article 13 of the Universal Declaration of Human Rights. The individual has also the right to seek and enjoy asylum under Article 14. Article 15 gives him the right to change his nationality. All these rights are reiterated in the International Covenant on Political and Civil Rights, 1966. It is given to the man to decide for himself whether to remain within the country of his birth or nationality or change the same by opting for a country of his choice. He should determine for himself as to what he wants.

Notes

1. P.C.I.J. Series B, No. 15 (1928).
2. Resolution No. 2106A (XX) of 21 December, 1965. It became effective from 4 January, 1969.

Chapter 22

TERRORISM

Terrorism, like sea piracy in old days, has become a great menace nowadays. Although, it is not absolutely new, it has recently acquired new dimensions in view of its frequency in the last few years. Killing of olympians in Germany is well known. Random shooting at Lydda airport resulting in the death of a number of innocent persons was gruesome. There was the murder of three diplomats at Saudi Embassy reception in Khartoum sometime back. Besides, there have been an number of hijackings. The Entebbe airport events in 1976 are historical in dramatics. There have been a number of hijackings from India. Two Indian airlines flights were diverted to Lahore in 1971 and 1976. While the first resulted in the burning of the aircraft, the second had a happy ending due to Pakistani cooperation. There was also the hijacking of a Lufthansa flight in 1972 when it left Delhi for Europe. It was diverted to an airport in the Middle East. In October, 1977, Japan Airlines was hijacked. It fetched the hijackers release of six terrorists and a ransom of six million dollars. Lufthansa hijacking during same month caused the death of German pilot.

These events have indeed been terrifying. Not that acts of terrorism had not occurred in the past. There have been a number of terrorist acts in the past. History of Indian struggle for independence could give a list of instances of such acts on British functionaries. King Alexander of Yugoslavia was assassinated in 1934 in France. Yugoslavia ambassador was assassinated sometime back in Stockholm. In 1970, Jordanian Prime Minister was assassinated in his Cairo hotel. A number of Indian diplomatic personnel have been subjected to acts of terrorism. The intensity and frequency of such events has worsened the situation to a saturating point.

Pained at these gruesome happenings, the U.N. Secretary General, Kurt Waldheim, remarked on 12th September, 1972 that the United Nations could not remain a "mute spectator" in the face of growing trend towards acts of terror and violence against innocent people all over the world. He, therefore, urged the inclusion of an item in the agenda for the General Assembly's twenty-seventh session in 1972.

The General Assembly was evenly divided on the issue. While the Western nations were in favour of an early action to combat terrorism, the Afro-Asian States were not in favour of a blanket ban on terrorism. These States wanted the study of the underlying causes while discussing any action on terrorism.

Terrorism depicts the deep-rooted motivation which prompts the terrorists to risk their lives. It may be a reflection of frustration and despair in the face of a determined enemy who is organised, armed and ruthless. In the process, there may be nothing left for a fragile fighter for the liberation of its country except to resort to acts of terrorism in order to keep the enemy on its toes and sometimes demoralise him also, as was done in Mozambique, Angola and South Rhodesia. No one would normally like to practice rituals in blood or live in a flurry of bullets. The cause-effect relationship in case of terrorism is like the perennial question as to which came first—the hen or the egg.

Black September, a Palestinian organisation named after King Hussain's (of Jordan) crackdown on Palestinians in September, 1970, is credited to have a special terrorist squad. Until then, and perhaps even till today, there is no central world organisation, to direct terrorist activities. The terrorist activities have been essentially localised and territorial as a reaction against colonial power or a ruthless dictator or enemy, or one may say as a reprisal against State terrorism.

However, Black September activities have added a new dimension to terrorist activities in the world. For the first time, there is something international about terrorism. Intelligence reports reveal informal contacts between terrorists of different countries for purposes of financing, gun running and guerilla training. Supply of forged travel documents and providing shelter to terrorists are other cooperative activities indulged in by terrorists in different countries. Terrorists have solicited and secured support of some governments and their embassies also.

What is the remedy to stop these acts of terrorism. In the past, there have been attempts at curbing them. The League of Nations

Experts Committee considered this problem in the wake of the assassination of King Alexander of Yugoslavia in France in 1934. A Convention was signed on 16th November, 1937 in Geneva. Under the Convention, terrorism, including conspiracy and incitement, was considered as a crime for which an accused could be extradited. Twenty-three States signed it. By another Convention, ten of the signatory States agreed to the creation of an International Criminal Court to try acts of terrorism when terrorists were not extradited or tried within the country of asylum. India was party to both the Conventions which never came into force.

With the spurt in aerial piracy and other acts of terrorism, there have been attempts to put a check on aerial piracy. Tokyo, Hague and the Montreal Conventions provide for sanctions for unlawful interference with aircraft. No attempt has been made to tackle other acts of terrorism. Besides, there has been a crisis of conscience among States. States normally advocate for the extradition of hijackers and terrorists. But a few States have some reservation about the duty of extradition of terrorists. The Conventions have not yet become generally acceptable.

The problem of terrorism has been considered at the Legal Committee of the General Assembly. It has also been considered at other forums like the International Law Association and World Association of Lawyers. These discussions have shown that while Afro-Asian States intend to differentiate between individual acts of terrorism and those committed by freedom fighters, Western powers are in no mood to recognise this difference. Nor are they ready to condemn State terrorism. Thus, the matter has been in a stalemate. It can only be solved when there is a change of mind. When the colonialists become stubborn and intend to crush the freedom fighters with the help of organised army and police, the only alternative left for the colonial people is to resort to acts of terrorism. This basic difference regarding motivation has got to be kept in view while making any Convention for preventing terrorism about which there is grave world concern. At the same time, the humanitarian aspect of jeopardising the lives of innocent people cannot be overlooked. Terrorism cannot be treated as a premium to cash dividends. Efforts should be made to differentiate between acts of anarchists and patriotic struggles.

CHAPTER 23

PEACETIME ESPIONAGE

Espionage is the collection (or attempt to collect) of strategic information regarding a foreign country for the benefit of the State which employs the spies. Previously, espionage was commonly undertaken during war-time by soldier scouts. Therefore, the Hague Regulations 1899 and 1907 provided that the spy may be tried and punished if he is caught in the act [1]. He cannot be tried if he has rejoined his forces after completion of his mission or even before such completion [2].

Espionage is as old as human history. It is said that Moses sent man to spy in the land of Cannan [3]. However, peacetime espionage has been on the increase in the post-World War II period. Mutual distrust and premium attached to surprise attack in the nuclear era have made the nations conscious of the problem of self-preservation. Nations resort to espionage even over friendly nations because one does not know how long the friendship will last. Embassies are the citadels of espionage activities because diplomats enjoy immunity from local jurisdiction. When caught, they can at the most be deported. They can, therefore, indulge in espionage with some impunity. One would find a number of news items regarding diplomats being deported by a host State on grounds of espionage or other subversive activities. A number of diplomats of a friendly State were deported and a number of governments functionaries were arrested in March, 1977 because of their suspected involvement in economic espionage in India.

Besides diplomats, a number of other personnel are engaged in espionage activities. The C.I.A. of the United States of America and K.G.B. of Russia are fairly famous for such activities. The Agency even indulges in toppling of foreign governments which are not responsive to the United States overtures. The U-2 or Pueblo affairs are too well known in the history of peacetime espionage.

The recent spurt in espionage activities has attracted the attention of world elites to this chronic problem.

There is quite a controversy about the legality of espionage. One school considers it as illegitimate because it tantamounts to the violation of sovereignty of the territorial State [4]. Others try to justify espionage on grounds of self-preservation. They contend that in this nuclear era, the first perpetrator of hostilities may have initial victory. They do not want to be taken unawares. Espionage forewarns about the evil intentions of an enemy, present or potential [5].

Espionage is one of the weapons to prevent the recurrence of the story of Pearl Harbour. It also forestalls evil intentions regarding surprise attack by enemies. Any dent in the enemy's intentions could be a saviour of the country's sovereignty as well as integrity. Confronted with the U-2 affair in 1960, President Eisenhower remarked: "It is distasteful but a vital necessity."

Law relating to espionage reflects the above claims and counterclaims. Under national law, it is a violation of territorial sovereignty involving acts prejudicial to national interests. International law does not consider espionage as an illegal act. States deprecate espionage activities of other States while indulging in the same elsewhere. A spy can be arrested only while he is within the territory of his activities. Once he has left the country, he is immune from that country's jurisdiction. There is no extradition of spies; only exchange.

Of late there has been swing from human espionage to electronic espionage by satellite, aircraft or vessel used for the purpose. U-2 was an aircraft; Pueblo was a vessel. There have also been satellite spies. U.S. satellite had detected impending Indian nuclear explosion in 1975. There is not much prevention against such devices. The States have come to live with them. There is a silent understanding among powers regarding the freedom to snoop over the other.

Espionage is not an international delinquency. No State asks for reparation or compensation from the State which sends its spies to the former. It only apprehends the spies when it becomes aware of their activities. In one way, every country knows that espionage activities are carried out within its territory. It is, therefore, safe to be on the watchout against such spies and their activities.

Spies are of three categories. Diplomats, local citizens and foreigners. Diplomats are deported. Local citizens are liable to be arrested under Official Secrets Act. The foreigners can only be apprehended while they are still within victim territory. Once they are out, they cannot be recalled through extradition. For one thing, it is an act authorised by sovereign State; secondly, it can be termed as a political offence. But once they are arrested, their conviction is almost sure. One has yet to know of an espionage case where the accused has been let off.

Notes

1. Article 30 of the Annex to the Hague Conventions, 1899 and 1907.
2. Article 31.
3. Hanson W. Baldwin, News of the week, New York Times, International Editor, 13 June, 1960.
4. Quincy Wright, Legal Aspects of the U-2 Incident, (1960) 54 A.J.I.L. 836.
5. Cohen, Espionage and Immunity—Some Recent Problems and Developments (1947) 24 B.J.I.L. 404 at p. 408 Oppenheim, op. cit. vol. I Section 455.

CHAPTER 24

CHARTER OF ECONOMIC RIGHTS AND DUTIES

Every since the emergence of new States from former colonies of the Western countries, there has been clamour for a new economic order in the world community. It has been alleged by developing countries that the present economic order helps the developed countries which are responsible for tailoring it to their own needs. This creates a situation of neocolonialism—transformation from political domination to economic domination by the Western States. The developing States have resented this state of affairs.

After persistent efforts by the Group of 77—an association of newly independent States itching for economic emancipation—succeeded in getting a Charter of Economic Rights and Duties of States passed by the General Assembly at its Twenty-ninth Session in 1974. The Charter was passed in Resolution 3281 (XXIX) by a vote of 120 in favour to six against with ten abstentions on 12th December, 1974. The Charter has a Preamble and 34 articles.

Preamble of the Charter states that its fundamental purpose is "to promote the establishment of the new economic order, based on equity, sovereign equality, interdependence, common interest and cooperation among all States, irrespective of their economic and social systems." The Preamble declares that all States are interdependent and there can be no international peace and stability in the midst of some States remaining very rich and others remaining very poor. The Charter aims at contributing to the creation of conditions for attainment of wider prosperity and higher standards of living, economic and social programmes of all countries, cooperation on the basis of mutual advantage and equitable benefits, economic development of developing countries by overcoming of main obstacles, acceleration of economic growth and bridging of the gap between the two sets of States and protection, preservation and enhancement of environment.

The Preamble further expresses that the world community is mindful of the need to establish and maintain a just and equitable economic and social order through more rational and equitable international economic relations and structural changes in the world economy, intensification of economic cooperation among States, strengthening of economic independence of developing countries and promotion of international economic relations after taking into account diversities and needs of their development.

Chapter 1 gives the fundamental principles which will guide economic, political and other relations among States. These principles are:

(a) sovereignty, territorial integrity and political independence of States;

(b) sovereign equality of States;

(c) non-aggression;

(d) non-intervention;

(e) mutual and equitable benefit;

(f) peaceful coexistence;

(g) equal rights and self-determination of peoples;

(h) peaceful settlement of disputes;

(i) remedying of injustices brought about by force;

(j) fulfilment in good faith of international obligation;

(k) respect for human rights and fundamental freedoms;

(l) no hegemony and spheres of influence;

(m) promotion of international social justice;

(n) international cooperation for development; and

(o) free access to and from the sea by landlocked countries.

Most of the above principles can be found in the Preamble or Article 2 of the U.N. Charter. Others are new innovations like mutual equitable benefits, peaceful coexistence, ban on hegemony, promotion of international social justice, international cooperation for development and free access to and from sea by land-locked countries. These new principles have been developed since the advent of the new Afro-Asian States into the world community.

Article 1 of the Charter reiterates the right of self-determination by which every State has the sovereign and inalienable right to choose its political, economic, cultural and social system without outside interference, coercion or threat thereof in any form.

It would mean that even economic threat is not admissible under this Article. The principle of self-determination and all its facets have been discussed earlier.

Article 2 gives the right to a territorial State to exercise full permanent sovereignty over its wealth, natural resources and economic activities. The Article empowers the State to regulate and exercise authority over foreign investments within its territory, supervise activities of multinational corporations which must comply with economic and social policies of the local State. Multinational corporations will not interfere in the local affairs of the host State. This ban is in the light of activities of some of the multinational corporations which try to dictate the activities of the territorial State. In some cases, these multinational giants have tried to topple the local governments which do not act according to their terms. In some cases, it has been found that some multinational corporations have bigger budgets than the budgets of many of the new States.

The State can nationalise foreign companies by giving appropriate compensation; quantum of compensation will be determined by its relevant laws and regulations and other circumstances which the local State considers pertinent. This would imply that local economic conditions may weigh while determining the quantum of compensation. This would demolish the Western demand that compensation must be prompt, adequate and effective. In case of any controversy over the quantum of compensation, Article 2(c) states that it shall be decided by local tribunals under the relevant domestic law on the point. However, the State may decide upon any other peaceful method for settling the question of compensation consistent with sovereign equality of States and free choice of means. There can be no compulsion at this juncture by the foreign company affected by local decree or its parent State.

Article 5 gives the right to producing States to form association for developing their national economies and accelerating their development. This would permit the formation of bodies like Oil Producing Exporting Countries and such other organisations. By implication this would give the right to these organisations to fix the prices of their commodities so that there is no unfair competition between producing countries. The article puts a corresponding duty on other States not to apply economic and political measures which would hamper the right of the producing States to form association and fix stable, remunerative and equitable prices under Article 6 of the Charter.

In the circumstances, it becomes clear that Kissinger's threat of intervention in 1975 if the Western economy were strangulated by further hike in oil prices was contrary to the spirit behind Articles 5 and 6 of the Charter and remniscent of the trigger-happy diplomacy of the European nations in earlier centuries. Article 6 specifically states that price fixation should contribute to an equitable development of the world economy. The interests of the developing countries should particularly be taken into account. Article 8 aims at facilitating the building of a "balanced world economy in harmony with the needs and interests of all countries, especially, developing countries."

Article 10 reiterates that all States are "juridically equal" and, therefore, all States should participate fully and effectively as equal members of the world community in the international decision-making process while solving world economic, financial and monetary problems. It should not be the privilege of the developed few to dictate monetary reforms which are advantageous to the developed countries only.

Article 13 ensures that every State has the right to benefit from development in science and technology in order to promote its economy and social development. It is in this context that developed States are expected to share scientific knowledge acquired from communications transmitted by satellites. International sea bed authority is also sought to be established in order to give the benefit of new funds from the sea bed and ocean floor.

Article 15 imposes a duty on all States to promote the achievement of general and complete disarmament under effective international control and channelise the saved resources for economic and social development of the world community.

Mutual distrust and consequent rearmament are the two tragic developments of this century. Technological developments have worsened the situation where all types of destructive weapons can be manufactured with the help of scientific know-how. Presently, experiments are going on to use weather as a military weapon. What is more in store could be anybody's guess. Nations spend more on military hardware than on basic needs of man. Conservative estimates on annual world military expenditure varies between

350 and 400 billion dollars. This is double of 1972 figures of 200 billion dollars.

Nations have built overkill arsenals which can destroy humanity a number of times. The nuclear stockpile had swollen from two in 1945 to 12,000 in 1975. Besides, a number of new weapons have been invented and manufactured. Detente and Helsinki European Security Pact have not deterred the States from incurring huge national military expenditures. Ominous development of recent years is the purchase boom of sophisticated armaments by West-Asian countries. More than half of the total arms supplied in 1975 went to the West-Asian countries which spent 16 per cent of their combined gross national products on weaponry [1]. It is indeed a tragic state for a developing country to be spending more on military purchase than on welfare activities for its peoples.

World concern for disarmament was reflected in twenty resolutions passed by the U.N. General Assembly on disarmament and related questions at its thirtieth Session on 9th December, 1975. Resolution 3254 exhorted upon nations to reduce military budgets by 10 per cent and utilise part of the savings for assisting the developing countries.

In resolution 3255 B, the General Assembly condemned the use of napalm and other incendiary weapons in armed conflicts which not only affect human beings but cause damage to environment and natural resources. The Assembly invited all States to refrain from the production, stockpiling, proliferation and use of such weapons. The Assembly vide its resolution 3256 reaffirmed its objective of reaching an agreement on the effective prohibition on the development, production and stockpiling of all chemical and biological weapons and called on all States to observe the principles of 1925 Protocol on the Prohibition of Use of Asphyxiating, Poisonous or other Gases and of Bacteriological Methods of Warfare.

In its resolution 3257, the General Assembly condemned all nuclear tests in whatever environment. The Assembly called for a comprehensive test ban treaty. It exhorted upon States to adhere to the 1963 Treaty Banning Nuclear Weapon Tests in the Atmosphere, in outer space and underwater, if they had not already adhered. The Assembly also approved Treaty of Tlatelolco of 1967 declaring Latin America as Nuclear Weapon Free Zone and exhorted upon the Soviet Union to sign and ratify Additional

Protocol II of 1967 as has been done by other nuclear powers. The Assembly vide its resolution 3261 E called upon States to consider and respect the continent of Africa as Nuclear Free Zone as declared by Organization of African Unity. The General Assembly welcomed the idea of making the Middle East as Nuclear Weapon Free Zone vide its resolution 3263.

The General Assembly reaffirmed its earlier resolution 2832 (XXVI) of 16 December, 1971 declaring the Indian Ocean as a zone of peace and asked upon States vide its resolution 3259 A to give tangible support to establishment of the Indian Ocean as a zone of peace. It called upon great powers to refrain from increasing and strengthening their military presence in the region. It is heartening to note in this connection the response of President Carter in March, 1977 and subsequent policy statements.

The General Assembly vide its resolution 3264 exhorted upon states to refrain from using environment and climate for military and other hostile purposes, pending conclusion of the international convention for the purpose.

Article 16 of the Charter condemns all types of colonisation, neo-colonialism, apartheid, racial discrimination, foreign aggression, occupation and domination. According to Article 16, every State has the right as well as duty to eliminate above nuisances in world community. These nuisances constitute impediments in the development of the State. Earlier these impediments are removed, better it will be for the world.

Article 17 makes international cooperation for development as the shared goal and common duty of all States. States should cooperate with each other for mutual development. UNCTAD (United Nations Conference for Trade and Development) is motivated to achieve all-round development, particularly of the developing countries. For this, Articles 18 and 19 require that developed countries should extend generalised preferential, nonreciprocal and nondiscriminatory treatment to developing countries.

Article 29 reiterates that the sea bed and ocean floor beyond national jurisdiction is the common heritage of mankind as declared in resolution 2749 (XXV) of 17th December, 1970. These areas must be used for peaceful purposes and benefit derived therefrom should be shared equitably by all the States.

Notes

1 In 1974, per Capita G.N.P. for West Asia was $ 845 out of which $ 135 was spent on military hardware. In 1975, leading importers of major weapons were Egypt, India, Iran, Iraq, Israel, Libya, South Africa Syria and Vietnam. All this has been disclosed by the 1976 Year Book of the International Peace Research Institute (Stockholm)—The Statesman, 19th July, 1976.

Chapter 25

MULTINATIONAL CORPORATIONS

Of late, there has been awakening regarding the role of multinational corporations in the world community. The activities of International Telegraph Corporation in Chile which contributed partly to the overthrow of Allende regime in 1973 are pointer to the activities of many other such multinational corporations. Already the Afro-Asian States which have recently achieved political independence from colonial European powers are itching for economic independence also. This requires quick industrialisation to promote economic growth. However, quick industrialisation is not possible without the inflow of foreign capital and technological know-how from industrialised States of Europe and the United States of America.

Multinational Corporations are not newcomers on the world political scene. One is fairly familar with the activities of the East India Company which came as a trading company to India during the Mughal period. It had the dual functions to trade and indulge in politics within the Indian subcontinent. It had the power to acquire and govern territory, maintain armed forces and make war and peace with native princes, who were not considered then as subjects of international law. Similar have been the activities of the Dutch East India Company in Indonesia. The Franco-British Company—Universal Company of Maritime Canal of Suez—controlled the east-west trade passing through the Suez and exercised immense political power in the Middle East. The Anglo-Iranian Petroleum Company in Iran or Aramco in Saudi Arabia wielded great political powers within the territories of their operations. International Telegraph Corporation, United Fruit Company, American Banana Company, Coca-Cola Company, Lockheed, General Motors and Ford Company of the United States are typically giant business concerns operating in different countries of the world. Surprisingly, the budgets of these companies far exceed the budgets of many newly independent States.

In this era of economic interdependence, foreign investment is essential for every State. Even well-developed States invite foreign investments. The Socialist States allow selective foreign investments. A number of Arab States have purchased shares in big companies of the United States and Europe. India has also launched individual as well as joint ventures abroad.

For newly independent States of the Third World, inflow of foreign capital is a "must" in order to facilitate quick industrialisation and avoid the otherwise inevitable imports. This can only be done by inviting foreign corporations from developed States to establish their subsidiaries or branches in these new States. The response has been quite encouraging. As of 1975, India had 482 branches and 171 subsidiaries of multinational corporations operating within its territory. But it only represented nine per cent of the total capital of the Indian corporate sector—Rs. 259 crores as against Rs. 5400 crores.

However, as there are always two sides of a coin, multinational corporations are not in anyway different. They have the plus points like global economic integration, importation of technical know-how, capital investment, quick pace of industrialisation, greater production and increased gross national product. All these things help in the reduction of national and individual poverty, promote more employment avenues and contribute to better utilisation of natural resources. Multinational corporations could be of great economic assistance; sophisticated foreign investment can promote exports and earn foreign exchange. The other side of the story is that multinational corporations are not free from indulging in malpractices. It has been noticed that some of the multinational corporations interfere in the affairs of the host State in order to maintain or gain political patronage of the powers that be within the State. They try to destabilise the host government if it is hostile to their interests or to the interests of the parent State. Multinational corporations contribute to convenient political parties and personalities in developing countries for ulterior motives. The Lockheed scandal of 1976 regarding huge payoffs to important political leaders of a number of States rocked a number of State capitals. Corruption at the political level makes the governmental functionaries vulnerable to economic and political blackmail. Developing States have also been victims of economic exploitation at the hands of multinational corporations as in the case of oil companies which have milked the Arab oil. Strangely enough, until recently American coca-cola was costing more than a litre of petrol. Things are no better today except that the recent trends are encouraging. Multinational corporations have also been sometimes considered as symbols of economic neocolonialism. It may not be an exaggeration to say that in some cases joint action by multinational corporations within a given country could cripple the economy of the nation-state. It is estimated that in some Latin American countries, U.S. investment constitutes about 70 to 80 per cent of total foreign investment. This kind of block investment of U.S. multinationals may cause the collapse of a national economy as and when they may take a joint action as a measure of political or economic pressure. In some countries, foreign investment exceeds total investment and this poses an economic and political threat. In some cases, parent States seek to intervene in the affairs of a host State on the pretext of protecting the interests of its nationals and the business they represent.

Alarmed at the wide scope of malpractices which multinational corporations are capable of inflicting on the host State to its economic and political detriment, the United Nations constituted a group of twenty experts in June, 1973 to study the problems pertaining to the functioning of multinational corporations and the impact of such functioning on development and international relations. The group gave its report after one year in June, 1974 which was adopted by the U.N. Economic and Social Council in July, 1974.

The report known as "Impact of Multinational Corporations on Development and International Relations" gives a number of clues to the thinking of the Group of Experts on the subject.

The Group acknowledges the role of foreign private investment towards international development strategy. Multinational corporations have distinct capabilities which can be put to service of development. However, there is clash of objectives as between those of developing nations and of the multinational corporations. Technological development and welfare of their citizens are the two main objectives of developing nations while the chief goals of multinational corporations are profit and growth. Multinational corporations, particularily the very large ones, possess considerable power, patronage and influence. Their activities may have far-reaching consequences for the society in which they operate.

Because of the desire on the part of developing nations for fast technological development, they have to depend on foreign know-how and investment. Therefore, they have a weak bargaining position. It was also noted by the Group that multinational corporations have a potential for interference in the domestic affairs of the host developing State. In some cases, multinational corporations become instruments of foreign policy of their home State.

The Group wanted to ensure that multinational corporations and their activities should not affect relations between two countries which may lead to confrontation between them. It was noted by the Group that there is great potential on the part of these corporations to influence the decision makers in the host country by utilising their vast financial power and their often cordial relationship with the local government cadre. The Group therefore condemned any political subversive intervention on the part of the multinational corporations to either serve the home country's policies or overthrow an unfriendly government in the host country.

The Group made a number of recommendations which are summarised below:

1. The host country should specify as precisely as possible the conditions under which multinational corporations should operate in their territory.

2. The host country should consider setting up of centralised negotiating committee to deal with all proposals for foreign investment by multinational corporations.

3. Developing countries should intensify their efforts for regional cooperation and establishment of joint policies with respect to multinational corporations.

4. The host country should clearly define permissible public activities of multinational corporations and prescribe sanctions against violations.

5. In case of political interventions by multinational corporations the host country should impose strict sanctions subject to due process of law.

6. The home country should refrain from involving itself in differences and disputes between host country and the multinational corporations.

7. In case of nationalisation of foreign investment, host country should ensure fair and adequate compensation.

8. Establishment of commission on multinational corporations under the auspices of U.N. Economic and Social Council.

9. Establishment of Information and Research Centre in the U.N. Secretariat.

10. Framing of Code of Conduct for multinational corporations.

11. These companies should not violate U.N. sanctions.

12. They preferred the name of Transnational Corporation for Multinational Corporation.

The Group's recommendations on the establishment of Commission on multinational corporations and Information and Research Centre have been accepted and they have already started functioning. Besides an Inter-Government Working Group of 48 countries has been established by the United Nations to prepare a code of conduct for them. Although the code of conduct has not been prepared, there is consensus among these countries that these corporations should;

1. observe local laws;
2. adhere to the economic and socio-cultural objectives of the host country;
3. respect human rights;
4. not interfere in internal and international policies of the host country; and
5. abstain from corrupt practices.

The Group's recommendations are welcome; so also the proposed code of conduct. However, developing countries should not be obsessed with only the dark side of some of the activities of some of the multinational corporations. There should be an objective assessment of each proposal for foreign investment and the returns which the host country expects. All multinational corporations are not monsters.

While determining the case of multinational corporations, it must be born in mind that they are not charitable institutions. They are after all business concerns and thier motivation is growth and profit. There is nothing missionary about them. But there should be no excessive profiteering. This should be added to the proposed code of conduct. A multinational corporation, therefore, should be ensured, that there would be no objection to its legitimate business motivation; it should not however indulge in unfair business practice; nor should it operate at the "cost" of the host country. These should be the two watchwords for multinational corporations. For the developing countries, it would be better to diversify foreign investment within its territory in the sense that there is no bulk investment originating from one country. Foreign investment should not constitute dominant economic force in any country. Nor should foreign investment be encouraged in sensitive areas and essential consumer goods.

CHAPTER 26

ENVIRONMENT CONSERVATION

There is growing concern about the deterioration of the natural environment around the world. Man has become conscious that the environment in which he is living is either not conducive to his healthy growth or is likely to threaten it. Population explosion and technological developments are two dominant factors responsible for environment pollution to the extent that it has become a health hazard. World population has grown from one billion in 1830 to an estimated four billion in 1980. Naturally, all this population requires more food, more space and more employment. Movement from rural to urban areas has caused unhealthy growth of towns surrounded by slums and shanties resulting in insanitary conditions and contamination of atmosphere. Affluence has no less contributed to the problem of dumping off a town's waste. Large cities have the problem of finding out places for dumping and disposing off their daily refuse and waste. In the United States, abandoned cars pose a great pollution problem.

River and sea water are contaminated by dumping of industrial-cum-nuclear waste, throwing of dead bodies, underwater nuclear tests, domestic waste, wreckage and oil pollution. Until recently, rivers and seas were considered as safe places for dumping all sorts of wastes. After World War II, canisters containing poisonous gases were dumped in the sea with an impression that the same will remain harmless in the sea. Deep-sea mining caused leakage of poisonous gases in 1976 near the Californian coast. In 1973, the Japanese people found to their horror that residents of Minamata fell sick after eating sea fish. It turned out that a chemical company had dumped mercury waste in adjoining waters. Mercury accumulates in the brain causing permanent neurological damage like blindness, paralysis and even death. Sixty-five residents died of the Minamata disease and it was spreading to other communities.

Enormity of sea pollution can be assessed from the fact that every year the Mediterranean Sea is polluted with 120 tons of mineral oils, 100 tons of mercury, 60 tons of detergents, 3800 tons of lead, 2400 tons of chromium, 21000 tons of zinc, 1120 tons of nitrogen and phosphorus and 2500 cusecs of radio nuclides. The eighteen Mediterranean States have agreed to do something about it in conjunction with United Nations Environmental Program. Already, they have ratified three conventions signed in 1976. One aims at protection of sea from pollution. The other outlaws dumping of dangerous substances and the third seeks to combat massive oil spills. The Conventions became part of International Environmental Law on 12th February, 1978.

Aerial atmosphere is polluted by emission of motor and industrial smoke, extensive use of pesticides and DDT and dust-causing urban diseases like asthma and cancer. Even the flight of aircraft causes ecological problems. Technological developments have made man conscious that the atmosphere he is living in is no more safe; the water he drinks is no more pure; the fish he is eating may be poisonous; he cannot take a dip in the water for fear of a skin disease. Mahatma Gandhi once remarked that while wild life was decreasing in the jungles, it was increasing in the cities. The problem is not local, it is global. A concerted international effort is required to tackle it because atmosphere transcends national borders and sea pollution affects all the nations.

Fortunately, there is worldwide consciousness to protect the natural environment as far as possible. Today, man dreads all kinds of pollution—earth, air and water. Individual States have already embarked upon national anti-pollution laws depending upon the extent of their development and requirements. Willy Brandt campaigned for "blue skies above Rhine and Ruhr." The Soviet Union has launched a billion rouble programme to clean up the Volga and Ural rivers by 1980. What is required is the standardisation and uniformity of legislation and efforts to prevent transmission of pollution beyond national borders lest it may be held responsible under the precedent of Trail Smelter Arbitration in 1941. This requires international cooperation on science, policy and law.

In recognition of world consciousness regarding international cooperation, the first U.N. Conference on Human Environment was held in June, 1972 at Stockholm (Sweden). The Stockholm

Declaration on Environment consists of 26 principles, besides the Preamble and is supplemented by 109 recommendations. The Declaration was reinforced by U.N. General Assembly Resolution 2996 adopted on 15th December 1972. Stockholm Declaration and U.N.G.A. Resolution depict the coming of an international environment law. Some of the important principles from the Stockholm Declaration are:

Principle 1 gives the man a fundamental right to adequate conditions of life. Principle 2 states that natural resources of earth, air, water, land, flora and fauna must be safeguarded for the benefit of present and future generations through careful planning and management. Principle 7 requires States to take all possible measures to prevent pollution of the seas. Principle 15 states that human settlements and urbanisation should be so planned so as to avoid adverse effects on environment. Principle 21 gives a territorial State the right to exploit natural resources subject to the condition that its activities do not cause damage to areas beyond their jurisdiction. Principle 22 enjoins upon a State to cooperate in developing international environmental law with regard to liability and compensation for the victims of pollution and other environmental damage caused by State activities beyond national boundaries. Principle 24 envisages international cooperation in protection and improvement of environment. Principle 25 endows the international organisation with coordinated, efficient and dynamic role for the protection and improvement of environment. Principle 26 declares that man and environment must be spared from the effects of nuclear weapons and other means of mass destruction.

The Stockholm Conference also recommended the establishment of Environmental Secretariat to deal with day-to-day work of the United Nations in the sphere. Another recommendation related to the creation of a 54-member Governing Council to be elected every three years by the General Assembly to work as an inter Governmental organ for seeking international cooperation under Principle 24. It was further recommended to establish an Environment Fund to be raised through voluntary contributions for meeting the cost of new environmental activities to be undertaken by the United Nations and it agencies. In pursuance of these recommendations, U.N. Environmental Programme has been launched to deal with protection and improvement of human environment.

SECTION IV

DISPUTES

CHAPTER 27

SETTLEMENT OF DISPUTES

Man is essentially selfish. The theory of social contract owes its existence to the fighting nature of man. Disputes between man and man are, therefore, natural. A State is not different from the man who manages it. Disputes between States are common occurrences. States are more prone to disputes due to their stand of self-righteousness and overconsciousness of national sovereignty.

There are various methods for settlement of international disputes between States. These may be peaceful or non-peaceful. The latter are also called compulsive methods short of war. All these methods are discussed below.

Peaceful Procedures for Settlement of Disputes

Important among the peaceful methods are negotiations, good offices, mediation, arbitration, reference to the International Court of Justice or to the United Nations. Besides these, Article 33 of the U.N. Charter recognises two more methods of inquiry and conciliation as peaceful methods. Article 2(3) of the Charter obliges members of the United Nations to "settle their disputes by peaceful means." The Charter lays its emphasis on peaceful settlement of international disputes. The Preamble of the Charter says that the United Nations is established to save the succeeding generations from the scourge of war. Article 2 Clause 4 obliges the States not to resort to use of force. Chapter VI of the Charter deals specifically with settlement of international disputes by peaceful means which are given in Article 33. Earlier, Article II of the Paris Pact of 27th August, 1928 said: "The settlement or solution of all disputes or conflicts of whatever nature or of whatever origin they may be which may arise among them shall never be sought except by pacific means." This was followed by General Act for the

Pacific Settlement of International Disputes of 26th September, 1928. This was reaffirmed with slight modification by General Act for the Pacific Settlement of International Disputes as passed by the General Assembly on 26th April, 1949. The revised General Act came into force from 20th September, 1950. Earlier, the Inter-American Treaty, popularly known as Bagota Pact, of 1948 emphasised on peaceful settlement of disputes.

Negotiations

Negotiations are by far the most popular mode which nations frequently resort to for settling their disputes *inter se*. "Negotiations" are direct contact between the disputing nations to sort out their contentions and settle them amicably. The 1971-72 detente between the United States of America and China was through negotiations. So also the detente between the Soviet Union and the United States. The Federal Republic of Germany established diplomatic relations with the Soviet Union through "ostopolitic" negotiations between the two countries. The Simla Accord was the result of negotiations between Indira Gandhi and Bhutto, Prime Ministers of India and Pakistan respectively in July, 1972. This was followed by three other agreements through negotiations between them in August, 1973, April, 1974 and May, 1976.

Negotiations may be open or secret or both. They may be short or protracted as in the case of negotiations which temporarily suspended the Vietnamese War in 1973. Kissinger-Tho parleys have shown the effectiveness of negotiations and for this they were justly awarded the Nobel Peace Prize for the year. The truce, however, proved to be short-lived and hostilities were restarted resulting in final victory of the Viet Cong Forces in 1975. But this does not falsify the effectiveness of negotiations as a means for settlement of disputes. The Sadat-Begin meet in November, 1977 was a historic step to settle the Arab-Israel conflict through negotiations.

Nations normally like to settle their disputes between themselves through negotiations. Negotiations may be preceded by correspondence and/or Commission of Inquiry to ascertain facts and sort out points of difference between the disputing nations. In other cases, negotiations are undertaken between plenipotentiaries to be formalised at Foreign Ministers' level or summit conference between the nations. This happened when the Iceland and British Prime Ministers met in London in September, 1973 to settle their dispute regarding unilateral extension of fisheries zone by Iceland from 12 to 50 miles in September, 1972. Kissinger-Brezhnev negotiations also resulted in the cessation of hostilities in the Middle East in October, 1973. Negotiations between Sri Lanka and India resulted in boundary demarcations in Falk Bay and surrender of India's claim over Kachhativu in July, 1974. In March 1976, Sri Lanka and India again settled their maritime boundaries in the Gulf of Mannar through bilateral negotiations.

Negotiations, which are symbol of bilaterism, have been recommended by the United Nations. In 1946, the United Nations advised the Iran and Soviet Union Governments to negotiate and report to it about the peaceful settlement of their dispute. Sometime back the United States and Cuba reached an agreement through negotiations for surrender of hijackers by Cuba to the United States. The Simla Accord of 2nd July, 1972 between India and Pakistan provided for settlement of their differences by peaceful means through bilateral negotiations or by any other peaceful means mutually agreed upon. The United Nations advised India and Bangla Desh for bilateral negotiation over Farrakka Barrage in December, 1975. Finally, they reached an agreement through negotiations in September, 1977.

Good Offices and Mediation

When parties fail to meet or reach an agreement through negotiations, a third party, may be a third State or person, may lend its good offices for arranging a meeting between the disputing States so as to resolve their differences amicably. It is possible that disputing parties may reach an agreement through negotiations after a meeting has been arranged between them through the good offices of a third party. This is what happened when Wilson, Prime Minister of the United Kingdom, lent his good offices to Lal Bahadur Shastri, Prime Minister of India and Ayub Khan, President of Pakistan to reach an agreement to refer the Kutch dispute to an arbitral tribunal.

A third party, lending its good offices, is naturally friendly and *persona grata* to both the disputing nations. It could also be an international organisation. The Security Council of the United Nations has lent its good offices in a number of situations. As early as in 1947, it offered to lend its good offices to Holland and Indonesia in the latter's fight to become independent. A comm itte of good offices was thus formed in 1947 by the Security Council consisting of Australia, Belgium and the United States to resolve Indonesia's dispute with the Netherlands. The main function of the party offering its good offices is to bring the disputing parties together when they have either failed to negotiate or where negotiations have failed.

Mediation is one step further. The third party which is friendly to the disputing States does not only try to bring the disputing parties together on the Conference table but also seeks to give some advice. Russo-American mediation in the Arab-Israel conflict in October, 1973 was responsible for the cease-fire call by the United Nations Security Council through its resolutions 338 and 339. Earlier, Russian leaders' mediation was responsible for the Tashkent Agreement between India and Pakistan in 1966. Dr. Jarring worked as a U.N. mediator for a number of years from 1967 to 1973 between the Arabs and Israelis. Post-October 1973 agreements between Egypt and Israel and Syria and Israel had been due to the efforts of Kissinger's shuttle diplomacy which was the combination of good offices and mediation.

It is difficult to say when good offices end and mediation starts. Even when a third party purports to lend its good offices, there may be subtle mediation. In many cases, mediation is done behind the scene and in some cases it is denied. Whether the Tashkent agreement was the result of good offices or mediation of the Soviet leaders has not been clear. But the circumstances, such as the death of the Prime Minister of India immediately after the agreement, lead to the presumption that there was mediation by the Soviet leaders. In any case, the main difference between good offices and mediation is that in the case of good offices, the third party, friendly to both, tries to bring the disputing nations to the negotiating table without offering any advice on the disputed matter while in mediation, the third party also suggests how the dispute could be settled. In the initial stages of Lebanese civil strife in 1975-76, Syria was lending its good offices as well as functioning as a mediator between the rightist and leftist factions.

Arbitration

Arbitration is a process by which the disputing States refer their dispute to an *ad hoc* tribunal consisting of one, three or more umpires. When States fail to settle their dispute through diplomatic channels like negotiations and mediation has not been possible or successful, States may refer the matter to an arbitral tribunal either on their own or through the good offices of some third party. India and Pakistan referred the Kutch dispute to the arbitral tribunal through the good offices of the British Prime Minister, Harold Wilson.

Arbitration may arise out of an arbitration clause in a particular treaty or through a treaty of arbitration referring a particular dispute, which has already arisen, to a given arbitral tribunal. This was the case between India and Pakistan when they referred the Kutch dispute to an arbitral tribunal. Such an agreement is called *compromis*. There may also be a general arbitration treaty providing for reference of all disputes, or some types of disputes, which may arise between the parties, to the panel of arbitrators to be appointed for the purpose. This type of general treaty of arbitration is a twentieth century development, following the recommendations of the Hague Peace Conferences of 1899 and 1907.

Permanent Court of Arbitration

There is no such thing as Permanent Court of Arbitration. It is neither a court, nor is it permanent. There only exists a panel of names suggested by States, party to the Hague Conventions of 1899 and 1907. Each such State has a right to recommend four persons well-qualified in the field of international law who can be entrusted with the task of being an arbitrator in a given dispute. Persons so suggested remain on the list for six years which can be renewed. Hague has been made the seat of the Court.

Although arbitration, as a process for peaceful settlement of international disputes, may be traced to antiquity, modern practices of arbitration can be traced to the Anglo-American Jay Treaty of 1794. Alabama Arbitration of 1870 is a landmark in modern arbitration. England and France referred the dispute, regarding the mistaken surrender of V.D. Savarkar, an Indian revolutionary, by the French police to the Captain of the British vessel, to the Permanent Court of Arbitration in 1910. Again it was resorted to in 1965 when India and Pakistan referred the Kutch dispute to the arbitral tribunal.

Arbitration takes place through appointment of arbitrators by the disputing parties. The disputing parties may also appoint a sole arbitrator who is *persona grata* to both the disputing parties.

However, appointment of a sole arbitrator is not a common practice. The general practice is that each party nominates his own arbitrator and the two arbitrators, so appointed, nominate the third arbitrator who is neutral in the right sense and who becomes the Chairman of the arbitral tribunal. It may also be provided in such arbitration treaty that in case of failure of two nominated arbitrators to appoint the third arbitrator, the President of the International Court of Justice or Secretary-General of the United Nations may appoint the third arbitrator. This happened in the case of Indo-Pakistan arbitration. India nominated a Yugoslav and Pakistan nominated a diplomat from Iran. Since they could not agree on the third arbitrator, the U.N. Secretary-General had to appoint the third arbitrator as Chairman of the tribunal from Sweden.

The arbitral tribunal applies international law and general principles recognised by the community of nations. However, it is left to the parties to permit the tribunal to apply principles of equity or decide the case *ex acquo et bono.* In some cases, the tribunal may apply principles of equity even without authorisation provided there is no restriction under the treaty. The Kutch Tribunal applied the principle *ex ecquo et bono* in Indo-Pakistan dispute. Parties may also stipulate as to law which the tribunal has to apply. In British Guiana-Venezuela Boundary Dispute, the *compromis* included a principle that fifty year occupation may entitle the occupant a prescriptive right.

Award is normally binding upon parties which must carry out the award in good faith. Otherwise, there is no purpose in referring the matter to the arbitrators. The award is final and operates as *res judicata* between parties. However, it is expected of the arbitrators to observe the terms of reference. If the arbitrators have been bribed or pressurised, any award given in such circumstances will not be considered as binding on such party whose interests have been prejudicially affected by such corrupt practices. In such cases, the award will be null and void. But the difficulty arises as to what is the criteria for considering the award as null and void and the agency which is competent to declare the award as null and void. There being no court superior to an arbitral tribunal, it is naturally the party affected which can challenge the award. This will necessarily be subjective like the invoking of the doctrine of *rebus sic stantibus* and is, therefore, liable to abuse and challenge.

Award can be challenged on ground of exercise of jurisdiction with regard to issue not referred to the arbitrator, or applying the law not authorised by the terms of reference. Allegations of corruption would also nullify the award.

Arbitration has not been a popular mode among nations for settlement of their differences with other States. States being too conscious of their sovereignty, are lethargic to refer the dispute to an arbitral or judicial tribunal whose findings will be binding upon them. States want scope for flexibility which is wanting in cases of arbitration. Instead, they are in favour of diplomatic procedures which abound in flexibility and face-saving devices. Rigidity is the greatest drawback of arbitration or adjudication as compared to diplomatic methods for settlement of disputes. No case has been referred to the Permanent Court of Arbitration since 1932.

Judicial Settlement

Judicial settlement is a mature system of settlement of legal disputes. This is particularly true of municipal law where there is a sovereign whom the people are in the habit of obeying and who administers justice through his courts. However, the system of judicial settlement in the world community is yet to ripen and inspire confidence in view of the fact that each State is equal and sovereign and there is no means of imposing compulsions and enforcing binding decisions. Nevertheless, efforts have been made to introduce this tried municipal law system in the working of international law also.

The question of establishing an International Court of Justice was discussed at the Second Hague Peace Conference in 1907. It was misconceived into Permanent Court of Arbitration which was far from what was desired. Coincidently during that year, a mini world court of justice was created at Cartage by five Latin American countries, namely, Costa Rica, Guatemala, Honduras, Nicargua and San Salvador. It consisted of five judges, one each from the contracting parties. This was the first experiment in international judicial settlement.

Article 14 of the League Covenant authorised its Council to adopt plans for the establishment of a Permanent Court of International Justice. An Advisory Committee of Legal Experts was appointed in 1920 to prepare a document for the establishment of such a court. The draft statute was accepted by the League Assembly in December, 1920. This was later to be converted into

Protocol of Signature of the Statute on 16th December 1920. It came into force in 1921 after ratification by the requisite number of States. The Permanent Court of International Justice was thus created in 1921. It started functioning from 15th February 1922. The Hague was selected as its seat. It worked up to early 1940, despite the outbreak of World War II. However, when Holland was occupied by Germany, the Court ceased to function. It was officially dissolved in 1946 by resolution of the Assembly of the League. The International Court of Justice started functioning from 18th April, 1948, with the same statute as that of the P.C.I.J. It also succeeded to acceptances of the optional clause made under Article 36 Clause 2 during P.C.I.J. period.

However, the International Court of Justice can only adjudicate upon legal disputes between States. It cannot pass its judgment on political disputes. Oppenheim defines legal disputes as one regarding which contending parties "base their respective claims and contentions on grounds recognised by international law."

Article 36 Clause 2 of the Court's statute says that States may confer jurisdiction on the Court in respect of legal disputes concerning:

(a) the interpretation of a treaty;
(b) any question of international law;
(c) the existence of any fact which, if established, would constitute a breach of an international obligation; and
(d) the nature and extent of reparation to be made for the breach of an international obligation.

Inquiry

Resort to Inquiry as a procedure for peaceful settlement of international disputes was advocated by the Hague Conference of 1899. Inquiry is nothing else but a process to ascertain facts from amongst disputing claims of the States concerned where no honour or vital interests of States are involved. The process of inquiry was successfully invoked for the first time in the Dogger Bank Incident in 1904 when Great Britain and Russia agreed upon the establishment of the International Commission of Inquiry. Commissions of Inquiry became very popular soon thereafter culminating in the establishment of a number of such commissions as envisaged in Bryan Treaties. The League of Nations appointed a number of fact-finding missions. However, this procedure soon fell into disuse. A commission of inquiry becomes useful when there are conflicting versions given by the disputing parties. In some cases, it serves as a cooling-off process. Article 33 of the Charter speaks of inquiry as one of the peaceful procedures for settlement of international disputes. But it has rarely been used.

Conciliation

Conciliation is a combination of inquiry coupled with suggestions for settlement of dispute between States. Such suggestions, however, are not supposed to be binding upon the disputing States. This procedure was boosted by a resolution of the Third Assembly on 22nd September, 1922 asking States to establish conciliation commissions consisting of five members. The two disputing States were to nominate two members—one its own national and the other from a third country. The fifth was to be nominated by the four members so appointed by the States. This was not, of course, to dilute the conciliatory functions of the Council of the League of Nations under Articles 15 and 17 of the Covenant. The Scandinavian countries were very enthusiastic about conciliation commissions. It almost became a fashion among States to form conciliation commissions in the post-World War I era. Several such commissions were established but without much results. The General Act (Pacific Settlement of International Disputes) 1928 recommended conciliation as one of the three peaceful procedures for settlement of international disputes.

Conciliation borders on arbitration with two points of difference. Arbitration is in respect of legal or quasi-legal issues. while conciliation may be in respect of political disputes also; secondly, while award given by the arbitrator is binding, the suggestions given by the conciliator or conciliation commission are not binding upon parties. It has some traits of mediation also.

The United Nations tried to recommend conciliation when the General Assembly passed such a resolution at its third session, despite Soviet opposition. However, the response has not been good. There have been some instances of resort to conciliation procedure among the Latin American States and African States. Charter of the Organisation of American States signed in Bagota on 30th April 1948 provides for conciliation between the disputing States. So also the Charter of the Organisation of African Unity adopted in Addis Ababa in 1963 which contemplates the establishment of a Commission of Conciliation, Mediation and Arbitration by a separate protocol which was adopted in Cairo in the succeeding year.

Recent instances of appointment of conciliation commission may be found in the formation of Belgo-Danish Conciliation Commission in 1952 and Greco-Italian Conciliation Commission in 1956. African States have also resorted to the use of conciliation commissions for settlement of disputes among themselves. Kissinger's role in the West-Asian dispute may be considered as an amalgam of being a mediator-cum-conciliator.

United Nations

United Nations may contribute to the peaceful settlement of an international dispute through its two main organs—Security Council and General Assembly. Article 33(2) authorises the Security Council to call upon the disputing States to settle their disputes by peaceful procedures as given in Article 33(1). Preamble and Article 2 Clause 3 and 5 provide that nations should settle their disputes by peaceful means. The United Nations was established to save the succeeding generations from the scourge of war. So nations must avoid war and resort to peaceful procedure for settlement of their disputes.

The United Nations is instrumental in stopping of hostilities in a number of situations. Chapter VI of the Charter enjoins upon the members to settle their disputes by peaceful means.

Non-Peaceful Methods

Non-peaceful methods are also called compulsive methods, short of war. These compulsive methods do not amount to war. They are short of war although it may involve the use of force or threat thereof. These compulsive methods do not by themselves settle the disputes. In some cases, these are pressure tactics to force a State to settle the dispute. There are six types of compulsive methods. They are retortion, reprisals, intervention, pacific blockade, embargo and limited force.

Retortion

Retortion has its basis on the principle of tit for tat. It is an unfriendly act by the State towards another State which has initially done some unfriendly act. Mostly, the unfriendly act is similar to that initiated by the victim State. If State A deports a number of nationals of State B and B deports A's nationals in order to bear upon State A to stop deportation of its nationals, it is called retortion. Similarly, State A may declare B's diplomat as *persona non grata* to be followed by State B declaring A's diplomat the same. Retortion is not an illegal action taken by the State; it is merely retaliatory.

Reprisals

Reprisals are hostile acts committed by one State against another State as a countermeasure to force stoppage of commission of illegal acts by the latter State. Reprisals are a forceful measure involving use of force intended to bear upon the other State which itself has earlier indulged in illegal acts against the State now resorting to reprisals. Reprisals differ from war because in case of reprisals, there is stray use of force which may be a solitary instance while in the case of war there is repeated use of force. Otherwise, reprisals has the semblance of war because use of force is common to both. Hindmarsh has aptly defined reprisals as "coercive measures taken by one State against another, without belligerent intent, in order to secure redress for, or to prevent recurrence of, acts or omissions which under international law constitute international delinquency." It differs from war because there is no belligerent intention in case of reprisals.

Since reprisals involve the use of force, its validity is often questioned. Thus, when Italy occupied the Corfu Island in 1923, which resulted in the death of 15 people, as a measure of reprisals against Greece, the matter was referred to a Special Committee of Jurists. The Commission was asked to reply whether coercive acts not constituting acts of war were consistent with Articles 12 to 15 of the League Covenant. The Committee gave an evasive reply in the following words:

> "Coercive measures which are not intended to constitute acts of war may or may not be consistent with the provisions of Articles 12 to 15 of the Covenant."

Article 2 Clause 4 of the U.N. Charter, of course, prohibits "threat or use of force against the territorial integrity or political independence of any State, or in any other manner inconsistent with the purposes of the United Nations." Reprisals which include threat or use of force would, therefore, be considered as having been prohibited by the U.N. Charter. Nevertheless, States have resorted to reprisals as and when necessary in order to get redress of their real or supposed grievances. States have resorted to reprisals even when they are specifically prohibited as against prisoners of war. But in time of war, prisoners of war are often the victims of reprisals.

Reprisals, illegal by themselves, are permitted as a counter-measure against illegal acts of the other State. In some cases, they have proved to be effective means of preventing recurrence of illegal acts by the other State. The two world wars bear witness to many acts of reprisals and counter-reprisals by the belligerents. In recent days, Israel has often resorted to reprisals against the so-called illegal acts by Palestine terrorists. Only sometime back in 1968, Israel attacked Beirut civil airport, resulting in the loss of many aircraft, as a measure of reprisals against the attack on an Israeli aircraft at Athens airport, by Palestinian terrorists based in Lebanon.

Reprisals are sought to be condoned if they fulfil two conditions:

(a) Demand for redress has been made and it has not been complied;

(b) Reprisals are proportionate to the injury suffered.

Validity of reprisals normally fails because reprisals are more often than not disproportionate to the injury sought to be redressed. The Israeli attack on Beirut civil airport was considered as disproportionate to the injury inflicted upon Israel. Reprisals are also the monopoly of a strong nation against weak nation. Therefore, reprisals are not recognised by the world community. Reprisals are reminiscent of the gun-boat diplomacy which should be discouraged as far as possible. In 1934, Institute of International Law adopted a resolution prohibiting resort to reprisals involving use of force except in the case of self-defence or an international action authorised by the world body. It was naive on part of some persons to justify the dropping of an atom bomb on Hiroshima and Nagaski by the United States in 1945 as a measure of reprisals against the illegal acts of the Axis Powers, including Japan. That may be an excuse but not a valid reason.

Pacific Blockade

Pacific Blockade is blockading of another State's coast in order to inconvenience the latter during peacetime and thus compel her to redress grievances of the blockading State. Pacific blockade, as a compulsive procedure short of war, has been resorted to for settling international disputes since the 19th century. It was first applied in 1827 by the British, French and Russian ships jointly against the coast of Greece in her fight for independence against Turkey. Since then, there have been a number of instances involving resort to use of pacific blockade as a means for getting redress from the blockaded State.

Jurists are divided over the validity of pacific blockade. There is, however, the Declaration by the Institute of International Law in 1887 making pacific blockade as valid. It cannot be denied that big nations have resorted to pacific blockade as a means to get redress for real or illusory grievances. In most of the cases, weak nations are the victims of pacific blockade. However, Cuban quarantine in 1962, as Kennedy called it, is a solitary instance where it was applied against another big State—the Soviet Union—to compel her to remove missiles from Cuban soil or face war. The gamble paid and Kruschev withdrew the missiles from Cuba. In that way surely, pacific blockade is a lesser evil than war.

Embargo

Embargo is another procedure which aims at getting redress for its grievances from the other. State Embargo is putting ban on export of goods from within its country to another country with which it is not on friendly relations. The United States put embargo on export of goods to China and Cuba when it did not have friendly relations with them. The embargo has been withdrawn in the seventies. The United Nations has also put general embargo on export of goods to South Rhodesia because the latter has refused to yield to majority rule. Arabs resorted to an oil embargo in 1973-74 to pressurise the Western Nations to take pro-Arab stance in the Arab-Israel conflict.

Embargo may not be as effective weapon as reprisals or pacific blockade but it is less hostile and there is less risk of it being escalated to war. Besides, it depends upon circumstances. Monopoly embargo may succeed as the oil embargo succeeded in 1973-74.

Limited Force

Limited force may be used as a measure of self-help to settle a dispute with another State. Iceland's use of force against British trawlers fishing within Iceland's controversial waters may be one way of settling the dispute. Violation of a State's border may be repulsed by use of force which is only intended to stop recurrence of border violations in the future. Limited use of force has sometimes become very effective and brought about desirable results. Syria used limited force to secure a durable cease-fire and comparative peace between the warring factions of Lebanon in 1975-76.

CHAPTER 28

INTERVENTION

Intervention may be defined as dictatorial interference in the affairs of another sovereign State [1]. Interference has got to be dictatorial in order to constitute intervention. If it is not dictatorial, it does not amount to intervention. Up to this point, there is a general consensus. Beyond this, we enter into the realm of uncertainty.

In a wide sense, any utterance by one State with respect to another State may constitute intervention. For example, if some State asks India to settle the Kashmir dispute with Pakistan, it may be interpreted as intervention. Economic aid may be used as a lever to pressurise another country into a particular course of conduct. Foreign broadcasts beamed at the people of another country may be termed as intervention. Sabotage or subversion could amount to intervention in the affairs of another State. Imparting military training to foreign nationals for fomenting trouble within their country may be termed intervention. So also when a State facilitates within its territory the formation of an exile government which aims at overthrow of the parent government abroad. The Indian Government has not allowed Dalai Lama to form an exile government of Tibet in India despite several pressures. Premature recognition, or non-recognition when it is due, may be interpreted as intervention in a loose sense. It was on this ground that the Indian Government did not recognise the Bangla Desh Government before 6th December, 1971 despite much local pressure brought on it to do so.

The difference should be reocgnised between one Government's intervention in the affairs of another State, and the freedom of press. In a democratic country, a free press or an individual may make statements which may not be desirable if the same were to be uttered by a governmental agency. Unfortunately, only democratic countries can appreciate this difference. Elsewhere, it is wrongly believed as intervention.

But in the legal sense, one understands by intervention such use of force or threat thereof to pressurise the foreign State to act according to the dictates of the former State. There must be something dictatorial in the State's behaviour towards another State. We are mainly concerned here with overt not subtle acts of intervention. Nor are we concerned here with the friendly advice given by one State to another State in good faith.

It is said that although intervention is contrary to international law as it violates State sovereignty, it may be justified in some situations. Oppenheim, and for that reason many other Western authors, are of the view that a State may have the right of intervention in some cases [2]. Whether or not such right exists is analysed below.

(1) It is said that a "State which holds a protectorate has a right to intervene in all the external affairs of the protected State" [3]. It is hard to call such an act as intervention. A State which has another State as a protectorate has the right to regulate external affairs of the protected State. Therefore, to call such regulation of affairs as intervention would be a misnomer. Besides, the institution of protectorate is normally the product of an agreement between the two States. Hence any act done with the consent of another State cannot be considered as intervention. Again, a protectorate is not a fully sovereign State. Therefore, it would not be called an act of intervention.

(2) It is said that a State has a right to intervene in the external affairs of another State if "an external affair of a State is at the same time by right an affair of another State".[4]

It may be submitted that no such right of intervention exists or should exist. If a State is interested in a particular external act of another State which has taken the action unilaterally, it will be better for the aggrieved party to protest and ask for adjudication rather than use force or threat thereof. This is exactly what happened when Nicargua and the United States entered into the Bryan-Chammorrow Treaty in 1914 which gave, besides cession of Great and Little Corn Islands in the Carribean Sea, an exclusive option to the United States to construct another interoceanic canal through the Nicaraguan territory. Costa Rica, El Salvador and Honduras protested against this treaty on the ground that it violated the rights of those States under an earlier treaty. The first two States also brought an action against Nicargua in the Central American Court of Justice where their stand was vindicated [5]. Perhaps, if a big power had been aggrieved, it would have assumed the right of intervention which is not correct. Similarly, when India prohibited passage of Pakistan aircraft through Indian airspace, Pakistan could not have the right to intervene. On the same grounds, when Uganda expelled Asians from within its territory, countries concerned could not intervene. Yet when India protested against the lifting of embargo on sale of arms to Pakistan by the United States in 1974, this was not intervention but only an expression of concern to the United States.

Something needs to be said about Deconcini's Amendment which was attached to Panama Treaty ratification by the United States Senate on 16th March, 1978. Arizona Senator's Amendment which was accepted by the U.S. Administration, was that "the United States of America and the Republic of Panama shall each independently have the right to take such steps as it deems necessary including the use of military force in Panama, to reopen the canal or restore the operations of the canal, as the case may be." To make the thing worse, the Senator explained during his floor speech in the Senate that his main motivation "is directed toward situation in which the canal is closed because of internal difficulties in Panama."

Deconcini doctrine (Amendment) was clarified by Senate vote on 18 April, 1978. According to it, any U.S. action "to assure that the Panama Canal shall remain open, neutral, secure and accessible...shall not have as it purpose nor be interpreted as a right of intervention in the internal affairs of the Republic of Panama or interference with its political independence and sovereign integrity."

How far this clarification is genuine or camouflage, it is yet to be seen. It may, however, be made clear that any action under the pretext of keeping the canal open will be construed as intervention, irrespective of any other name given to its action. Deconcini Doctrine smacks of interventionist tone and is reminiscent of Article 7 of the Treaty of Habana, 1903, discussed in the next paragraph. It was unfortunate for Carter administration to accept this reservation.

(3) Intervention is said to be justified if the State does not

comply with the restrictions imposed upon her exercise of internal or external sovereignty [6]. The United States action in Panama in 1904 under the Treaty of Habana, 1903 is sought to be justified under this clause. Article 7 of the U.S. Panamian Treaty provided that "the same right and authority are granted to the United States for the maintenance of public order in the cities of Panama and Colon, and the territories and harbours adjacent thereto, in case the Republic of Panama should not be able to maintain such order" [7]. The Franco-British and Russian intervention in Greece in 1917 for purposes of re-establishing constitutional government there in pursuance of the Treaty of London, 1863 was also sought to be justified on the above pretext.

In fact no such right of intervention exists in international law. Self-assumed rights do not create customary rules of international law. Britain, France and Israel invaded Egypt in 1956 when Egypt nationalised the Suez Canal. The two big powers tried to justify their intervention on the plea of protection of its vital interests and violation of the Constantinople Convention, which made the Suez Canal an international waterway, by Egypt. The pleas were rejected by the United Nations which condemned the adventure. There are instances of unequal treaty which lack validity in the modern world community.

(4) Some States assume the right to intervene if they have guaranteed by treaty or otherwise a particular form of Government or particular dynasty to rule in a given State. Of course, the validity of this premise is doubled by Hall [8] although Oppenheim is of the view that such a right can exist [9].

Nothing can be farther from the truth than this assertion. Every State has a right to determine for itself the form of government within its territory. No other State can have a right to intervene in the internal affairs of another State which has chosen a particular form of government even if it is not palatable to the former State. If it were not so, we would not have blamed the Soviet Union for intervening in Hungary and Czechoslovakia. The Brezhnev doctrine of limited sovereignty of socialistic communities cannot be fitted in the customary rules of international law [10].

The legal position is that the people of a State have a right to determine for themselves whether they would have a liberal, conservative or socialist form of government. Any outside intervention would be the negation of the right of self-determination. The right of self-determination includes the right to decide its political setup. It would indeed be prepostrous to think if the United States or the Soviet Union were to tell us as to which form of government we should have. It is on this account that the United States is disliked in Latin American States for trying to install or perpetuate pro-American Governments in those countries.

The situation may be different if some States have guaranteed sovereignty and territorial integrity of any State and that has been violated by one of the guaranteeing States or any other State either through direct use of force or incitement of internal forces. This problem arose when Archbishop Makarios, President of the Republic of Cyprus, was ousted by the National Guards commanded by Greek officers in July, 1974. As per the 1960 Tripartite Agreement, the Governments of the United Kingdom, Turkey and Greece guaranteed the independence, territorial integrity and security of the island. The Zurich Agreement also prohibited the union of the island with any other country. The purpose of a *coup d'etat* was to install a pro-Greek Government which may eventually facilitate the merger of the island with Greece.

Although, Turkey invaded the island on the plea of restoring a constitutional government and secure safety of the Turkish minority there, such an action lacks validity in international law. However, if Turkey and the United Kingdom had taken a joint action in pursuance of the Zurich Agreement in order to restore independence and constitutional government and maintain territorial integrity, the action may have been justifiable because of the earlier subtle intervention of Greece through its officers.

(5) It is alleged that a State can intervene if a State violates any universally recognised rule of custom whether in time of peace or war [11]. If such a right were to be recognised, it would open a floodgate of intervention in the affairs of another State on one pretext or another. The real remedy for the victim State would be to claim reparation from the offending State. Beyond that stage, no further right exists. This has been amply stated by the International Court of Justice in the Corfu Channel Case. In that case, the United Kingdom had asserted the right of intervention to preserve its right of innocent passage. As the Court observed: "The Court can only regard the alleged right of intervention as the manifestation of a policy of force such as has in the past given rise to most serious abuses and such as cannot, whatever be the present

defects in international organisation, find place in international law". [12]

(6) Many big nations have intervened in the affairs of another State on the pretext of protecting their nationals [13]. The United States is a great champion of this right, and it has intervened innumerable times in Latin America on the pretext of protecting the life, property and honour of its nationals. Britain comes next in claiming this right.

It may be made clear here that no such right exists or could be assumed. It is on this ground that the Calvo Clause was introduced to bar the intervening attitude of big States on the pretext of protecting business interests of its nationals. The principle was enunciated by a Argentine jurist. The purpose of the principle is that a foreign national who invests abroad has to agree that all his disputes with the host country will be decided by the municipal courts there. His State would not intervene.

It is true that one of the functions of a diplomat is to protect the interests of his conationals in a foreign country and this every State does. But diplomatic protection is one thing and should not be confused with intervention. The Calvo Clause does not bar diplomatic dialogue. India has entered into agreements with Burma and Sri Lanka on the treatment of Indians and protection of their properties in these countries. But to say that India could rightly intervene in the affairs of Burma and Sri Lanka on the pretext of the treatment of Indians and protection of their interests and properties in these countries would be negation of territorial sovereignty and political independence of another State. It is on this account that the British and Indian Governments felt helpless when the Ugandan Government expelled Asians having British or Indian passports in 1972. The life of a British Lecturer, Mr. Hill who had been sentenced to death by the Ugandan authorities in 1975, was saved by diplomatic efforts rather than by intervention. The sending of a four-man delegation from Islamic Secretariat to the Philippines in August, 1973 to advise the latter Government for equal treatment of its Muslim nationals was initially full of misgivings. Later on it turned out to be good will mission to bring rapprochement between the Muslims and Christians in that country. The Libyan President used his good offices with the Muslim rebels in South Philippines to patch up with Marcos. No State or group of States has a right to advise a sovereign government as to how it should treat its nationals who are in minority. However, any friendly advice rendered in good faith by one State to another State should not be miscontrued as intervention. Thus, when some Arab States advised Prime Minister Bhutto of Pakistan to patch up with his opposition, it was not intervention.

Something need to be mentioned here about Franco-Belgian armed action in Kolwezi in May 1978 to save the lives of their nationals and other foreigners. Reportedly they were being held hostages by Anglo-based secessionists who had raided the province of Sheba of the State of Zaire. Ordinarily, it is the duty of both the warring groups in civil strife to afford protection to foreigners within their territory provided foreigners observe neutral role. Things become difficult if the revolting group holds foreigners as hostages—as was the case in Kolwezi. In such a situation if the parent State or a group of States take a limited action to rescue their nationals, that would be justified. Rebel group would be ill-advised to harass the foreigners which may compel the foreign State to resort to rescue actions.

(7) There was also some talk of threatened intervention by the Western powers in 1974-75 if there was further hike in oil prices. Kissinger threatened United States' intervention by taking over Arab oil wells if there was strangulation of the Western economy by oil embargo or hike in oil prices. This threat was equally misconceived. It is the right of every State to exploit its natural resources and fix a price for its commodities. It does not lie in the power of a foreign State to dictate prices of a given commodity in another State except through international competition or unless there is agreement to supply a given commodity at a given price for a stipulated period. Can the Western nations be compelled to sell armaments or manufactured goods at reduced rates? Surely they would resist any such attempts. Why then threaten Arab countries which are not so military strong? Could the United States have thought in such terms if the Arab World were military strong? Such intervention is unlikely to be acceptable to the developing nations.

(8) There is talk of the right of intervention to protect violation of human rights in a given State. The International Commission of Jurists thinks there could be humanitarian intervention under

some conditions [14]. Others assert the right of humanitarian intervention if there is imminent or existing gross human rights violations and all non-intervention remedies have been exhausted. According to them, there should be the least interference with the authority structure of concerned State [15].

However laudable humanitarian intervention may be to protect the violations of human rights in a given State, any such right will facilitate an unscrupulous State to intervene in the affairs of a neighbouring State on the pretext of the latter having violated human rights. This will not be a welcome step. It will result more in the violation of territorial integrity than in the preservation of human rights. After all who will determine the violations. The assessment is bound to be subjective and motivated. Therefore, it would be better to deny any such right of humanitarian intervention, whatever be the motivation.

(9) Some States claim the right of intervention in the interest of self-preservation, self-defence and national security [16]. Israel threatened Syria in 1975 and 1978 not to interfere in Lebanese affairs or else it would have also intervened in Lebanon. President Ford, while speaking in Stanford University, in September, 1975, did not rule out intervention in the affairs of any foreign State if interests of national security require it. Brezhnev claimed that the Soviet Union has the right to intervene in Socialist countries if any of their leaders went stray and tried to take out a given Socialist country from the orbit of Soviet influence.

It may be of interest to mention here the Monroe Doctrine which President Monroe of the United States declared in a message to the U.S. Congress on 2nd December, 1823. In this message, he warned the European nations not to interfere or colonise the American Continent in return for American promise of non-interference in Europe. The purpose of the Doctrine was to impress upon the European States, particularly Spain to keep her hands off its erstwhile colonies on the American continent which the United States conceded as its sphere of influence. There was nothing wrong on the part of President Monroe to warn the European States against interfering in the American States which were struggling for independence. But it was not proper for Monroe to consider the American Continent as the United States sphere of influence and subject to its hegemony. The notion was misconceived although the United States has claimed this right even in the twentieth century. Cuban quarantine was resorted to in 1962 partly because of the U.S. fear that the Soviet Union was extending its net to the Latin American States and this was not liked by the United States Government. Of late, there has been some loosening of the U.S. grip over the Latin American States which have become emboldened with the support of the newly independent States. If Monroe doctrine meant to leave the American continent to itself, it was a good doctrine. But if it purported to replace European hegemony with that of the United States of America, it was indeed bad. The Third World badly needs the invocation of Monroe Doctrine in the sense that they want to be left alone without being interfered with by big powers or ideological diplomacy as is being witnessed presently in the African continent.

All these claims are ill-founded and misconceived. There is no such right of intervention. These claims are based upon outdated big power rivalry, trying to establish or maintain their own hegemony or sphere of influence in a given area or maintain balance of power. The Charter of Economic Rights and Duties of States as adopted by the U.N. General Assembly on 12th December, 1974 deprecated practices of establishing hegemony zones or spheres of influence. The earlier these notions are discarded, the better it will be in the interest of the world community. Days of hegemony of any power are gone and no State should consider it as its right to intervene in the affairs of another State on the pretext of self-preservation, self-defence, interests of national security or maintenance of a balance of power.

(10) Intervention may, however, be permitted under the U.N. Charter when the Security Council takes any action under Chapter VII of the Charter after determining the breach or peace or threat to international peace. Similar action may be taken by the General Assembly under the "Uniting for Peace" Resolution of 1950 when the Security Council has failed to take action due to veto.

From the above discussion, it can safely be deduced that intervention is a violation of international law as it is repugnant to territorial supermacy and sovereignty of a State. It was in the earlier centuries when the strong nations assumed the right of intervention in the affairs of weak nations. One has yet to see a weak nation intervening in the affairs of another State although its rights have been violated or are in jeopardy. It is an innovation of the Western nations to justify their illegal actions in the Afro-

Asian and Latin American States. There is no customary right of intervention. If any strong nation does assume such a right, it arises from a conceited notion of self-righteousness. Intervention violates Article 2(4) of the Charter which forbids use of force or threat thereof against the territorial integrity and political independence of another State.

It is in pursuance of this principle of non-intervention that the General Assembly has adopted the same in its Declaration in 1965. It provides that "No State has the right to intervene directly or indirectly, for any reason whatever, in the internal or external affairs of other State" [17]. This was again reaffirmed by another Declaration on the Principles of International Law Concerning Friendly Relations and Cooperation Among States in accordance with the Charter of the United Nations vide its Resolution 2625 (XXV) during the Silver Jubilee celebration of the United Nations in 1970. This Declaration said:

> "The Principles concerning the duty not to intervene in matters within the domestic jurisdiction of any State, in accordance with the Charter.
>
> No State or group of States has the right to intervene, directly or indirectly, for any reason whatever, in the internal or external affairs of any other State. Consequently, armed intervention and all other forms of interference or attempted threats against the personality of the State or against its political, economic and cultural elements, are in violation of international law.
>
> No State may use or encourage the use of economic, political or any other type of measures to coerce another State in order to obtain from it the subordination of the exercise of its sovereign rights and to secure from it advantages of any kind. Also no State shall organise, assist, foment, finance, incite or tolerate subversive, terrorist or armed activities directed towards the violent overthrow of the regime of another State, or interfere in civil strife in another State.
>
> The use of force to deprive peoples of their national identity constitutes a violation of their inalienable rights and of the principle of non-intervention.
>
> Every State has an inalienable right to choose its political, economic, social and cultural systems, without interference in any form by another State.
>
> Nothing in the foregoing paragraphs shall be construed as affecting the relevant provisions of the Charter relating to the maintenance of international peace and security."

The duty of non-intervention has been reiterated by the Charter of Economic Rights and Duties of States as adopted by the General

Assembly on 12th December, 1974. The former Prime Minister of Britain, Mr. Wilson, also warned against intervention at the Helsinki Conference in July, 1975. According to him, none of the 35 participating States will have any excuse in future to intervene in the internal affairs of others. He warned that "No excuse can henceforth be found for any participating State attempting to prevent any other State from exercising its sovereign rights or to intervene in its internal affairs." [18]

So-called Intervention by Invitation

Something need to be said here about intervention by invitation. As a matter of fact, the words, "intervention" and "invitation" are contradictory when used together. Nevertheless, they are used when a foreign State helps another State on the latter's request. Such a situation may arise when a State is threatened by internal disturbance or external invasion. If a lawful government is threatened by a rebel group which is supported by outside elements, the lawful government may seek assistance of a foreign government in such a situation. Similarly,if a comparatively weak State is invaded by a strong nation, the former may seek foreign assistance to ward off external threat to protect its political independence and territorial integrity.

Instances of intervention by invitation are mostly found in civil strifes. A legal government may be threatened by local revolt whereupon a foreign friendly power is invited to assist the legal government in quelling the internal revolt. In such a situation, if any foreign power does help the legal government, that is termed as intervention by invitation.

In a purely local strife between two or more hostile groups, the legal government should not seek foreign assistance. Any such assistance is capable of being misunderstood as intervention against the rebel group. Thus, if State A were to intervene in State B during civil strife between the legal government and local revolting group or community, it would be construed as intervention even if it is at the invitation of the legal Government. However, if the revolting group is basically helped by a foreign power, the other foreign power may justifiably help the legal government, if invited to do so. For example, Russian intervention in Czechoslovakia in 1968 could not be permissible in international law because Dubcek Government was not aided by any foreign power, even if Russia was claiming that it was invited by some of their Czech comrades which, of course, they equally failed to substantiate. Brezhnev's doctrine of limited sovereignty of socialist countries has no place in international law.

What had been the role of Syria in the Lebanese civil strife in 1975-76. Initially, Syria lent its good offices to the warring factions of Lebanon because it enjoyed the confidence of the Maronite Christians as well as the Arab leftists and 450,000 Palestinians stationed in Lebanon. Gradually, Syria became the mediator and was responsible for persuading President Franjieh to agree to resign (which did not materialise) before the expiry of his term as was the minimum demand of leftists and Palestinians. It agreed to police the various cease-fires from January, 1976 in cooperation with the Lebanese army and Palestinian guards. However, when cease-fires became illusory and ineffective, Syria used limited force when the Palestinians, leftists and Arab defectors from the Lebanese army under Lieutenant Khatib tried to harass and beseige the Christian villages.

In context of the above events, should Syria's use of limited force be considered as pure and simple intervention, which is unjustifiable in international law, or just assisting its neighbour at the invitation of the ruling President and Maronite Christians? Syria claimed that it came at the invitation of the above two to restore law and order in the country in the face of PLO support to local leftists.

It seems Syria launched its police action at the invitation of the *de jure* President of Lebanon to restore law and order which had been deteriorating since April, 1975. The situation became complicated in view of Palestinian involvement in favour of the local leftists. If it had been a purely local affair between two groups, Syria's participation would have amounted to intervention. In the given circumstances, it could not be considered as intervention. It may be termed either as assistance or an amalgam of mediation-cum-conciliation. Later adoption of the Syrian forces as Arab Peace forces reinforced the mediatory role of Syria.

It may be of interest to mention here the Zaire situation in April-May 1977. It is alleged that former expatriates from the province of Katanga invaded the State from Angola and ransacked some of the towns. The Zaire President, Mobutu, alleged that these expatriates were supported by Cuban forces stationed in Angola. Thereupon, he solicited logistic support from Morocco, France and Egypt. The triparty support could not be considered as intervention if Mobutu's allegations were correct. In that case, it could be considered as assistance to the legally constituted and recognised government.

NOTES

1. Oppenheim: International Law, vol. 1 (1955), p. 305 (Edited by H. Lauterpacht). He defines intervention as "dictatorial interference by a State in the affairs of another State for the purpose of maintaining or altering the actual condition of things."
2. Ibid, Brierly lists three situations for intervention and they are self-defence, reprisals and treaty right.—Brierly, Law of Nations (Sixth Edition) 402-03.
3. Oppenheim, Ibid, p. 306.
4. Ibid.
5. 10 American Journal of International Law, pp. 344-51.
6. Oppenheim op., cit. 307.
7. As cited by Oppenheim, Ibid, and Footnote 4 on that page.
8. Hall, Treatise on International Law (1924) Section 93.
9. Oppenheim, op. cit, p. 309 and Footnote 1.
10. According to the Brezhnev Doctrine, Socialist countries cannot go beyond the Communist orbit. Therefore, if any Socialist country wants to be independent of Soviet influence, other Communist countries have a right to intervene.—Soviet Land, December, 1968. It seems that the doctrine has been abandoned at the Helsinki Conference in July, 1975.
11. Oppenheim, op. cit., 308.
12. 1949 International Court of Justice Reports, p. 4.
13. E. Borchard, Diplomatic Protection of Citizens Abroad (1915); Dunn, The Protection of Nationals (1932).
14. Mr. Neal McDermot, Secretary General of the International Commission of Jurists, laid these requirements as below :
    (1) The State against which measures are to be taken must have shown itself manifestly guilty in respect of its citizens of systematic cruelty and persecution to the point at which :
        (a) their fundamental human rights are denied them, and
        (b) the conscience of mankind is shocked and finds that cruelty and persecution intolerable.
    (2) The circumstances must be such that no practical peaceful means of resolving the problem is available such as negotiations with the State which is at fault, intermediation or submission to a competent international organisation.
    (3) The international community must have had the opportunity within the limits imposed by the circumstances:
        (a) to ascertain whether the conditions justifying humanitarian intervention do in fact exist, and

(b) itself to solve the problem and change the situation by applying such measures as it may deem appropriate.

(4) If the international community does not avail itself of the opportunities offered and fails to act in order to prevent or put a stop to widespread violations of human rights which have been called to its attention, thereby leaving no choice but intervention then a State or group of States will be justified in acting in the name of humanity provided that:

(a) before resorting to force it will deliver a clear ultimatum of preemptory demand to the State concerned insisting that positive actions be taken to ameliorate the situation;

(b) it will resort to force only within the strict limits of what is absolutely necessary in order to prevent further violations of fundamental human rights;

(c) it will submit reports on its actions to the competent international agency to enable the latter to know what is being done and to intervene if it sees fit to do so;

(d) it will withdraw the troops involved in the intervention as soon as possible—

1972 Report of the Fifty-fifth Conference of the International Law Association (1972), p. 555.

15. See International Law Association, New Delhi, Conference (1974-75), Report of the International Committee on Human Rights, p. 17.
16. Strake J.G., Introduction to International Law (Seventh Ed. 1972) p, 111.
17. United Nations General Assembly Resolution 2131 (XX) of December 21, 1965.
18. The Statesman, July 31, 1975.

CHAPTER 29

WAR—USE OF FORCE

War is said to be an ultimate mode for settlement of international disputes between States. The world community is not as perfect as a national society. Under municipal law a person can get his dispute settled through courts which decide the disputing claims through judgment. International law is not so well organised as to settle all disputes between nations through the legal process. In this regard, international law has yet to achieve perfection like municipal law. States normally strive to settle their disputes through peaceful means; failing that, through compulsive measures, short of war. Both these procedures have been discussed earlier. If the dispute still remains unsolved, some nations take to war to settle their account with another.

Concept of War

War is an armed contention between two or more States. It is different from measures short of war. In war, the armed clashes are continuous and reciprocal; in compulsive measures short of war, use of force is stray, irregular and many a time unilateral. War is a trial of strength between the armed forces of two or more States, each trying to outwit and overpower the other with a view to settle some dispute or gain some territory or advantage which the other party is not willing to do in the absence of armed pressure. That is why war is different from reprisals and blockade which may involve the use of the armed forces on a limited scale.

War was once considered as an attribute of sovereignty and an instrument of national policy. Nations resort to war in the belief that they would be able to overpower the adversary. They are sometimes mistaken in their belief; consequently, the initiators of war are over-powered in the process. This is what happened in

World War II and the Indo-Pakistan War in 1971 when Pakistan started the war by bombarding Indian airfields. Nevertheless, strong nations have always looked at war as the ultimate weapon to redress some wrong or annexe some territory. It is also resorted to as an instrument of national policy. In some cases, war is not waged to overpower the other but with the limited aim of recovering some lost territory or getting one's country liberated from the metropolitan country.

War is waged by States, irrespective of whether they are recognised or not. It is enough if it is an organised group having the semblance of State. War should be distinguished from skirmishes or border clashes which may not be termed as war but only hostile acts involving the use of force.

War is a mutual involvement of the armed forces by both the parties. Unilateral use of force by one State against another without retaliation from the opposite direction may either be in the case of reprisals, military occupation or aggression. War is a contention, not a unilateral use of force.

Civil war is a war within one country between the established government and a rebel group which either wants to replace the established government or secede from the central government. The Spanish Civil War was of the first category while American civil war, the Biafran war and Bangla Desh war of 1971 were of the second category. Civil war may also be waged to unify the two divided wings of the country as happened in Vietnam. But this third category of civil war is not of common occurrence.

War is labelled as self-help which was very much prevalent in primitive societies. Today, a person is not allowed to take the law in his own hands because law is fully developed. Some consider war as an attribute of sovereignty of a nation. This makes the word "sovereignty" much maligned.

A war could be considered as synonym or apostle of destruction. A U.N. study has revealed that between 1600 and 1945, about 54 million people died due to war. World War II alone accounted for 30 million deaths; World War I for 9.1 million deaths; French Revolutionary and Napoleanic Wars from 1789 to 1815 were responsible for the third highest casualties amounting to five million deaths of civilians [1].

It is a fallacy to say that war settles disputes. Rather, it gives rise to other disputes and leaves scars which linger on. Banning of war has been a perennial problem. King Ashoka was so fed up with war that he took to Buddhism. The two Hague Conferences of 1899 and 1907 tried to limit the right to have recourse to war. The Hague Convention of 1907 prohibited recourse to war for recovery of contractual debts. The Bryan treaties tried to create a cooling-off period to ease tensions and prevent armed hostilities. The Locarno Treaty of 1925 obliged the contracting States not to resort to war against each other. In 1928 came the famous Kellog-Briand Pact. It was signed on 27th August, 1928 and is known as Pact of Paris and Renunciation of War treaty. Although it was originally signed by only 15 States, a number of other States accepted it. It was considered as near universal treaty before World War II broke out. The pact had two Articles. Article 1 banned the use of force:

> "Article 1—The High Contracting Parties solemnly declare in the name of their respective people, that they condemn recourse to war for the solution of international controversies and renounce it as an instrument of national policy in their relations with one another."

Although, the Pact banned resort to war as an instrument of national policy, war was still considered lawful in self-defence, as between contracting and non-contracting parties and as against contracting party which has violated the Pact.

Historically, the Pact was a very important development in the renunciation of war as an instrument of national policy. When Japan occupied Manchuria in 1931 and Italy occupied Ethiopia in 1935-36 after the Pact, these were considered as only setbacks. However, the Pact came to a tragic end with the outbreak of World War II which involved all the signatory powers in offensive or defensive hostilities. Nevertheless, the Atlantic Charter exhorted upon the States to abandon the use of force.

At the close of World War II, the international elites realised that States try to make distinctions between 'war' and 'use of force'. Therefore, the framers of the Charter avoided the word 'war' and substituted it by the phrase 'use of force'. Article 2 Clause 4 of the Charter says that "All members shall refrain in their international relations from the threat or use of use of force against the territorial integrity or political independence of any State or in any other manner inconsistent with the purposes of the United Nations."

The ban on use of force is one of the principles of the United Nations Charter. The U.N. Charter states in its Preamble that "armed force shall not be used, save in the common interest . . . ." The word 'use of force' is wider than the word 'war'. It is, therefore, implied that war is outlawed, irrespective of the fact whether nations use the word or not. The United Nations abjures resort to threat or use of force and does not permit any nation to reap the fruits of use of force. This is clear from the fact that the United Kingdom and France had to vacate Egyptian territories occupied in 1956 during the Suez Canal war. The United Nations Security Council has asked the Israeli Government to vacate territories occupied in the 1967 war vide its various resolutions. Israel has since vacated some of the occupied territories and handed over the same to Egypt. India vacated the Pakistani territories occupied by her during the 1965 and 1971 wars. No State is allowed to retain the fruits of war. This naturally makes the war partly unfruitful.

Legality of War or Use of Force

Today, war has become an enigma. Even States resorting to war do not label it as war. They call it armed conflict or hostilities. They are afraid lest they may be labelled as aggressors by the U.N. Security Council or the world community. War as an attribute of sovereignty is gradually receding. By theory of auto-limitation, States have undertaken not to resort to the use of force as an instrument of national policy. When Kissinger threatened to occupy Arab oil fields in 1974 if Western economy were strangulated, there was all round condemnation of his threat and no State or world leader could come forward to Kissinger's rescue. War is, therefore, a rare phenomenon. It is no more a sovereign act of a State. Nor can a State reap the fruits of war. However, use of force may still be resorted to in some very exceptional cases which are stated as follows:

(1) *Self-defence*

Every State has an inherent right of self-defence in the same way as every individual has an inherent right of self-defence to protect his person and property. Article 51 of the Charter reiterates this right of self-defence which may be exercised individually or collectively.

However, preemptive attack as a means of self-defence is not permissible. Israel tried to justify its attack on Egypt in 1967 as a means of self-defence in order to forestall an Egyptian attack which, according to Israel, Nasser was threatening. It had argued that in case of an Arab attack on Israel, it could have been swamped merely by the enormity of the Arab armed forces. No one has taken the Israeli arguments seriously. The Israeli attack was considered as naked aggression and she was asked to return the occupied territories to the Arab States.

Article 51 envisages the inherent right of self-defence in case of "an armed attack". Therefore, preemptive invasion cannot be considered as self-defence although some jurists have argued that States cannot have patience to wait for taking counter-measures in self-defence until it is actually attacked. It is enough to say that if the nation is threatened with immediate hostilities which look imminent, the threatened State may take preemptive action in self-defence. As Thomas Frank has said. "No nation, it is safe to suppose, would willingly sit by while another prepares its doom" [3]. According to McDougal, a State may resort to use of force in self-defence if it is "intolerably threatened by the activities of another" [4]. The argument has some substance and reasoning behind it but the difficulty may arise in case of an unscrupulous adventurer who in the guise of defensive war launches aggressive hostilities. The wording of Article 51 is intended as a safeguard against such excuses which the nations have given in the past in order to justify adventurist activities beyond their frontiers. It is, therefore, safe to assume that preemptive self-defence is not permissible in international law. This is the literal interpretation of Article 51. Any other interpretation will open a floodgate of excuses whereby nations will fulfil their evil designs by raising the bogey of self-defence against apprehended attack.

(2) *Decolonisation*

The U.N. Charter gives the right of self-determination to peoples of colonies to become independent. This right of self-determination can be exercised peacefully when by mutual consent, the metropolitan country grants independence to its colonial territory. This has happened in the case of many former British colonies like India, Pakistan, Sri Lanka, Burma and many other States in Africa.

However, if the colonial power does not read the writing on the wall and persists in keeping the colonial people under its yoke, as Salazar did in respect of the erstwhile Portuguese colonies, there is no other alternative for the colonial people to secure independence, except through use of force and guerrilla warfare. This is what happened in Mozambique and Angola. Indonesia, Algeria and Indo-China also secured independence through resort to force.

Many Western jurists assert that there is a blanket ban on the use of force under the U.N. Charter. Hence colonial people cannot resort to use of force to gain independence. Their argument can hardly be tenable. For one thing, there are a number of U.N. General Assembly resolutions permitting all necessary means to colonial people to gain independence. This would include resort to use of force against a reluctant liberator [5]. Besides, a colonial State cannot claim immunity from use of force for decolonisation because they themselves acquired control over colonies through the use of force. It is one of the principles of equity that one who seeks equity must come with clean hands. Since a colonial State has no clean hands, it cannot claim that the colonial people have no right to use of force to become independent. India had also to use force to liberate Goa, Daman and Diu from Portuguese rule when the latter refused to grant independence peacefully. It is also asserted that the U.N. Charter puts a ban on the use of force on States only and people are not affected by it They can, therefore, resort to use of force to liberate themselves [6]. In view of the above, it can be safely assumed that use of force is permissible to gain independence from a recalcitrant colonial State.

(3) *Recovery of lost territory*

If one State has lost some of its territory of a State which has used force in violation of Article 2(4) of the Charter, the former State has a right to have recourse to use of force to recover the lost territory, in case peaceful means have failed. The case becomes stronger if the U.N. Security Council has asked the aggressor nation to return the territory but it has refused or failed to do so. No State is entitled to retain the fruits of its aggressive activities.

Thus when Egypt crossed the Suez Canal in October 1973 in an assault on Israel, there was all-round approval of the Egyptian action in the world community and no State called Egypt an aggressor because she used force to recover lost territory. Use of force in such situations is justified on the ground that occupied territory is just like a colony and the parent State has a right to liberate the colony and drive away the aggressor from its occupied territory.

(4) *Under the Charter*

United Nations Charter envisages use of force under three conditions. Preamble of the Charter says that "armed force shall not be used, save in the common interest." Under Article 42, the Security Council is authorised to resort to use of armed forces if other means as envisaged under Article 41 have not produced the desired results. Article 51 gives the inherent right of self-defence.

It is thus clear that the United Nations may sanction the use of force in some circumstances. So far, the U.N. Security Council has authorised the use of force in Korea in 1950 and in Congo in 1960 although it has sent U.N. Emergency Forces to a number of States like the Indo-Pakistan border in Kashmir, the Middle East and Cyprus.

It is possible that the United Nations may take recourse to armed force in Nambia and South Rhodesia where U.N. mandates are openly violated by South Africa and the Smith regime of South Rhodesia. These will be instances of taking to armed force in the common interest to free Nambia from the South African rule and introduce the black majority rule in South Rhodesia.

Concept of Just War [7]

Although the use of force has been considered as an attribute of State sovereignty, it has been argued that there could be just and unjust causes of war. In ancient days, nations were exhorted to help the State which has been a victim of unjust war. A State which was involved in just war was to be helped, irrespective of the fact as to who initiated the war. Saint Augustine, the Christian philosopher, propagated distinction between just and unjust wars. Grotius said that nations had the right to intervene in favour of a State which is defending against unjust war. According to ancient Hindu philosophy also, wars were distinguished between just and unjust wars. Lord Krishna helped the Pandavas because they were involved in a just war.

From the eighteenth century, however, the wars ceased to be just or unjust. All wars were considered as an exercise of State sovereignty and the other States had to remain neutral. Things began to change with the signing of the Kellog-Briand Pact, 1928 which renounced war as an instrument of national policy. The United States assisted Britain in its war effort on the plea of Germany's unjust war and violation of the Kellog-Briand Pact of 1928. The plea however was not convincing.

The Charter of the United Nations has revived the concept of just war inasmuch as it is designed to save the succeeding generations from the scourge of war and member States have undertaken to settle their disputes by peaceful means and in accordance with the U.N. Charter. Article 2(3) declares the principle of peaceful settlement of disputes and Article 2(4) enunciates the principle of the non-use of force for settlement of international disputes. Articles 2(5) and 25 oblige the member States to assist the Security Council in its implementation of any action taken under Chapter VII of the Charter.

Today, use of force or threat thereof has been banned. Therefore, if any State threatens or uses force, it is a violation of the U.N. Charter and the other States are bound to take action in favour of the victim nation if called upon to do so by the Security Council under Chapter VII. That is the reason that Israel's invasions in 1956 and 1967 were considered as instances of unjust war and nations were allowed to take positive stands in favour of victim nations. This is also the reason that Sadat was not criticised when he crossed the Suez in October, 1973 in a bid to drive out Israel from occupied Arab territories. Similarly, wars of liberation are also just war. Again, if the Security Council takes action against South Africa or South Rhodesia, that will be treated as a just war.

Aggression

Since war has been outlawed, there has been search for definition of the word "Aggression". Aggression has been considered as the gravest crime against peace and security [8] and yet it defied definition for half a century. The first attempt was made by the Soviet Union when it defined aggression in 1933 in a number of treaties with it neighbours [9]. The U.S. Counsel at the Nuremberg Trials accepted the Soviet concept of aggression given in 1933. It defined aggression as:

(1) Declaration of war against another State;
(2) Invasion by its armed forces, with or without declaration of war, of the territory of another State;

(3) Attack by its land or air forces, with or without declaration of war, on the territory, vessels or aircraft of another State; and

(4) Provision of support for armed bands formed in the territory of another State, or refusal, notwithstanding the request of the invaded State to take in its territory all the measures in its power to deprive those bands of all assistance and production.

The International Law Commission in its first ever attempt to define aggression said that aggression would include "employment by authorities of a State of armed forces against another State for any purpose other than national or collective self-defence or in pursuance of decision or recommendation by a competent organ of the United Nations" [10]. The definition was not exhaustive.

Not satisfied with the I.L.C. definition of aggression, the General Assembly appointed the First Special Committee to define aggression in 1952 consisting of 15 States. This was followed by Second Committee consisting of 19 States in 1954. In 1957 a Third Special Committee was appointed to determine when it would be appropriate for the General Assembly to define aggression. The Committee after its casual deliberations for almost a decade decided in 1967 that the time was not ripe to define aggression.

However, the matter was again initiated at the Twenty Second Session of the General Assembly in 1967 by the Soviet representative to expedite the process of defining aggression. This resulted in the appointment of a Fourth Special Committee in the same year consisting of 35 members for considering all aspects of the question for preparing adequate definition of aggression.

In 1968, the Fourth Special Committee started its first session dealing with preliminaries like whether it would be worthwhile to have a definition, whether it be a general definition or enumerative or a combination of both. There were four proposals before the Committee. In the first year of its functioning, there was confrontation between those who wanted the Committee to continue and others who wanted the winding up of the Committee. Anyway, it survived; while the Soviet Union was in favour of its continuation, the Western group was not enthusiastic about it.

In 1969, these proposals were put forward one by the Soviet Union, second by a combination of Latin American and African States and third by the Western nations. This was followed by annual sessions in 1970, 1971, 1972, 1973 and 1974 when it ultimately recommended on eight article definition of aggression to the General Assembly. It was adopted by the Assembly on 14th December, 1974 after a debate on the subject for 51 years from 1923. In view of its importance the eight article text is given below.

Article 1: Aggression is the use of armed force by a State against the sovereignty, territorial integrity or political independence of another State or in any other manner inconsistent with the U.N. Charter, as set out in this definition.

In this definition, the term "State" (A) is used without prejudice to questions of recognition or to whether a state is a member of the United Nations; (B) includes the concept of a group of States where appropriate.

Article 2: The first use of armed force by a State in contravention of the Charter constitutes *prima facie* evidence of an act of aggression although the Security Council may, in conformity with the Charter, include that a determination that an act of aggression has been committed would not be justified in the light of other relevant circumstances including the fact that the acts concerned or their consequences are not of sufficient gravity.

Article 3: Any of the following acts, regardless of a declaration of war, shall subject to and in accordance with the provisions of Article 2 qualify as an act of aggression:

(a) The invasion or attack by the armed forces of a State or the territory of an other State, or any military occupation, however temporary resulting from such invasion or attack, or any annexation by the use of force of the territory of another State or part thereof;

(b) Bombardment by the armed forces of a State against the territory of another State, or the use of any weapons by a State against the territory of another State;

(c) The blockade of ports and coasts of a State by the armed forces of another State;

(d) An attack by the armed forces of a State on the land, sea or air forces or marine and air fleets of another State;

(e) The use of armed forces of one State which are within the territory of another State with the agreement of the receiving State, in contravention of the conditions provided for in the agreement or any extension of their presence in such territory beyond the termination of the agreement;

(f) The action of a State in allowing its territory, which it has placed at the disposal of another State, to be used by that other State for perpetrating on act of aggression against a third State;

(g) The sending by or on behalf of a State of armed bands, groups, irregulars or mercenaries, which carry out acts of armed force against another State of such gravity as to amount to the acts listed above, or its substantial involvement therein.

Article 4: The acts enumerated above are not exhaustive and the Security Council may determine that other acts constitute aggression under the provisions of the Charter.

Article 5: No consideration of whatever nature, whether political, economic, military or otherwise, may serve as a justification for aggression. A war of aggression is a crime against international peace. Aggression gives rise to international responsibility. No territorial acquisition or special advantage resulting from aggression are or shall be recognised as lawful.

Article 6: Nothing in this definition shall be construed as in any way enlarging or diminishing the scope of the Charter including its provisions concerning cases in which the use of force is lawful.

Article 7: Nothing in this definition, and in particular Article III, could in any way prejudice the right of self-determination, freedom and independence, as derived from the Charter, of peoples forcibly deprived of that right and referred to in the Declaration on Principles of International Law Concerning Friendly Relations and Cooperation among States in accordance with the U.N. Charter, particularly peoples under colonial and racist regimes or other forms of alien domination; nor the right of these peoples to struggle to that end to seek and receive support in accordance with the principles of the Charter and in conformity with the above mentioned Declaration.

Article 8: In their interpretation and application, the above provisions are interrelated and each provision should be construed in the context of the other provisions.

Analysis of the text

Article 1 defines aggression as use of armed force by one State against the sovereignty, territorial integrity or political independence of another State. The aggressor State or the victim State may or may not have been recognised. Nor does it need to be a member of the United Nations. There could also be aggression by a group of States against another group of States.

Article 2 makes the first user of force as *prima facie* aggressor unless the Security Council determines otherwise in the light of other relevant circumstances.

Article 3 deals with specific acts which are considered as constituting acts of aggression irrespective of the fact whether there was declaration of war or not. These include armed attack or invasion, military occupation or annexation of foreign territory.

Bombardment of or use of weapons against foreign territory or military of another State would amount to an act of aggression. Blockade of a foreign part or coast or attack on land, sea or air force of another State would constitute an act of aggression. Similarly, use of armed forces of one State which are already in foreign territory in contravention of agreement would amount to an act of aggression. A State allowing its territory to foreign armed force to attack a third State would be treated as having committed an act of aggression. Again if any State supports armed bands, groups, irregulars or mercenaries who carry out acts of armed forces against another State would be treated as having committed an act of aggression. Article 4 empowers the Security Council to determine other acts as constituting aggression.

Article 5 makes aggression as a crime against international peace. Besides, no territorial acquisition or advantage resulting from aggression will be recognised as lawful. Aggression cannot be justified on grounds of political, military, economic or other considerations.

Article 7 is a very important Article which says that various acts of aggression as enumerated in Article 3 will not prejudice the right of self-determination, freedom and independence of peoples against colonial and racist regimes. This would imply that if people of colonies, Nambia and South Rhodesia, resort to acts enumerated in Article 3, they will not be construed as acts of aggression.

Article 8 is a guideline for interpretation of the whole text. It says that no article is self-contained. All articles are interdependent. Each article, therefore, need not be interpreted independently but in context of the entire text.

NOTES

1. New York Herald (International) February 15, 1972.
2. Oppenheim, op. cit. vol. II, pp. 182-83.
3. Thomas Frank, Who killed Article 2(4) (1970) 64 A.J.I.L., 820.
4. 1963 Proceedings of A.S.I.L. 164.
5. U.N.G.A. Resolution: also see Hingorani, International Law Through United Nations (1972), p. 6.
6. Max Sorenson, Manual of Public International Law (1968) pp. 771-72.
7. Y. Melzer, Concepts of Just War (1975).
8. U.N.G.A. Resolution, 380 (V) of Nov. 17, 1950.
9. (1933) 27 A.J I.L. Supplement.
10. Vide its report in 1951.

CHAPTER 30

REGULATION OF WAR

Although war is an apostle of destruction and misery, it is not an absolute anarchy. It has always been the endeavour of international elites to minimise the rigours of war by regulating its conduct as far as possible. These regulations may be found in the Declaration of Paris, 1856, Geneva Convention of 1864, Declaration of St. Petersburg, 1868, the two Hague Conventions of 1899 and 1907, Geneva Protocol of 1925, and Geneva Conventions of 1929 and 1949. These documents relate to declaration of war, lawful combatancy, extent of injury, permissible weapons and war crime trials. They are all discussed below.

Declaration of War

It has been said that declaration of war is necessary for commencement of hostilities. Grotius considered it as an essential requirement for initiating war. He was supported by Vattel in this. While declaration of war may be desirable, State practices have not fortified this desire. Since waging of war was considered to be an attribute of sovereignty, nations did not bother to make a declaration of war before initiating hostilities. In some respects, surprise attack gave the warring State an initial advantage over its adversary. In 1906, the Institute of International Law, an important body of academic international lawyers, adopted the principle of declaration of war before initiation.

The second Hague Conference of 1907 was prompted by an earlier Russo-Japanese War in 1904 to consider the modality for initiating hostilities. Article I of Convention III of 1907 tried to fill the gap by saying: "The contracting powers recognise that hostilities between them must not commence without a previous and unequivocal warning which shall take the form of either of a declaration of war, giving reasons or of an ultimatum with a conditional declaration of war." Unfortunately, no war since then has ever been initiated by prior declaration of war. Declaration of war was, of course, handed over during World War I after commencement of hostilities [1]. The situation in subsequent wars has not been too different. Japan occupied Manchuria in 1931. Italy occupied Ethiopia in 1937. There were undeclared hostilities between China and Japan in 1937. The Soviet Union occupied Finland in 1938 quietly. Germany and the Soviet Union invaded Poland in 1939 without any warning. Japan attacked Pearl Harbour on December 7th, 1941 thus sparking off the spreading of World War II to the Asian region without prior declaration of war. Israel bombarded Egyptian airfields without prior warning in June 1967 war. Pakistan bombarded Indian airfields without a declaration of war on 3rd December, 1971. Communication of an ultimatum with a conditional declaration of war as a second alternative required under Article 1 of Convention III has been equally absent in most of the wars in the twentieth century.

Matters have worsened with regard to declaration of war in view of the renunciation of war as an instrument of national policy in 1928 and ban on use of force under Article 2 Clause 4 of the U.N. Charter. States have, therefore, intentionallly avoided issue of a declaration of war on grounds of political and strategic considerations. Politically, States do not want to be branded as aggressors or first initiators of hostilities. They would prefer to initiate war or use force without much ado and be able assert their act as self-defence or self-preservation. Strategically, surprise attack partly cripples the adversary which may not be the case when the war commences with prior declaration. The United States had an initial shock when Pearl Harbour was bombarded by Japan and similarly the Egyptian armoury was crippled in the June 1967 war. It took Egypt a number of years to recover from the 1967 shock suffered from surprise attack. Pakistan tried to take India unawares when it bombarded a number of Indian airfields simultaneously in December, 1971 but failed in its mission. However, India had suffered severe reverses from China's surprise attack in 1962.

The absence of a declaration of war or ultimatum with conditional declaration of war does not have the effect of altering the rules of war. Uniform rules of war are applicable to each war situation irrespective of the declaration or not. The initiator of hostilities may incur penalty, whatever that be, for violating Article I of Convention III. Beyond that, declaration or no declaration makes no difference as far as the conduct of war is concerned.

Commencement of War

When does war commence? If there is declaration of war, it solves the problem as to commencement. War starts with the issue of the declaration of war. In some cases, even the issue of ultimatum may be helpful in the determination of the timing of the commencement. Difficulty may, however, arise as to the commencement when there is neither a declaration nor ultimatum.

Every use of force is not war. Nor each engagement of armed forces between two or more States. There may be a limited use of force without amounting to war as in the case of retortion, reprisals, blockade or skirmish. War is an extended use of force between two or more States with a view to impose its will on another. In order to constitute war, there must be *animo belligerendi*—intention to wage war in order to outwit the other. It is possible that a State may have resorted to limited use of force in the hope that it would achieve the objective in view but the other State may have resisted the use of force against it and this may have sparked off the commencement of war.

Complications may sometime arise when both the warring nations deny the existence of a state of war between them. This happened during the Sino-Japanese war in 1937 when both Japan and China denied being in a state of war against each other. Surprisingly, some third States accepted their version and did not have to announce neutrality.

Determination of commencement of war is necessary to invoke the application of rules of warfare to the hostilities and enable the third State to announce their neutrality with its attendant rights and duties.

Lawful Combatants

War is waged by a State through combatants. The armed forces constitute the major bases of power of any State. Warring nations employ the members of their armed forces to commit hostilities.

Homicide is not normally excusable. However, in times of war, members of armed forces of one belligerent are entitled to inflict injury or kill their counterparts in the opposite camp. Any such homicide is permissible provided it is committed by such persons who are lawfully authorised to commit hostilities. These persons are called lawful combatants. They can inflict injury and it can be inflicted on them. Categories of lawful combatants are discussed as follows.

(a) *Armed forces*

They consist of members of the army, navy and air force. What constitutes members of army, navy or air force is entirely an internal affair of a State. Armed forces may consist of permanent cadres in the armed forces or even national militia or volunteer corps if the State treats them as such. Of late, it has become a fashion among States to maintain a standing army. Previously, only big States used to have a standing army while small states used to maintain national militia and volunteer corps which could be called up for duty at short notice. Even now some States which cannot afford to have big armed forces maintain a reserve list of trained personnel who can be enlisted at short notice. Iceland, Gabon and Togo have no standing armies but only national militia. On the other hand, Isreal has a large reserve list of trained personnel, besides its standing army. In some other countries, apart from the regular members of armed forces, there are paramilitary forces which can be termed second line of defence inasmuch as they can be trained for war purposes within a short spell of time. In India, such forces consist of members of the Border Security Force, Central Reserve Police, State Military Police, members of the territorial army, members of the National Cadet Corps and the Home Guards. A State may treat all such personnel as members of its armed forces and as such lawful combatants if they are so authorised and carry letters of identification as required of them under the Hague Regulations [2]. It is immaterial if the members of the armed forces are nationals of the country or mercenaries from foreign countries. India has a large number of Gorkhas from Nepal in its army and they are as much members of the armed forces in India as any Indians. Some Gorkhas may be found in the British armed forces also. They are renowned for bravery and good soldiership.

(b) *Paratroopers*

There are some airborne soldiers who are trained to operate within enemy line singly or in groups. Their mission is to commit acts of sabotage behind enemy lines or transmit any information through wireless to their base. Such troops are also known as commando troops. Each belligerent has such troops. In World War II, the German High Command ordered shooting of such troops even when they were found in uniform and were ready to surrender. In 1971, Pakistan also dropped some such personnel in India. They are all lawful combatants.

(c) *Irregular forces*

Irregular forces may comprise such personnel who do not belong to the regular cadre of the State armed machinery but they supplement the regular armed forces. Such irregular forces may be turned into lawful combatants if they are: (i) commanded by a person responsible for his subordinate, (ii) wear a fixed distinctive emblem recognisable from a distance, (iii) carry arms openly, and (iv) conduct their operations in accordance with the laws and customs of war [3]. Guerilla forces, members of resistance movements in occupied territories and members of liberation movements in colonial country belong to this category.

(d) *Levee en masse*

Residents of a town which is threatened by advancing enemy may lawfully take up arms against the invading army if they otherwise carry out hostilities openly and in accordance with laws and customs of war [4]. In 1962, when the Chinese army was advancing towards Tejpur (India), residents of Tejpur had the right to rise and fight against the Chinese army and be treated as lawful combatants. However, this facility of *levee en masse* is given to only such persons whose town has not been occupied by the enemy. In case, their town has been occupied, they can benefit if they organise resistance movements and fulfil the four requirements of irregular forces, as discussed above.

Oppenheim says that once the territory has been invaded, although not occupied, right of *levee* ceases. He has argued that *levee* is entitled to lawful combatant status only on approach of enemy and since enemy has already invaded, there is no right of *levee* [5]. It is difficult to agree with what Oppenheim says. *Levee* can be raised when the enemy has invaded the country and a given town is threatened with occupation by the invading army. In such a situation, people can rise in *levee* to defend their town from falling into the hands of the enemy. There is bound to be confrontation between the invading army and the *levee* when the enemy reaches the town and tries to capture it. Thus, although the town has been invaded, but if it has not yet been occupied, the people of the town have the right to rise in *levee* without being led by a Commander, and wearing a distinctive emblem for which they may have no time.

Resistance movements

As opposed to *levee en masse*, which rises spontaneously on the approach of the enemy army, resistance movements operate within occupied areas. The objective of resistance movements is to harass the occupying forces and keep the morale of the residents high until such time when they can force out the occupying forces from their territory. Resistance movements may consist of the remnants of armed forces of the occupied State who have escaped capture at the hands of the occupying power and some other patriotic citizens who do not mind sacrificing their lives for the liberation of their State.

Resistance movements were witnessed during World War II in territories occupied by the Axis powers, particularly in France, Greece, Yugoslavia, the Netherlands and Belgium. The occupying power refused to give them prisoner of war status on their capture because they were not considered as lawful combatants. As a matter of fact, resistance movements were successful only in Greece and Yugoslavia and partly in France. After World War II, resistance movements were accorded lawful combatant status on the analogy of members of the irregular forces if they fulfil the four requirements of being commanded by a responsible officer, wearing distinctive emblem recognisable from a distance, carrying arms openly and conducting hostilities in accordance with rules and customs of war. This was perhaps a concession to post-World War II leadership of liberated countries because most of them were former members of the resistance movements in their country during World War II. How far they could fulfil the four requirements is a debatable point.

Difference between Combatants and Non-combatants

War, it is said, is between States and not between citizens of the two countries. Rousseau, the famous French political philosopher, was responsible for such differentiation. He could be right during his days. One has to assess this statement in modern days of total war when war is not merely fought between professional soldiers of the two warring nations only but between the citizens of the two countries on a number of levels. Jawaharlal Nehru once said that every farmer in the field and worker in the factory is a soldier. He was not exaggerating. They also contribute to the prosecution of war by supplying the accessories or tools of war. Who is more dangerous? The scientist who invented the atom and hydrogen bombs and the continental ballistic missile, or a soldier who uses them? Undoubtedly the scientist who is responsible for inventing such a deadly weapon. Again, how can a worker in an ordinance factory, which manufactures armaments, be considered different from the soldier who uses them? Should the worker be considered as an innocent civilian to be spared from the rigours of war while the soldier be killed because he uses the rifle or weapon manufactured by the worker? For that reason, how can you spare a political commissar who incites the soldier in the name of religion or ideology.

As stated earlier, Rousseau may have been correct during his days that war is a contest between States and not between individuals. Those were the days of monarchy and it made little difference for the common man whether he was ruled by monarch A or B. Today in the days of democracy where people have a say in shaping the destiny of their country, it is neither a war between States, nor between soldiers. It is a peoples' war where the people of one country are set against the other. Everyone contributes in his humble way in the success of war. A poet who composes patriotic songs is as much a participant in war as the one who sings it or the soldier to whom it is sung.

The concept of total war and aerial bombardment have further diminished the difference between combatants and non-combatants. An engineer who designs a bridge over the river for easy transportation of troops and war material and the persons who build the bridge could all be targets of aerial bombardment in times of war. There could also be aerial bombardment of an electric power house and water works to deprive the armed forces and civilians alike the necessaries of modern life. Scientific laboratories and factories, which augment war potential, could also be justifiably bombarded.

Nevertheless, the age old difference between combatants and non-combatants is still maintained. While combatants are the primary and direct targets of enemy attack, civilians only run the risk of modern warfare by being targets of aerial attacks if they work in or live near sensitive spots which can legally be targets of aerial bombardment. Aerial warfare however greatly affects the civilian population. Atomic war could be worse, as it levels off all differences between the two categories. All said and done, injury can be validly inflicted by lawful combatants only on their counter parts in the enemy camp. Non-combatants cannot inflict injury lawfully, although they can well be victims thereof.

Extent of Injury

The right of a belligerent to inflict injury on another belligerent is not unlimited. Article 22 of the Annexe to the Hague Regulations is pertinent on this point. It reads as follows: "The right of belligerents to adopt means of injuring the enemy is not unlimited."

While members of belligerent forces have the right to kill or wound the opposite numbers, the right is regulated by the above article as well as other rules of warfare. Violence can only be directed towards combatants of the other belligerent. Non-combatants are to be spared from violence. Even in the case of combatants, they can be killed or wounded so long as they are fit and willing to fight. Combatants who have become *hors de combat* (unfit to fight) or who surrender cannot be killed or wounded.

Refusal of Quarter

Article 23(d) of the Annexe to the Hague Regulations prohibits refusal of quarter to enemy soldiers who have become unfit to fight or have shown their intention to surrender. Denial of quarter has been considered as a war crime [6]. It has been alleged that there can be justificable refusal of quarter as a means of reprisal, or where it will imperil the security of the potential captor [7]. If the surrendering troops or some individuals therefrom are at fault, they can be tried for war crimes instead of treating the whole bunch of surrendering troops as cannon fodder.

Prohibition on Use of Particular Weapons

Nations have tried to ban use of such weapons which cause more agony than killing. Declaration of St. Petersburg in 1868 prohibited the use of projectiles of less than 400 grams which are loaded with inflammable substance [8].

The Hague Conference of 1899 adopted two Declarations—one banning use of Dum Dum bullets which expanded in the body [9], and the other banning projectiles diffusing asphyxiating or deleterious gases.

In 1925, nations adopted the Geneva Protocol banning use of chemical and biologically-stuffed weapons. It is heartening to note that the United States, a major producer of such weapons, ratified this Protocol in 1972.

It may be of interest here to remark that the banning of weapons causing unnecessary agony is not a new phenomenon. This was done even during the war of the Epic Ramayana between Lord Rama and Ravan where Ram exhorted upon Laxman not to use poisonous weapons.

Legality of the Use of Atomic Bomb

In the light of above observations, the question is naturally asked here if the use of the atom bomb by the United States in Hiroshima and Nagasaki in August 1945 was legal and whether such weapons can be used in future wars.

Oppenheim has considered the use of the atom bomb as permissible as a reprisal against a blatant violator of rules of warfare [10]. The United States has also justified its use in World War II against Japan because it hastened the surrender by Japan and thus saved many lives which may have been lost if the war had continued [11]. Some nations may justify the use of the atom bomb on the pretext of self-preservation.

The use of atom bomb was in violation of Articles 22 and 23 of the Hague Regulations. It was also against the spirit of the Geneva Protocol of 1925 to which of course, the United States was not party then. It was against the proposed rules relating to aerial warfare enunciated at the Washington Conference of 1923. The Conference prohibited aerial bombardment of towns, cities and civilian targets for causing devastation and terrorising the enemy and its population. Nor could it be justified as a means of reprisal which cannot be disproportionate to the injuries inflicted by illegal acts of the Axis Powers. No belligerent in World War II was free from blame regarding the indiscriminate aerial bombardment of civilian populations. Fortunately for the Allied Powers, they won and therefore all their misdeeds during World War II were covered by victory. Unfortunately for the Axis Powers, they lost the war and therefore their misdeeds were exposed in the form of war crime trials.

Nations may also seek to resort to the use of the atom or hydrogen bomb on the pretext of self-preservation. There could hardly be justification for the same. One's conscience revolts when one is reminded of the immediate and consequential devastation caused around Hiroshima and Nagasaki by the dropping of the bomb on these two cities. The United Nations General Assembly, which has been the enunciator of the principles of international law, passed a resolution in 1961 making the use of nuclear weapons as inadmissible in the conduct of war [12].

War Crime Trials

If war is not to be an anarchy, the rules and customs of war are to be observed scrupulously. Any violation of the rules of warfare has, therefore, to be condemned and perpetraters punished. This has given rise to war crimes and war crime trials.

War crimes are violations of the laws and customs of war [13]. These violations may consist of grave breaches of the Hague Regulations of 1899 and 1907 and various other Conventions relating to conduct of war including the four Geneva Conventions of 1949 relating to the protection of war victims.

War crime trials are not new innovations, although they have been very rare. Instances of war crime trials can be traced down the ages to the present century. The ancient war crime trial has been reported to have been in 405 B.C. when after the surrender of the Athenian fleet at Aegespotamos, the prisoners were charged with the commission of premedidated war crimes of which they were sentenced to death [14]. The fifteenth century witnessed the trial of Sir Peter of Hagenbug in 1474 for creating a reign of terror in the town of Breisaeh as its Governor. The Breisaeh trial has been considered as a forerunner of war crime trials of the twentieth century [15]. Some war crime trials were held in the eighteenth century also. In recent history, World War I was followed by the Leipzig Trials and World War II was followed by the

Nuremberg and Tokyo Trials, besides many other minor trials.

The Hague Regulations do not have any provision for war crime trials. Article 3 to the Hague Convention (II) of 1907 provided for pecuniary compensation for any violation. The Leipzig trials were based on Articles 228 and 229 of the Treaty of Versailles. Under Article 228, Germany recognised the right of the Allied Victor Powers to try persons accused of violation of laws and customs of war before military tribunals. The same article obliged the German Government to hand over wanted criminals to the Allied Powers. However, the German Government insisted on trying the war criminals by its own courts. The Allied Powers having consented, only six persons were convicted out of forty-five cases submitted by the Allied Powers. These were more or less shadow trials.

When the Allied Powers thought of holding war crime trials after World War II, there was no existing law providing for any such trial. They had, therefore, to draw a special Charter providing for war crime trials after World War II [16]. It set up an International Military Tribunal under the Charter to try war criminals. The Nuremburg Trials were held under the Charter. The Tokyo Trial was held under the Potsdam Declaration of 26th July, 1945 and special Proclamation of 19th January, 1946 by the Allied Supreme Commander in the Pacific.

The Legality of the Nuremberg and Tokyo Trials was not above question. Many doubted the legality and validity of such trials. Late Senator Taft had remarked that the Nuremberg Trials "while clothed with forms of justice were in fact an instrument of government policy, determined months before at Tehran and Yalta" [17]. Kelsen criticised it as "captor" show who was the creater of law, the prosecutor and the judge [18]. Radha Binod Pal's dissenting opinion in the Tokyo trial still remains as a classic [19].

However, soon after these trials, international elites tried to prepare a code which could be the basis for future contingencies. The U.N. General Assembly vide its resolution 177 (ii) of 21st November 1947 asked the International Law Commission to codify the Nuremberg Principles. The International Law Commission submitted its report in 1950 in the form of seven Nuremberg Principles which were adopted by the General Assembly in its Resolution 488 (V) on 12th December 1950. These principles are:

Principle I

Any person who commits or is an accomplice in the commission of an act which constitutes a crime under international law is responsible thereof and liable for punishment.

Principle II

The fact that domestic law does not punish an act which is an international crime does not free the perpetrator of such crime from responsibility under international law.

Principle III

The fact that a person who committed an international crime acted as Head of State or public official does not free him from responsibility under international law or mitigate punishment.

Principle IV

The fact that a person acted pursuant to order of his government or of a superior does not free him from responsibility under international law. It may, however, be considered in mitigation of punishment, if justice so requires.

Principle V

Any person charged with a crime under international law has the right to a fair trial on the facts and law.

Principle VI

The crimes hereafter set out are punishable as crimes under international law:

(a) Crimes against peace;

(1) Planning, preparation, initiation or waging of a war ot aggression, or a war in violation of international treaties, agreements or assurances;

(2) Participation in a common plan or conspiracy for the accomplishment of any of the acts mentioned under (1).

(b) War crimes: namely, violations of the laws or customs of war. Such violations shall include, but not be limited to murder, ill-treatment or deportation to slave labour or for any other purpose of civilian population of or in occupied territory, murder or ill-treatment of prisoners of war or persons on the seas, killing of hostages, plunder of public or private property, wanton destruction of cities, towns or villages, or devastation not justified by military necessity.

(c) Crimes against humanity: namely, murder, extermination, enslavement, deportation and other in-human acts done against a civilian population, or persecutions on political, racial or religious grounds, when such acts are done or such persecutions are carried on in execution of or in connection with any crime against peace or any war crime.

Principle VII

Complicity in the commission of a crime against peace, a war crime or a crime against humanity, as set forth in Principle VI, is a crime under international law.

Article 85 of the Geneva Convention (iii) of 1949 relating to Prisoners of War envisages trial of prisoners of war for war crimes. Article 99 of the Convention upholds the principles of *Nullum Crimen Sine Lege* which means that a person cannot be tried for any act which was not an offence at the time of commission. This was the main complaint regarding the Nuremberg and Tokyo trials.

No war crime trials have been held after the adoption of the Nuremberg Principles by the General Assembly in 1950. The Eichmann trial in Israel and a few other trials in Europe were the remnants of World War II. This is despite the fact that there have been a few wars like the Korean, Vietnam, the Arab-Israeli conflict and the Indo-Pakistan wars of 1965 and 1971.

The world community had at least two opportunities to sanctify war crime trials after World War II. One was the "My Lai" affair where the United States forces were alleged to have liquidated the whole village of My Lai in Vietnam. When the lid was lifted off the incident, the United States staged the trials of the accused who were either discharged or acquitted, except Lieutenant Caley who was convicted, acquitted and again convicted.

The other great opportunity afforded was in 1972 when Bangla Desh wanted to try Pakistani military personnel under its custody for war crimes alleged to have been perpetrated by Pakistani soldiers from March 1971 to December 1971 in erstwhile East Pakistan, now Bangla Desh.

It was indeed surprising that world opinion was not too enthusiastic about such trials in contrast to manoeuvres at the United Nations to waive the statutory limitations for trying war criminals of World War II after a lapse of more than three decades [20].

This raises the basic question—whether there should be war crime trials or not? If the answer is in the affirmative, it was wrong to miss the two opportunities afforded to the world community to sanctify the Nuremberg Principles. If the answer is in the negative as recent events have shown, were the Nuremberg and Tokyo trials justifiable? Moreover is it fair to resort to witch-hunting and to continue to hound the alleged war criminals of World War II [21].

In my opinion, whatever the initial controversial nature of war crime trials after World War II, war crime trials have been a part of conventional international law after the adoption of the Nuremberg Principles in 1950. It was, therefore, a mistake in not holding war crime trials in respect of recent hostilities. Nevertheless it is equally overenthusiastic to hound the alleged World War II criminals after a lapse of three decades.

Notes

1. Oppenheim, International Law, vol. II, p. 293 F. No. 4.
2. Article 1 of the Annexe to the Hague Regulations, 1907.
3. Ibid.
4. Article 2 of the Annexe to the Hague Regulations.
5. Oppenheim, op. cit., vol. II p. 258.
6. In Abbaye Ardene Case, Commander of German regiment was convicted by Canadian Military Court for exhorting upon his troops to refuse quarter to surrendering Allied troops—(1948) 4 W.C.R. 97.
7. Oppenheim, op. cit., pp. 338-39.
8. The Declaration was signed on 11th December 1868 by seven States.
9. These bullets were manufactured by the British Government in Dum Dum, near Calcutta.
10. Oppenheim, op. cit., vol. II, p. 351.
11. War ended within four days of the first dropping of the atom bomb on Hiroshima on 6th August, 1945. The second bomb was dropped on Nagasaki on 9th August, 1945 and Japan surrendered the next day.
12. U.N. G.A. Resolution 1653 (XVI) of 24th November, 1961.
13. Report of the International Law Commission (Third Session) p. 13.
14. As reported by Woetzel, The Nuremberg Trials in International Law, p. 17.
15. Schwarzenberger, International Law (1949) vol. I, p. 310.
16. Charter was drawn under the London Agreement of 8th August 1945.
17. As cited by Woetzel, op. cit. XII.
18. Kelsen, Hans, Will the Judgment in the Nuremberg Trial Constitute

a Precedent in International Law, 1947 International Law Quarterly 169-70.

19. Dissenting opinion of Justice Radha Binodh Pal in book form.
20. The General Assembly passed a Resolution, 2391 (XXIII) in 1968 for non-application of statutory limitation, with regard to war crime trials arising out of World War II events. In 1971, the General Assembly exhorted upon nations to cooperate in extradition of war criminals and noted that any refusal to do so was contrary to purposes and principles of the United Nations—Resolution 2840 (XXVI) dated 18th December, 1971.
21. World War II hangover still persists. Only on 14th December, 1977, Pieter Menten (78) was sentenced to 15 years imprisonment for taking part in mass executions by Nazi forces in Poland by special Court in Amsterdam (Netherlands)—The Statesman, 16th December, 1977.

CHAPTER 31

EFFECTS OF WAR

War brings in its trail a number of consequences which follow the commencement of hostilities. War is an all embracing event which affects national as well as international life insofar as relations with warring nations are concerned. These effects may be broadly divided into two categories—as between warring nations *inter se*, and as between warring nations and third States.

As Between Warring Nations

With the commencement of hostilities, all pending transactions between warring nations come to an end. This would include official as well as private transactions. They are analysed as follows.

(1) *Diplomatic relations*

There is rupture of diplomatic relations as soon as hostilities commence. In some cases, severence of diplomatic relations is a prelude to commencement of hostilities. In other cases, diplomatic relations are severed after hostilities have started. India and Pakistan severed diplomatic relations as soon as war started between them in December 1971. In some cases, when hostilities are for a very short while, diplomatic relations are not severed but only frozen just as in the case of the Sino-Indian war of 1962. During that war, both the countries continued with their legations but in a low key because the relations had already been downgraded from ambassadorial level to that of charge d' affaires since 1961. Besides, the war lasted for a few days only during which there was hardly any time to discuss modalities for closure of respective embassies. Normally during war, belligerents negotiate with each other through the good offices of a third country. Even when legations are not closed, diplomatic personnel remain confined to their chanceries and do not come out for fear of hostile demonstrations.

(2) *Trade relations*

Trade relations between warring nations come to an end with the commencement of hostilities [1]. This is but natural because all borders become war zones and traffic is suspended between the countries. Hence, there is no scope for trade between them Nevertheless, nations issue notification to the effect that trade with enemy is suspended. In many cases any clandestine trade with enemy is made punishable. War is a valid reason for termination of a contract either on the basis of supervening impossibility, frustration of contract or supervening illegality [2]. Even trade treaties come to an end. In the Zenso Arakawa versus Clark case, it has been held by the U.S. Court that war between Japan and the United States terminated the U.S.-Japan Treaty of Commerce and Navigation [3].

(3) *Enemy aliens*

Nationals of enemy country living within one's country are termed as enemy aliens. The warring nation may either deport or intern them or put them under strict security. In the eighteenth and nineteenth centuries, enemy aliens were allowed to withdraw. Oppenheim says that it has become customary law to enable enemy aliens to withdraw from enemy country, if their services will not help the enemy country [4]. However, with the advent of total war concept, it is difficult to accept such a position as a customary rule of international law. The Twentieth century practices go against any so-called customary rule of international law. In modern times, enemy aliens are either detained or strict watch is kept on them and if it is found that any enemy alien's movements are prejudicial to national security, he may be interned without enabling him any access to move courts for *habeas corpus*. Such right is normally suspended in respect of enemy aliens during war [5]. The United States detained many Japanese during World War II on the western coast. In some cases, the United States detained many U.S. citizens of Japanese ancestory. Sometimes, enemy aliens may be taken in protective custody to save them from local harassment. For this, they may be grouped and housed in camps. Some belligerents abuse this right and house enemy aliens in concentration camps just as it was done during World War II.

Enemy aliens may also include nationals of foreign territory occupied by the enemy. However, this does not always happen. It is left to the discretion of the territorial State to determine for itself whether to detain nationals of occupied territory. In such situations, only such aliens are interned whose movements are considered suspicious and prejudicial. Others are not affected particularly when these nationals of occupied territories owe allegiance to exile government which is an ally of the territorial State.

The Geneva Convention (IV) of 1949 relative to Protection of Civilians During War permits enemy aliens to leave the country unless their departure is prejudical to the security of the country. They are permitted to take with them reasonable funds for their journey. If detained, information regarding them should be given to their Protecting Power and they should not be asked to work which may increase war potential of the territorial enemy.

(4) *Enemy property*

Enemy property within the territorial limits of warring nations is either managed by enemy aliens under strict watch or taken over by the local government. Normally, a custodian of enemy property is appointed during the war to look after the properties which are left by enemy aliens. The property may also be taken over by the Government under Acquisition of Enemy Property Regulations if it is required by the Government for prosecution of war. The property may either be returned to its owner after the war is over or he is given some amount in lieu thereof. In some cases, it could also be seized by the government for any prejudical activities pursued by the alien. However, enemy property cannot be confiscated without any reasons as was the earlier practice. It makes no difference whether enemy property is within the territory or on its merchantmen. It was, therefore, a wrong British practice to confiscate enemy property on British merchantmen by making a convenient distinction between property on land and property on sea [7]. There is no justification for making such distinctions. Of course, public enemy property can be confiscated wherever it may be.

Regarding enemy merchantmen in enemy ports, although the Hague Convention VI of 1907 provided for enabling them to leave the port, practices during the two World Wars showed apathy to such Convention. It may, therefore, be said that enemy merchantmen may be taken over by the belligerent on the basis of *jus angary* but returned after the termination of war. Analogically, the same rule should be applicable to civil aircraft at a belligerent's airport.

(5) *Treaties*

Bilateral treaties between warring States come to an end with commencement of hostilities. However, bilateral treaties concerning boundary fixation on a permanent basis between warring nations continue to remain effective. They are not affected by a State of war between the two countries unless they can be categorised as unequal treaties which may be disowned by the erstwhile weak State which accepted the treaty under economic, political or physical pressure from the big brother. It may be that an unequal treaty relating to boundary fixation may be the basis of *cause belligerendi*. In such a situation, the position remains fluid.

As far as multilateral and general treaties are concerned, they continue to be effective despite war between two States which are party to the same treaty. However, in case of multilateral treaties, *inter se* obligations between warring nations may remain suspended if this could be implied from terms of the treaty.

As Between Warring Nation and Third State

War affects third States in a number of ways. First of all, they have to declare their neutrality expressly or impliedly. Their course of action is normally determined by their attitude towards warring nations which reciprocate in the same way. Nevertheless, neutral property in belligerent country as well as neutral trade suffers from the pangs of war. Some such effects are given below.

(1) *Right of angary*

A belligerent State has a right to requisition neutral property, including vessels and aircraft, within its territory for prosecution of war. Any such requisiton must be duly compensated and the property returned after war. The right to requisition neutral property by the belligerent within its territory is called the right of angary. It was originally applicable to vessels which were requisitioned for purposes of transportation of troops and munition. This is a customary rule of international law based on the principle of self-preservation. Belligerent has a right to acquire neutral property found within its territory if it helps her in the prosecution of war. Neutral property may either be used for offensive or defensive purposes. Similarly, it may be used or destroyed as the exigency of situation may require. This customary rule of international law was codified in Article 19 of the fifth Hague Convention of 1907.

Instances of exercise of right of angary were witnessed during the France-German war of 1870 when Germany sank a number of British vessels in the Siene in order to block French warships from using the river. Later on, Bismark paid compensation to the owners of the sunken vessels. It also used a number of Austrian and Swizz railway rolling stock found in France.

The right of angary is applicable not only to foreign property within belligerent's territory but also any such property which might be in transit through its territory, unless the belligerent has undertaken its safe transit through its territory. Even the property seized as contraband which has been brought within its territory for adjudication by prize court may be requisitioned pending decision by the prize court. This was so in the case of Zamora where the cargo of timber and copper was requisitioned while it was pending adjudication by the British Prize Court [8].

There was extensive use of this right during the two world wars. The Allied Powers seized the Dutch merchant fleet lying within the ports of various Allied Powers despite Dutch protests. The Allied Powers paid compensation for the services of these vessels which were returned to their owners after war. Compensation was given for such vessels which were destroyed during war. In 1967, a number of foreign vessels were sunk by Egypt in the Suez Canal in order to prevent traffic through the Canal. The canal was cleared only in 1975.

(2) *Contraband* [9]

Contraband is made up of two words—"contra" which means contrary and "band" which means ban—thing which is being sought to be delivered despite ban. During war, each belligerent makes up a list which it notifies to the neutrals and warns them that any delivery of contraband goods to the enemy will be intercepted and confiscated by it.

During war, neutrals are allowed to trade with the belligerents subject to the condition that any supply of contraband goods to one of the warring nations will be intercepted by the other belligerent. This is one of the risks of war which the neutrals have to accept in case they want to trade in contraband goods. It is naturally the effort of each belligerent to see that the enemy does not augment his firing power by receipt of such goods from neutral nations.

Contraband consists of such goods which the belligerent considers as helpful to the enemy in the prosecution of war. Goods are, therefore, divided into three categories—absolute, conditional and free. According to British practices, absolute goods comprise armaments which are of military advantage to the warring nations and about which there could be no dispute whether goods will be useful to the belligerent or not. Armaments, including vessels and aircraft, come in this category.

Conditional contraband consists of such goods which could be of use during war as well as during peace. These goods may include gold, silver, cotton, cloth, foodgrains and such other things. These goods are conditional contraband if their destination is for the warring nations.

Free goods may comprise such articles which have no relation with war efforts and may consist of watches, transistors, crockery, cosmetics, toys, etc.

Declaration of London, 1909 supports the British viewpoint although it has not been ratified. American viewpoint supports the British stand. The U.S. Supreme Court divided the goods in three categories in Peterhoff's case [10].

There is, however, the French view which divides the goods into two categories—contraband or non-contraband. According to this view, goods are either contraband or not. There is no such thing as conditional contraband. The French view is supported by the countries in Europe and, therefore, it is also known as the Continental viewpoint.

There seems to be some truth about the Continental view. The goods are either contraband or free. The same goods cannot be contraband as well as non-contraband depending upon circumstances. State practices also support the French viewpoint. Normally, the belligerent declares a list of contraband articles which is notified to neutral nations for non-supply of the same to the other belligerent. Goods are contraband when they belong to a given category and are destined for the belligerent port. This is necessary in case of contraband goods. Goods meant for neutral ports cannot be considered as contraband unless the neutral destination is only a detour and not the ultimate destination.

Whether goods are contraband or not and as to what is the destination of the goods is to be determined by the prize court. Essentials for successful confiscation of contraband may be summarised as war, declaration of list of contraband goods by the belligerent, notification of the list to neutral nations and enemy destination. Enemy destination does not only include belligerent territory but also occupied territory. If these essentials are fulfilled, the goods will be ordered to be confiscated as prize by the prize court of the capturing State.

Doctrine of continuous voyage: One of the essentials for valid seizure of contraband goods is that it should have enemy destination. Attempt is, therefore, sometime made to cover-up such destination by showing some neutral port as destination. The purpose for such ostensible destination is to avoid *en route* seizure of the contraband cargo by the belligerent. The contraband cargo is later on transported to its real owner, the warring nation, either through land route or continuing journey to the enemy port by the vessel or by transferring the contraband to an other vessel. Carriage of contraband goods in above circumstances would invoke the doctrine of continuous voyage and circuitous carriage of contraband. The contraband cargo, therefore, is liable to seizure during the first leg of its voyage if it is proved that the ultimate destination is enemy port, notwithstanding its ostensible neutral stopover.

Belligerents apply the doctrine of continuous voyage to check surreptitious supply of contraband cargo to enemy without risk of interception. This is based on the principle that what is prohibited to be done directly cannot be done indirectly [11]. In the case of "The Bermuda" which involved a carriage of contraband through the doctrine of continuous voyage during the American civil war, it was held as:

> "A transportation from one point to another remains continuous, so long as intent remains unchanged, no matter which stoppages or trans-shipments intervene". [12]

During World War I, contraband cargo bound for Denmark in a convoy of vessels belonging to different nationalities was seized by British men-of-war on the plea that it was really meant for Germany. The seizure was adjudged as lawful [13].

However, the problem may arise if the consignor and the shipping company honestly believed that the cargo was meant for a neutral country and it was to be discharged by the captain in a neutral port. It is possible that a neutral consignee had ordered it for a bordering belligerent or may have thought or intended to resell it to the nearby belligerent after it was discharged at the neutral port. Will the doctrine of continuous voyage be applicable to such a case?

Probably the doctrine should not be applicable in such a situation because the consignor and the shipping company were to discharge the cargo at neutral port. Besides, it was only the intention or wish of the consignee to make a huge profit by selling it to the nearby belligerent. That intention or wish may or may not materialise. However, if the bargain has already been struck between the neutral consignee and belligerent's agents for supply of the contraband cargo after its unloading at the neutral port, the cargo may be categorised as contraband liable to seizure. In the absence of any such bargain, the cargo cannot be seized. An additional factor which may be considered is the volume of trade in that commodity between the two neutral countries during peace time.

Prize courts: A prize court is an *ad hoc* court established by the belligerent country to determine the validity or invalidity of captures made by belligerent warships on the high seas in respect of so-called contraband cargo. Whenever belligerent warships seize any contraband cargo on the high seas on the plea that it has enemy destination, the prize court of the capturing State is called upon to adjudicate upon the validity of the seizure of the cargo. Although, prize courts are essentially concerned with seizure on the high seas, nothing prevents them from adjudicating upon aerial seizures in view of aerial gun-running in recent days. No contraband cargo can be condemned by the belligerent without the prize court putting a seal of its approval on such capture. Property in captured cargo remains in the name of the consignee until it is condemned as valid seizure by the prize court. Property in condemned cargo passes on to the belligerent as soon as the judgment is given by the prize court. Condemned cargo is called prize. Captured property can, however, be an object of right of angary pending decision by the prize court. If it is condemned, no compensation is due to its original owner. If it is released, compensation must be paid and cargo returned after hostilities.

Prize court is a national court of the belligerent appointed for specific purposes of determining the validity of capture. Each belligerent has a right to establish its own prize courts after the commencement of hostilities. In the Katrantsior versus Bulgaria case, the arbitral tribunal upheld the right of every belligerent to appoint its prize courts [14]. It lies within the power of the belligerent to confer the powers of prize courts on already established courts or constitute *ad hoc* tribunals which may be termed as prize courts. Both practices are prevalent. These courts may be final courts or there may be some superior courts also which may be empowered to hear appeals from lower prize courts. Prize courts may be set-up from civilians or military officers or from both. No criteria is fixed regarding the personnel of the court.

Whenever any contraband cargo is seized on the high seas, it is brought to the belligerent port for adjudication by prize court. If the facts are simple, the contraband is condemned and confiscated. But if the cargo is taken under the cover of neutral destination, it becomes complicated and the prize court is asked to adjudicate whether it could be condemned under the doctrine of continuous voyage. For this, evidence is to be led and facts ascertained.

A prize court is a national court but it applies an amalgam of international as well as municipal law. Since it is established by national decree of the belligerent, it has to apply the relevent municipal law along with the notification giving the list of contraband goods. But since it has to adjudicate upon the rights of neutral and enemy States, it has to apply international law also, including general principles of the law as are recognised by States. No prize court applies international law or municipal law exclusively.

Decisions of prize courts are a good source of international law. In order to form a persuasive precedent, judgments should be elaborate with proper reasoning. Short judgments without reasoning are likely to be misunderstood and treated as arbitrary and cannot serve as a good precedent. Nor should the decisions smack of a national bias. Once appointed by a State, the prize court judge should administer justice impartially without national consideration.

Prize court decisions have international implications. The decisions are final and cannot be questioned in a foreign court or in any international forum. It is on this account that some publicists plead for the establishment of international prize courts during war. As an alternative, warring nations may nominate *ad hoc* prize courts consisting of jurists from neutral countries. This may prevent the element of national bias or personal prejudices of the judges of a national prize court.

(3) *Right of visit and search*

Every belligerent has a right to visit neutral merchantmen to ascertain if it is engaged in any contraband trade or unneutral service for the enemy country [15]. The right can be exercised on the high seas or within the territorial waters of the belligerent. The belligerent has also the right to search the merchant vessel for contraband goods if the commander of the belligerent warship is not satisfied with the vessel's log books and bills of landing. The right of visit and search is exercisable by belligerent warships or aircraft as the case may be.

The right is supplementary to the right of capturing contraband cargo. The latter right cannot be exercised without the right of visit and search. Only neutral merchantmen can be visited and searched. This should include State-owned merchantmen although it is contended in some quarters that public vessels are exempted from visit and search. Neutral State-owned merchantmen do not enjoy such immunity. There is a recent tendency to form State-owned shipping companies. If such merchantmen were to be exempted from visit and search, the right can be sidetracked by engaging State-owned ships for contraband trade or unneutral service.

Neutral warships are immune from visit and search. So also the neutral merchantmen under the convoy of neutral warships. Article 61 of the Declaration of London (1909) reiterates this limitation on the belligerent's right of visit and search. Of course, if the belligerent's commander is suspicious of trafficking in contraband cargo by the neutral merchantmen under convov, he can seek assurance from the neutral commandant who is leading the convoy. As a matter of reassurance, the belligerent's commander may ask the neutral commander to verify if contraband cargo is taken by the merchantmen under the convoy and later on certify that merchantmen under convoy are not engaged in contraband cargo.

Neutral merchantmen must submit to a belligerent's exercise of right of visit and search. If the captain of the merchantmen resists any such right, the vessel can be seized and directed to the belligerent's port. Article 63 of the London Declaration makes the resisting vessel liable to condemnation. However, if the neutral warship resists any such visit and search, it does not commit any breach of customs and laws of war. It was, therefore, wrong on the part of the British prize court to condemn 'Maria' under convoy of Swedish warships which resisted such a visit. Britain claimed the right of visit and search of Swedish merchantmen under convoy of the Swedish warships during the Franco-British war in 1799. The incident was severely criticised.

The right of visit and search is criticised because it causes harassment of neutral merchantmen and impedes neutral's right of trade with both the belligerent States. Criticism is sometimes justified when the right of visit causes undue delay due to search of vessel on slight suspicion and towing it away to belligerent's port for the purpose. This was particularly so during the two world wars which caused great hardship to neutral trade. While abuse of exercise of right should be checked, there is nothing basically wrong with the right.

Since World War I, Navicert system has been developed in order to save the neutral merchantmen from going to the belligerent's port for search of contraband cargo. Under Navicert system, the belligerent's representative (Consul or diplomat) in the neutral country to whom the merchantman belongs certifies absence of contraband cargo on the neutral merchantman. This saves the merchantman from the botheration thereafter. The Navicert system was operational during World War II also. It was initiated during World War I in 1916 by the United States for carrying trade between the States and Scandinavian countries.

(4) *Blockade*

During war, every belligerent tries to block the coast of another belligerent in order to prevent supply of potential goods to the enemy and also stop its commerce with other countries No state is self-sufficient. It requires some goods from outside in exchange of its exports. Many States, particularly the developing countries, depend upon foreign armaments for their survival. They buy their arms by selling their raw materials and indigenous products. The purpose of blockade is to cripple the enemy's war potential by crippling her militarily and economically.

Blockade occurs almost in every war, depending upon the strength of the belligerent's navy which enforces the blockade. Only strong naval States resort to blockade of enemy coast. Neutral States have to bear with it despite the fact that neutral States have freedom of commerce. Blockade is an old institution practised during war, sometimes successfully sometimes unsuccessfully. Over the years a number of essentials of blockade have been established.

(a) *Existence of state of war*: Blockade is resorted to in time of war only. Therefore, there must be a state of war between the two or more contending States. Blockade in time of peace is called pacific blockade meant for settling some mutual disputes.

(b) *Blockade of enemy coast by men-of-war*: Blockade of enemy coast must be by men-of-war or aircraft or by both. It cannot be by enemy's merchantmen although it may supplement the men-of-war.

(c) *Notification*: Any intention of blockade must be notified by the belligerent to various neutral States stating its intention to blockade enemy coast. Article 8 of the Declaration of London 1909 provides for such notification. Although the Declaration remains unratified and, therefore, not binding, practices reveal that blockading States inform the neutral States about a blockade through diplomatic channels. British, American and Japanese authorities do not subscribe to the idea of notification.

(d) *Effective*: Blockade, in order to be a valid one, must be effective. This means that belligerent's men-of-war should be capable of enforcing the blockade. If it is not capable of enforcing it, the blockade is not valid. Dcclaration of Paris, 1856 made "effectiveness" as one of the essentials of blockade. Declaration of London confirmed it. Effective blockade is differentiated from paper blockade which is only on paper and, therefore, considered as invalid. Neutral States insist on effective blockade in order to be valid. In the seventeenth, eighteenth and nineteenth centuries there were a number of paper blockades which were only on paper and ineffective. There must be show of force and its occasional exercise to make the blockade effective. Effectiveness is also necessary to avoid long distance blockades which are normally ineffective. Blockade is considered to be effective, if it poses danger to neutral vessels trying to evade the blockade [16].

(e) *Universal*: The blockade should be applicable to all States. Blockade cannot be enforced against one set of States only. Any such partial blockade is not valid.

Blockade, pure and simple, is a wartime phenomenon. It should be distinguished from pacific blockade which is resorted to during peacetime in order to settle some dispute with the blockaded State or remedy some wrong done to the blockading State. President Kennedy called it 'quarantine' when he ordered the blockade of the Cuban coast in order to pressurise the Soviet Union to remove its missiles from the Cuban soil. The gamble succeeded.

Breach of blockade: If any State attempts to break the blockade by trying to get into the blockaded port, the blockading State may condemn the men-of-war which seek to bully the blockading men-of-war. During the American civil war, a number of British vessels were condemned on the suspicion that they were bound for Confederate ports. *De facto* or *de jure* knowledge of blockade on the part of the captain of the vessel is necessary for such condemnation. Any resistance to blockade may also spark off war between the blockading State and the State which seeks to dent into the blockade.

Long distance blockade: Two world wars witnessed long distance blockades of the German ports by Great Britain. Long distance blockade means blockade by one belligerent of sea routes on the high seas leading to enemy ports. This sometimes resulted in the blockade of even neutral ports. When Great Britain declared long distance blockade of German ports during World War I as a retaliation against the German declaration of the British Isles as a war zone, the United States protested against such a blockade as discriminatory and ineffective. Long distance blockade was repeated by Great Britain during World War II also as a measure of retaliation against German mining of British coast and submarine warfare.

Long distance blockades are not valid in international law. Britain justified such blockades in the two world wars as a measure of reprisals against illegal acts of Germany and as a measure of economic warfare. Such blockades affected neutral trade with belligerents and neutral merchantmen were greatly harassed by the British measures. In some cases, blockade covered a 1000 miles area from enemy ports and included even neutral ports. Such blockades were also not very effective. Such blockades, therefore, did not fulfil the essentials of a valid blockade although Britain justified the same in the context of modern developments of total war. However, it is difficult to accept the British viewpoint.

Termination of blockade: Blockade is terminated in a number of ways:

(a) *On cessation of hostilities*: Since blockade is the outcome of war, it terminates as soon as hostilities cease.

(b) *Withdrawal of blockade by the initiating State*: When the belligerent which has blockaded withdraws the same, it automatically comes to an end.

(c) *When it is ineffective*: It has been said earlier that a blockade in order to be valid must be an effective one. If the blockade has become ineffective, it has no validity in international law.

(d) *When the blockading contingent is defeated*: This is supplementary to effective blockade. If the belligerent warships cannot enforce the blockade, it ceases.

(e) *When the blockading State occupies the blockaded port*: This may be only by partial occupation of the enemy territory including the blockaded port or the whole enemy territory. In both the cases, blockade ceases with the occupation of the blockaded port.

NOTES

1. Oppenheim, vol. II, pp. 318-19.
2. Ibid., 322.
3. (1947) F. Supp. 468.
4. Oppenheim, vol. II, 306.
5. Ibid., pp. 308-10.
6. Ibid., pp. 326-27.
7. Ibid., p. 331.
8. The Zamora (1916) 2 A.C. 77.
9. Hingorani, R.C., French Seizure of Yugoslav Arms and the Principle of Contraband, 1959, India Quarterly 165-69.
10. (1866) 5 Wallace 58.
11. In case of Polly (1800) 2 C.R. 362.
12. (1865) 2 Wallace 551.
13. Kim (1915) Probate Division 215.
14. (1928) 7 M.A.T 39.
15. The right of visit and search was confirmed by the Permanent Court of Arbitration in the case of *Carthage*.
16. The Franciska, as per Lord Lushington; also see Geipel vs Smith (1822) 7, Q.B. 404.
17. Bermuda, Stephen Hart and Peterhoff vessels.

CHAPTER 32

BELLIGERENT OCCUPATION AND POSTLIMINIUM

Belligerent occupation means occupation of enemy territory with an intention to administer it. It has two essentials—physical control over enemy territory and intention to govern it. Sufficient military force is necessary for controlling enemy territory and enforcing law and order within the territory. There may be symbolic capture of capital of the enemy country from where orders are issued to other areas for compliance. Other areas may either comply with orders or resist. In the latter case, such resistance is to be silenced in order to occupy the territory effectively. In other cases the invader may occupy only part of the enemy territory. Article 42 of the Hague Regulations, 1907 says that there should be establishment and exercise of authority in occupied enemy territory in order to constitute belligerent occupation. Occupation should be distinguished from invasion. Invasion is an attack on enemy territory. Occupation is control over the territory with intention to administer it. Occupation is preceded by invasion unless it is the invaded country which repulses the invasion and follows the invading army into its own territory.

Belligerent occupation should be distinguished from occupation of enemy territory after war. Belligerent occuption means occupation of enemy territory while the war still continues in other theatres. Occupation of enemy whose territory after war implies defeat of and surrender by the enemy whose territory has been occupied by the victorious army. Here only belligerent occupation is being discussed. A number of countries were objects of belligerent occupation during World War II. They were France, Poland, Belgium and the Netherlands, to name a few. When Germany and Japan surrendered, these territories were occupied after cessation of hostilities. In some cases, occupation may be termed as belligerent despite the fact that hostilities may have ceased. Israel is still considered as in belligerent occupation of territories gained by her in the six days war of June, 1967. In the absence of a peace treaty between the Arabs and Israelis, it is a state of no peace, no war which may well be called a state of intermediacy. Technically, a state of war still prevails in the Middle East.

Belligerent occupation is one of the immediate aims of each belligerent because it can then bargain with the other belligerent from a position of strength. Besides, if the territory is rich in minerals or agriculture, it can derive benefit from such products as Israel got from the occupation of oilfields in the Sinai area and West Bank from the Jordan side which is rich in agriculture.

Occupation is not a state of anarchy. Days of anarchy are gone when the occupying power could deal with the territory and its occupants in any manner that it suited its caprice. Gone are the days of Genghis Khan and Mohammad Gouri when the invaders and occupiers could devastate the territory and use the inhabitants as cannon fodder. In the past centuries, occupying power could even cede the occupying territory or portion thereof to another State. Thus, Denmark sold Bermen and Verden to Hannover in 1715 while the war was still raging. Great Britain sought to transfer the island of Guadeloupe to Sweden in 1810 while it was still fighting France. Now, of course, belligerent occupation is governed by two specific documents, the Hague Regulations of 1907 and Geneva Convention IV of 1949, besides many other general documents. The Law of Belligerent Occupation gives a number of rights to the occupying power along with some duties also. These are analysed as follows:

(1) *Right to govern the territory*: When one belligerent occupies enemy territory effectively, it is its right to govern the occupied territory. For this, it can establish police posts and courts for maintaining law and order within the territory. The right gives the occupying power a handle to punish the law breakers. Article 1.3 of the Hague Regulations says that the occupying power shall "re-establish and ensure, as far as possible, public order and safety." It has the right to seek and enforce obedience to its orders.

(2) *Ensuring safety of its forces*: An occupying power has a right to ensure safety of its forces against guerilla activities of some of the inhabitants of the occupied territory and the remnants of enemy army within the occupied territory. In the process, it is possible that the occupier may resort to some ruthless measures

as military expediency may require.

(3) *Right to issue decrees and orders*: An occupying power has right to issue decrees and orders for proper administration of the territory under its control. In the process, it may be permissible for it change the preoccupation law if the situation so demands. For example, it can introduce rationing for conserving essential commodities for its forces. But, it cannot starve local inhabitants under the garb of rationing, although its armed forces may be its first priority.

(4) *It can impose and collect taxes* for purposes of administration and other functions which go with administration. Article 48 of the Annexe to the Hague Convention IV, 1907 provides for that.

(5) *The occupying power may impose levies* for the needs of the occupying army or of the administration of the territory. Article 49 envisages imposition of such levies. However, such levies cannot be exhorbitant and disproportionate to the local needs.

(6) *It can make requisition for goods and housing* needed either for local military needs or for proper administration of the territory. Article 52 permits such requisitions so long as these are compensated for. There were alleged complaints by the Allied Powers against the German practices in occupied territories in World War I and World War II which were denied by the German authorities [1]. As a matter of fact, no warring power during the two world wars was free from blame because both the sides violated rules of war to some degree. German lapses have however been highlighted because they *lost* both the wars.

(7) *The occupying power has the right to seize its predecessor's assets* like cash, funds and securities which it comes across during occupation. Article 53 permits such seizures. It also acquires control over depots of arms, means of transport, stores and supplies found within the territory. The occupier is entitled to all public or State properties. However, if it acquires any private property, it has to give compensation to individuals.

(8) *The occupier has a right to punish and impose penalties* for violation of its orders. But local inhabitants cannot be punished vicariously for acts for which they are not jointly or severally liable.

(9) *The occupying power is entitled to the usufruct of State property* like public buildings, real estate. forests, agricultural estate

and State enterprises without touching or spoiling the capital under Article 55 of the Annexe.

(10) Whether a belligerent occupant has a right to change the currency of the occupied territory or not is a bit controversial. If the occupation is brief and the active war is continuing, the occupant has no right to change the currency of the territory. However, if the occupation is to last for some time or the hostilities have ceased and the occupied territory is adjacent to that of the occupying power or there is apprehension of running inflation, the occupying power may change the system of currency. Even in other cases where the legitimate government has dumped large amounts of local currency before vacating in order to create problems for the occupying power, the latter may change the currency in order to stabilise the economy and prevent chaos within the territory.

Duties of the Occupying Power

(1) The duty to maintain law and order within the territory.

(2) Compensation must be paid for whatever is requisitioned [2].

(3) Uphold respect of family honour and rights, individual lives, private property and religious convictions [3].

(4) Defray administration expenses of the territory in lieu of taxes collected [4].

(5) Safeguard the capital of State properties seized during occupation. The usufruct of these properties can only be used under Article 55.

(6) Ensure and maintain medical and hospital establishments and services within the territory [5].

Limitations of the Occupying Power

(1) An occupying power is a temporary administrator of the enemy territory. While it would seek obedience from the local populace, it cannot ask them to owe allegiance to it. This is forbidden under Article 45.

(2) It is prohibited to force the local inhabitants to partake in military or prejudicial operations against their own country under Article 44 of the Annexe [6].

(3) The occupying power is forbidden to indulge in acts of pillage under Article 47.

(4) It is forbidden under Article 54 to seize or destroy submarine

cables connecting the occupied territory with neutral territory except in case of absolute necessity.

(5) The occupier is forbidden to change the existing law of the territory unless it is inconsistent with the law of occupation or it becomes an absolute or military necessity.

(6) It is forbidden to introduce political measures to divide the local population.

(7) The occupying power is prohibited from deporting local people to the territory of the occupying power for any work whatsoever [7]. Germany seemed to have deported thousands of civilians from occupied territories during the two world wars and there have been a number of war crime trials involving punishment for deportation or use of deported labour from occupied territories for military operations [8].

(8) The occupying power is forbidden to compel the local population from giving information [9].

(9) It cannot destroy any individual or public property except when it is absolutely necessary to do so for military reasons [10].

Rights and Duties of Civilians

Civilians in occupied territory have a number of rights and duties vis-a-vis the occupying power.

Rights of civilians

(1) Civilians have the freedom of conscience and they can practise any religion. The occupying power cannot compel them to subscribe to a particular religion [11]. Nor any ideology.

(2) Civilians enjoy their private rights even during occupation. The occupying power cannot interfere with these rights.

(3) They are entitled to compensation for any property, moveable or immoveable, acquired by the occupying power.

(4) Civilians accused of any crime are entitled to the right of defence under Article 72 of the Geneva Convention IV (1949) relative to Protection of Civilians During War.

Duties of civilians

(1) They must obey the lawful orders of the occupying power. Any disobedience thereof may haul them up for disobedience during martial law.

(2) They must pay taxes which are due from them.

(3) They must maintain public order during occupation.

(4) They must submit to lawful requisitions made by the occupy ing power for which it should pay.

Position of Government Officials and Judges

When a legitimate government evacuates from its territory because of its imminent occupation by enemy forces, most of the functionaries of the legitimate government also evacuate from the territory, particularly so when they have got some time to do so and there is imminent danger of occupation of only part of the territory. However, if there is belligerent occupation of all territory, a problem may arise regarding the position of officials and courts functioning under the former regime.

Article 54 of the Geneva Convention (IV) of 1949 relative to Protection of Civilian During War states that the occupying power "may not alter the status of public officials or judges in the occupied territories." It may also not apply sanctions or take any measures of coercion against them if they abstain from fulfilling their functions.

It is, therefore, clear that two situations may arise in case of occupation. It may be that some of the former public officials may resign if they do not like to work for the occupying power. In any case, public officials who continue to function under the regime of a hostile belligerent have to swear obedience to the occupying power and carry out its orders and decrees. Of course, if their conscience revolts against some orders of the occupying power, it would be better for the officials to resign than to resist the compliance of orders while still serving them. Article 54 forbids the occupying power from taking any coercive or discriminatory measures against the resigning officers.

The occupying power normally appoints some of its own personnel as functionaries within the occupied territory to maintain law and order and supervise the functioning of state. In the process, it may even establish some military courts to try offences against military occupation or acts prejudicial to the successful prosecution of war by the occupying power. Otherwise also, it may make fresh appointments against vacancies which may occur due to the unwillingness of some of the local officials to work under the occupying power. It may also appoint judges to man the local courts.

The question is some time asked whether the officials of the legitimate government continue on their old terms or the occupying power can alter the emoluments. While Article 54 is somewhat prohibitive in this regard, in my opinion, in days of war, it would be within the domain of the occupying power to revise and lower the salaries of the continuing officers with an option to them to resign if they do not want any reduction in their salaries. The occupying power cannot be blamed if it reduces the salaries of officials of the occupied territory in order to continue with its war effort.

Position of Laws of the Legitimate Government

Article 43 of the Annexe attached to the Hague Convention IV, 1907 says that the occupying power must respect the existing law, unless it is absolutely necessary to change or annul the same. Articles 64 and 65 of the Geneva Convention IV of 1949 enable the occupying power to introduce new laws for its own security and maintaining an orderly government within the territory. However, these penal laws must be published and brought to the notice of the local inhabitants. Article 65 prohibits its retroactive effect. The first proclamation of the Allied Powers after occupying Germany in 1944 was to change the German law which was discriminatory and against the rule of justice [12]. However, the Allied position was different before the surrender by Germany.

Postliminium

When a territory occupied by a belligerent is retaken by the erstwhile legitimate government of the territory, the old legal order is re-established. The coming back of old legal order—*status quo ante*—is called *postliminium*. Restoration of territory to its legitimate owner may be effected by the State itself or its allies. It may be done during war or after it when the belligerent occupant is defeated or is so much pressed for his own security that he vacates the territories occupied by him. Belgium, the Netherlands and France were occupied by Germany during World War II. When Germany vacated these territories, the doctrine of *postliminium* became applicable to such territories.

Doctrine of *postliminium* is derived from Roman Law where it meant "revert back." In the literal sense, it means reverting back to an old legal order. In international law, doctrine of *postliminium* is applied in respect of territory and the acts of belligerent occupant during his occupancy. The effect of the doctrine on both these aspects is as follows:

Territory

When a territory is returned to its legitimate sovereign, it comes back to its old status. If it was a colony it becomes a colony again. Burma and Malaysia were occupied by Japan during World War II. When Japan vacated them after its defeat, they became British colonies again. If the territory was sovereign, it again becomes a sovereign State as it happened in respect of France, Belgium, the Netherlands and Poland after World War II. With the reversion of the old order, the country retains its old colour or flag.

Old laws

Normally, old laws which were operative prior to occupation are restored by the legitimate sovereign on its coming back. Some laws are not changed even by the occupant. They continue as before. Regarding other laws which happen to be changed by the belligerent occupant, the legitimate sovereign restores them by promulgation of an order to that effect.

New laws

New laws introduced by the belligerent occupant are examined by the legitimate sovereign. Laws which were made in the context of occupation of territory by hostile army are withdrawn. Laws which were made for administration of territory and which are not found prejudicial to the interests of the legitimate government may be retained.

Restoration of other things

The coming back of the legitimate sovereign does not nullify all the acts of the belligerent occupant. The acts of the occupant may be broadly divided into two categories—legitimate and illegitimate acts. Legitimate acts of the occupant are approved by the legitimate sovereign and they continue to be valid. Illegitimate acts of the occupant may be rescinded by the sovereign and so also its effects. Thus, if the occupant has collected taxes and has performed a few other acts in the normal course of affairs, these acts continue to be valid. So also if legitimate sentences have been passed by the occupant. However, if some property has been permanently disposed off by the occupant without any justification, the property has to be restored to its original owner without any compensation to its purchaser.

Position of officials

Officials who were appointed by the occupying power may be removed. So also such old officers who cooperated with the enemy during period of occupation. Officers who resigned during occupation period may be reinstated to their old position or may even be promoted. This applies equally to judges depending upon their attitude during the period of occupation.

NOTES

1. Oppenheim, op. cit., vol. II. pp. 410-11.
2. Article 52.
3. Article 46.
4. Article 48.
5. Article 56 of the Geneva Convention (IV-1949) Relative to Protection of War Victims During War.
6. Also see Article 51 of the Geneva Convention above.
7. Article 4 of the Geneva Convention above.
8. Krupp Trials, (1949), 10 W.C.R. 144.
9. Article 44 of the Annexe.
10. Article 53 of the Geneva Convention (IV-1949).
11. Article 46 of the Annexe.
12. Military Government Proclamation No. 1, dated 18th September, 1944 as given in Oppenheim, op. cit., vol. II, pp. 446-47.

CHAPTER 33

PRISONERS OF WAR

Enemy armed personnel captured by a belligerent are called prisoners of war [1]. In the olden days, captured personnal were either summarily killed or were converted into slaves by their captors who treated them as their booty. As time passed and humanitarian law was brought in to humanise laws of war, the conditions of prisoners of war improved. Over the years, prisoners have been well-treated and mal-treated. The intensity of war and concomitant hatred generated during war has had its repurcussions on the treatment of prisoners of war. In fact, the treatment of prisoners has been arbitrary. Cruelty to prisoners has not been the monopoly of the past alone. Present-day wars are no exceptions. Atrocities have been perpetrated on prisoners throughout the centuries despite proclamations of humanity by those very perpetrators. All religions preach love for the enemy but during war there is only lip sympathy for the prisoners.

Since the last few centuries, prisoners have been considered as unfortunate casualties of war and, therefore, objects of compassion. Slavery having been universally outlawed, prisoners cannot be enslaved. Nor killed summarily. Of course, killings have occurred but under some pretext like self-preservation, deceit or attempted escape. Sometimes, these pretexts are exposed; at other times, these are considered as incidents of war.

Several attempts have been made to ameliorate the lot of prisoners. Previously, they were considered as the captives of individual captors. The practice was stopped when they were treated as captives of the capturing State and not of an individual. Earlier they were treated as criminals, not any more. The outlook towards prisoners began to change from the eighteenth century when international law began to take concrete shape. It was then felt that prisoners were not criminals. They are instruments for waging war and, therefore, need to be prevented for the period of war. The Treaty of Friendship between the United States and Prussia in 1870 provided for their confinement in healthy places, to be fed properly and lodged in barracks like their own troops. The Brussels Conference, 1874 called at the instance of Czar Alexander II of Russia adopted a convention which was not ratified. But it recognised prisoners as lawful and disarmed enemies in the power of the hostile government who must be humanely treated [2]. Towards the end of the nineteenth century, Hague Regulations provided for proper treatment of Prisoners of war. However, they proved to be inadequate during World War I. Experiences and deprivations during World War I gave rise to the conclusion of the Geneva Convention relating to Prisoners of War, 1929. This convention was tested during World War II but also proved to be inadequate in many respects. It was, therefore, felt necessary to bring about an entirely new convention which may be all-inclusive. Thus a new Geneva Convention III was concluded in 1949 as a result of deliberations from 21st April to 12th August, 1949. It was one of the four Conventions concluded for the protection of war victims. Convention III related to prisoners of war. The Convention has been almost universally accepted and applied in almost all the post-Convention wars. However, treatment of prisoners of war during some wars has been none-too-envious. In some cases, prisoners of war were intentionally labelled as war criminals and, therefore, treated worse than ordinary criminals. This is not a happy state of affairs. The following pages will deal with some aspects of prisoners of war in some details.

Prisoner of War Status

Prisoner of war status is a privileged status which gives some privileges to the captured personnel of the belligerent at the hands of another belligerent. Every enemy person captured by the belligerent is not treated as a prisoner of war; only some categories of enemy personnel are treated as prisoners of war. Article 4 of the Geneva Convention gives the categories of captured personnel to be treated as prisoners of war:

(a) Members of armed forces of belligerent as well as members of national militia or volunteer corps forming part of such armed forces, irrespective of the fact whether the belligerent is recognised or not.

(b) Members of other militia or volunteer corps including members of resistance movements if they fulfil the following conditions:

(i) they are commanded by a person responsible for the acts of his subordinates;

(ii) wear a distinctive sign recognisable from a distance;

(iii) carry arms openly;

(iv) observe laws and customs of war.

(c) Civilian personnel who accompany the army units to render them essential services like cooks, barbers, contractors, labour, engineers and correspondents.

(d) Crew and master of the merchant marine or civil aircraft who do not benefit by any more favourable treatment.

(e) *Levee en masse*: Inhabitants of a town who raise spontaneously and carry arms openly at the approach of the enemy having no time to organise themselves provided they carry arms openly and observe rules and customs of war.

There is no difficulty regarding treatment of members of armed forces as prisoners of war. However, some artificial difficulties may be created by the belligerent when even regular members of the armed forces of one belligerent are not treated as prisoners of war on the plea that they are war criminals. This is not warranted by any stretch of law. If some members of the belligerent armed forces are war criminals, they should be tried for such war crimes with the guarantees which they enjoy under the Geneva Convention. Even after conviction, they are entitled to minimum treatment as prisoners of war under Article 85 of the Convention. The socialist countries have reservations with regard to Article 85.

Members of the armed forces would also include such personnel whose duty is to operate behind enemy lines like commandos and paratroopers. They are entitled to prisoner of war status when they are captured.

Regarding members of militia or voluntary corps not forming part of the armed forces and members of resistance movements, they have to fulfil the four requirements of being commanded by a responsible officer, wear a sign distinguishable from a distance, carry arms openly and observe the rules and customs of war. This category may include guerilla forces whose activities are similar to those of resistance movements.

Resistance movements were formed during World War II in

territories occupied by the Axis Powers. These were witnessed in France, Greece, Yugoslavia and Netherlands. None of these movements strictly fulfilled the four requirements. Germany treated members of the resistance movements rather harshly because their main functions were to harass the occupying forces and commit acts of sabotage wherever possible. However, after World War II, leaders of the resistance movements became the rulers of the country. At the Geneva Diplomatic Conference in 1949, they claimed prisoner of war status for their activities. Since there was not much opposition, the resistance movements were given pow status. It is, however, doubtful if members of resistance movements, stationed as they are mostly in occupied territories, can really fulfil the four requirements. As Oppenheim writes, operation of resistance movements is "clandestine and sporadic" [3]. They discard their uniform or distinctive sign at convenient moments. These characteristics of resistance movements cause difficulty for the occupying power. Activities of these groups lack "military cohesion" and the "elusive force" has greater potentiality for mischief [4]. While conceding these defects, Oppenheim justifies the activities of the resistance movements by saying that "in modern global warfare the complete occupation of a country may be but an episode in the campaign in which the legitimate government though compelled to withdrew from national territory continues to fulfil its responsibilities in conjunction with its allies" [5]. Oppenheim seeks to justify the activities of the resistance movements in case of global wars which do not occur frequently.

In the post-World War II era, P.O.W. status has been granted to members of liberation movements in colonies where the colonial State is averse to grant independence to its colonies. Such liberation movements have operated in former French Indo-China, Algeria, Mozambique and Angola. The Palestine Liberation Organisation which works for the creation of a separate State of Palestine has been given the status of "full State" and recognised as such by a number of States. Naturally, its armed are entitled to P.O.W. status. as and when captured in hostilities.

Mercenaries

Something need to be said about the status of mercenaries. They have been found to be taking part in secessionist activities like when Katanga tried to secede from the Congo (now Zaire). Some mercenaries were also found in the Angolan civil strife on the eve of independence. South Rhodesia also engages mercenaries against terrorist activities of coloured majority.

There are some tribes or races which are professional warriors like Gorkhas of Nepal. India and Britain employ Gorkhas in their armies. They form part of their national armies. They are entitled to P.O.W. status when captured. However, they should be distinguished from mercenaries who are pure and simple adventurists, employed for *ad hoc* purposes or a limited period. They are promised a free hand in loot. They cannot be treated as prisoners of war.

At the Geneva Diplomatic Conference in 1977, Additional Protocol I to the Geneva Conventions of 1949 was adopted in June, 1977. Article 47 of the Protocol defines a mercenary as specially recruited to fight in an armed conflict, who takes direct part in hostilities and is motivated by the desire for private gain and is promised material compensation in excess of that paid to members of the regular armed forces. He is neither a national of the belligerent State, nor a member of its armed forces, nor has he been sent by a State on official duties as a member of its armed forces to the conflict. In such a situation, Article 47 (i) disqualifies him to be a lawful combatant. When captured, he cannot be treated as a prisoner of war.

Armed Forces of Unrecognised States

Members of the armed forces of an unrecognised belligerent power are also entitled to P.O.W. status. Thus, if the Arab countries capture any Israeli personnel during war, they are entitled to P.O.W. status even though State of Israel has not been recognised by the Arab States. Similarly, if any PLO members are captured by Israel, they are to be P.O.W. although the PLO is not recognised as belligerent by Israel. Members of the Mukti Bahini of Bangla Desh were also entitled to P.O.W. status in 1971 although it was denied to them by Pakistan.

Levee en Masse

Residents of a given town who rise on the approach of enemy forces are entitled to P.O.W. status if they rise spontaneously and carry arms openly and observe the laws and customs of war. This privilege is applicable to an invaded town but not to an occupied town. As far as occupied territory is concerned, P.O.W. status can be given to only members of resistance movements who fulfil the four requirements. The Geneva Conference of 1949 rejected the proposal of permitting *levee en masse* in occupied territories. In 1962 when the Chinese army was advancing towards Tejpur, residents of that town could have risen against the Chinese army and would have secured P.O.W. status subject to their carrying arms openly and the observance of laws and customs of war. This is just a hypothetical example.

Other Categories

Under Article 4 Clause 5 of the Geneva Convention, officers and men of the merchant marine and civil aircraft are given P.O.W. status in case of their capture if they are not given better status and are not released on condition that they do not engage themselves in war operations during the current hostilities. Personnel of road transport who are requisitioned by the government for transport of army military personnel and equipment should also be treated as prisoners of war.

Commencement of P.O.W. Status

Army personnel of one belligerent become prisoners of war when they are captured by the other belligerent. This may happen when they become *hors de combat* or they appeal for surrender. Article 5 of the Convention says that the Convention becomes applicable from the time enemy personnel fall into the power of the enemy. Enemy exercises control over its opponents when they have been rendered *hors de combat* and they do not pose any menace to the captor. A combatant may either be overpowered or his weaponry exhausted or he may surrender. He becomes a prisoner of war as soon as the other belligerent secures control over him.

Refusal of Quarter

Some belligerents refuse to accept enemy personnel who signal for their readiness to surrender. Although there is no specific provision in the Geneva Convention regarding ban on refusal of quarter, there is ban on killing or wounding an enemy soldier who has laid down arms or has no longer means of defence and has surrendered. Article 23 (c) of the Annexe to the Hague Regulations, 1907 prohibits such killings. Article 23(d) prohibits any declaration that no quarter will be given. Enemy personnel must be given quarter as soon as they signal their readiness for surrender. Refusal of quarter to a surrendering or wounded enemy soldier would amount to a war crime.

Treatment of Prisoners of War

Geneva Convention provides for internment of prisoners of war in similar conditions as armed forces personnel of the captor. Quarters must be free from dampness and must be adequately heated and lighted [6]. They must not be placed in close confinement unless it is necessary on health grounds [7]. Premises must be hygienic and conducive to healthfulness [8]. Prisoners are to be given food sufficient in quantity, quality and variety to keep them in good health [9]. Prisoners will be supplied with clothing, underwear and footwear by the captor [10]. The captor will install canteens in P.O.W. camps where they can purchase soap, tobacco and other articles of daily use [11].

Prisoners must be humanely treated. They are not to be subjected to physical mutilation or to medical experiments. During World War II, many prisoners were made medical guinea pigs. Nor are they to be subjected to acts of violence, intimidation and insults Captor should not exhibit them as objects of curiosity. Reprisals are prohibited against them [12]. Prisoners are entitled to respect for their person, position and honour [13]. Due consideration is to be given to their rank and sex [14]. They are entitled to medical care [15]. There shall be at least a monthly medical check up of every prisoner of war [16]. They shall be entitled to freedom of religion and they will have complete latitude in the exercise of their religious rites [17].

Discipline

Prisoners of war are subject to discipline in the P.O.W. camps. Each camp is to be headed by a camp commandant who must be a regular army officer of the captor. Prisoners must salute the officers of the captor power. Officer prisoners will salute only such officers of the captor who are senior to them in rank [18]. Prisoners shall maintain discipline in the camp.

Transfer

Prisoners may be transferred from one place to another. Article

46 of the Convention requires that transfers shall be made while taking into account the interests of the prisoners. Transfers shall be made under humane conditions to places which have similar climatic conditions to which the prisoners are accustomed. Provision for *en route* food and water shall be made. Prisoners shall not be subjected to long marches nor any deprivations during transfers. Article 47 requires that sick and wounded prisoners shall not be transferred if it would affect their health and recovery. Prisoners shall be informed in advance about their transfer and they shall be allowed to take their personal effects. Arrangements shall be made for redirecting their mail to their new place [19].

There is provision of transfer of prisoners by one State to another State. Article 12 of the Convention permits such transfers if the transferee State is willing and able to apply the Convention. However, if the transferee State defaults in the observation of the Convention, the transferring State can adopt corrective measures or ask for the return of prisoners for eventual treatment under the Convention.

Labour

Detaining power may utilise the labour of prisoners who are physically fit, after taking into account their age, sex, rank and physical aptitude. A noncommissioned officer shall be given only supervisory work. Beyond that, noncommissioned officers and officers may be given suitable work if they so ask [20]. Article 50 enumerates authorised types of work. It may be in respect of agriculture, commercial business, domestic service, nonmilitary transport or public utility service and industries. Prisoners may complain about the nature of work under Article 78 either to the detaining power or to the protecting power.

Prisoners must be given suitable working conditions with particular reference to accommodation, food, clothing and equipment. Conditions of working shall not be inferior to those enjoyed by the nationals of the detaining power employed in similar work. Regulations of safety as applicable within the State well be equally applicable to the prisoners [21].

Prisoners shall not be given dangerous, unhealthy and humiliating work unless they volunteer to do so [22]. The duration of labour hours shall not be excessive and they shall be given rest at midday for at least one hour [23]. They shall be paid a fair working pay and shall receive due attention if they sustain any injury or contact any disease in consequence of their work [24].

Financial relations

Detaining power may decide about the maximum amount which a prisoner may have on his person. Any extra amount on his person at the time of his capture may be kept by the detaining power on account of the given prisoner [25].

Detaining power does not want much money to be left with the prisoner because it may help him in his escape. Article 60 provides for monthly allowances to be given to prisoners according to their rank and status. Belligerents will adjust the amounts given by them to prisoners of war, with each other. Besides, the parent belligerent may send amounts for distribution among his captured personnel with the other belligerent. Prisoners may receive individual or collective remittances [26]. The detaining power shall maintain detailed account of each prisoner. The account may be inspected by the protecting power and prisoners' representative.

Relations with outside world

Prisoners are allowed to communicate with their family and Central Prisoners of War Agency about their capture. Such communication shall not be delayed by the detaining power [27]. They are further allowed to correspond with their family and friends with a minimum of two letters and four cards unless themail is reduced by the parent government. Prisoners may send telegrams in case of urgency or when the distances are long or there has been no news from home for quite some time. For this, they have to pay the cost of the telegram [28]. Prisoners may also receive gift parcels containing clothing, food, medicines, books, musical instruments, religious articles, etc. [29].

All incoming and outgoing correspondence between prisoners and the outside world will be subject to censorship which shall be carried out with minimum delay [30].

Judicial Proceedings Against Prisoners

Prisoners are subject to discipline and laws of the detaining power [31]. Any violation of discipline or laws of the country would land the prisoners into disciplinary or judicial proceedings against them. Choice of disciplinary or judicial proceedings rests with the detaining power. Prisoners shall ordinarily be tried by military courts unless their counterparts could be tried by civil courts for similar wrongs. The detaining power shall ensure independence and impartiality of the court and afford the right and means of defence to the accused prisoners. Article 86 provides that no prisoner shall "be punished more than once for the same act or on the same charge." However, the article is defective. It should be that no prisoner may be *tried* (not *punished*) more than once for the same act or on the same charge. While punishing the prisoners, it must be borne in mind that prisoners are unfortunate victims of war in the custody of hostile country to which they do not owe any allegiance. Captivity is by itself a great misfortune and deprivation for the prisoner. Therefore, he may be awarded minimum penalty as warranted by circumstances and law.

War crimes

There is no specific provision in the Geneva Convention for the trial of prisoners of war for war crimes alleged to have been committed by them. This is despite the fact that the Geneva Convention was concluded in 1949 when a number of war crime trials were already over in respect of prisoners of war. The Nuremberg Principles had been established although they had not been codified until the Geneva Convention. However, since the Nuremberg Principles were codified in 1950, it is quite likely that perpetrators of war crimes, including prisoners of war, may be tried for war crimes in future.

While it may be difficult to secure custody of perpetrators of war crimes who are at large, prisoners of wars become easy targets for being proceeded against for war crimes, being already in the custody of the detaining power which may seek to stage war crime trials more for political purposes than for administering justice. So far only prisoners of war, nationals and dignitaries of the Axis Powers have been subjected to war crime trials. They are being hounded even now after a lapse of three decades. No one else has been tried for war crimes although there have been a number of wars since World War II. It is hard to believe that only the Axis Powers and their nationals committed war crimes. Stories of war crimes were heard of during the Vietnamese War but not a single war crime trial was held. During the Indo-Pakistan war in 1971, Bangla Desh wanted to hold trial of 196 Pakistani prisoners for war crimes alleged to have been perpetrated by them during the freedom struggle from March 1971 to December 1971. However, such a trial could not materialise because world opinion was conspicuously quiet over this issue. Besides, Bangla Desh withdrew the threat of war crime trials by gaining some concessions from Pakistan in the form of its recognition and repatriation of Pakistani nationals from Bangla Desh.

There is a subtle reference about the possibility of prisoners of war being tried for war crimes in Article 85 of the Convention. It says that "Prisoners of war prosecuted...for acts committed prior to capture shall retain, even if convicted, the benefits of the present Convention." Crimes prior to their capture could be either war crimes or ordinary crimes.

There is a controversy around Article 85. While it provides that prisoners will benefit by the provisions of the Geneva Convention even after their conviction for war crimes, the socialist countries around the world have made reservations to this Article to the effect that prisoners convicted of war crimes will not benefit by the provisions of the Convention [32].

Safeguards in judicial proceedings

Articles 99-108 deal with safeguards afforded to a prisoner of war during judicial proceedings sought to be initiated against him. Article 99 presents three basic tenets of criminal law: (1) No prisoner can be tried for acts which were not crimes at the time of commission. This is a rule against *ex post facto* laws. This was one of the major complaints against the Allied Powers who tried war criminals after World War II. German and Japanese war criminals had argued that offences attributed to them were not offences at the time of commission; (2) No prisoner shall be pressurised, morally or physically, to admit his guilt. Voluntary admission of guilt is permitted but not by compulsion; and (3) A prisoner should have opportunity to defend himself with the assistance of a competent lawyer before he is convicted.

Article 104 enjoins upon the detaining power to give at least three weeks' notice to the prisoner as well as the protecting power regarding its intention to try the given prisoner of war for a given offence before a particular magistrate. This notification shall contain the identity of the accused prisoner, place of his internment, specification of charges and designation of the court which will try him along with date and place of trial.

Article 104 is a general article dealing with the procedure to be adopted by the detaining power when it has decided to initiate judicial proceedings against any prisoner of war. The article should therefore, be applicable to trials for ordinary crimes as well as for war crimes. However, in a number of cases after World War II, it was decided by courts from various countries that Article 104 (its counterpart Article 60 of the Geneva Convention, 1929) was not applicable to cases of war crimes [33]. Even the United States Supreme Court held likewise in the case of Yamashita [34]. Their stand could hardly be tenable. Noncompliance with the procedure contained in Article 104 may not vitiate the conviction on ground of miscarriage of justice but it casts a great shadow on the independence and impartiality of tribunals.

Article 107 provides that any judgment and sentence pronounced by court shall be communicated to the protecting power with information whether there is any right of appeal. If the sentence is that of death, the protecting power is entitled to a detailed report including the place of execution of sentence. Article 101 provides that death sentence shall not be executed for at least six months from the date of receipt of communication under Article 107 by the protecting power. Article 103 provides that in case of any other sentence, the period of confinement will be deducted.

Escape

It is a natural desire of the prisoner to escape from captivity. It is equally the duty of the detaining power to thwart any escape attempts on the part of prisoners of war. This results in clash of interests which manifest themselves in actual clashes. The Geneva Convention takes a realistic note of the interests of parties. Article 91 of the Convention gives out a number of situations which shall amount to successful escape—joining the forces of the parent State or its allies, leaving the territory of the detaining power or its ally, joining a ship of the parent State or its ally even within the territorial waters of the detaining power but not under its control.

Article 92 makes unsuccessful attempts at escape as subject to disciplinary punishment, besides surveillence not affecting his health. The difficulty arises when some crime is committed in order to effect one's escape. Article 93 says that offences connected with escape not involving violence against life or limb, like theft without intention of self-enrichment, offences against public property and preparation of false papers shall entail only disciplinary punishment. This was an improvement upon the Geneva Convention of 1929 under which offences in pursuit of effecting escape were treated as offences liable to judicial proceedings [35]. Consequently, a number of prisoners were punished for ordinary crimes in Canada during World War II [36]. Article 93 reflects the realisation on the part of world elites that prisoners should not be punished heavily for escape attempts and crimes associated with such attempts. The article further states that even when prisoners are liable to judicial proceedings in respect of ordinary crimes associated with escape attempts, the latter should not be considered as aggravating circumstance even when there have been repeated attempts.

It may be mentioned here it has been found that a captor's guards are sometimes ruthless in preventing escape on the part of prisoners with the result that many prisoners are killed in the process. While no one doubts the right of the captor to prevent escape by prisoners, there should be judicious use of force while preventing escapes. Many a time, it is said that undesirable prisoners are shot dead on the pretext of their attempts to escape. Although, it is difficult to enquire in these cases of excesses because the factual evidence is entirely under the control of the captor, one can only appeal to the captor to impress upon its personnel to use restraint while dealing with prisoners who should not be shot dead for ulterior purposes.

Protecting Power

Article 8 of the Convention envisages the appointment of the protecting power who shall be responsible for safeguarding the interests of the parties to the conflict. The Convention is to be applied in cooperation with and under security of the protecting power.

Any neutral State enjoying the confidence of both the belligerent parties may be nominated as a protecting power to see that the prisoners are well treated and there are minimum possible lapses on the part of the detaining power. The task of the protecting power is to see that the Convention is applied in law as well as in spirit. For this, representatives of the protecting power can visit

P.O.W. camps and enquire about any complaints or suggestions from P.O.W. representatives. Protecting power need not appoint its own nationals only as its representatives. It may appoint even nationals of other neutral countries, subject to no objection on the part of the territorial belligerent where it is looking after the interests of prisoners or interned civilians of another belligerent State. The services of the protecting power become necessary to redress the grievances of prisoners in camps and protect them in judicial proceedings.

The institution of the protecting power was introduced for the first time in the Geneva Convention of 1949 after the experiences of World War II during which there were large-scale deprivations on the part of prisoners of war. It was thought that there should be some State which enjoys the confidence of both the belligerents and which can act as an intermediary to see that there are minimum deprivations of unfortunate victims of war, whether they are interned civilians or captured soldiers. The protecting power was, therefore, given the task of safeguarding the interests of the prisoners of war after taking into consideration the imperative necessities of security of the detaining power. Article 10 provides that when P.O.Ws. do not benefit or cease to benefit by the activities of the protecting power, the detaining power may designate any neutral State or an impartial organisation to carry out the functions of the protecting power. The Socialist countries have made reservation to this Article to the effect that no neutral State or organisation shall be designated to discharge the functions of the protecting power unless the other belligerent also agrees.

Strangely enough, no protecting power has been appointed in any of the post-Convention period. One reason may be short duration of wars except the Vietnamese war. Regarding the Vietnamese war, experience relating to P.O.W. treatment has not been too happy. It is hoped that future wars will not treat the Vietnamese war as its model.

International Committee of Red Cross

Any discourse on the treatment of prisoners of war would be incomplete without discussing the role of the International Committee of Red Cross situated in Geneva, Switzerland. It is always in the vanguard of ameliorating the conditions of war victims, including prisoners of war. The International Committee of Red Cross is a Swiss registered body consisting of exclusively Swiss nationals. It is dedicated to the welfare of victims of disasters, particularly caused by war. It is responsible for the 1929 and 1949 Geneva Conventions on war victims. It has rendered a yoeman's service during many wars, the latest being the Lebanese civil war in 1975-76. The Geneva Conventions of 1949 were concluded on the basis of the Stockholm Draft prepared at the Conference of the International Committee of Red Cross in 1948.

Article 9 of the Convention says that nomination of protecting power does not prevent the International Committee of Red Cross from undertaking humanitarian activities in P.O.W. camps or in relation thereto. Article 10 further says that where prisoners of war do not benefit by the activities of the protecting power, the detaining power may either request the ICRC or accept the offer of the ICRC to undertake the functions otherwise performed by protecting power. Besides, the ICRC is responsible for organising massive relief parcels to be sent to prisoners of war in order to keep them in good spirits and thus prevent them from developing psychological disorders.

Termination of Captivity

Captivity of prisoners may be terminated in two ways—either during war or after war. During war, prisoners may end their captivity by grant of parole, repatriation, stay in neutral territory, escape or death. Defection to the enemy would also terminate captivity. Prisoners may be repatriated after war. All these situations are discussed below.

Parole

Article 21 visualises release of prisoners on parole if it is permissible under the Armed Forces Manual of the parent State. Parole in present situation means an undertaking given by prisoner not to engage in war-like activities during the current war if he is released. This is a departure from the 1929 Geneva Convention which did not contain any provision regarding release on parole. Article 10 of the Annexe to the Hague Convention on Land Warfare, 1899 and 1907 provided that prisoners may be released on parole if laws of their country so permit. In the past, there were practices of release on parole. But there have been no releases on parole during the twentieth century. There may be stray release of prisoners of war during war for propaganda purposes.

Repatriation of seriously sick and wounded prisoners— Article 110 of the Convention provides that the following categories of prisoners shall be repatriated to their home State:

(a) Incurably sick and wounded prisoners whose mental or physical fitness seems to have been gravely deteriorated;

(b) Sick and wounded prisoners who are not likely to recover within one year and whose mental or physical fitness seems to have been gravely deteriorated;

(c) Sick and wounded prisoners who have recovered but whose mental or physical fitness seems to have been gravely and permanently diminished.

Repatriation of sick and wounded prisoners has always received priority. Both the belligerents are interested in getting back their sick and wounded prisoners. Since they do not pose any military threat, belligerents mutually repatriate seriously sick prisoners.

Stay in neutral territory

Article 110 provides that sick and wounded prisoners whose treatment in a neutral country might increase the prospects of more certain and speedy recovery or whose mental or physical health is seriously threatened by continued captivity but whose accommodation in a neutral territory may remove such a threat may be allowed to be sent to a neutral country.

Besides, Article 111 provides that the belligerents may conclude an agreement for stay of prisoners in neutral territory until the close of hostilities. This may be in respect of prisoners who have been in captivity for a long time.

Escape, defection and death

Escape of prisoner results in gaining his freedom without conditions. Prisoner may also defect to the side of the detaining power and thus gain freedom. This normally happens only in civil or ideological war. Death of a prisoner naturally has its own finality.

Repatriation after Hostilities

Prisoners are normally released and repatriated after the cessation of hostilities. Article 118 provides that they shall be released and repatriated "without delay after the cessation of active hostilities." Article 118 was inserted in the light of experience gained after World War II where the Allied Powers detained the prisoners of the Axis Powers for quite some time even when the War had ended and there was unconditional surrender.

The wording of Article 118 has created some misgivings in the wake of experiences of the post-Convention period. In 1953, controversy was raised in the Korean war whether prisoners must be released and repatriated to the parent State without ascertaining their desire whether they want to be repatriated to the home State. The parent State was citing Article 7 of the Convention which says that prisoners will not give up rights under the Convention. The other side was against forcible repatriation of unwilling prisoners to their home State. The controversy ended when India was appointed as the screening country to ascertain the wishes of prisoners without fear of reprisals. This would mean that prisoners who really do not want to return home may stay away in the territory of the detaining power or elsewhere.

The controversy was again raised in 1972 when after liberation of Bangla Desh in December 1971, about 92,000 Pakistani prisoners could not be repatriated immediately after the cessation of active hostilities. India which was the detaining power was accused of having delayed the repatriation of prisoners. However, India had its own reasons for not repatriating the prisoners immediately. For one thing, Bangla Desh where Pakistani soldiers were taken as prisoners, was contemplating trial of some prisoners for war crimes. Investigations were going on in this connection. Any immediate repatriation would have hampered investigations, collection of evidence, production of witnesses and identification of accused prisoners who were required as war criminals. The unusually large number of prisoners also posed security problem to India because in a situation of intermediacy—no war, no peace—India wanted to be reassured that any release of such a large number of prisoners, which was equivalent to one fourth of the Pakistan army, would not expose her to the threat of insecurity. India had also to settle accounts with Pakistan on account of advance of pay given to Pakistani prisoners under Article 60 of the Convention.

This raises the question as to what is the meaning of phrase—"without delay after the cessation of active hostilities."

In the light of experiences gained during the post-Convention era, it may be said that prisoners should be repatriated as soon as possible after the cessation of active hostilities. Any contrary interpretation emphasising upon immediate repatriation would be taking an unrealistic attitude of the situation. However, repatriation should not be delayed on account of political reasons to extract some concession from the prisoner's State as has been our experience in the past.

NOTES

1. For detailed study of the subject, see Hingorani, R.C. Prisoners of War (1963).
2. Article 23 of the Brussels Conference 1874.
3. Oppenheim's International Law, vol. II, p. 212.
4. Ibid., 214-15.
5. Ibid., 215-16.
6. Article 25.
7. Article 21.
8. Article 22.
9. Article 26.
10. Article 27.
11. Article 28
12. Article 13.
13. Article 14.
14. Article 15.
15. Article 30.
16. Article 31.
17. Article 34.
18. Article 39.
19. Article 48.
20. Article 49.
21. Article 51.
22. Article 52.
23. Article 53.
24. Article 54.
25. Article 58.
26. Article 63.
27. Article 70.
28. Article 71.
29. Article 72.
30. Article 76.
31. Article 82.
32. They are Soviet Union, Poland, Bulgaria, China, Hungary, Vietnam, Romania, German Democratic Republic, North Korea, Czechoslovakia and Algeria.
33. Oppenheim's International Law vol. II. p. 390 footnote 3.
34. (1946) 327 U.S. 1. at p. 7.
35. Article 51 of the Geneva Convention of Prisoners of War (1929).
36. R.V. Schindler, 1944 A.D. Case No. 135; R.V. Brosig, 1945 A.D. Case No. 136.

CHAPTER 34

NEUTRALITY

Neutrality is an attitude of impartiality adopted by third States in an armed conflict between two warring States or group of States. Whenever war breaks out between States, the other States remain neutral and do not participate in hostilities. While some States practice strict neutrality, others while professing neutrality may be sentimentally inclined towards one or the other belligerent. In the process, they give some benefits to the warring State of their choice to the prejudice of another warring nation. Neutrality, however, should not brook such practices.

History of Neutrality

War is an old institution; so is neutrality. In ancient days, neither were the rules of war firmly established nor the precepts of neutrality. But it would be wrong to say that the modern concept of neutrality was unknown in ancient days. Third States did practice neutrality but tilted the balance in favour of one or the other belligerent in self-interest. In ancient days, wars were mostly localised between neighbouring States. Therefore, it affected only the bordering States. Non-bordering States were not that much affected by localised conflicts due to lack of transport and communication facilities. Arms were mostly locally made and there was no practice of import of arms from third States as is the practice today. There was also not much of maritime trade between distant countries in ancient days. Therefore, there was no question of maritime warfare; nor the problem of blockade or contraband. The problem of declaring neutrality was also confined to nearby States bordering belligerent States. Distant States would not know of the war. In any case, they remained indifferent to wars waged by distant States. The attitude of neighbouring States was determined partly by the justness or unjustness of the cause of respective belligerents, the extent of pressure on non-warring States and self interest. Self interest outweighed the justness of cause. If the pressure of the warring nation was overwhelming, the weak neighbouring State succumbed to it and sided with the pressurising State. This process continued until the sixteenth century.

In the seventeenth century, Grotius emphasised more upon righteousness and justness of war. There was no question of neutrality between just and unjust war. The question of neutrality could only arise when the justness of any warring party could not be ascertained. In such a situation, both the warring nations may be given equal treatment in order to maintain neutrality. Neutrality then meant equal treatment, negatively as well as positively. Beyond that, no rules of neutrality could be evolved. Nor did the warring nations consider the neutral territory inviolable. Neutral countries had some duties but no rights which they could exercise against the warring groups.

The concept of neutrality became little crystallised during the eighteenth century with the writings of two great international lawyers, Bynkershoek and Vattel. But it was not considered as violation of neutrality if some assistance was given under a treaty [1]. By this time, the means of communication between distant nations had greatly improved and there were commercial as well as political exchanges between them. In the circumstances, wars did not affect the war zones only. It affected all-round which precipitated a decision on nations to maintain neutrality or otherwise.

During the eighteenth century, maritime warring States tried to cripple each other's trade with other States as well as their colonies. In the absence of recognised rules, nations prescribed their own rules. Thus, France and Spain considered it legal to seize neutral goods on enemy vessels as well as enemy goods on neutral vessels. England released neutral goods on enemy vessels but applied the rule of sabotage. Thus in 1756, when the Netherlands tried to do business with the French colonies, its fleet was seized by England on the plea that its fleet had merged with the French fleet although the Netherlands had declared neutrality. This kind of assimilation by Britain was called the rule of 1756 [2]. The rule had no earlier precedent; nor was it justified. It was purely a British-oriented rule sought to be imposed on the Netherlands by sheer naval superiority of Britain. It was but natural that if the French could not trade with its colonies, some neutral power would fill the gap. This did not warrant treatment of the Netherlands as an enemy when it had declared its neutrality. A neutral State is entitled to do business with a belligerent and its colonies. As a matter of fact one of the reasons for adopting neutrality is motivation to trade with the belligerents. Britain also insisted on the visit and search of merchantmen headed by neutral men-of-war in eighteenth century. Although, this was resisted by Russia, Denmark, Prussia and Sweden, it exhibited archaic conditions of neutrality in the eighteenth century.

Neutrality was effective in the nineteenth century with the emergence of the United States of America as a strong neutral power in European conflicts. In Europe, Switzerland was recognised as a neutral State. This was followed by Belgium. Norms of neutrality also began to take shape. The Declaration of Paris, 1856 partly covered the rights and duties of neutral State.

The twentieth century has witnessed the rise and fall of neutrality. There was concretisation of rules of neutrality at the Hague Conference of 1907. The Hague Conventions V and XIII deal with Rights and Duties of Neutral States in war on Land and Sea respectively. Declaration of London, 1909 also dwelt on rights and duties of neutral States in naval wars. This Declaration was never ratified but it had incorporated many recognised customary rights of neutral States. On the other hand, there was collapse of the concept of neutrality during the two world wars.

In World War I, although the United States had declared neutrality, it later on joined hands with Great Britain on the plea that due to extensive sea warfare on the part of Germany it affected the freedom of the seas and its commerce as a neutral State. This changeover was also sought to be justified on the ground that a neutral State should not shirk from its share of the burden of humanity in the Wilsonian words.

In World War II also initially, the United States declared neutrality. However it took a partisan attitude in favour of the United Kingdom. In 1940, it transferred destroyers to Britain in return of lease of naval bases in Bermuda, Bahamas and Jamaica. Subsequently, under the Lend-Lease Act, 1941, the United States provided essential supplies to Great Britain. The United States justified these acts of un-neutrality on the ground of self-defence, the Kellog-Briand Pact, 1928 and excessive submarine war by Germany. Violation of territories of neutralised States in Europe like Belgium, Holland and Luxemburg was additional reason for the United States to tilt in favour of Great Britain.

While Germany already remains condemned for violation of the rights of neutral State, it may be said in retrospect that the United States policy of partisanship in favour of Great Britain in both the world wars was not consistent with accepted notions of neutrality. While Lauterpacht admits the unneutral acts of the United States, he seeks to justify these acts in view of its entirety and in its true historic perspective. They were adopted as measures of discrimination against a belligerent who had resorted to war in violation of international law [3].

Either a State is neutral or not neutral. There is no half way house. Nor is there any such thing as qualified neutrality. There is only one neutrality—an absolute neutrality as in the case of Switzerland. United States neutrality was camouflage neutrality in the same way as it was said to be neutral during the Indo-Pakistan war of 1971. There is no such thing as tilting neutrality.

Just War and Neutrality

Of and on, it is said that there is no scope for neutrality where one is waging a just war against another. In ancient days, moral issues did dominate the question of neutrality. In the seventeenth century, Grotius advocated support for just war. However soon thereafter, the concept of just war disappeared and States were required to be neutral without caring to know the justness or otherwise of the belligerent. This position dominated the world scene until World War I when Wilson sought to intervene to share the burden of humanity and promote justice. American tilting in favour of Great Britain during World War II was a repeat performance which was sought to be justified on the ground that Hitler had violated the Treaty of Versailles and the Kellog-Briand Pact of 1928 on Renunciation of War as an Instrument of National Policy. Whether the U.S. actions during the two wars fitted into the concept of support of just war is debatable. Articles 41 and 42 of the U.N. Charter which speak of enforcement action against a State impliedly supports the resurrection of the concept of just war, when read with Article 2 Clause 5 and 25 of the Charter.

While it is easy to champion that in just war, there should be no neutrality, it may be difficult to determine the nature of war. Theoretically, the difference is between good and evil but the obvious difficulty is of the agency to be endowed with the job. Any unilateral determination may be subjective and biased. There is no third agency to determine the issue. Even the decision of the Security Council cannot be said to be judicial. It is more political than judicial. Therefore, it may be desirable to bury the concept of just war, at least for the time being.

Neutrality and the United Nations

The United Nations Charter has not abolished neutrality as a concept. It has, however, affected neutrality in case the Security Council decides to take action against a State under Article 41 or 42 as the case may be. In such a situation, the member States of the United Nations are bound to carry out their obligation under Article 2(5) and Article 25 of the Charter. The Security Council may ask only a few States to lend their armed forces for restoring or maintaining international peace and security under Articles 43 and 48. The question thus will be as to the status of the remaining member States. Should the non-participating States be considered as neutral? In my opinion, all States which as members of the Security Council have voted for the enforcement action cannot be called neutrals. Besides, States which have been called upon to give assistance of any kind under Article 43 may also be excluded from neutrals. Barring these two categories, all other States remain as neutral States under the Charter.

Neutrality may also be maintained in case there is no unanimity among the five permanent members of the Security Council. Similarly, action recommended by the General Assembly under the Uniting for Peace resolution does not deprive the States from remaining neutral.

Notion of Neutrality

What is the meaning of neutrality? Oppenheim calls it impartiality which is a negative attitude. It may perhaps be better to say that neutrality is equal treatment of both the belligerents by the neutral. Equal treatment may comprise both negative and positive acts on the part of the neutral. It includes actions as well as utterances. Thus, a neutral State may supply military hardware to both the countries without violating its neutrality. But equal treatment does not mean supply of sophisticated hardware to one and less sophisticated or outdated hardware to another. But if a neutral State has sentimental attachment with one belligerent, it is immaterial so long as it is not converted into adverse action or utterance.

Neutrality of the State Government should not be confused with the attitude of individuals in a free democratic society. In such a society, there is freedom of expression of opinion and freedom of Press. Individuals as well as the Press in a neutral nation have a right to express their opinion regarding the belligerents without affecting the official neutral attitude of the State. This is the personal opinion of an individual or a newspaper, and the government has nothing to do with it and has no control over it.

Neutrality and Non-alignment

Neutrality should not be confused with non-alignment. Neutrality is equal treatment of both the belligerents in time of war. Non-alignment is an attitude of equidistance from the bipolar powers in time of peace. Non-alignment is exclusively a peacetime attitude of not taking the side of one or the other bipolar power. It is an offshoot of the cold war generated by the United States and the Soviet Union soon after World War II. Non-alignment has now become a creed with newly independent States which have formed a block of non-aligned nations.

Kinds of Neutrality

Some international lawyers have categorised neutrality into perfect, imperfect, absolute, qualified and benevolent. These names are just a jugglery of words motivated to justify one or other type of violation of neutrality. There is no such distinction. There is only one neutrality, pure and simple. Any aberration of neutrality is violation of neutrality itself. Thus, if the United States supplied essential material to Great Britain, it ceased to be neutral. Similarly, if the Soviet Union were to support India in time of war on the basis of the Indo-Soviet Treaty of 1971, it ceases to be neutral. Its attitude cannot be called imperfect neutrality because it was supporting India on the basis of a pre-existing treaty. International law does not make such distinctions. Only States seek to make distinctions to justify their un-neutral acts.

Rights and Duties of Neutrals and Belligerents

The main concern of a neutral nation is to see that it does not get involved in the war, and its trade with outside world, including belligerents, is not disturbed. On the other hand, the main concern of belligerents is that a neutral State does not do anything which favours one belligerent to the detriment of the other belligerent. For this reason, neutral States and belligerents both have rights and duties which are discussed as follows:

Rights of neutral nations

(1) Neutral territory is inviolable. Article 1 of the Hague Convention V of 1907 makes neutral territory inviolable. Belligerents are under a duty not to do anything on neutral territory which may compromise its neutral position. Neutral territory cannot be used as a staging ground for war activities by one belligerent against another belligerent.

(2) Neutral nations are free to trade with the outside world including belligerents subject to law of contraband and blockade.

(3) Nationals of a neutral State within belligerent's territory remain free and are entitled to fair treatment.

(4) Neutral State has a right to disarm and detain belligerent forces which have taken shelter on neutral territory; such forces cannot be released during the current war.

Duties of neutral nations

(1) To acquiesce to the exercise of rights of angary, visit and search of its merchantmen on the high seas, capture of contraband goods and declaration of blockade of an enemy coast by the belligerent nation.

(2) To prevent any belligerent from staging hostile acts from within its neutral territory. If any belligerent forces have transgressed into its territory, they must be disarmed and detained for the duration of hostilities.

(3) To prevent its territory being made a recruiting base by one belligerent. Article 16 of the Hague Convention (V) 1907 prohibits this. However, a neutral nation is not under a duty to prevent its individual nationals from leaving the country and join the armed forces of one or the other belligerent.

(4) Abstain from helping or assisting one belligerent to the detriment of another belligerent. Nor can it tilt the balance in

favour of one belligerent to the disadvantage of another belligerent.

Rights of belligerents

(1) A belligerent has a right of angary by requisitioning any neutral property within its territory for successful prosecution of war.

(2) A belligerent has a right to visit and search neutral merchantmen on the high seas to check if they are carrying any contraband goods to enemy and capture it if it is so found.

(3) A belligerent has a right to declare blockade of enemy coast which must be respected by neutrals.

Duties of belligerents

(1) Not to violate neutral territory.

(2) Not to launch hostile acts from within neutral territory.

(3) Not to disturb neutral trade subject to rights of contraband and declaration of blockade.

(4) Not to disturb the activities of neutral State's nationals within its territory subject to right of angary.

(5) Not to use neutral territory as a recruiting base for its armed forces. The duty remains although it may be traditional for belligerent to recruit from neutral nationals for its armed forces as in the case of Indian and British armies which recruit Gorkhas from Nepal for their armed forces.

Un-neutral Service

Un-neutral service may be defined as rendering such services by neutral agencies which assist one belligerent in prosecution of war to the prejudice of another belligerent. Such services may be in the form of transporting belligerent troops, important individuals or other individuals destined for induction in belligerent's war effort, either as members of armed forces or as technical experts on military and allied affairs. Transmission of military or quasi-military intelligence by neutrals would also be categorised as un-neutral service.

If un-neutral service is rendered by a neutral State, it is a violation of neutrality by that State which may entail some action by the belligerent. However, if it is rendered by some private agency or business company of a neutral nation it becomes liable to capture and confiscation or such other penalty as may be warranted by the situation.

Un-neutral service is considered as analogous to contraband with this difference that while in case of contraband, it is carriage of goods, in case of un-neutral service, it is carriage of person or transmission of intelligence.

There have been instances of un-neutral services during World War I and World War II. London Declaration of 1909 on Naval Warfare dealt with un-neutral service in Articles 45-47 of Chapter III. Article 45 makes neutral vessel liable to condemnation if she is involved in the transport of members of armed forces of military detachment or enemy or persons who assist the operations of the enemy during the course of war.

Article 46 made the neutral vessel liable to condemnation if it takes part in hostilities, is under control of an agent of a belligerent, is in exclusive employment of a belligerent, or is engaged in transport of enemy troops or transmission of intelligence in the interest of the enemy.

Article 47 provides that enemy soldiers found on neutral vessel may be captured and detained as prisoners of war. The London Declaration was never ratified although many of its provisions were declaratory or customary rules of international law respecting law of naval war.

In the Asama Maru Case, the Japanese Vessel was on its way to Yokohama when it was challenged by a British man-of-war in 1940 while Japan was neutral. Twenty-one German civilians were disembarked by Britain on the plea of their being of military age.

Earlier international law envisaged un-neutral service could only be committed by neutral vessels. The advent of the aircraft has made it possible to resort to un-neutral service by air in the same way as in the case of a vessel earlier. Now an aircraft is more capable and efficient in rendering un-neutral service and quicker service to belligerents than the vessel. In such circumstances, an aircraft may also be subjected to the same rules as have so far been made applicable to vessels for committing un-neutral service or contraband. Aircraft are known to be engaged in gun-running and so also in transmission of intelligence and transport of important persons of belligerents. As a matter of fact, an aircraft has replaced a vessel in this regard. Soon, it may be supplemented by a satellite.

Notes

1. Lauterpacht, H., Oppenheim's International Law (Seventh Edition, 1952) vol. II, p. 627.
2. Ibid., pp. 628-29.
3. Ibid., pp. 638-39.

Section V

INTERNATIONAL INSTITUTIONS

CHAPTER 35

THE UNITED NATIONS ORGANISATION

The United Nations Organisation was born in 1945. It was formed initially with 51 States as founding members. By December, 1977, it had 149 members. The U.N.O. was the result of the Moscow Declaration of 1st November 1943 in which Foreign Ministers of China, Russia, the United Kingdom and the United States decided to establish an international organisation at an early date. The talks were continued between the above representatives in Washington in September-October, 1944. These are better known as Dumbarton Oaks talks named after the villa where the talks were held. On 7th October, 1944 the proposed framework of the U.N.O. was tentatively published. These proposals were further discussed at the Yalta Conference in February, 1945 between the three Heads of State, Churchill, Roosevelt and Stalin. It commanded the convening of a U.N. Conference to be held in San Francisco from 25th April 1945. Eventually, the document was signed on 26th June 1945. The U.N. Charter came into force on 24th October, 1945 when it was ratified by a requisite number of States. Twenty-fourth October is, therefore, celebrated as U.N. Day every year since then.

Objects of the United Nations Organisations

Objects of the U.N.O. are given in the Preamble of the Charter. There are four objects for which the U.N. has been formed: (i) to save the succeeding generations from the scourge of war, (ii) to reaffirm faith in fundamental human rights, in the worth and dignity of human person and equal rights of men, women and nations, (iii) to establish conditions in which justice and respect for international obligations are maintained and (iv) to promote social progress and a better standard of life.

These objects are sought to be secured to peoples of the world through practising tolerance and living together in peace with one another as good neighbours. This has given rise to the concept of peaceful coexistence among States despite political, economic and ideological differences between them. The principle of collective security is enshrined in the Preamble to maintain international peace and security. It abjures the use of armed force, except in common interest.

The Preamble promises to employ international machinery for the promotion of the economic and social advancement of all peoples. This has given rise to a new world economic order which does not exploit the less developed nations for the enrichment and welfare of more developed nations.

Special Characteristics of the Charter

The U.N. Charter has departed from the usual practice prevalent in respect of conclusion of international agreements. Whereas, a treaty is entered into in the name of High Contracting Parties, the U.N. Charter starts with "We the peoples of the United Nations". This shows the importance given to peoples of the world instead of importance being given to States. It is said that States are the only subjects of international law. In that case, there is a distinct departure made by the United Nations Charter for the first time in any international agreement. The Organisation's concern about the peoples, dignity and worth of human person and fundamental human rights is borne out by the Preamble, Articles 1 and 55 of the Charter. Subsequent developments have fortified the recognition of human values and rights.

Purposes of the Charter

There are four purposes of the U.N. Charter given in Article 1. These are:

(i) Maintenance of international peace and security;

(ii) Development of friendly relations among nations;

(iii) International cooperation in solving problems of economic, social, cultural and humanitarian character; promotion and encouragement of respect for human rights and fundamental freedoms; and

(iv) Centre for harmonising the actions of nations to achieve the above ends.

(i) *Maintenance of international peace and security*

This is the first and primary purpose of the United Nations as given in the Preamble and reiterated in Article 1. The United Nations was established to save the succeeding generations from the horrors of war. The United Nations may take effective collective measures for the prevention and removal of threats to peace. It shall, therefore, be the endeavour of the United Nations to prevent any occurrence of events which may threaten peace. But if some situations have arisen which threaten peace, the U.N. would remove such threats. The U.N. would also suppress any acts of aggression or acts involving breach of peace.

The U.N. would try to bring about adjustment of settlement of international disputes by peaceful means as given in Article 33 in conformity with justice and international law. Pacific settlement of international disputes would naturally eliminate chances of eruption of war.

(ii) *Development of friendly relations*

The second purpose of the United Nations is to develop friendly relations among nations. Such relations can be developed on the basis of equal rights for all States, irrespective of their size, economic development, race, religion or colour.

It was realised that there can be no peace in the world unless peoples of the world are given the right of self determination to decide about their fate, form of government and economic ism.

The U.N. General Assembly appointed a Committee to chalk out the principles governing friendly relations among nations. These principles are now incorporated in the U.N. General Assembly Resolution 2625 of 24th October, 1970. Coincidentally, this day was being celebrated as the twenty-fifth anniversary of the United Nations. The committee enunciates seven principles:

(1) States shall refrain from use of force in their international relations against territorial integrity and political independence of any State; (2) States shall settle their disputes by peaceful means in such a manner that international peace, security and justice are not endangered; (3) non-intervention in the domestic relations of another State; (4) international cooperation among nations; (5) equal rights to all States and right of self-determination of peoples; (6) sovereign equality of States; and (7) States to fulfil in good faith the obligations assumed under the Charter. All these principles are

well entrenched in international law for developing friendly relations among nations. Earlier, these were noticed in the Indo-Chinese Declaration of five principles of peaceful coexistence (The *Panchsheel*).

(iii) *International cooperation and promotion of human rights*

The U.N. is established to achieve cooperation in solving international problems of an economic, social, cultural and humanitarian character. States should promote and encourage respect for human rights and fundamental freedoms for all without distinction as to race, sex, language or religion. This has been borne out by the Universal Declaration of Human Rights adopted by the General Assembly on 10th December, 1948 and two International Covenants on Political, Civil, Economic and Social Rights, commended by the General Assembly in 1966 but which became effective from 1976.

(iv) *International forum for harmonisation*

The United Nations is to function as a centre for harmonising actions of different States in order to maintain international peace, develop friendly relations and secure international cooperation among members of the organisation. Here the things are talked out to ease international tensions.

Principles Recognised by the U.N.

Article 2 enumerates the principles which will guide the organisation in persuit of its purposes. In all, seven principles are given:

(1) *Sovereign equality*

It is a recognised principle of international law that all States are sovereign and therefore equal. The Charter reaffirms this principle irrespective of size and extent of development of nations. This principle has, however, been compromised in the formation of the Security Council where there are five permanent members with right of veto to torpedo any resolution of the Security Council from becoming binding on member States.

(2) *Fulfilment of obligation*

All members undertake to fulfil in good faith the obligations assumed by them. This is a basic principle of international law that they must carry out their obligations which they have undertaken. The principle is better known as *Pacta Sunt Servanda.*

(3) *Peaceful settlement of disputes*

Member States are to ensure that they settle their disputes by peaceful means without endangering international peace, security and justice.

(4) *Non-use of force*

Members undertake to adjure violence and refrain from use of force or threat thereof against territorial integrity and political independence of any State whether it is a member of the U.N. or not. Use of force is, therefore, banned. Clause 4 is complimentary to Clause 3 urging the States to settle their disputes peacefully.

(5) *Assistance to the U.N.*

All members undertake to give assistance to the U.N. as and when it is demanded of them under the Charter. Negatively, members shall refrain from giving assistance to any State against whom the United Nations is taking action under Articles 41, 42 or any other provision. Members have assumed this obligation under Articles 2, 25 and 43 of the Charter.

(6) *Non-member States*

This is a real controversial principle enunciated in the Charter. Normally, only those States are bound by commitments which are party to an agreement. Consent is the basis of any obligation. Article 2 Clause 6 seeks to ensure that non-member States do not violate the Charter or commit acts which are inconsistent with the Charter. The Security Council took action against North Korea in 1950 when it invaded South Korea. Both the States are not members so far. The U.N. has also taken action against Rhodesia for its perpetrating minority racial rule on a black majority. This shows that the U.N. means business regarding Article 2 Clause 6.

Surely Article 2 Clause 6 incorporates a welcome principle. Today use of force and racial discrimination are universally banned. No State would be allowed to use force or practice racial discrimination on the plea of it being outside the United Nations. None of the purposes of the United Nations are controversial. Therefore, even non-member States are bound to act in accordance with the purposes and principles of the Charter.

(7) *Domestic jurisdiction*

This is yet another controversial Clause which has been debated a lot. The Charter provides that the U.N. will not intervene in matters which are essentially within the domestic jurisdiction of any State; nor shall it require the members to submit such matters for settlement under the present Charter. This Clause has raised a number of storms, particularly in respect of South Africa for its racial discrimination. States are quick to raise the "domestic jurisdiction" bogey whenever there are allegations of violation of human rights.

There is, however, one redeeming provision in Article 2 Clause 7. It says that the plea of domestic jurisdiction will not be applicable to enforcement measures under Chapter VII. It is on this ground that the Security Council is taking action against Rhodesia under Chapter VII although Rhodesia argues that the form of government is one essentially within domestic jurisdiction. The plea has not been accepted.

Membership

There are two categories of members of the United Nations, of course, without any kind of distinction of privileges between them. Article 3 speaks of original members which participated in San Francisco Conference or had signed earlier the Declaration by United Nations of 1st January, 1942 and signed the Charter and ratified it also. In all, 51 States are considered as original members. India, Iran, Thailand, China were from Asia. South Africa was the solitary member from Africa.

Subsequent members are elected under Article 4 by the General Assembly on the recommendation of the Security Council. While it requires nine votes, including concurring votes of the permanent members of the Security Council, it requires two-third majority in the General Assembly.

Article 4 puts only two conditions necessary for membership. It should be a peace-loving State and is in the opinion of the organisation able and willing to carry out the obligations under the Charter. The International Court of Justice in its Advisory Opinion on Conditions of Membership in the United Nations gave five conditions: (i) State, (ii) Peace-loving, (iii) Acceptance of obligations of the Charter, (iv) Ability to carry out these obligations, and (v) Willingness to do so [1].

However, there is some politicking in the case of admission of new members. A number of States were denied membership in the fifties because of objections made by one or the other big power. Resultantly, sixteen States belonging to both the blocks were admitted in a package deal in 1955. Curiously, concurring vote was given conditionally in case of one set of States subject to concurring vote given by the other big power in case of another set of States. There was again politicking in 1972 in the case of admission of Bangla Desh when China vetoed it on the plea that until Bangla Desh returned the Pakistani prisoners of war, it would not be admitted. Bangla Desh was admitted only after the prisoners were repatriated to Pakistan. United Vietnam was not admitted during 1975 and 1976 due to the United States veto. It was admitted only in 1977 when there was a change of regime and heart in the United States. The United Nations has consistently refused admission to Rhodesia because of its minority rule and racial policies.

Representation of China

There has been some confusion with regard to Chinese representation at the United Nations. The Republic of China was a founding member of the United Nations with a permanent seat in the Security Council. It was the only Asian power as a permanent member of the Security Council. However, Chiang's Government was overthrown by Communists on the Chinese mainland in 1949. Resultantly, Chiang withdrew to Formosa, also known as Taiwan. The Communist regime took over the administration in main China. Both the regimes claimed to represent the Republic of China. Partly because the Peking regime was not recognised by some and mainly because of the United State's pressure, every time the question of Chinese representation came up, the United States manoeuvred to see that Peking did not enter the United Nations by raising the plea that it was an important matter which required two-third majority under Article 18 Clause 3.

In 1971, Kissinger visited China and he tried to bring about a thaw in the Sino-United States relations. With mounting pressure for Peking's representation at the United Nations, the United States advocated for Peking's entry into the United Nations along with the non-expulsion of Taiwan from the United Nations. However, the United States strategy failed and Albania's 22-nation resolution asking for Peking's representation as the sole representative of the Republic of China was accepted. Thus, the Peking regime entered the United Nations in November 1971 consequent upon Taiwan's expulsion from the United Nations. This was no admission of a new member. It was the question of Chinese representation at the United Nations. With this ended the idea of the two China theory which the United States wanted to import into the question.

Suspension

Article 5 provides that any member State may be suspended from the exercise off rights and privileges of membership by the General Assembly on the recommendation of the Security Council if any preventive or enforcement measure has been taken against that State. No State has so far been suspended from membership. Suspension can be revoked by the Security Council.

Expulsion

Article 6 provides that a member State may be expelled from the organisation if it has persistently violated the principles of the Charter. Expulsion is done by the General Assembly on the recommendation of the Security Council. So far no State has been expelled although of and on there is talk of Israel's expulsion for not vacating the occupied territories of West Bank, Golan Heights and Jerusalem.

In 1974, the Credentials Committee rejected the credentials of the delegation of South Africa. Later on, the General Assembly called on the Security Council to review South Africa's relations with the U.N. The African effort to expel South Africa from the United Nations was thwarted in the Security Council by a triple veto by the United States, the United Kingdom and France on 30th October, 1974. On 12th November, 1974, the President of the U.N. General Assembly ruled that in view of the rejection of credentials of the South African delegation, the South African delegation could not participate in the General Assembly. The ruling of the President was approved by the Assembly with 91-22-19. This amounted to *de facto* expulsion of the State. Rejection of the credentials of the South African delegation and ouster of South

Africa from the General Assembly thereafter, lack legal validity. What would have happened if the President of the Assembly had been a Westerner instead of the Algerian is debatable. It was also beyond the scope of the Credentials Committee to disqualify a duly authorised delegation.

Suspension of Voting Rights

Article 19 of the Charter provides that a member State may be deprived of its voting right in the Assembly if the member is in arrears equivalent to its two-year contribution. The Article does not say whether the voting right of member, including permanent members, can be suspended in the Security Council. Ostensibly, there is no such suspension in case of the Security Council membership. So far there has been no suspension of the voting rights of any State. At one time, there was a fear that France and the Soviet Union may be deprived of their voting rights if they did not pay their share of expenses incurred in connection with the United Nations Emergency Forces in the Middle East and Congo. Although, the International Court of Justice in its Advisory Opinion held that these expenses were part of the U.N. expenses [2], the dissenting States were asked to give voluntary contribution instead of the same being treated as normal budgetary contribution.

Withdrawal

The Charter has no provision regarding withdrawal of any member of the organisation. The Covenant of the League had such provision in Article 1 Clause 3. The question of withdrawal arose in 1964-65 when Indonesia expressed its desire to withdraw from the United Nations as a protest against Malaysia's election as a member of the Security Council for 1965 and 1966. Indonesia was at that time claiming Brunie as its territory.

At the San Francisco Conference on the United Nations, the Sub-Committee had said that if a member State feels constrained to withdraw from the organisation and leave the burden of maintaining international peace and security to others, the organisation has no intention to compel the State to remain in the organisation.

This was a logical statement because Charter is nothing but a consensual agreement among nations and no nation can be bound infinitely against its wishes. The right of withdrawal is inherent in every treaty, irrespective of the fact whether there is such provision or not in the treaty. It was on this ground that the U.N. Secretariat considered Indonesia's withdrawal as valid although it was welcomed back without the formalities for new membership. As a token, it had to pay 17 per cent arrears of its normal dues while it had withdrawn.

Observer Status

A new tribe of States has been created by practice at the United Nations. It has been noticed that if a State is not admitted to the United Nations or it is not willing to become a member of the U.N. for whatever reason, it is given the status of "Observer". Such a State is allowed a number of facilities at the U.N. Secretariat without right of active participation and voting. It is given on the basis of the acceptance of "Observer" State as a nation by world community.

Presently, Switzerland, Monaco, the Vatican, two Koreas and the Palestine Liberation Organisation have been given the status of Observer. Earlier, West Germany and Bangla Desh had been given Observer status before their admission as members of the United Nations.

General Assembly

The General Assembly is the main body of the United Nations. It consists of all members of the United Nations. It meets at least once a year from September to December. This is called the annual session of the Assembly. There could also be special sessions. So far there have been six special sessions. It meets at U.N. Headquarters in New York. Barring the third session which was in Paris in 1948, the Assembly has not held its session anywhere since then.

Function and Powers

General Assembly has a number of functions and powers. Some are specific; others are implied. Its main functions are given in Articles 10, 11, 13, 14, 15, 17 and 19.

(1) *Omnibus functions*

The General Assembly has omnibus functions and powers under

Article 10. The Article empowers the Assembly to discuss any question or matter "within the scope of the present Charter or relating to the powers and functions of any organs provided for in the present Charter and may make recommendations" to its members or Security Council or both. Under this Clause, the General Assembly may discuss anything under the sun and has discussed many things from the occean floor and sea bed to pollution and outer space.

(2) *Maintenance of international peace and security*

Although the maintenance of international peace and security is the primary responsibility of the Security Council, under Article 11, the General Assembly may discuss steps to be taken to maintain international peace and security. It may consider the general principles of cooperation, and principles governing disarmament and regulation of armaments.

The matter regarding international peace and security may be brought before the Assembly or the Security Council by any member or even by a non-member under Article 35 Clause 2. It can make recommendations to States concerned or the Security Council or both. The General Assembly cannot take any enforcement action which may be referred to the Security Council. The General Assembly may draw the attention of the Security Council to situations or questions which endanger international peace and security.

Uniting for Peace Resolutions: The Security Council is primarily responsible for maintaining or restoring international peace and security. It was hoped that the five permanent members of the Security Council would forge a united front against any violator of international peace. They were required to work in unison. Else the Security Council could not function. However, soon after the establishment of the United Nations, cracks began to appear in the unity of the Big Powers. The cold war had already started and the world community had a taste of it in 1948 over the Berlin Blockade which was a matter of "touch and go". In 1949 Nationalist China was overrun by the Peking regime. Then started the Korean War. In the initial stage, the United States could get the things done from the Security Council because the Soviet Union had boycotted the Security Council meetings. But things did not look bright. Every Big Power could dangle veto to scuttle Security

Council's efforts to maintain international peace and security. Uniting for Peace Resolution was sought to remove the *impasse*.

On 3rd November 1950, the General Assembly passed the resolution which ran as under:

> "If the Security Council, because of lack of unanimity of the permanent members fails to exercise its primary responsibility for the maintenance of international peace and security in any case where there appears to be a threat to the peace, breach of peace, or act of aggression, the General Assembly shall consider the matter immediately, with a view to make appropriate recommendations to members for collective measures, including in the case of a breach of the peace or act of aggression, the use of armed force, when necessary. If not in session at the time, the General Assembly may meet in emergency special session within twentyfour hours of the request therefor. Such emergency special session shall be called if requested by the Security Council on the vote of any seven members, or by a majority of the members of the United Nations."
>
> (Now, seven members of the Council as originally in the text of the resolution should be read as nine members after the increase in the membership of the Security Council from 11 to 15 with effect from 31st August, 1965.)

The resolution was vehemently opposed by the Soviet Union and its group which was then not in happy position in the General Assembly. It thought that its right of veto in the Security Council was being sidetracked. Instead, the power was being given to the General Assembly where it feared that the United States of America could get things done according to its convenience by mechanical majority which it was then enjoying.

However, things have since changed. The resolution was first invoked in October, 1956 when the United Kingdom, France and Israel launched a joint attack on the Suez Canal consequent upon nationalisation of the canal by Nasser. In November, 1956, the Soviet action in Hungary was discussed by the Assembly. In August, 1958, the situation in Lebanon and Jordan was discussed. The Congo situation was discussed in September, 1960. Consequent upon the Arab-Israeli war in June 1967 the Emergency Assembly Session was called by the Soviet Union in June, 1967 to discuss the Middle East situation. It was again called in December, 1971 to discuss the situation in the Indian sub-continent.

The record of Emergency Sessions of the General Assembly to tackle peace situation has not been happy. In November, 1956, the United Kingdom and France agreed to respond to the Assembly's call for cease-fire only after the U.N. could assure them to secure their objectives for which they had launched their action. In the same month, the Soviet Union rejected the Assembly's demand that U.N. observers be stationed on Hungarian soil. In 1958, the United States and United Kingdom withdrew their troops from Lebanon and Jordan after they were sure that results of their action would not be disturbed. In 1960, Congo (now Zaire) unity was maintained and Katanga prevented from secession due to identity of views between the U.N. and the Central Congo Government. It, of course, cost the life of then U.N. Secretary General Hammarskjöld who died in an air crash in the Congo. In 1967, the Middle East question was again referred to the Security Council which adopted the Resolution 242 for the solution of Arab-Israel conflict. In 1971, the Assembly's call for cease-fire and withdrawal of military forces and the stationing of U.N. observers in Bangla Desh became redundant in the wake of the birth of Bangla Desh which had been recognised by India on 6th December 1971.

There has been some controversy about the constitutionality of the "Uniting for Peace" Resolution. Maintenance of international peace and security is the primary responsibility of the Security Council. The General Assembly can discuss this problem under Article 11 and recommend measures for peaceful adjustment of a situation. It can only make recommendations. It cannot take any enforcement action. For that, it has to refer the matter to the Security Council under Article 11 Clause 2. The International Court of Justice has held in its Advisory opinion in Expenses Case that any enforcement action cannot be taken by the General Assembly, although stationing of UNEF may be done by the Assembly with the consent of the States concerned. The powers that sponsored the resolution do not seem to be enthusiastic now because they cannot muster automatic two-third majority in the Assembly in view of change in its complexion. The Afro-Asian States also do not seem to be enthusiastic about it due to bilateral disputes between them, lest it may boomerang on them.

(3) *General functions*

The General Assembly has been empowered under Article 13 to initiate studies and make recommendations for:

(i) promoting international cooperation in political, economic, social, cultural and educational fields;

(ii) encouraging progressive development of international law and its codification; and

(iii) promoting human rights and fundamental freedoms without restriction as to race, sex, language or religion.

It is on the basis of these functions that the General Assembly has created the International Law Commission for making drafts to codify international law. It has commended a number of Conventions and declarations relating to human rights.

There is a duty imposed upon the General Assembly under Article 55 to promote international economic and social cooperation. This has become necessary for creating conditions of stability and well-being of mankind which are conducive to peaceful and friendly relations among nations. The General Assembly is to champion the principles of equal rights and self-determination of peoples. For this, it shall promote:

(a) higher standards of living, full employment and conditions of economic and social progress and development;

(b) solution of international economic, social health and related problems; and

(c) universal respect for, and observance of, human rights and fundamental freedoms.

(4) *Elective functions*

The General Assembly elects new members of the U.N. on the recommendation of the Security Council. It is entrusted with the election of members to a number of bodies. It elects five non-permanent members of the Security Council every year under Article 23(2). It elects five judges for the International Court of Justice every three years in conjunction with the Security Council. It elects eighteen members of the Economic and Social Council every year under Article 61(3). It elects members of the Trusteeship Council under Article 86. It elects (appoints) the Secretary-General of the United Nations every five years on the recommendation of the Security Council under Article 97. It elects members for various Committees and subsidiary organs created by it under Article 22.

(5) *Receptive, debating and recommending functions*

The General Assembly is to receive annual reports from the

Secretary-General, Security Council, Economic and Social Council, Trusteeship Council, High Commissioner for Refugees and various other organs and Committees sponsored by the organisation, debate on them and make such recommendations as may be deemed necessary under Article 15.

(6) *Financial functions*

The General Assembly is to approve the annual budget of the organisation under Article 17. Until 1977, the practice was that the Secretary-General was to present budgetary proposals to the Assembly every year. At the Thirty-second Session of the Assembly in 1977, the Secretary-General departed from earlier practice and presented two-year budget for 1978 and 1979.

The General Assembly has to apportion the budgetary expenses among its members.

(7) *Voting pattern in the Assembly*

Each member of the Organisation has one vote in the Assembly under Article 18. Resolutions of the Assembly are carried by simple majority of the members, present and voting. However, important questions require two-third majority of those present and voting. Important questions would include:

(a) Recommendations with respect to maintenance of international peace and security;

(b) Election of non-permanent members of the Security Council;

(c) Election of the members of the Economic and Social Council;

(d) Election of the judges of the International Court of Justice:

(e) Admission of new members;

(f) Suspension of rights and privileges of membership;

(g) Expulsion of members;

(h) Operation of Trusteeship System;

(i) Budgetary questions; and

(j) Any additional important question as determined by the Assembly through majority decision.

Security Council

Security Council is the most important body of the United Nations Organisation. It originally consisted of eleven members but its membership was raised to fifteen in 1965 when amendments with respect to Article 23, 27 and 61 became effective on 31st August, 1965. The General Assembly had earlier adopted these amendments on 17th December 1963. Out of fifteen members, five are permanent members of the Council. They are the United States of America, the Union of Soviet Socialist Republics, Republic of China, France and the United Kingdom of Great Britain and Northern Ireland. The other ten members remain for a term of two years but each year five members drop out after completing their two-year term.

Article 23 mentions two considerations for election of non-permanent members of the Council. These are : (i) Contribution to maintenance of international peace and security and other purposes of the U.N., and (ii) geographical distribution. However, geographical considerations have dominated the election of the members. Practices show that one member is elected from Eastern Europe, two from Western Europe, Canada and Australia, three from Asia preferably, one from the Far East, another from South-East Asia, third from West Asia, two from Africa and two from Latin America.

The main function of the Security Council is to see that international peace and security is maintained or restored where there has been a breach. Article 24 of the Charter says that its members confer primary responsibility on the Security Council for maintenance of international peace and security. This has been done because the Security Council is a small body of fifteen members which can be convened at a short notice. This will ensure prompt and effective action in comparison to the convening of the General Assembly's special session which will be time-consuming and will be unwieldy in view of its composition. Article 28 requires that the Council will be in session for all the twelve months. States, which are members of the Council, shall station their diplomats in New York so as to be easily available whenever any contingency arises as to the convening of the Council meeting to discuss urgent matters of international peace and security.

The Security Council, while discharging its primary responsibility, works as a representative of the whole body. The Council has to keep in view the purposes and principles of the Charter while discharging these duties. The Council has to consider pacific methods for settlement of any dispute which comes up before it. It may recommend appropriate measures and procedures under Article 36 for amicable settlement or adjustment of disputes through negotiation, enquiry, mediation, conciliation, arbitration, judicial settlement, resort to regional agencies or arrangements as provided under Article 33. It may make recommendations to the parties with a view to pacific settlement of the dispute under Article 38.

However, if pacific methods fail and there is a threat to peace, breach of peace or act of aggression, the Security Council may make recommendations under Articles 39 and decide on measures which the occasion may require. It may decide to take measures involving the non-use of force under Article 41 or measures involving use of force under Article 42. Measures under Article 41 may include economic embargo, severance of communications and diplomatic relation. Measures under Article 42 may include demonstrations, blockade or military operations. The Security Council may also decide upon provisional measures under Article 40 before taking action under Article 41 or 42.

Article 27 speaks about the voting pattern in the Security Council. While decision of the Security Council on procedural subjects requires simple majority of nine members, all important decisions of the Security Council require nine votes, including "concurring votes of the permanent members."

Concurrence of permanent members in all important decisions was made essential under Article 27(3) on the assumption that the permanent members who were allies during World War II would work unitedly to preserve international peace and security, However, the assumption was soon falsified. The Soviet Union and the Western powers—the United States, the United Kingdom and France—began to drift apart since 1948 with resulting disunity in the Security Council which has made it ineffective in most of the crucial issues.

The concurring vote of permanent members for any decision of the Council is called right of veto. These States can torpedo any resolution of the Security Council if it is carried against its wishes. None of the five States likes to be swamped by a majority vote to which it is not party. Rigours of concurring vote have been easened by interpreting that there need not be an affirmative vote by the permanent member so long as there is no dissenting vote and note. Mere abstaining from voting by any permanent member does not make the Security Council decision invalid. Thus was held in an Advisory Opinion by the International Court of Justice in the South West Africa Case in June, 1971 [3].

Article 27(2) says that procedural matters will be decided by a majority of nine members and the permanent members do not have veto in such matters. But whether the matter is procedural or not is to be determined by the concurrent vote of the permanent members. This has given rise to "double veto". Thus the dissenting permanent member may first assert that the matter is not procedural but substantial and important. Then it may dissent again on the merits of the matter. This double veto has been responsible for many inactions on the part of the Security Council.

Once the Security Council takes a decision, the members are bound to carry it out. Article 2 Clause 5 obligates them to give to the United Nations all assistance required of them under the Charter. Under Article 25, members agree to accept and carry out the decisions of the Security Council. Under Article 43, members undertake to make available to the Security Council armed forces which they may be called upon to contribute. Under Article 48, members may be asked to take any action which may be required of them to carry out decisions of the Security Council. Article 49 calls upon members to give mutual assistance in carrying out the decisions of the Council.

Apart from the Security Council's primary function for maintaining international peace and security, the Security Council recommends new members of the United Nations, recommends the appointment of the Secretary-General, selects judges of the International Court of Justice in cooperation with the General Assembly, expels any member for consistent violation of the Charter and suspends the members for default in payment of its dues for two years or more.

Some Important International Issues before the Security Council

(1) *Indo-Pakistan dispute over Kashmir*

When India became free in 1947, the princely States were allowed to accede to India or Pakistan or declare independence. The Maharaja of Jammu and Kashmir, instead of acceding to India or Pakistan, entered into a standstill agreement with both of them. The Pakistani government tried to pressurise the Maharaja to accede to Pakistan. Having failed to pressurise the Maharaja, Pakistan sent raiders and Pakistani soldiers in tribal dress and attacked Kashmir in October, 1947. The Maharaja of Jammu and Kashmir appealed to India to come to its rescue. India, however, refused to assist unless the Maharaja acceded to India. The next day, the Maharaja acceded to India, who in turn sent air-borne troops to save Srinagar which was being threatened by raiders. Kashmir had now become a part of India, and India complained to the U.N. Security Council about Pakistan's invasion of her territory. While the Security Council could arrange cease-fire in the sub-continent, and station U.N. Observers on the Indo-Pakistan border in the Kashmir sector, it did not resolve the issue.

The matter became explosive again in August, 1965 when Pakistan tried to capture Kashmir through infiltration and subversion. On September 1st, 1965, Pakistan launched a massive attack in the Jammu aud Kashmir Sector. India retaliated by advancing towards Lahore and captured vantage points in Kargil and Haji Pir Pass. The Security Council called upon India and Pakistan to cease-fire on 4th September 1965 and again on 6th September, 1965. This was followed by another resolution of 20th September, 1965 ordering for cease-fire from 22nd September, 1965. Accordingly, there was cease-fire from 22nd September, 1965.

In the meantime, Soviet leaders had offered their good offices to resolve the Indo-Pakistan differences. They arranged the meeting between Lal Bahadur Shastri, Indian Prime Minister and Ayub Khan, Pakistani President in Tashkent in January, 1966. Their meeting resulted in the issuance of the Tashkent Declaration of 10th January, 1966. The two leaders agreed to promote friendly relations and refrain from resort to use of force to settle their disputes. Besides, India agreed to vacate vantage points in Kargil and Haji Pir which were occupied by the Indian forces during the 1965 hostilities. The tragedy for India was the loss of its Prime Minister in Tashkent who died there soon after the agreement.

There was a third round of hostilities between India and Pakistan in December, 1971 over the question of Bangla Desh. Pakistan bombarded Indian airfields on 3rd December, 1971. India retaliated. The Security Council could not act because of Nixon's tilting in favour of Pakistan and America's partisan attitude at the Security Council meetings. The Soviet Union came to India's rescue by vetoing the resolutions of the Security Council on 4th,

6th and 12th December, 1971. The U.N. General Assembly, which was then having its 25th Session, also exhorted upon the parties to cease-fire on 7th December, 1971. India declared a unilateral cease-fire on 16th December, 1971 following the emergence of Bangla Desh on that day through the unconditional surrender of Pakistani forces in Bangla Desh. The cease-fire was accepted by President Yahya Khan of Pakistan and it became effective on 17th December, 1971.

Genesis of the Indo-Pakistan dispute over Kashmir is that Pakistan claims Kashmir because it has muslim majority. India refutes such a claim because of its secular character. The Indian Prime Minister had declared in 1947 while accepting the accesion letter of the Maharaja of Kashmir that the wishes of Kashmiris will be ascertained when things become normal. Kashmir has had a number of general elections since then and a pro-Indian majority has emerged ever since. Thus although the accession was unconditional and final it has been reinforced by the unequivocal voting pattern in subsequent elections. The issue seems to have lost its lustre in the U.N. corridors.

(2) *Middle East*

The Middle East has been the centre of an explosive situation since 1947 when the United Kingdom brought the matter before the United Nations in April. The General Assembly's Special Session established a Committee on Palestine which recommended the partition of former British mandate—Palestine—into Arab State, Israel and international regime for Jerusalem. The recommendations were opposed by the Arab States which resisted. The U.N. Palestine Commission was established to carry out the recommendations of the Committee on Palestine. The Security Council was requested to implement the plan and deal with any situation involving a breach or threat of breach of peace. The Security Council called for truce in April 1948 The State of Israel was proclaimed on 4th May, 1948 amidst armed action by Arab States. The Security Council ordered truce effective 11th June, 1948. Hostilities were renewed on 8th July, 1948. The Security Council proclaimed cease-fire. But fighting continued in the Negev area. Despite cease-fire and truce, there were continual hostilities until there were general armistice agreements signed between Israel and the Arab States in February-April, 1949. In between, the U.N.

mediator, Bernadotte, was killed in Jerusalem.

There was unsteady truce prevailing in the area with intermittent skirmishes between Israel and the Arab States from time to time. On 18th May, 1967, the U.A.R. requested for the withdrawal of the UNEF which ceased operating from 19th May following Secretary-General's agreeing to withdraw the force. The situation exploded on 5th June, 1967 when Israel launched a massive attack on the Arab countries—Egypt, Syria and Jordan and occupied large chunks of their territory—Sinai and Gaza in Egypt, Jerusalem and West Bank in Jordan and Golan Heights in Syria. The Security Council called for immediate cease-fire on 7th June, 1967. Cease-fire was effected from 9th June, 1967. Eventually, the Security Council adopted Resolution 242 of November, 1967 which runs as under:

> The Security Council,
> Expressing its continuing concern with the grave situation in the Middle East,
> Emphasising the inadmissibility of the acquisition of territory by war and the need to work for a just and lasting peace in which every State in the area can live in security,
>
> 1. Affirms that the fulfillment of Charter principles requires the establishment of a just and lasting peace in the Middle East which should include the application of both the following principles:
>   (i) Withdrawal of Israeli armed forces from territories occupied in the recent conflict;
>   (ii) Termination of all claims or states of belligerency and respect for and acknowledgement of the sovereignty, territorial integrity and political independence of every State in the area and their right to live in peace within secure and recognised boundaries free from threats and acts of force;
> 2. Affirms further the necessity:
>   (a) For guaranteeing freedom of navigation through international waterways in the area;
>   (b) For achieving a just settlement of the refugee problem;
>   (c) For guaranteeing the territorial integrity and political independence of every State in the area, through measures including the establishment of demilitarised zones. . . .

While the hostilities ceased, the stalemate continued. On 6th October. 1973, Egypt and Syria launched attacks across the Suez and took Israel unawares while the latter was celebrating its national festival. After the initial setback, Israel recovered from the shock and launched offensives against Egypt and Syria. The Security Council ordered cease-fire and passed Resolution 338 on 22nd October, 1973 which runs as under:

The Security Council:

1. Calls upon all parties to the present fighting to cease all firing and terminate all military activity immediately not later than 12 hours after the moment of the adoption of this decision, in the positions they now occupy;
2. Calls upon the parties concerned to start immediately after the cease-fire the implementation of Security Council Resolution 242 (1967) in all its parts;
3. Decides that, immediately and concurrently with the cease-fire, negotiations shall start between the parties concerned under appropriate auspice aimed at establishing a just and durable peace in the Middle East.

Since then, there was a Geneva Conference between Israel and the Arab States under joint Chairmanship of the United States and U.S.S.R. in December, 1973. The Conference remains adjourned and efforts are being made to reconvene it with Palestinian participation. In the meanwhile, Israel has vacated the Sinai area of Egypt and Egypt has opened the Suez to Israel. President Sadat of Egypt visited Israel in November, 1977 and had talks with Israeli leaders.

The crux of the matter is that Arab Palestinians want their national home in the form of State of Palestine on the West Bank. Israelis refuse to negotiate with the Palestinians whom they label as terrorists. Colonialists also initially refused to negotiate with members of liberation fronts in colonies. They were labelled as traitors. Eventually, they had to. Israel also interprets Resolution 242 by asserting that it does not demand evacuation from all occupied territories.

(3) *Congo crisis* (*now Zaire*)

Belgium granted independence to Congo on 30th June, 1960 reluctantly. It did not want to leave the copper-rich colony. The Congolese in turn were least prepared for independence. Belgium had not imparted any political or administrative training to the Congo people to run the government. Literacy rate was incredibly low. There were only a handful of Congolese university graduates who could be counted on fingertips. Before leaving, Belgium had fanned intertribal and interstate rivalries. Resultantly, when Belgium left, the army revolted and chaos prevailed. In the melee, a number of Europeans were killed. Kasavubu, President and Lumumba, Prime Minister, tried to dominate each other. The balancing factor was Mobutu who was then Commander in Chief of the armed forces. Belgium had also sponsored Tshombe, Chief Minister of Copper-rich Katanga Province, to secede from Congo. Belgium deployed its military forces on the plea of protecting the lives of Europeans. The Congolese Government complained to the United Nations about Belgian use of its armed forces on Congo soil.

Initially, the Security Council by its resolution authorised the Secretary-General on 14th July, 1960 to provide the local government with military assistance and asked the Belgian Government to withdraw its forces from the Congo. This was reiterated by the Security Council resolution on 22nd July, 1960 with a request to States not to do anything which may threaten the territorial integrity or political independence of the State. The Security Council by its third resolution on 9th August, 1960 called upon Belgium to withdraw its forces from Katanga which had accelerated its seccession demand with active Belgian support.

Although, a United Nations Force was formed by the Secretary-General on the basis of 14th July, 1960 resolution, the crisis got bogged down due to Soviet preference for Patrice Lumumba, the Prime Minister of Congo who developed differences with the U.N. Secretary-General. Resultantly, the controversy arose whether the U.N. Force should be under the control of the Security Council or Secretary-General. Besides, the role of the United Nations Force became controversial—whether it should interfere in the civil war or protect the lives of foreigners within the territory.

Division became apparent when Kasavubu and Lumumba dismissed each other in September, 1960. The West supported Kasavubu while the Soviet Union supported Lumumba. A special General Assembly session was called in September to discuss the Congo situation. The General Assembly asked the Secretary-General to maintain law and order in the Congo where Mobutu installed a care taker government. The General Assembly admitted the Congo without deciding upon its representation. Premier Kruschev asked for dismissal of the Secretary-General while addressing the General Assembly. In November, the U.N. accepted Kasavubu's credentials and in December, Lumumba was arrested by Mobutu. Lumumba died in February, 1961 but the strife continued. In March, the Soviet Union stopped recognising Dag Hammarskjöld as the U.N. Secretary-General. In July, 1961, the Congolese Parliament met. In August, Adoula was elected as Prime Minister. The mercenaries were apprehended in Katanga. In September, the Secretary-General was killed in an air accident while in Congolese airspace. In December, 1961, I.C.J. was approached for advisory opinion regarding the financing of U.N. action in Congo. In July 1962, I.C.J. in his advisory opinion considered the Congo expenses as part of the regular budget under Article 17. The stalemate continued up to 1964.

(4) *South Africa and apartheid*

South Africa's policy of apartheid—racial segregation—has also been one of the burning problems faced by the United Nations ever since its inception. The matter has been before the U.N. since 1946 in one or another form. Apartheid has been condemned by the world community as a "crime against humanity", which threatens international peace and security. South Africa has consistently maintained that it is essentially within its domestic jurisdiction and thus outside the purview of the U.N.

In 1962, the General Assembly appointed a special Committee Against Apartheid to keep South African policies under review. In 1963, Security Council called on States to stop sale and shipment of arms to S. Africa. It called upon the South African Government to release persons opposed to apartheid. In 1970, the Security Council condemned violations of arms embargo. Later on, the General Assembly advised for termination of diplomatic or official relations with South Africa and stoppage of any cooperation. It condemned the establishment of Bantu as a homeland for Blacks. In 1972, Security Council recognised the legitimacy of the anti-appartheid struggle. In 1973, the General Assembly adopted International Convention on the Suppression and Punishment of the Crime of Apartheid. 1973-1983 has been called as Decade for Action to combat Racism and Racial Discrimination. Twenty-first March has been declared as International Day for Elimination of Racial Discrimination. It is the anniversary day of 69 murders at Sharpeville in South Africa in 1960. Struggle against South African apartheid continues despite veto of the United States, the United Kingdom and France of any mandatory sanction against South Africa. In November, 1977, these three powers joined in unanimous mandatory arms embargo.

Economic and Social Council

There is an Economic and Social Council consisting of fifty-four members to be elected by the General Assembly for a term of three years. Eighteen of its members retire every year. The powers and functions of the Council are given in Article 62 of the Charter. These relate to making of recommendations and initiating studies in respect of economic, social, cultural, educational, health and related matters. In particular, it "may make recommendation for the purpose of promoting respect for, and observance of, human rights and fundamental freedoms". It may convene international conferences and recommend draft conventions to the General Assembly.

Article 66 confers further powers on the Council. It shall carry out the recommendations of the General Assembly in respect of such functions given to it under Article 62. Besides, it shall perform other functions which the General Assembly may confer on it.

In the course of years, the Economic and Social Council has assumed great importance. It has been noticed that except for matters of international peace and security, the Council has dealt with a variety of subjects. It has been singularly successful in the domain of human rights where it has piloted a number of draft conventions. It has been responsible for the two International Covenants on Economic, Social, Political and Civil Rights. It recommended the Draft Declaration on Principles Governing Friendly Relations Among Nations. It has dealt with rights of national minorities. There is hardly anything under the sun which it cannot deal with. All matters are decided in the Council by simple majority, present and voting.

Trusteeship Council

Article 86 establishes Trusteeship Council comprising of administering states, the five big powers who are permanent members of the Security Council and other member including five permanent members, equivalent to administering States. The Council composition has decreased progressively with most of the trust territories having become independent. Resultantly, only the big powers constitute the Trusteeship Council today.

Article 87 states the powers and functions of the Council. These are to consider reports by administering power, examine petitions from residents of trust territories, visit trust territories periodically and take any other action in conformity with Trusteeship Agreement.

Of the eleven trust territories which were put under trusteeship system, ten have attained independence or integrated with other States. Only the Pacific Islands remain with the United States of America. South West Africa (New Nambia) has not been categorised as trust territory because South Africa never accepted that position. Besides Nambia is being separately dealt with.

Nambia was one of the seven African territories held under mandate system of the League. In 1950, the International Court of Justice in its Advisory Opinion held that South Africa held international obligations regarding the territory and the United Nations should exercise supervision over its administration. In October, 1966, the U.N. General Assembly terminated the South African mandate authority over Nambia due to persistent violations of its international obligations. In May, 1967, Council for Nambia was created.

In October, 1971, the Security Council in the pursuance of International Court of Justice opinion declared that presence of South Africa in Nambia is illegal, that it should withdraw its administration immediately and put an end to its occupation of Nambia. Pressure on South Africa for its withdrawal from the territory is ever mounting.

In December, 1973, the General Assembly recognised SWAPO (South West African People's Organisation) as the people's representative of Nambia. In December, 1974, the Security Council called upon South Africa to vacate Nambia. In January, 1976, the Security Council called for the establishment of a machinery to organise people politically. There was also an international conference on Nambia held in Dakar, Senegal in January, 1976 where South African presence in Nambia was considered as a threat to international peace. In December, 1976, the General Assembly supported the armed struggle led by SWAPO for liberation of Nambia.

Secretary-General

Secretary-General is the Chief administrative officer of the organisation under Article 97 of the Charter. He works in that capacity in all meetings of the General Assembly, Security Council, Economic and Social Council and Trusteeship Council. He is appointed by the General Assembly on the recommendation of the Security Council which means the concurring vote of the five permanent members. Kurt Waldhiem is fourth Secretary-General. The earlier ones were Tryge Lie (Norwegian), Dag Hammorskjöld (Swedish), U Thant (Burmese).

The Office of the Secretary-General has grown to be a very important office. He is the chief executive who appoints the other staff under regulations established by the General Assembly. He sends annual reports to the General Assembly regarding working of the organisation as well as his proposals for its future working. He is the implementing authority for any recommendations made by the General Assembly and decisions of the Security Council. He prepares items of agenda for General Assembly's annual sessions. He has a hand in preparing Security Council agenda also. He can take part in deliberations of the General Assembly and Security Council by giving the truly world picture of a given situation agitating the minds of world elites. The Secretary-General may bring to the attention of the Security Council any matter which in his opinion may threaten the maintenance of international peace and security. The Secretary-General uses his discretion while deciding to draw the Security Council's attention to any situation. In some cases, he may prefer not to draw the Security Council's attention to a given situation because no useful purpose may be served in doing so. Thus, U Thant did not draw the Security Council's attention to Vietnam although full war was raging there.

The Secretary-General is a true international civil servant and should work as such. He should not seek, nor receive instructions from any Government or external authority. Once he is appointed, he should work as independently as he can in the circumstances without submitting too much to pressures of the five permanent members of the Council. Trygve Lie became unpopular with the Soviet Block on the Korean issue. Hammarskjöld incurred the wrath of Kruschev when the former did not support Patrice Lumumba as Prime Minister of Congo (Zaire). U Thant chose a middle path giving no cause of annoyance to the bipolar powers.

Therefore, he was a little weak. Waldheim has so far acquitted himself creditably, taking no rigid sides which may annoy the one or other big power. It is indeed a crucial assignment demanding real international outlook devoid of national or regional bias without caring for favours or frowns of nationally biased world leaders.

NOTES

1. 1948 I.C.J. Reports 61.
2. The Expenses Case, 1962 I.C.J. Reports 151.
3. 1971 I.C.J. Reports 22.

CHAPTER 36

THE INTERNATIONAL COURT OF JUSTICE

Establishment of the International Court of Justice is a great experiment in settlement of international disputes which may be justiciable. The idea is not new. The Hague Conventions of 1899 and 1907 had envisaged the establishment of an international court for peaceful settlement of international disputes. Article 14 of the Convenant of the League of Nations visualised the establishment of such a court. This matured into the establishment of the Permanent Court of International Justice which started functioning from 1922. It continued to function until the initiation of World War II. During the war, it ceased to function although it continued to exist on paper. This state of affairs continued until the present International Court of Justice was created under the United Nations Charter.

Unlike the United Nations which is not the successor of the League of Nations, the International Court of Justice is the successor of the Permanent Court of International Justice. Article 92 of the U.N. Charter states that the Statute of the Court is "based upon the Statute of the Permanent Court of International Justice." Article 36(5) of the Statute of the Court considers Declarations made under the Statute of the Permanent Court as valid between the parties to the present Statute. In point of continuity also, Judges of the Permanent Court resigned on 31st January, 1946 and the Court was formally disbanded by a Resolution of the Assembly of the League of Nations on 18th April, 1946. Coincidentally, the new Court had its inaugural function on the same date, 18th April, 1946 at the Peace Palace in Hague which was also the seat of the former Court. The retiring President of the Permanent Court, Judge Guerrero, was also the first President of the new Court. The basic difference between the two courts is that while the Statute of the present Court is an integral part of the U.N. Charter, this was not the case regarding the Statute of the Permanent Court.

The United Nations Organisation, which is dedicated to the cause of maintenance of international peace and security and settlement of international disputes by peaceful means, has a number of organs. The International Court of Justice is its principal judicial organ under Articles 7 and 92 of the U.N. Charter and Article 1 of the Court's Statute. Its main functions under the Charter are to settle legal disputes referred to it by parties under Article 36(3) or give advisory opinions under Article 96.

Parties: Article 93(1) of the Charter provides that all members of the United Nations "are *ispo facto* parties to the Statute of the International Court of Justice." This is a departure from the practice prevalent during the League days. Members of the League were not party to the Statute of the Permanent Court automatically by virtue of their membership of the League. They had to subscribe to the Protocol of the Court separately.

Article 93(2) of the Charter permits non-member States of the United Nations to become party to the Statute under conditions as fixed by the General Assembly upon recommendation of the Security Council. Switzerland was the first non-member State to become party to the Statute under this Clause. The General Assembly by its Resolution of 11th December, 1946 permitted Switzerland to become party to the Statute on the fulfilment of three conditions as recommended by the Security Council at its 80th meeting on 15th November, 1946. These three conditions were: acceptance of the Statute, acceptance of the obligations under Article 94(1) of the Charter relating to compliance with the decision of the Court to which it may be party, and equitable contribution to the Court's expenditure [1]. Switzerland became party to the Statute on 28th July, 1948 with the deposit of instrument of accession with the Secretary-General on that date.

Switzerland was followed by Liechtenstien which filed its application on 14th March, 1949. The same was approved by the General Assembly by its Resolution of 1st December, 1949 [2], as recommended by the Security Council at its meeting on 27th July, 1949. The conditions laid down were the same as in the case of Switzerland. Leichtenstein became party to the Statute on 29th March, 1950 with the deposit of instrument with the Secretary-General on that date. Few years later, San Marino and Japan requested for becoming party to the Statute. Accordingly, they became party to the Statute on 18th February, 1954 and 2nd April, 1954 respectively in pursuance of the General Assembly's recommendation on 9th December, 1953 [3]. In 1956, Japan became member of the United Nations. Consequently, as of today, there are only three States which are not members of the United Nations but are party to the Statute. Out of these three, the full statehood of Leichtenstein and San Marino is doubtful.

Question may be asked as to the rights and duties of States which are party to the Statute. Frankly speaking, being party to the Statute does not mean much. The Court is equally open to States which are party to the Statute as well as to States which are not party to the Statute. In the latter case, the Security Council may have to fix some conditions under Article 35(2) of the Statute to enable access to such States [4].

It may nevertheless be said that a State which is party to the Statute has two rights and one duty. Thus, such States have the right to participate in the election of Judges to the Court [5] and subscribe to the compulsory jurisdiction as provided under Article 36(2) of the Statute. These rights are followed by the duty to contribute to the expenses of the Court. Beyond this, States being party to the Statute, do not have any other right or duty. It may be argued that they have also the duty to comply with any decision of the Court to which they may be party. But this duty is equally incumbent on such States which are not party to the Statute but which have availed of the forum of the Court under Article 35(2) of the Statute.

Composition of the Court

Article 3 of the Statute fixes the number of Judges at fifteen. They are to be elected by securing two-third majority vote in the General Assembly as well as in the Security Council. Both these organs of the United Nations must proceed to elect the members of the Court simultaneously. The Judges are to be elected from the "list of persons nominated by the national groups in the Permanent Court of Arbitration" or by special groups in case of countries not represented at the Arbitration Court [6]. Members of the United Nations and other States which have become party to the Statute are entitled to participate in the election [7].

Article 2 of the Statute provides that the Court shall consist of independent Judges, irrespective of their nationality, from among persons of high moral character, who are either qualified to become judges of the highest judicial tribunal in their respective countries or they are noted jurisconsults. This would mean that candidates must be men of integrity and competent international lawyers. Article 9 of the Statute provides that while electing judges, the electors shall bear in mind that prospective judges are not only qualified but they also represent the mainstreams of civilisation and principal legal systems of the world.

It may be noted that there is no restriction on the nationality of a prospective judge. His country may not be member of the United Nations; nor need it be party to the Statute. A person may be elected solely in his individual capacity. However, there has been no instance in which a person may have been elected without national backing. On the contrary, many a competent lawyers have been defeated because their countries could not muster enough support from among the U.N. members for the election of the sponsored candidates.

The normal term of members of the court is nine years. But they are eligible for re-election [8]. Judges filling the casual vacancies are elected for the remainder of the term of their predecessor [9].

Members of the Court are irremovable except in the case of unanimous vote by the remaining 14 Judges to the effect that "he has ceased to fulfil the required conditions" [10]. The required conditions may be that he may have exercised some political, administrative or professional functions in contravention of Articles 16 and 17 of the Statute [11], or may not be acting impartially and conscientiously as required of him under an oath while assuming membership of the court [12]. Since there has been no chance of invoking Article 18 of the Statute so far, and since Rules of the Court are also silent on this point, it is doubtful to know the scope of the words that "he has ceased to fulfil the required conditions" as envisaged by Article 18.

There is provision for the appointment of national judges, known as *ad hoc* judges by the litigating States which are not represented at the Court [13]. Only such persons can be nominated as *ad hoc* judges who are otherwise qualified to be members of the court. They have also to take an oath of office as required of other judges under Article 20 [14]. No person may, however, be appointed as an *ad hoc* judge if "he has previously taken part as agent, counsel or advocate for one of the parties or as a member of a national or international court, or of a commission of inquiry, or in any other capacity" [15]. He may also be subject to restrictions as given in Article 24 [16]. His tenure of office is coextensive with the period of litigation and until the decision has been rendered in the case.

All the members of the Court, regular or *ad hoc*, are entitled to diplomatic privileges and immunities [17]. Article 19 does not specifically mention about the privileges and immunities of *ad hoc* judges. But these can be fairly implied from the fact that the national judge is as much a member of the Court as any other judge and he participates in the proceedings on terms of equality [18]. Besides, when agents, counsels and other representatives enjoy privileges and immunities under Article 42, it will indeed be difficult to imagine that a national judge would not enjoy the same. Article 105 of the Charter provides for functional immunity for the officials of the United Nations and its organs. Therefore, *ad hoc* judges have also privileges and immunities while they are functioning as such and are drawing their allowances from the U.N. exchequer. In practice also, they enjoy privileges and immunities.

A bench of nine judges and national judge(s) forms a quorum for ordinary hearings [19]. The Court also constitutes few Chambers comprising of three or more judges, for dealing with labour cases and cases relating to transit and communications or any other particular case with the approval of parties [20]. The Court may also constitute a Chamber of five Judges for speedy disposal of cases if the parties so desire [21].

Access to the Court

Article 34(1) stipulates that only "States may be parties in cases before the Court." This would mean that individuals would have no access to the Court. The word State, however, does not necessarily mean independent State only because India was party to the Statute before it was independent. Similarly, Liechtenstien and San Marino could become party to the Statute despite the fact that they are not considered as full States.

Article 35(1) limits the application of Article 34(1). This would mean that the Court is open to only such States which are party to the Statute; this would include the members of the United Nations and Switzerland, Liechtenstein, and San Marino. In fact, Liechtenstein utilised the forum of the Court in the Nottebohm case which it filed in 1952 against Gautemala.

Article 35(2) permits States, which are not party to the Statute, to have recourse to the Court on such conditions as may be fixed by the Security Council. The Security Council at its 76th meeting held on 15th October, 1946 resolved that non-party States may avail the forum of the Court provided:

> "the said State shall previously have deposited with Registrar of the Court a declaration by which it accepts the jurisdiction of the Court, in accordance with the Charter of the United Nations and with the terms and subject to the conditions of the Statute and Rules of the Court, and undertakes to comply in good faith with the decision or decisions of the Court and to accept all the obligations of a Member of the United Nations under Article 94 of the Charter."

Besides, the non-party State will have to contribute such amount to the expenses of the Court as the Security Council may fix under Article 35(3).

Apart from States, some International Organisation may have access to the Court by seeking its advisory opinion [22]. Article 96(1) of the Charter permits the General Assembly and the Security Council to seek advisory opinion of the Court on any legal question. Article 96(2) permits other organs of the United Nations and specialised agencies, which are so authorised by the General Assembly, to request for advisory opinion on any legal question "within the scope of their activities." [23]

Article 34(2) stipulates that the Court "may request of public international organisations information relevant to cases before it, and shall receive such information presented by such oranisations on their own initiative." This Clause does not make the international organisation as party to the case but it can surely appear as *amicus curie*, if permitted by the Court under Article 57(4) of the Rules of the Court.

Individuals have no access to the Court. Neither the Statute nor the Rules of the Court permit the individual to file a petition in the Court. This is due to the traditional concept of international law which deals only with States and not with individuals. Nevertheless, there have been a few instances where the cause of an individual has been sponsored by the State which has brought his matter before the Court. The Asylum case involved the fate of Haya de la Torre. Nottehohm is another instance. Nevertheless, but for the State sponsoring any individual's case, the individual by himself has no *locus standi* in the world court.

Jurisdiction of Court

Article 36 of the Statute confers jurisdiction upon the court. It runs as under:

1. The jurisdiction of the Court comprises all the cases which the parties refer to it and all matters specially provided for in the Charter of the United Nations or in treaties and conventions in force.
2. The States parties to the present Statute may at any time declare that they recognise as compulsory *ipso facto* and without special agreement, in relation to any other State accepting the same obligation, the jurisdiction of the Court in all legal disputes concerning:
(a) the interpretation of a treaty;
(b) any question of international law;
(c) the existence of any fact which, if established, would constitute a breach of an international obligation;
(d) the nature or extent of the reparation to be made for the breach of an international obligation.

The reading of the Article shows that the Court's jurisdiction may be divided into (i) *ad hoc*, (ii) voluntary, and (iii) compulsory. All this jurisdiction is based upon the consent of parties. Nations being sovereign, they cannot be subjected to any jurisdiction without their consent, express or implied. All jurisdiction of the Court is voluntary and amounts to self-imposed limitation upon the State's sovereignty. In some cases, the jurisdiction is vested in the Court when the dispute has already arisen; in other cases, jurisdiction is vested in the Court in advance. Besides, Article 65 of the Statute confers upon the Court the jurisdiction of giving advisory opinion to some organs of the United Nations and authorised specialised agencies. All these categories of jurisdiction are being discussed as follows:

Ad hoc jurisdiction

This kind of jurisdiction is assumed by the Court when States refer to it any dispute which has arisen between them if the same is justiciable. The Asylum case of Haya de la Torre, involving Colombia and Peru, is typical of this jurisdiction. The two States, having failed to reach an understanding over the asylum granted to Haya de la Torre by the Colombian embassy in Lima (Peru), they agreed to refer the matter to the Court.

Another case which may be said to have been referred to the Court by parties to the dispute was the Corfu Channel case which was the first case handled by the Court. In this case, the Security Council had asked the parties, the United Kingdom and Albania, to refer the case to the Court under Article 36(3) of the Charter. In pursuance of this, the United Kingdom filed the application with the Court on 22nd May 1947. The Government of Albania did not initially object to the Court's jurisdiction although it resented the unilateral application by the United Kingdom. Later on, when Albania disputed the jurisdiction of the Court, the latter held that Albania had consented to the Court's jurisdiction on the basis of forum prorogatum.

Voluntary jurisdiction

Some treaties, bilateral as well as multilateral, provide that in case of any dispute relating to interpretation of treaty or default thereunder, the same may be decided by the International Court. The latter part of Article 36(1), therefore, confers jurisdiction on the Court with respect to such contingencies. This kind of jurisdiction may be termed as voluntary inasmuch as the parties to a given treaty agree in advance that disputes with regard to that treaty will be determined by the Court. One will find a number of treaties like this which confer jurisdiction on the Court. The Treaty of Peace with Japan dated 14th November, 1951 is one of such treaties. Finland, Norway and Sweden have a number of treaties between them which provide for reference to the Court in case of any dispute which may arise relating thereto. European Convention for the Settlement of Disputes signed on 29th April, 1957 provides for reference of disputes to the Court. Earlier, the General Assembly by its Resolution (171-II) of 14th November, 1947 had exhorted upon States to encourage the insertion of a clause in their treaties or conventions for refering disputes arising thereunder to the International Court.

Article 36(3) of the Charter also provides that while making recommendations for peaceful settlement of international disputes, the Security Council should take into consideration that legal disputes should as a rule be referred by parties to the International Court. The Corfu Channel case arose out of recommendation by the Security Council to the parties that the matter may be referred to the Court.

Compulsory jurisdiction

As it has been noted above, Article 36(2) stipulates that States, party to the Statute, may accept compulsory jurisdiction with respect to legal disputes concerning any question of international law, interpretation of treaty, breach of international obligation, and nature and extent of reparation for such breach.

Compulsory jurisdiction has been the most controversial jurisdiction of the Court. In fact, vesting of compulsory jurisdiction in the Court ensures that all international legal disputes would be resolved by the Court. Therefore, each time when the Court's Statute was being drafted, attempts were made to see that the States acceded to the compulsory Clause. However, both the times, the attempts failed. It has been noticed that States have been averse to compulsory jurisdiction. It has, therefore, been left to the States to accede to the compulsory Clause or not. The results, however, have not been encouraging.

As of December, 1975, only 45 States have subscribed to the optional Clause relating to compulsory jurisdiction, although the number of States, party to the Statute, at that time was 144 [24]. In fact, the number of such States has retrogressively decreased. In 1960, when 85 States were party to the Statute, 39 States had subscribed to the compulsory jurisdiction. In 1970, when 129 States were party to the Statute of the Court, 46 States had subscribed to the compulsory jurisdiction. In 1975 the number was reduced to 45 [25].

Besides general decline in the acceptance of compulsory jurisdiction, States, which have subscribed to the same, have prefaced it with many reservations. For example, the condition of reciprocity is very common although the same may be implied from the wording of Article 36(2), which says that the optional clause may be accepted "in relation to any other States accepting the same obligation." Other conditions relate to time limit (with variables), power of denunciation [26] and exclusion of matters within the domestic jurisdiction of a State or matters relating to a particular period.

From among the reservations, reservation as to domestic jurisdiction is the most controversial one. For instance, the United

States' acceptance of the optional Clause is subject to the exclusion of "disputes with regard to matters essentially within the domestic jurisdiction of the United States as determined by the United States of America" [27]. France, India, Mexico, Liberia, Pakistan and South Africa have followed the American pattern.

Validity of the American type of reservation with respect to domestic jurisdiction is doubtful because the power to determine whether a particular dispute is within the domestic jurisdiction of the State is assumed by the State which is in the dock. This, apart from being against the rule of natural justice, is also in contradiction with Article 36(6) which says that in "event of a dispute as to whether the Court has jurisdiction, the matter shall be settled by the decision of the Court." However, the Court has never had the chance of adjudicating upon this reservation.

Something need to be said here about the latest Indian acceptance of compulsory jurisdiction of the Court (text given in Annexure I). It consists of 11 Clauses purporting to exclude the Court's jurisdiction under those Clauses.

Clause 1 bars disputes regarding which there is agreement to have recourse to some other procedure of settlement. However, the words "shall" are ambiguous, bordering on contradiction. Clause 2 purports to bar reference of disputes between Commonwealth countries to the Court. The inclusion of past Commonwealth members is intended to bar Pakistan from referring any dispute to the Court. Clause 3 bars disputes with regard to matters which are essentially within its domestic jurisdiction. Clause 4 bars disputes in relation to hostilities and fulfilment of obligations imposed by international bodies. The bar is equally applicable to past, present and future hostilities as well as international obligations.

Clause 5 seeks to bar reference of disputes by such countries which have accepted the jurisdiction for the special purpose of refering some dispute to the Court or have become a member within last twelve months from the date of application.

Clause 6 bars such disputes which are based on any treaty entered into under the auspices of the League of Nations. Clause 7 bars any dispute of interpretation of multilateral treaty unless all the contracting parties are also party before the Court. Clause 8 bars disputes with such States which are either not recognised or with which the Government has no diplomatic relations. Clause 9 bars disputes with non-sovereign States.

Clause 10 bars disputes relating to status of territory boundaries, frontiers including maritime boundaries. This has become necessary in view of recent developments in the law of sea and unilateral declarations by nations regarding exclusive economic zone.

Clause 11 seeks to bar disputes which may have arisen before the Declaration. The Clause is all embracing inasmuch as that the court will have no jurisdiction if the foundations, reasons, facts, causes, origins, definitions, allegations or bases of disputes had arisen before the Declaration.

Totality of the Declaration is that if it is taken to its logical end, no dispute can be referred to the Court. This is an unfortunate position but it seems to arise out of distrust of the Court.

Two questions are often asked with respect to the acceptance of the optional Clause: value of such acceptance and its effect.

As to the first question, it may be stated that it is a unilateral undertaking by the accepting State that all legal disputes which may arise between her and other similarly placed States which have also accepted the optional Clause will be determined by the Court if the dispute is brought before the Court.

The effect of such acceptance is that any finding which the Court may render is binding upon the accepting State which must comply with the same in accordance with Article 94 of the Charter. This leaves no scope for manoeuvring on the part of a big power which is in the habit of overawing the small State in case of a dispute between the two.

Advisory Opinions

The Court may give advisory opinion to some of the international organisations. As it has been said above, the Court is the principal judicial organ of the United Nations. As such, organs of the United Nations may obtain advisory opinion from the Court. Article 96(1) of the Charter specifically permits the General Assembly and the Security Council to request for advisory opinion on any legal question. Other international organisations may also seek advisory opinion from the Court if they have been so authorised by the General Assembly under Article 96(2). Important international organisations which have been so authorised are International Labour Organisation, UNESCO, International Civil Aviation Organisation, International Monetary Fund and World

Health Organisation.

It may be noted here that while the General Assembly and the Security Council may ask for advisory opinion on any legal question, other organs of the United Nations or specialised agencies which have been authorised to seek advisory opinion can do so only with regard to such legal questions which arise "within the scope of their activities." This means that the power to seek advisory opinion is restricted in case of such organisations.

Law to be Applied by the Court

Article 38(1) of the Statute says that the Court shall decide the disputes submitted to it "in accordance with international law." It clarifies it further by saying that it shall apply international conventions, particular or general, as recognised by litigating States, international custom, as evidence of general practice accepted as law, general principles of law as recognised by civilised nations, judicial decisions and teachings of noted international publicists.

Article 59 of the Statute, however, makes the decision of the Court binding only on the parties to the dispute. Therefore although the decision of the Court does not create a precedent in the sense of Common law, nonetheless it is entitled to great respect. In fact, earlier judgments have been relied upon by the Court in many cases [28].

The Court also recognises the general principles of law as recognised by civilised nations. This is in accordance with the Roman concept of *jus gentium* which consisted of such laws which were commonly recognised by all States. The use of the word "civilised" looks anachronistic in the present world context.

Article 38(2) provides that if the parties so agree, the Court may decide the dispute *ex acquo et bono.* The phrase means that the Court may decide the dispute equitably and not strictly according to law. So far, no case has been decided on the basis of this maxim although Gautemala wanted the problem of Belize between her and United Kingdom to be decided *ex acquo et bono* [29]. Colombia was also ready that Haya dela Torre's case may be decided on humanitarian and equitablc grounds but Peru did not agree [30].

Decision of the Court

The Court decides the case, in absence of unanimity, by majority of Judges present. In case of a tie, the President of the Court has a casting vote [31]. This was done in the case between Liberia and Ethiopia on one side and South Africa on the other side [32].

Article 59 of the Statute makes the decision binding upon the parties to the case. Article 60 makes the judgment final and non-appealable.

Enforcement of Judgment [33]

Article 94(1) of the Charter provides that every member of the United Nations undertakes to comply with the decision of the Court to which it is party. Non-member States also undertake to comply with the decision to which they are party. This is one of the conditions for their becoming party to the Statute.

Article 94(2), however, provides that in case of failure of any party to comply with the decision of the Court, the aggrieved State may request the Security Council which may take any action which it deems necessary.

In the days of the Permanent Court, no problem of execution of judgment arose because most of the decisions were complied with [34]. However, some doubts have been cast upon the post-United Nations era which has witnessed a number of instances where States have not complied with the decisions of the Court. Perhaps, the start was inauspicious in the very first case because Albania did not comply with the decision. It has been followed by other States not complying with some decisions of the Court. This has been the case not only with regard to decisions of the Court in contentious cases but also in advisory opinions rendered by the Court. For example, South Africa has failed to submit reports to the Trusteeship Council regarding South West Africa despite the Court's advisory opinion which obliges Africa to do so. Similarly, France and the Soviet Union did not accept the advisory opinion regarding peace keeping expenses. This raises the problem of execution.

Problem of enforcement of decision is of vital importance in international law. It has been noticed that the function of any international court or arbitral tribunal has so far been to declare legal position of parties on a particular question of international aw. Having determined that, the court or arbitral tribunal becomes *functus officio*; it is then left to parties to comply with the decision of the court. In world community there is no enforcement agency to order compliance with the decision of the Court. Any such agency would be inconsistent with the traditional concept of sovereignty of nations which do not know of any superior to them.

States which participated in the San Francisco had given thought to the problem of enforcement of decisions of the Court. While Australia had proposed the text of Article 94(1), Bolivia was of the view that non-compliance with the decision of the Court may be treated as an act of aggression. Eventually, the Australian view prevailed and its suggestion adopted in the form of Article 94(1). Perhaps, it was not found desirable to be more specific because that may discourage States from subscribing to the optional Clause.

Article 94(1) leaves it to the goodwill of the State to comply with the decision. If the State chooses to ignore the decision, as has been done in some cases, the aggrieved State may have recourse to the Security Council.

At this stage, an otherwise legal question is transformed into a political question. As the wording of Article 94(2) is, the Security Council may take action "if it deems necessary." This would mean that the Council may not take any action if it so desires. Besides, the Court's decision may be subjected to political pressures as are prevalent in the Council. It is also possible that the recommendations of the Council may be frustrated by any one of the five big powers. This may leave the question of enforcement abegging.

Evaluation

I have discussed above the composition and functions of the International Court. Now may arise the question as to how far the Court has succeeded in its mission.

Undoubtedly, the establishment of the Court has been a progressive step towards maintenance of the rule of law in the world community. However, the experience of the three decades has not been very happy regarding the working of the Court. It has been noticed that like the composition of the Security Council, the Court is also dominated by the five big powers whose nationals have been members of the Court since its inception. In 1956, there was a serious attempt to break the domination when the General

Assembly elected the Japanese representative to the Court but the Security Council thwarted the attempt. Eventually, the Assembly gave up. Eligibility of judges to seek re-election after the expiry of their term of nine years has the semblance of perpetuating given persons to continue as judges so long as they like. This is not a good practice. No judge should continue beyond one full term.

Judges also, it may be submitted, have not acquitted themselves creditably in the discharge of their judicial functions. They are enjoined upon by oath of office to act impartially and conscientiously. However, the performance of Judges in some cases has been patently partisan. This is a very unfortunate development. This has shaken the faith of the people of the world in the impartiality of the Court which received a great setback after its decision in the petition by Ethiopia and Liberia against South Africa.

Nations have also not shaken their traditional concept of sovereignty. This has resulted in the decreasing number of declarations accepting the optional Clause. It is indeed distressing to note that the number of declarations in the last three decades has almost remained static despite the fact that there are presently 152 States which are party to the Statute. This has frustrated the very idea of making the Court as an international judicial organ. The problem will not ease unless the States are ready to reconcile themselves to the institution of judicial settlement of international disputes which may be justiciable. Besides, it may also be provided that nationals of only such States shall be eligible for election as members of the Court which have accepted the optional Clause without reservations.

The problem of enforcement of the decisions of the Court also deserves the attention of international elites. So far, it has been left to the discretion of parties to comply with the decision. The Security Council steps in when the party is not willing to comply with the decision. This makes the question of enforcement an entirely political question. It is possible that the party may feel justified to take measures of self-help to enforce the decision in its favour. This may disturb international peace and security for the prevention of which States refer the matter to the Court. Paradoxically, the parties may find themselves in the same situation in which they were before referring the matter to the Court. Something ought to be done with regard to this.

Notes

1. Vide United Nations General Assembly Resolution 91 (1).
2. General Assembly Resolution 363 (IV).
3. General Assembly Resolution 805 (VIII) with regard to Japan and 806 (VIII) with regard to San Marino.
4. Article 35(2) of the Statute runs as follows: "The conditions under which the Court shall be open to other States shall, subject to special provisions contained in treaties in force, be laid down by the Security Council, but in no case shall such conditions place the parties in a position of inequality before the Court."
5. Article 4(3) of the Statute.
6. Article 4.
7. Article 8. Non-member State, which are party to the Statute participate in the election of judges on the basis of General Assembly's Resolution dated October 8, 1948.
8. Article 13.
9. Article 15.
10. Article 18.
11. Articles 16 and 17 run as under: Article 16(1) "No member of the Court may exercise any political or administrative function, or engage in any other occupation of a professional nature.

    (2) Any doubt on this point shall be settled by the decision of the Court."

    Article 17—"1. No member of the court may act as agent, counsel or advocate in any case.

    2. No member may participate in the decision of any case in which he has previously taken part as agents counsel or advocate for one of the parties, or as a member of a national or international court, or of a commission of inquiry, or in any other capacity.

    3. Any doubt on this point shall be settled by the decision of the Court."

    In the case between Ethiopia and Liberia versus South Africa, the President in persuance of power vested in him under Article 24 of the Statute, asked the Pakistani Judge, Mr. Zafrullah, not to sit on the Court because he was considered disqualified under Article 17 on the ground that he was at one time nominated as *ad hoc* Judge by the applicants although he did not sit on the Court as such. However, he did not force the decision of the Court.

    It is of significance to note that Judge Padilla Nervo of Mexico was also disqualified by the President on the ground that he actively participated in the U.N. debates on the matter. He challenged the order of the President with the result that the Court's decision permitted him to sit on the Court.
12. Article 20 of the Statute and Article 5 of the Rules of the Court.
13. Article 31 of the Statute.
14. Article 31(6).

15. Article 17(2).
16. Article 24 of the Statute runs as follows:
"1. If, for some special reason, a member of the Court considers that he should not take part in the decision of a particular case, he shall so inform the President.
2. If the President considers that for some special reason one of the members of the Court should not sit in a particular case, he shall give him notice accordingly.
3. If in any such case the member of the Court and the President disagree, the matter shall be settled by the decision of the Court."
17. Article 19.
18. Article 31(6).
19. Article 25.
20. Article 26.
21. Article 29.
22. Wilfred Jenks, The Status of International Organisations in relation to the International Court of Justice, (1946) 32 Proceedings of the Grotius Society 1.
23. Four organs of the United Nations—Economic and Social Council, Trusteeship Council, Interim Council of the General Assembly and the Committee on Applications for Review of Administrative Tribunal Judgments—have been permitted by the General Assembly to seek advisory opinion from the Court. Besides, a number of Specialised Agencies have been authorised to do so.
24. This number includes such States whose declaration is pre-1945 but whose declaration is valid under Article 36(5) of the Statute. These States are—Canada, Colombia, Dominican Republic, El Salvador, Haiti, Luxembourg, New Zealand, Nicargua and Uruguay.
25. International Court of Justice (1976). p. 37.
26. See particularly the Portugese Declaration.
27. See American Declaration of 14-8-1946.
28. Oppenheim, International Law, (Seventh Edition) volume ii, pp. 71-1.
29. See Gautemala's Declaration dated 27.1.1947.
30. As given by Rosenne, op. cit., p. 271.
31. Article 55 of the Statute.
32. See judgment of the Court dated 18.7.1966.
33. Oscar Schacter, The Enforcement of International Judicial and Arbitral Decisions, (1960) 54 American Journal of International Law. 1-24.
34. Rosenne, op. cit., p. 73.

ANNEXURE I

INDIA'S DECLARATION UNDER THE OPTIONAL CLAUSE OF THE ICJ STATUTE (15 September 1974)

Excellency,

I have the honour to declare, on behalf of the Government of the Republic of India, that they accept in conformity with paragraph 2 of Article 36 of the Statute of the Court, until such time as notice may be given to terminate such acceptance, as compulsory, *ipso facto* and without special agreement, and on the basis and condition of reciprocity, jurisdiction of the International Court of Justice overall disputes other than:

(1) disputes in regard to which the parties to the dispute have agreed or shall agree to have recourse to some other method or methods of settlement;

(2) disputes with the government of any State which is or has been a Member of the Commonwealth of Nations;

(3) disputes in regard to matters which are essentially within the domestic jurisdiction of the Republic of India;

(4) disputes relating to or connected with facts or situations of hostilities, armed conflicts, individual or collective actions taken in self-defence, or resistance to aggression, fulfilment of obligations imposed by international bodies, and other similar or related acts, measures or situations in which India is, has been or may in future be involved;

(5) disputes with regard to which any other party to a dispute has accepted the compulsory jurisdiction of the International Court of Justice exclusively for or in relation to the purpose of such disputes; or where the acceptance of the Court's compulsory jurisdiction on behalf of a party to the dispute was deposited or ratified less than 12 months prior to the filing of the application bringing the dispute before the Court;

(6) disputes where the jurisdiction of the Court is or may be founded on the basis of a treaty concluded under the auspices of the League of Nations, unless the Govern-

ment of India specially agree to jurisdiction in each case;

(7) disputes concerning the interpetation or application of a multilateral treaty unless all the parties to the treaty are also parties to the case before the Court or Government of India specially agree to jurisdiction;

(8) disputes with the Government of any State which, on the date of an application to bring a dispute before the Court, the Government of India has no diplomatic relations or which has not been recognised by the Government of India;

(9) disputes with non-sovereign States or territories;

(10) disputes with India concerning or relating to:

(a) the status of its territory or the modification of delimitation, its frontiers or any other matter concerning boundaries;

(b) the territorial sea, the continental shelf and the margins, the exclusive economic zone, and other zones of national maritime jurisdiction including for the regulation and control of marine pollution and the conduct of scientific research by foreign vessels;

(c) the condition and status of its islands, bays and that of the bays and gulfs that for historical reasons belong to it;

(d) the airspace superjacent to its land and maritime territory; and

(e) the determination and delimitation of its maritime boundaries.

(11) disputes prior to the date of this declaration, including any dispute the foundations, reasons, facts, causes, origins, definitions, allegations, or bases of which existed prior to this date, even if they are submitted or brought to the knowledge of the Court hereafter.

2. This Declaration revokes and replaces the previous declaration made by the Government of India on 14th September, 1959.

Yours sincerely,
(Swaran Singh)
Minister of External Affairs.

ANNEXURE II

CASES DECIDED BY INTERNATIONAL COURT OF JUSTICE FROM 1946 TO 1975

	Case	Year
1.	Corfu Channel	1947-49
2.	Asylum case	1950-51
3.	Anglo-Norwegian Fisheries case	1951
4.	Rights of Nationals of the United States in Morocco	1952
5.	Ambatielos	1952
6.	Minquiers	1953
7.	Right of Passage over Indian Territory	1957-60
8.	Application of the Convention of 1902 Governing the Guardianship of Infants	1958
9.	Sovereignty over Certain Frontier Land	1959
10.	Arbitral Award Made by the King of Spain on 23.12.1906	1960
11.	Temple of Preah Vihar	1961
12.	North Sea Continental Shelf	1969
13.	Appeal Relating to the Jurisdiction of the ICAO Council	1972
14.	Fisheries Jurisdiction	1972, 1973 & 1974

Cases Terminated by Judgment on Preliminary Objection or Other Interlocutory Order

	Case	Year
1.	Anglo-Iranian Oil Co.	1951-52
2.	Nottebohm	1953-55
3.	Monetary Gold Removed from Rome in 1943	1954
4.	Certain Norwegian Loans	1957
5.	Interhandel	1957
6.	Aerial Incident of 27 July, 1955	1959 & 1960
7.	Northern Cameroons	1963
8.	South West Africa	1962-66

9.	Barcelona Traction, Light and Powers Company	1961, 1964 & 1970
10.	Nuclear Tests	1973 & 1974

Cases Discontinued

1.	Protection of French Nationals and Protected Persons	1950
2.	Electricite de Beyrouth Company	1954
3.	Compagnie du port, des Quais et des Entreports de Beyrouth and Societe Radio Orient	1960
4.	Trial of Pakistani Prisoners of War	1973

Advisory Opinions Delivered by the Court

1.	Conditions of Admission of State to Membership in the U.N.	1947-48
2.	Reparation of Injuries suffered in the Service of the United Nations	1949
3.	Competence of the General Assembly for the Admission of a State to the United Nations	1950
4.	Interpretation of Peace Treaties with Bulgaria, Hungary and Romania	1950
5.	International Status of S.W. Africa	1950
6.	Reservations to the Convention on the Prevention and Punishment of the Crime of Genocide	1951
7.	Effect of Awards of Compensation Made by the U.N. Administrative Tribunal	1954
8.	Voting Procedure on Questions relating to Reports and Petitions concerning the Territory of S.W. Africa	1955

9.	Admissibility of Hearings of Petitioners by the Committee on S.W. Africa	1956
10.	Judgment of the Administrative Tribunal of the ILO upon Complaints Made Against UNESCO (UNESCO)	1956
11.	Constitution of the Marine Safety Committees (IMCO)	1960
12.	Certain Expenses of the U.N.	1962
13.	Legal Consequences for States of the Continued Presence of S. Africa in Namibia. (S.C.)	1971
14.	Application for Review of Judgment No. 158 of the U.N. Administrative Tribunal (U.N. Committee)	1973
15.	Western Sahara	1975

INDEX